# The Cambridge Companion to Wordsworth

*The Cambridge Companion to Wordsworth* provides a wide-ranging account of one of the most famous Romantic poets. Specially commissioned essays cover all the important aspects of this multi-faceted writer; the volume examines his poetic achievement with a chapter on poetic craft, other chapters focus on the origin of his poetry and on the challenges it presented and continues to present. The volume ensures that students will be grounded in the history of Wordsworth's career and his critical reception. Further contributions include discussions of *The Prelude* and *The Recluse*, Wordsworth as philosophic poet, his writing in relation to European Romanticism, and Wordsworth as Nature poet. The collection, by an international team of established specialists, concludes with a lucid account of the history of Wordsworth's texts, and offers students invaluable reference material including a chronology and guides to further reading.

D0060811

# THE CAMBRIDGE
# COMPANION TO
# WORDSWORTH

EDITED BY
STEPHEN GILL

CAMBRIDGE
UNIVERSITY PRESS

PUBLISHED BY THE PRESS SYNDICATE OF THE UNIVERSITY OF CAMBRIDGE
The Pitt Building, Trumpington Street, Cambridge CB2 1RP, United Kingdom

CAMBRIDGE UNIVERSITY PRESS
The Edinburgh Building, Cambridge, CB2 2RU, UK
40 West 20th Street, New York, NY 10011–4211, USA
477 Williamstown Road, Port Melbourne, VIC 3207, Australia
Ruiz de Alarcón 13, 28014 Madrid, Spain
Dock House, The Waterfront, Cape Town 8001, South Africa

http://www.cambridge.org

First published 2003

Printed in the United Kingdom at the University Press, Cambridge

*Typeface* Sabon 10/13 pt      *System* LATEX 2$_\varepsilon$   [TB]

*A catalogue record for this book is available from the British Library*

ISBN 0 521 64681 2 hardback
ISBN 0 521 64116 0 paperback

#50669821

# CONTENTS

CONTENTS

CONTRIBUTORS

JAMES A. BUTLER is Professor and Chair of English at La Salle University in Philadelphia. He is an associate editor of The Cornell Wordsworth Series in which he has edited *The Ruined Cottage* and *The Pedlar* (1979) and co-edited *Lyrical Ballads and Other Poems* (1992). His most recent book is an edition of *Romney and Other New Works About Philadelphia* by Owen Wister (2001).

FRANCES FERGUSON is Mary Elizabeth Garrett Professor of English and the Humanities at Johns Hopkins University. She has written on the eighteenth century, Romanticism, and literary theory, and is the author of *Wordsworth: Language as Counter-Spirit, Solitude and the Sublime: Romanticism and the Aesthetics of Individuation*, and *Pornography: The Theory*.

STEPHEN GILL is a Professor of English Literature at Oxford University and a Fellow of Lincoln College, Oxford. His edition of Wordsworth's *Salisbury Plain Poems* inaugurated the Cornell Wordsworth Series. He has written *William Wordsworth: A Life* (1989) and *Wordsworth and the Victorians* (1998).

PAUL HAMILTON was a Fellow of Exeter College, Oxford, for ten years and is now a Professor of English at Queen Mary, University of London. He has written books on Coleridge, Wordsworth, Shelley, Historicism, and related subjects, and is currently working on the philosophy and political theory of European Romanticism.

KEITH HANLEY is Professor of English Literature at Lancaster University, where he directs the Ruskin Programme. He is co-editor, with Greg Kucich, of the interdisciplinary journal *Nineteenth-Century Contexts* and the book series Interdisciplinary Nineteenth-Century Studies. Among his publications are *An Annotated Critical Bibliography of William Wordsworth* (1995) and *Wordsworth: A Poet's History* (2000). With Amanda Gilroy, he has recently edited a selection of the plays and poems of Joanna Baillie.

KENNETH R. JOHNSTON is Ruth Halls Professor of English at Indiana University. He is the author of *The Hidden Wordsworth* (1998) and *Wordsworth and 'The Recluse'* (1984). He is currently studying the effects of the British Government's repression of the 1790s reform movement.

LUCY NEWLYN is a Fellow of St Edmund Hall, Oxford. She is the author of three books published by Oxford University Press: *Coleridge, Wordsworth and the Language of Allusion* (1986), *Paradise Lost and the Romantic Reader* (1993), and *Reading, Writing and Romanticism: The Anxiety of Reception* (2000). She co-edited with Richard Gravil and Nicholas Roe *Coleridge's Imagination: Essays in Memory of Pete Laver* (1985); and she is editor of the *Cambridge Companion to Coleridge*. She is now working on the poetry of Thomas Hardy.

JOEL PACE is Assistant Professor of British and American Romanticism at the University of Wisconsin-Eau Claire and a Fellow of the John Nicholas Brown Center of American Civilization, Brown University. He is working on a book on Wordsworth in America for Oxford University Press and he has published further on the subject in *Romanticism on the Net*, *Symbiosis*, and *Romantic Circles Praxis Series*.

JUDITH W. PAGE teaches in the English Department at the University of Florida, where she is also affiliated with the Center for Research on Women and Gender and the Center for Jewish Studies. She is the author of *Wordsworth and the Cultivation of Women* (1994) and numerous articles on Romanticism. Her current research includes work on women's life-writing in the Romantic period and on British Romanticism and Judaism.

SEAMUS PERRY is a Fellow of Balliol College, Oxford. He is author of *Coleridge and the Uses of Division* (1999), editor of *Coleridge: Interviews and Recollections* (2000), and co-editor, with Nicola Trott, of *1800: The New Lyrical Ballads* (2001). He is an editor of the Oxford journal *Essays in Criticism*.

RALPH PITE, University of Liverpool, has published on Dante's importance to Romantic poetry, on Wordsworth and ecology, and on Coleridgean biography. He has recently completed a book, *Hardy's Geography*, and is working on a biography of Hardy, *The Guarded Life*.

NICHOLAS ROE is Professor of English at the University of St Andrews. His books include *Wordsworth and Coleridge: The Radical Years* (1988), *John Keats and the Culture of Dissent* (1997), and, as editor, *Keats and History* (1995) and *Samuel Taylor Coleridge and the Sciences of Life* (2001).

NICOLA TROTT is Lecturer in English Literature at the University of Glasgow. She is co-editor, with Seamus Perry, of *1800: The New 'Lyrical Ballads'* (2001), and has published several articles on Wordsworth and Coleridge, as well as essays on Romantic aesthetics, periodical criticism, gothic fiction, Lamb, Keats, 'Christopher North', Mary Shelley, and Wollstonecraft.

SUSAN J. WOLFSON is Professor of English at Princeton University, a contributor to several volumes in the Companion series and the editor of the volume on John Keats. Her publications on Wordsworth include *The Questioning Presence* (1987), *Formal Charges* (1998), essays in *Le Questionnement*, a special issue of *Revue Internationale de Philosophie*, ed. Nigel Wood (1993), *'The Prelude': Theory in Practice*, ed. Nigel Wood (1993), and *Men Writing the Feminine*, ed. Thaïs Morgan (1994).

DUNCAN WU is a Fellow of St Catherine's College, Oxford, and Professor of English Literature. His books include *Wordsworth's Reading 1770–1815* (2 vols., 1993–5) and *Wordsworth: An Inner Life* (2002).

# CHRONOLOGY

| | |
|---|---|
| 1770 | William Wordsworth (WW) born 7 April at Cockermouth, Cumberland, in the English Lake District. |
| 1771 | Dorothy Wordsworth (DW) born 25 September at Cockermouth. |
| 1778 | Mother, Ann Wordsworth, dies *c*. 8 March. |
| 1779 | WW enters Hawkshead Grammar School, lodging with Hugh and Ann Tyson. |
| 1783 | Father, John Wordsworth, dies 30 December. |
| 1785–6 | First surviving verse, 'Lines Written as a School Exercise at Hawkshead' (1785) and composition towards *The Vale of Esthwaite*, not published by WW. |
| 1787 | WW's first published poem, 'Sonnet on Seeing Miss Helen Maria Williams Weep at a Tale of Distress' appears in *The European Magazine* in March. WW enters St John's College, Cambridge. |
| 1788–9 | Composition of *An Evening Walk*, published 1793. Storming of the Bastille, 14 July 1789. |
| 1790 | Walking tour in France and Switzerland with Robert Jones, July–October. Edmund Burke's *Reflections on the Revolution in France* published. |
| 1791–2 | WW in London. In November 1791 returns to France and sees Revolutionary fervour in Paris. Is influenced by Michel Beaupuy. Love affair with Annette Vallon and birth of their daughter, Caroline, 15 December 1792. Composes *Descriptive Sketches*, published 1793. Returns to England to seek a livelihood. |
| 1793 | Louis XVI executed in January. War declared between England and France in February. WW feels an outcast in his own country. Writes but does not publish a seditious *Letter to* |

*the Bishop of Llandaff*. After wandering across Salisbury Plain in a journey to Wales, WW composes *Salisbury Plain*. Sees Tintern Abbey. William Godwin's *Political Justice* published, as Government suppression of dissent intensifies.

1794      WW reunited with DW in stay at Windy Brow, Keswick in Cumberland. In August–September stays at Rampside on the southern coastal tip of the Lake District and sees Peele Castle. Nurses Raisley Calvert, who leaves W £900 on his death in January 1795. Execution of Robespierre 28 July.

1795      Samuel Taylor Coleridge (STC) lectures in Bristol on politics and religion. WW a familiar figure in radical circles in London in spring and summer and regularly meets Godwin. Meets STC and Robert Southey in Bristol in August. Settles with DW at Racedown in Dorset and rewrites *Salisbury Plain*.

1797      Completes play, *The Borderers* and moves to Alfoxden to be nearer STC. First version of *The Ruined Cottage* and plans for joint composition with STC.

1798      The year remembered at the end of *The Prelude* as the *annus mirabilis*. WW completes *The Ruined Cottage* (incorporated eventually into *The Excursion*, 1814), and composes the bulk of the verse published anonymously in September as *Lyrical Ballads*. Plans for *The Recluse* first mentioned. WW, DW, and STC go to Germany and over winter WW writes autobiographical verse, the foundation of *The Prelude*.

1799      By end of April WW back in England. Move into Dove Cottage, Grasmere, in December.

1800      Begins *Home at Grasmere* (not published in WW's lifetime) and probably composes lines printed in 1814 as a 'Prospectus' to *The Recluse*. Works on poems for second edition of *Lyrical Ballads*, published January 1801, and writes 'Preface'.

1802      Much lyrical poetry composed. Publication in April of further edition of *Lyrical Ballads*, with revised 'Preface'. Peace of Amiens enables WW and DW to visit Annette and Caroline in August. WW marries Mary Hutchinson (b. 1770, d. 1859) 4 October.

1803      War resumes and fear of invasion grows. Birth of first son, John. WW, DW, and STC tour Scotland from mid-August. The Ws meet Sir Walter Scott 17 September. STC ill and planning to leave for better climate.

1804     Much composition, especially on *The Prelude*, enlarged after March from planned five-book structure. 'Ode to Duty' and completion of 'Ode: Intimations of Immortality'. STC sails to Malta. 18 May Napoleon crowned Emperor. Daughter, Dorothy (always known as Dora) born.

1805     WW's brother John, b. 1772, drowned in the wreck of his ship, *The Earl of Abergavenny*. The Wordsworth circle very deeply affected. WW completes *The Prelude*.

1806–7     Birth of son, Thomas, 1806. Visits London. The Wordsworths spend winter in a house of Sir George Beaumont at Coleorton, Leicestershire. STC at last returns, much changed by ill-health. WW reads *The Prelude* to him. *Poems, in Two Volumes* published in 1807. WW staggered by critical abuse. Composes *The White Doe of Rylstone*, but does not publish it until 1815.

1808–9     Birth of daughter, Catherine, 1808. The Wordsworths leave Dove Cottage for Allan Bank, a larger house but still in Grasmere. WW publishes, 1809, *The Convention of Cintra*.

1810     Son, William, born. Misunderstanding leads to breach with STC, not healed until 1812. First version of *Guide to the Lakes* published as anonymous Preface to Joseph Wilkinson's *Select Views in Cumberland, Westmorland and Lancashire*.

1811–12     Death of children, Thomas and Catherine. The Wordsworths move from Allan Bank to Rectory, Grasmere.

1813     Appointed Distributor of Stamps for Westmorland (a post in the revenue service). Moves to Rydal Mount, home for the rest of his life. Completes *The Excursion*.

1814     *The Excursion* published; the project of *The Recluse* announced in the Preface. Poem attacked by reviewers. Tour of Scotland, including a visit to the Yarrow.

1815     First collected edition of poems published, with new Preface. *The White Doe of Rylstone* (written 1807) published.

1816     Publishes prose *Letter to a Friend of Robert Burns*.

1817     STC's *Biographia Literaria* published. WW moves more widely in London circles; meets Keats.

1818     For the General Election WW campaigns energetically for the Tory interest in Westmorland, to the distress of family and many admirers.

1819     Publishes *The Waggoner* and *Peter Bell*, poems written long before in 1806 and 1798 respectively.

| 1820 | Publishes *The River Duddon* sonnet sequence and a further collected works. Regular updating of his collected edition now becomes a feature of WW's writing life – 1827, 1832, 1836, 1845, 1849–50 being the most important editions. Tours Europe and revisits memorable places from the 1790 tour. |
| --- | --- |
| 1822 | *Memorials of a Tour on the Continent, 1820* published and *Ecclesiastical Sketches*. First separate publication of *Description of the Scenery of the Lakes* (later *Guide to the Lakes*). |
| 1829–35 | Catholic Emancipation greatly troubles WW, as does the Reform Bill of 1832. Enters period of greatly exaggerated alarm at the state of the country. Tours Scotland once more, September–October 1831, and sees Sir Walter Scott (d. 1832) for the last time. Death of STC, 25 July 1834. *Yarrow Revisited* published 1835, with important prose Postscript. |
| 1836–43 | Tours France and Italy in 1837. Sonnets collected as one volume in 1838. In 1839 WW conducts last of many revisions of *The Prelude*. Poems written in youth, notably *The Borderers* and *Salisbury Plain*, revised for publication in *Poems, Chiefly of Early and Late Years*, 1842. Resigns Stamp Distributorship in 1842 and following year becomes Poet Laureate on death of Robert Southey. WW now widely celebrated figure, receiving honorary degrees from Durham and Oxford. |
| 1844–50 | Supervises with great care one-volume collected edition in 1845. Deeply stricken by death of Dora, 9 July 1847. WW dies 23 April 1850. *The Prelude* published by his wife and executors. |

KEY   *1800*    The 'Preface' to *Lyrical Ballads* (1800)

         *1802*    The revised 'Preface' to *Lyrical Ballads* for the 1802 edition

         *1815*    'Preface' to the *Poems* (1815)

         *1815 Supplement*    'Essay Supplementary to the Preface to the *Poems*' (1815)

         *IF*    'Isabella Fenwick Notes', 1843. *The Fenwick Notes of William Wordsworth*, ed. Jared Curtis (1993)

'There is little need to advise me against publishing; it is a thing which I dread as much death itself.' *Letter to James Tobin, 6 March 1798*

'I think publications in which we formally & systematically lay down rules for the actions of Men cannot be too long delayed...I know no book or system of moral philosophy written with sufficient power to melt into our affections, to incorporate itself with the blood & vital juices of our minds, & thence to have any influence worth our notice...' *'Essay on Morals' 1798 in Prose I*

'It has been said of poets as their highest praise that they exhausted worlds and then imagined new, that existence saw them spurn her bounded reign, etc. But how much of the real excellence of Imagination consists in the capacity of exploring the world really existing...' *Annotation in Wordsworth's copy of 'Paradise Lost'*

'It is the honourable characteristic of Poetry that its materials are to be found in every subject which can interest the human mind.' *'Advertisement' to 'Lyrical Ballads'(1798)*

'Words, a Poet's words more particularly, ought to be weighed in the balance of feeling and not measured by the space which they occupy upon paper. For the Reader cannot be too often reminded that Poetry is passion: it is the history or science of feeling.' *Note to 'The Thorn' (1800)*

'Low and rustic life was generally chosen [for *Lyrical Ballads*], because in that condition, the essential passions of the heart find a better soil in which they can attain their maturity, are less under restraint, and speak a plainer and more emphatic language; because in that condition of life our elementary feelings co-exist in a state of greater simplicity, and, consequently, may be more accurately contemplated, and more forcibly communicated...' *1800*

'For all good poetry is the spontaneous overflow of powerful feelings: but though this be true, Poems to which any value can be attached, were never produced on any variety of subjects but by a man, who being possessed of more than usual organic sensibility, had also thought long and deeply.' *1800*

'it is proper that I should mention one other circumstance which distinguishes these Poems from the popular Poetry of the day; it is this, that the feeling therein developed gives importance to the action and the situation, and not the action and situation to the feeling.' *1800*

'The end of Poetry is to produce excitement in co-existence with an over-balance of pleasure.' *1800*

'... the language of a large portion of every good poem, even of the most elevated character, must necessarily, except with reference to the metre, in no respect differ from that of good prose, but likewise... some of the most interesting parts of the best poems will be found strictly the language of prose, when prose is well written.' *1802*

'What is a Poet?... He is a man speaking to men: a man, it is true, endued with more lively sensibility, more enthusiasm and tenderness, who has a greater knowledge of human nature, and a more comprehensive soul, than are supposed to be common among mankind; a man pleased with his own passions and volitions, and who rejoices more than other men in the spirit of life that is in him; delighting to contemplate similar volitions and passions as manifested in the goings-on of the Universe, and habitually impelled to create them where he does not find them.' *1802*

'Among the qualities which I have enumerated as principally conducing to form a Poet, is implied nothing differing in kind from other men, but only in degree.' *1802*

'Aristotle, I have been told, hath said, that Poetry is the most philosophic of all writing: it is so: its object is truth, not individual and local, but general, and operative; not standing upon external testimony, but carried alive into the heart by passion...' *1802*

'The Poet writes under one restriction only, namely, that of the necessity of giving immediate pleasure to a human Being possessed of that information which may be expected from him, not as a lawyer, a physician, a mariner, an astronomer or a natural philosopher, but as a Man.' *1802*

'The Man of Science seeks truth as a remote and unknown benefactor; he cherishes and loves it in his solitude: the Poet, singing a song in which all human beings join with him, rejoices in the presence of truth as our visible friend and hourly companion. Poetry is the breath and finer spirit of all knowledge; it is the impassioned expression which is in the countenance of all Science.' *1802*

'...a great Poet ought...to a certain degree to rectify men's feelings, to give them new compositions of feeling, to render their feelings more sane pure and permanent, in short more consonant to nature, that is, to eternal nature, and the great moving spirit of things. He ought to travel before men occasionally as well as at their sides.' *Letter to John Wilson, 7 June 1802.*

'...if I were disposed to write a sermon...upon the subject of taste in natural beauty...all of which I had to say would begin and end in the human heart, as, under the direction of the divine Nature conferring value on the objects of the senses and pointing out what is valuable in them.' *Letter to Sir George Beaumont, 17 and 24 October 1805*

'...to be incapable of a feeling of Poetry in my sense of the word is to be without love of human nature and reverence for God.' *Letter to Lady Beaumont, 21 May 1807*

'never forget what I believe was observed to you by Coleridge, that every great and original writer, in proportion as he is great or original, must himself create the taste by which he is to be relished; he must teach the art by which he is to be seen...' *ibid.*

'Every great Poet is a Teacher: I wish either to be considered as a Teacher, or as nothing.' *Letter to Sir George Beaumont [Feb. 1808]*

'Words are too awful an instrument for good and evil to be trifled with: they hold above all other external powers a dominion over thoughts . . . Language, if it do not uphold, and feed, and leave in quiet, like the power of gravitation or the air we breathe, is a counter-spirit, unremittingly and noiselessly at work to derange, to subvert, to lay waste, to vitiate, and to dissolve.' *Essays upon Epitaphs, III, 1810*

'. . . the mighty difference between seeing & perceiving.' *'The Sublime and the Beautiful', 1811–1812. Prose II*

'. . . the mind gains consciousness of its strength to undergo only by exercise among materials which admit the impression of its power . . .' *The Convention of Cintra, 1809*

'. . . the range of poetic feeling is far wider than is ordinarily supposed, and the furnishing new proofs of this fact is the only *incontestable* demonstration of genuine poetic genius.' *Letter to R. P. Gillies, 22 December 1814*

'[Imagination] recoils from everything but the plastic, the pliant, and the indefinite.' *1815*

'Fancy is given to quicken and to beguile the temporal part of our Nature, Imagination to incite and to support the eternal.' *1815*

'The appropriate business of poetry (which, nevertheless, if genuine, is as permanent as pure science), her appropriate employment, her privilege and her *duty*, is to treat of things not as they *are*, but as they *appear*; not as they exist in themselves, but as they *seem* to exist to the *senses*, and to the *passions*.' *1815 Supplement*

'Thus the Poetry, if there be any in the work [*The White Doe of Rylstone*], proceeds whence it ought to do from the soul of Man, communicating its creative energies to the images of the external world.' *Letter to Francis Wrangham, 18 January 1816*

'. . . even in poetry it is the imaginative only, viz., that which is conversant [with], or turns upon infinity, that powerfully affects me, – I mean to say that, unless in those passages where things are lost in each other, and limits vanish, and aspirations are raised, I read with something too much like indifference . . .' *Letter to W. S. Landor, 21 January 1824*

'... the logical faculty has infinitely more to do with Poetry than the Young and the inexperienced, whether writer or critic, ever dreams of. Indeed, as the materials upon which that faculty is exercised in Poetry are so subtle, so plastic, so complex, the application of it requires an adroitness which can proceed from nothing but practice, a discernment, which emotion is so far from bestowing that at first it is ever in the way of it.' *Letter to William Rowan Hamilton, 24 September 1827*

'blank verse... is infinitely the most difficult metre to manage...' *Letter to Catherine Grace Godwin [Spring 1829]*

'words are not a mere *vehicle*, but they are *powers* either to kill or to animate.' *Letter to William Rowan Hamilton, 23 December 1829*

'If my writings are to last, it will I myself believe, be mainly owing to this characteristic. They will please for the single cause, That we have all of us one human heart!' *Letter to Henry Crabb Robinson [c. 27 April 1835]*

'Admiration & love, to which all knowledge truly vital must tend, are felt by men of real genius in proportion as their discoveries in Natural Philosophy are enlarged; and the beauty in form of a plant or an animal is not made less but more apparent as a whole by a more accurate insight into its constituent properties & powers.' *IF note to 'This Lawn'*

# SOURCES AND SHORT FORMS OF CITATION

The authoritative edition of Wordsworth's poetry is the Cornell Wordsworth, general editor Stephen Parrish. Wherever possible quotation from the poems throughout this *Companion* will be keyed to the 'Reading Text' in the relevant volume of this multi-volume edition, but where there can be no mistaking what is being referred to, quotations will not be encumbered with unnecessary citation notes. Line numbers will only be added at the end of quotations from longer poems – no one needs a line number to find a quotation from a sonnet. Bibliographical details for each volume of the Cornell Wordsworth referred to are given below in the list of short forms of citation. As this *Companion* goes to press the Cornell Wordsworth is not yet complete and for certain poems – most notably *The Excursion* – it is necessary to refer to the previously standard edition of Wordsworth's poetry, edited by Ernest de Selincourt and Helen Darbishire, details of which appear below.

*Short Forms of Citation*
Place of publication is London unless otherwise noted.

| | |
|---|---|
| *1799* | *The Prelude, 1798–1799*, ed. Stephen Parrish [Cornell Wordsworth] (Ithaca, 1977) |
| *1805* | *The Thirteen-Book Prelude*, ed. Mark L. Reed [Cornell Wordsworth] (2 vols.; Ithaca, 1991) |
| *1850* | *The Fourteen-Book Prelude*, ed. W. J. B. Owen [Cornell Wordsworth] (Ithaca, 1985) |
| BL | Samuel Taylor Coleridge, *Biographia Literaria*, ed. James Engell and W. Jackson Bate (2 vols.; 1983) |
| DS | *Descriptive Sketches*, ed. Eric Birdsall [Cornell Wordsworth] (Ithaca, 1984) |
| Borderers | *The Borderers*, ed. Robert Osborn [Cornell Wordsworth] (Ithaca, 1982) |
| BW | *Benjamin the Waggoner*, ed. Paul F. Betz [Cornell Wordsworth] (Ithaca, 1981) |

DW   Dorothy Wordsworth

EP   *Early Poems and Fragments, 1785–1797*, ed. Carol Landon and Jared Curtis [Cornell Wordsworth] (Ithaca, 1997)

H@G   *Home at Grasmere*, ed. Beth Darlington [Cornell Wordsworth] (Ithaca, 1977)

LB   *Lyrical Ballads, and Other Poems, 1797–1800*, ed. James Butler and Karen Green [Cornell Wordsworth] (Ithaca, 1992)

LP   *Last Poems, 1821–1850*, ed. Jared Curtis [Cornell Wordsworth] (Ithaca, 1999)

PB   *Peter Bell*, ed. John E. Jordan [Cornell Wordsworth] (Ithaca, 1985)

P2V   *Poems, in Two Volumes, and Other Poems, 1800–1807*, ed. Jared Curtis [Cornell Wordsworth] (Ithaca, 1983)

Prose   *The Prose Works of William Wordsworth*, ed. W. J. B. Owen and Jane Worthington Smyser (3 vols.; Oxford, 1974)

PW   *The Poetical Works of William Wordsworth*, ed. Ernest de Selincourt and Helen Darbishire (5 vols.; Oxford, 1940–9)

RC   *The Ruined Cottage and The Pedlar*, ed. James Butler [Cornell Wordsworth] (Ithaca, 1979)

SP   *The Salisbury Plain Poems of William Wordsworth*, ed. Stephen Gill [Cornell Wordsworth] (Ithaca, 1975)

SPoems   *Shorter Poems, 1807–1820*, ed. Carl H. Ketcham [Cornell Wordsworth] (Ithaca, 1989)

STC   Samuel Taylor Coleridge

STCL   *Collected Letters of Samuel Taylor Coleridge*, ed. Earl Leslie Griggs (6 vols.; Oxford, 1956–71)

TT   Samuel Taylor Coleridge, *Table Talk*, ed. Carl Woodring (2 vols.; London, 1990).

Tuft   *The Tuft of Primroses, with Other Late Poems for The Recluse*, ed. Joseph F. Kishel [Cornell Wordsworth] (Ithaca, 1986)

WD   *The White Doe of Rylstone*, ed. Kristine Dugas [Cornell Wordsworth] (Ithaca, 1988)

WL   The Wordsworth Library, Grasmere.

WL   *The Letters of William and Dorothy Wordsworth* (8 vols.; Oxford, 1967–93). Individual volumes: *The Early Years 1787–1805*, ed. Chester L. Shaver (1967); *The Middle Years*, pt 1: *1806–1811*, ed. Mary Moorman (1969); *The Middle Years*, pt 2: *1812–1820*, ed. Mary Moorman and Alan G. Hill (1970); *The Later Years*, pt 1: *1821–1828*, ed. Alan G. Hill (1978); *The Later Years*, pt 2: *1829–1834*, ed. Alan G. Hill

(1979); *The Later Years*, pt 3: *1835–1839*, ed. Alan G. Hill
(1982); *The Later Years*, pt 4: *1840–1853*, ed. Alan G. Hill
(1988); *A Supplement of New Letters*, ed. Alan G. Hill (1993).
The edition referred to serially as *WL*, I–VIII.

WW   William Wordsworth

STEPHEN GILL

# Introduction

After struggling in his middle years to win more than a coterie readership, William Wordsworth lived to savour success. He died full of honours in 1850, Poet Laureate to Queen Victoria, a man recognized, in John Keble's words, as 'raised up to be a chief minister, not only of noblest poesy, but of high and sacred truth'.[1] Over the next fifty years his status as an English classic was confirmed in innumerable printings of his works, anthologies, and eventually scholarly studies. By 1950, however, it seemed that his time was over. At an event to mark the centenary of Wordsworth's death, Lionel Trilling, one of the foremost American critics of his generation, summed up what he took to be the current perception of the poet: 'Wordsworth is not attractive and not an intellectual possibility.'[2] Although Trilling's lecture went on to demonstrate that this was not his own view, his decisive and memorable formulation sounded right, as if Keble's words on the plaque in Grasmere Church were being given their sad but inevitable addendum. But such has not been the judgement of history. Since the muted celebrations in 1950, shifts in intellectual concerns have brought the Romantics into new focus and have rediscovered Wordsworth as a fully 'intellectually possible' figure. Western culture's preoccupation with identity and the self; the linguistic turn of much current theory; the interest in power and politics and nationhood; the return to history; environmental issues – all of these dominant features of the cultural landscape of the last half-century have been mapped across the terrain of Wordsworth's poetry and prose.

That today's 'Wordsworth' (the name constituting the object of study in its totality – poetry, prose, biography, historical context, critical history) is substantially different from that of 1950 is partly due to the labours of editors. As Keith Hanley's chapter in this collection spells out, multi-volume editions of Wordsworth's poetry and prose, as well as editions of his letters and of Coleridge's and of other members of their circle, have enormously enlarged our factual knowledge. As far as Wordsworth the poet is concerned we can say more: editorial interventions have reconfigured 'Wordsworth'.

Students now routinely refer to poems which Wordsworth did not publish. *The Prelude* in thirteen books completed in 1805, was not brought to light until seventy-six years after his death. Since then other texts have emerged through scholarly activity, such as *Salisbury Plain, The Ruined Cottage, The Pedlar, The 1799 Prelude, The Recluse*. And this is not a case of editors beavering away at trivia. No one would doubt that the 1805 *Prelude* is Wordsworth's finest poem; recent criticism has treated the others mentioned as central to Wordsworth's achievement.

So strongly have these texts emerged, in fact, poems Wordsworth did not publish, that Jack Stillinger, himself an experienced editor, has warned against the effacement of the poetic canon Wordsworth did choose to authorize (for details see Hanley). But what is actually happening is not effacement – *Lyrical Ballads* and *Poems, in Two Volumes*, for example, are too powerful to accept relegation – but rather a realignment of texts in relation to one another as readers encounter an enlarged poetic corpus, with all the uncertainties inherent in the new apprehension that such an encounter must involve.

Something of the same sense of continuity bracketed with newness must strike us when we consider 'Wordsworth' more largely. I will consider three examples, but more could easily be adduced. In 1916 it was at last revealed publicly (scholarly insiders had known for some time) that Wordsworth had fathered a daughter on a French Royalist sympathizer when he was twenty-two years old. To some it was a relief to learn that Wordsworth had been like Keats and Shelley and Byron, a man with flesh and blood appetites, and not just a solitary visionary communing with Nature and the Universe, which is the figure most of the late portraits, busts, and statues conveyed. For others, though, the news had a more exciting meaning. Now one could see why Wordsworth's early poetry is peopled with abandoned women and destitute figures and haunted guilty men. The haunted, guilty one was the poet himself. Further speculation about Wordsworth's relations with his sister, Dorothy, added to the sense that the poetry up to, say, 1803 was the product of a tormented spirit.

That Wordsworth was a driven man in the 1790s is not in dispute, but more recently scholars struggling to penetrate the opacities of *The Prelude*'s account of those years have focused on the poet's politics, on his allegiances and betrayals as they can be inferred, and in so doing have wonderfully thickened our sense of what it meant to be a radical poet in a country gearing up for a war of survival. But as Kenneth Johnston's *The Hidden Wordsworth* (1998) persuasively demonstrates, it is not the case that a newer, more fashionable *angst* has just supplanted the old. Johnston reminds us how complex the relation was in the 1790s between the private and the public and his work – as does that of David Bromwich in *Disowned by Memory* (1998) – invites still further investigation of Wordsworth in the most turbulent decade of his life.

Or consider the issue of Nature's healing power. In *The Prelude* it is claimed that 'Nature's self, by human love/Assisted' (*1805* X 921–2) guided Wordsworth out of the labyrinth of error in which he was bewildered in the 1790s and one might say that in a sense his whole creative output is a thank-offering. Following up the question of quite how Nature's self saved the poet must lead us into Metaphysics, but it also must lead into appreciation of what the poetry does with Nature in the form of rocks and stones and trees. Wordsworth's poetry is about the 'sense sublime / Of something far more deeply interfused', but much of it is immediately and overtly about mountains and lakes, about clouds and weather and growing things. This immediately attractive aspect of the poetry eventually became the primary identifier of 'Wordsworth' – Wordsworth the 'Nature poet'. His spirit brooded over the foundation in Great Britain of the National Trust, charged with the preservation of landscape of exceptional beauty, and in America over attempts by John Muir (1838–1914) to persuade his contemporaries that the survival of wilderness was vital for the nation's soul. But it was also invoked by anyone wanting to persuade town-dwellers to part with their money on a day out in the country. 'One impulse from a vernal wood' ('The Tables Turned') can be the text for a monograph on Wordsworth's religion, but it can also be used to sell hiking boots.

Until recently it seemed that this bifurcation could only become more pronounced. Wordsworth's 'sense sublime' was increasingly alien, or simply unintelligible, to a post-Christian, urbanized readership. What has come to be called 'eco-criticism', however, has begun one kind of recuperation. Victorians found reassurance in their 'Prophet of Nature'; a few fanatical Wordsworthians testified that they carried a *Poetical Works* along with their Bible. Few if any readers in the twenty-first century are going to return to that. But it is with a sense of urgency that much criticism is reconsidering Wordsworth's writings about the natural world and the place of human beings in it. Coleridge thought it part of the special power of Wordsworth's poetry that it could nourish us 'by awakening the mind's attention from the lethargy of custom, and directing it to the loveliness and the wonders of the world before us; an inexhaustible treasure, but for which, in consequence of the film of familiarity and selfish solicitude we have eyes, yet see not, ears that hear not, and hearts that neither feel nor understand'.[3] As Ralph Pite's essay in this collection ably shows, the eco-criticism of our own time reaches across the centuries to Coleridge here.

A final example: Wordsworth and the New World. After Wordsworth's death American admirers raised money for a memorial in Ambleside Church in the Lake District, confirming, what was already clear from the stream of visitors to the poet's home at Rydal Mount, that his work continued to be esteemed in America. Quite what the esteem amounted to, though, has been the question, one whose challenge was not adequately met by routine gestures towards Emerson and Thoreau. Recent work, however – and the pioneering studies of Alan G. Hill deserve tribute here[4] – has begun to convey some sense of the diversity of response Wordsworth elicited in the new Republic, and Joel Pace's essay in this collection indicates how much more fascinating evidence is waiting to be investigated. But there is more work to be done, as Pace implies, not only on what Wordsworth meant to America but on what America meant to him.

What I am trying to suggest in these examples is that contemporary Wordsworth scholarship is vibrant because it is alive to its continuity with that of the past whilst being fully aware of historical distance, and in this respect it honours, in fact, a primary force in the creative powers of the poet himself. Wordsworth was obsessed with ensuring that nothing was lost from his past: 'I look into past times as prophets look / Into futurity'. Memory reaches, chains bind, bonds sustain, links link – the poetry and much of the prose celebrates whatever preserves affinities 'Between all stages of the life of man'.[5] But the intensity of Wordsworth's gaze as he hangs 'Incumbent o'er the surface of past time' (*1805 Prelude*, IV, 263), is a function of his equally obsessive awareness that making sense of the past calls for a lifetime's revisiting, open to the possibility of and recognizing the necessity for reinterpretation. All of the specially commissioned essays in this Companion share something of the same awareness. Their topic, too, is Wordsworth past and present.

## NOTES

1 The tribute from the dedication to Keble's Oxford lectures on poetry, *De Poetica Vi Medica: Praelectiones Academicae Oxonii Habitae* (1844), was inscribed on the plaque to Wordsworth in Grasmere Church, where he is buried.
2 Lionel Trilling, 'Wordsworth and the Rabbis', in *The Opposing Self* (London, 1955), p. 118.
3 *Biographia Literaria*, chapter XIV.
4 Alan G. Hill, 'Wordsworth and his American Friends', *Bulletin of Research in the Humanities*, 81 (1978), 146–60. Much freshly researched information is also compressed into the footnotes of Hill's volumes of the Wordsworth letters.
5 *PW* II 481.

# I

NICOLA TROTT

# Wordsworth: the shape of the poetic career

In sketching Wordsworth's life, two portraits might be drawn, almost as mirror images of one another. The first would present a child who was orphaned by the age of thirteen, and to whose family the first Lord Lonsdale refused to pay the substantial debt (over £4500) that was owing to Wordsworth senior at his death; a boy who rebelled against his guardians, slashed through a family portrait with a whip,[1] and failed, first to gain anything more than an unclassified BA (from St John's College, Cambridge, 1791), and then to take orders or enter one of the professions; a graduate who in 1792 travelled to revolutionary France, where he was converted to its cause and fathered an illegitimate child; a 'vagabond' who returned to England and several years of apparently aimless roving, leading, in 1796, to some kind of nervous breakdown; a young 'democrat' who kept dubious, if not actually dangerous company, and in 1798 was thought worthy of surveillance by a government spy;[2] a republican who laid plans for a radical monthly called the *Philanthropist*, and may have been involved in a liberal London weekly of that name, which ran for forty-two issues, 1795–6;[3] an author of oppositional political tracts, the unpublished *Letter to the Bishop of Llandaff* (1793), written in defence of the regicide in France and rights of man at home, and *The Convention of Cintra* (1809), which accepted that fighting imperialist France constituted a just war, but was highly critical of the deal by which a Spanish revolt ended with Britain allowing the defeated French army to evacuate Portugal without loss; a '*Semi*-atheist' whom Coleridge persuaded into an unspecific form of Unitarianism, and who in 1812 still had 'no need of a Redeemer';[4] a would-be populist who argued that poetry was not the exclusive property of the middle and upper classes, and attributed to his own work the polemical purpose of showing that 'men who do not wear fine cloaths can feel deeply' (letter to Charles James Fox, 14 January 1801); a financially insecure poet who until his mid-forties lived in relative poverty, adopting a lofty defensiveness against an uncomprehending 'public' and the diffuse notoriety provided by hostile Tory critics, among whom he was synonymous at once with childishness and insubordination.

And yet a quite different silhouette might be drawn. This would outline a Wordsworth who was the second son of a well-to-do law-agent of the wealthiest peer in Westmorland; who, as a boy, was educated at Hawkshead, one of the best grammar schools in the country, with a string of Cambridge entrants to its name; who, as a young man, mixed with the foremost radical intellectuals of his day, and formed a profound friendship with Coleridge, a 'seminal' mind of the age; who was learned in Latin and Italian, as well as English literature, had many thousands of lines of poetry by heart, and came to possess a substantial library; who sent his edition of the *Lyrical Ballads* (1800) to the leader of the Whig Opposition, was recognized as a founder of the 'Lake School' of poetry, and, on Southey's death in 1843, rose to be Poet Laureate; who had a friend in Sir George Beaumont, a leading patron of the arts, and, as a landscaper, designed both the Beaumonts' winter garden at Coleorton in Leicestershire (1806–7) and his own grounds at Rydal Mount (where the Wordsworths moved in 1813); who was an influential arbiter of taste in rural scenery and who, as well as insisting on rights of way, campaigned for the Lake District to be spared the despoliations of rail-borne industry and tourism; who signed up for the Grasmere Volunteers when there was threat of French invasion in 1803, and addressed a sequence of sonnets to the theme of national moral and martial renewal; who in 1813 accepted a government post as Distributor of Stamps for Westmorland (which made him responsible for the tax raised on the stamped paper used in legal transactions); who became intimate with the second Lord Lonsdale, and in 1818 electioneered tirelessly on his behalf in the Tory interest, earning the nickname 'Bombastes Furioso' (as well as publishing *Two Addresses to the Freeholders of Westmorland* against agitation and press freedom); who latterly emerged as a defender of the Church of England and the Anglican tradition; who lived, as Stephen Gill has shown,[5] to be still more central to the Victorian than he had been to the Napoleonic age; who had as brothers a London lawyer and a Master of Trinity College, Cambridge, was a regular presence among the London literary and social élites, and, at long last, in his sixties, found himself world-famous.

The entire career, and with it the path from anonymity to household name, is momentarily visible in George Eliot's *Middlemarch*, published in 1871–2, two decades after the poet's death, and set just prior to the first Reform Bill of 1832: as chapter 2 opens, Mr Brooke is reminiscing about how he and Wordsworth missed each other as contemporaries at Cambridge (*c.* 1790), but dined together 'twenty years afterwards at Cartwright's', and in the company of the chemist Sir Humphry Davy. From the radical years of the 1790s to the no less turbulent period of the late 1820s, Mr Brooke has remained, albeit confusedly, on the liberal side of politics. Wordsworth, (in)famously, did not; and this break in the career has made him a pivotal and controversial representative of those who came of age at the onset of the French Revolution (1789). Just lately, some powerful revisionists (Jerome J. McGann, James K. Chandler, and Marjorie Levinson, among others) have produced readings of the early poetry in terms of its hidden clues to tergiversation, or silent evasions of 'history' (the most notorious test case being 'Tintern Abbey', whose title elaborately, almost teasingly, draws attention to its composition on 13 July, and so to the very eve of the Bastille Day anniversary). Such readings have kept Wordsworth at the centre of 'Romanticism', however much the concept may have shifted its ground around and beneath him.

The conscious liberal in Wordsworth died harder than has sometimes been suggested. He was understood to be 'strongly disposed to Republicanism' and '*equality*' in 1806,[6] and advocated 'a thorough reform in Parliament and a new course of education', in 1809 (letter to Daniel Stuart, *WL* ii 296). *The Excursion* (1814) drew to an end with a swingeing attack on child labour (Book VIII), and a call for a system of national education (Book IX). *The Prelude* allowed the 'Bliss' of witnessing the 'dawn' of Revolution to stand alongside an apostrophe to the 'Genius of Burke', added in 1832 (*Prel.1850* xi 108, vii 512–43). Even in 1836 Wordsworth could be heard praising the Sheffield poet Ebenezer Elliott, whose *Corn-Law Rhymes* (1828) spoke for the impoverished labouring classes and, incidentally, was being regarded by Henry Crabb Robinson as a fellow-traveller in Whiggish politics (*Diary* iii 87–8, 83).

Nevertheless, the late Toryism is hard to overestimate. Wordsworth was dead against Catholic Emancipation (1829) and the 1832 Reform Bill. His lifelong sympathy with the poor and appreciation of Ebenezer Elliot did not, as we might expect, extend to support for the Anti-Corn Law League's challenge to the protectionist policy of taxing imported corn, the effect of which was to maintain the incomes of landowners at the expense of artificially high prices for bread. Nor was Wordsworth any better disposed towards the utilitarian and laissez-faire economics which sought to free trade and systematize welfare: his hostility to the 1834 Poor Law Amendment Act, which promoted workhouses over outdoor relief, gave a vivid political colouring to preferences he first articulated in *The Old Cumberland Beggar*, 1798. As this last example suggests, the late Wordsworth found new relevance and impetus for the radically inclined poetry of his youth. When the *Salisbury Plain* poems written in the 1790s were finally revised and published as *Guilt and Sorrow* (1842), they were placed in the context of the *Sonnets upon the Punishment of Death*, which argued in favour of the penalty and were published in the Tory *Quarterly Review*, for December 1841. As a result, a work which began life under the shadow of William Godwin's *Political Justice* (1793) as an attack on war and law (that is, on human sacrifices to 'Superstition', and a penal code which creates the crimes it punishes), instead ended by asserting the justice of sentencing a murderer to swing. The merciful – or squeamish – reader was reassured that, in this case, judgement was not marred by arbitrary cruelty, which in the eighteenth century demanded that the body be hung 'in iron case' as an entertainment, or warning, to the masses (the fate which had indeed formed the last outrage of the unpublished interim text, *Adventures on Salisbury Plain*, 1795–9).

Wordsworth's shifts to the right may be gauged by the fact that the 'Sonnets Dedicated to Liberty' (1807 and 1815) were progressively devoted, first 'to National Independence and Liberty', and then 'to Liberty and Order'. Among the sonnets eventually collected in this sequence, one was written against the introduction of voting by ballot;[7] another 'recommended to the perusal of the Anti-Corn Law Leaguers, the Political Economists, and of all those who consider that the Evils under which we groan are to be removed or palliated by measures ungoverned by moral and religious principles' (1843 Fenwick Note to 'Feel for the wrongs'); and three were offered *In Allusion to Various Recent Histories and Notices of the French Revolution*, the last of which addressed the nation thus:

> Long-favoured England! be not thou misled
> By monstrous theories of alien growth . . .

This suspicion of the foreign and theoretical was sparked by the appearance of Carlyle's *French Revolution* (1837); but reached back to those patriotic and traditional allegiances which were first activated by the founding document of modern conservatism, Edmund Burke's *Reflections on the Revolution in France* (1790). Such tenacities of the memory, both for language and for feeling, had been the great strength of Wordsworth's writing. What became at last a panicky rigidity – a favourite line from Spenser, 'All change is perilous and all chance unsound',[8] could well serve as the motto of old man Wordsworth – was once a lively fear of perishability, transience, and loss, a fear that may be related to the poet's acute anxiety for his own powers, and which shapes the massive achievements of 'Tintern Abbey' and *Resolution and Independence*, the 'Intimations Ode' and *The Prelude*. For all the evident dislocation between radical and reactionary Wordsworths, the poetry insists on its own revival as the evidence of undiminished imaginative life, and, faced with that vital threat of mortality, asserts a remarkable continuity of vision:

> I thought of Thee, my partner and my guide,
> As being past away. – Vain sympathies!
> For, *backward*, Duddon! as I cast my eyes,
> I see what was, and is, and will abide;
> The Form remains, the Function never dies...
>     ('Conclusion' to *The River Duddon*, 1820)

Any account of the 'shape' of Wordsworth's career has to reckon with the fact that it has already been amply reflected upon by the poet himself. Wordsworth's chosen metaphors for this shape are the river and the church. The river flows through the central self-explorations, 'Tintern Abbey' and *The Prelude* (*1805* i 271–304, ix 1–9, xiii 172–84), to say nothing of *Essays upon Epitaphs* I and the lines just quoted. The church is publicly asserted as a model in the Preface to *The Excursion* (1814), where it places all the poet's works as contributions to a single evolving gothic building. Both metaphors offer themselves as organic, counter-classical modes of organization. Yet, while each is insightful on its own account, these analogies are most interesting for the conflicts that emerge between them. The one is drawn from a natural, the other from a man-made, structure. If the rivery self-image suggests an identity of unceasing process and free-flowing form, ever-changing and yet continuous through time, then the cathedral of works is dedicated to the idea of a completed whole, an architectonic arrangement as final and incontestible as the claims of religion itself.

As it happens, we know (as Wordsworth's contemporaries did not) that, for all the confident aspirations of the architect, the edifice announced in *The Excursion* would never be built. Of the epic project of *The Recluse*, only the glorious 'Prospectus' and the – often impressive – fragments of false starts, remain: *Home at Grasmere*, 1800; 'St Paul's', 'To the Clouds', and 'The Tuft of Primroses', 1808; and the vital 1798 drafts, which were incorporated into *The Excursion* (see *William Wordsworth*, ed. Stephen Gill (Oxford: Oxford University Press, 1984), pp. 676–81). When *The Recluse* was first devised, with Coleridge, in 1798, Wordsworth excitedly speculated that it would prove an all-inclusive shape: 'I know not any thing which will not come within the scope of my plan' (letter to James Webbe Tobin, 6 March 1798). By 1814, it has become the very *raison d'être* of the poet's enterprise, the great 'body' of the Wordsworthian church. But the 'blissful hour' never arrives.

As is now familiar from the work of Kenneth R. Johnston and others,[9] this absence haunted Wordsworth's writing life and was fundamental in shaping his career. It also brings us to another way in which we have stolen a march on his contemporaries. Unlike them, we possess the 'biographical' poem which the Preface to *The Excursion* mentions as 'preparatory' to the unwritten

*Recluse*. The 'history of the Author's mind' had by 1814 long since assumed epic proportions, but did not get published until 1850. This second absence marks the great oddity of Wordsworth's presentation of his career: that it is a shape which deliberately refuses to reveal itself in its most important form – *The Prelude* – until after the poet's death. Wordsworth's longest and most ambitious work to date was kept back as merely the 'ante-chapel' to the church, as a 'prelude' to, and preparation for, the one true epic. For most of us, it is on the contrary *The Prelude* which seems to make Wordsworth a true poet, and of the Romantic party without knowing it, because it shows how he wrote in fetters when striving to fulfil that hard task, *The Recluse*, and at liberty when exploring the self in all its rich and unphilosophic perplexity. It is *The Prelude* that has come to seem truly 'Wordsworthian'.

A crucial aspect of this re-shaping of Wordsworth is that the results are neither univocal nor uniform. For we can speak, as (once again) original readers could not, of more than one *Prelude*. The retrieval from manuscripts of the earliest full-length version of the poem, completed in 1805, has been followed by the two-part version of 1798–9 (the former was first presented by Ernest de Selincourt, in 1926; the latter in the Norton Critical Edition, ed. Jonathan Wordsworth, M. H. Abrams, and Stephen Gill, 1979). These texts, both of which are now standard 'Preludes', were just the start of a thorough-going rejuvenation of the Wordsworth corpus. The survival of a huge archive (now preserved by the Wordsworth Trust) has enabled scholars to present reading texts of many more early versions (the Cornell Wordsworth Series, under the General Editorship of Stephen Parrish). Thanks to this new-look Wordsworth, we can observe the precise moment at which Coleridge's influence begins to be felt, in the development of *The Ruined Cottage* (now disentangled from its original place of publication as the first book of *The Excursion*); and the first stirrings of a poetry that traces the 'Growth of a Poet's Mind', in the related biography of *The Pedlar*. We also have a wealth of material that is newly promoted to the status of 'text' rather than being allocated to footnotes or appendices: the juvenilia; the 1794 revisions of *An Evening Walk*; the multiple stages of *Salisbury Plain* and *The Prelude*; the full complexity of the early notebooks, and the drafts surrounding the *Lyrical Ballads* and *Poems, in Two Volumes*.

This versioning of Wordsworth (which far surpasses the variant readings supplied by old-fashioned editing) has altered his shape in two main ways. First, it has assumed that early is best. That assumption has turned readers and editors into textual primitivists and archaeologists: the accretions of a lifetime's rewriting have been removed, so as to reveal the pristine, often pre-publication, and as it were unsocialized, Wordsworth. Putting it crudely, the youthful Romantic needed to be rescued from the 'bleak old bore'

(W. H. Auden's phrase) who went on tinkering long after age and habit had atrophied the body and closed the mind – a slow fade that bears a striking resemblance to Wordsworth's own self-diagnosis in the 'Ode' and elsewhere. Secondly, the recent shape-shifting has tended to privilege the poet of process. In terms of Wordsworth's own metaphors, its model is the river, its method a chronology of writing which itself assumes the rivery course of an on-going, linear development through time. A minute attention to the historical details of composition, year-by-year, and almost hour-by-hour, would seem to fit in, not only with our own prejudices in favour of the open-ended, the undogmatic, and the inconclusive, but also with the facts of the case as we now know them. After all, *The Recluse* was never completed. By a supreme irony, the Wordsworthian church turned out to be a castle in the air. What survives are the ruins of that dream – or, to put it more positively, a 'body' that is forever in process: 'Who that shall point, as with a wand, and say, / 'This portion of the river of my mind / Came from yon fountain?'' (*Prel.1805* ii 213–15).

And yet the rivery form has its limitations. As an exclusive shape, it is seriously distorting. In foregrounding the design of *The Recluse, The Excursion* signalled a turn, which Wordsworth's remaining years largely confirmed, towards the finished product, and away from the process of its making. Modern textual scholarship has enabled readers' preferences to run in the opposite direction; and we have very good aesthetic reasons for this preference. But it is nevertheless crucial to our understanding of the shape of the career that the emergence of the second metaphor – the church – be acknowledged. Its practical meaning as a principle of organization is revealed almost immediately, by the publication of the two-volume *Poems* (1815), Wordsworth's first collected edition, and the first in which his works are, as the Preface to *The Excursion* anticipates, 'properly arranged'. This arrangement introduces the categories under which, with modifications, he will group all future collections.

The chronological sequence has taught us a great deal about composition (and has its apotheosis in the work of Mark Reed). It has had less to say about publication, or the carefully orchestrated dissemination of the works, by volume, by class, and by genre. The four corner-stones of the Wordsworthian church are *Lyrical Ballads* (1800), *Poems, in Two Volumes* (1807), *The Excursion* (1814), and *Poems* (1815). (For those who lack the originals, facsimiles of all four have recently appeared under the Woodstock Books imprint.)

As Wordsworth's first substantial single-author publication, *Lyrical Ballads* (1800) is of the greatest symbolic importance. It does away with the anonymity and partnership of the 1798 volume, and indicates Wordsworth's discovery of his settled vocation as a poet, which came about when he and Dorothy moved into Dove Cottage at the end of 1799. This moment was the fulfilment of a cherished ideal in which poetry and the Lake District fuse. Wordsworth's hour of 'dedication' is always set in the Lakes; in the Fenwick Note to *An Evening Walk* it is dated to his fourteenth year, and in *The Prelude* iv 314–45 to the Cambridge summer vacation. The ambitious new start is apparent from the substantial essay prefacing the 1800 volumes, which as a statement of poetical principles and declaration of a specific mission was an unwitting hostage to Wordsworth's critical fortune, and passport to his lasting influence. However, since Volume I more or less reproduces the contents of 1798, only the second of the 1800 volumes contains fresh material. Here, the novelty is partly generic, involving a Lake District take on the ancient forms of pastoral and fable. To the psychological dramatizations of 1798 are added the new varieties of Goslar and Grasmere: the provocative enigma of the Lucy poems, the quelled tragedy of 'Michael' and 'The Brothers', the significant inconsequentiality of the 'Poems on the Naming of Places', the bizarrely poignant Mathew poems, the exemplary mind-and-nature interchange of 'There was a Boy', and the disturbing sexuality and spirituality of 'Nutting' and 'Ruth'.

Poems, *in Two Volumes* (1807) is nothing if not mixed. Volume I leads off by juxtaposing the mercurial lyrics of 1802, whose poet is prepared to fraternize with birds and flowers, with the high-mindedness of the 'Ode to Duty', whose poet 'supplicate[s]' for the 'controul' of a 'Stern Lawgiver'. Volume II, for its part, moves from the butterfly 'Moods of My Own Mind' to the baffling heights of the 'Ode'. Between these two voices lies a conscious recognition of change – a recognition that is already underway in 'Resolution and Independence', and is summed up, in 'Elegiac Stanzas', the penultimate poem of the collection, by the terrible fracture caused by the drowning of Wordsworth's seaman brother John: 'I have submitted to a new controul: / A power is gone, which nothing can restore'. The new seriousness of temper has a public dimension also: Wordsworth's first venture in the sonnet-sequence, and in a consciously Miltonic persona, is dedicated to 'Liberty', under whose banner all who oppose the Napoleonic regime must enlist.

For all this, the reception of Poems, *in Two Volumes* nearly destroyed Wordsworth's reputation. It was here, ironically, that his 'jacobinical' past, and the critical animus generated by his Preface to *Lyrical Ballads*, caught up with him. The collection was judged by the slighter lyrics with which it opened, and by the Augustan criteria which still persisted among periodical reviewers. Significantly, these criteria united the liberal Lord Byron and the Whig Francis Jeffrey in common disdain: both used a mock-nursery rhyme, 'namby-pamby', to ridicule what they saw as the 'puerility' and 'affectation' of the Wordsworth system (Byron, *Monthly Literary Recreations*, July 1807; Jeffrey, *Edinburgh Review*, October 1807).

After the 1807 disaster, Wordsworth fell silent. His next major production, all of seven years later, was seemingly designed to be critic-proof. *The Excursion* could not be less childish. It is, perhaps, the nearest thing we have to a Wordsworthian church (indeed, it has a pastor for one of its central characters). It also marks Wordsworth's arrival socially: the work was dedicated to Lord Lonsdale. None of this prevented Jeffrey from mounting a further attack; but his famous and devastating opener, 'This will never do', is belied by the fact that it *did* do, both at the time of publication (Keats called *The Excursion* one of 'three things to rejoice at in this Age', letter to Haydon, 11 January 1818) and beyond: for the Victorians, *The Excursion* was *the* long Wordsworth poem. Dissenting voices were raised, privately, by Coleridge, who blamed *The Excursion* for not being *The Recluse* (letter to Wordsworth, 30 May 1815); by Blake, who refused 'to believe' the Wordsworth doctrine of mind and world 'fitting and fitted' (annotation to the Prospectus to *The Recluse*); and by the Shelleys, who categorically pronounced 'He is a slave' (Mary Shelley's Journal, 14 September 1814) – thus beginning the 'lost leader' syndrome that culminates in Robert Browning's 1845 poem of that name, where the Distributor of Stamps is glibly conflated with Judas Iscariot: 'Just for a handful of silver he left us.'

*The Excursion* alters our sense of Wordsworth's shape in three main ways: it uses the peripatetic form of a Tour to organize a long series of interlocking narratives; it adapts both Lake District pastoral and philosophical blank verse to a wide-ranging survey of contemporary society; and it introduces, in the story of the French Revolution and the ideological debate surrounding its events, the master-narrative of the age (which we know from *The Prelude* to have been shaped by a personal experience unique among the major Romantic writers).

*Poems* (1815), dedicated to Beaumont, hopes to replace the discredited system of *Lyrical Ballads* with one that will make the works invulnerable to the 'senseless outcry' of the critics ('Essay, Supplementary'). To this end, Wordsworth introduces a new theory and a new order: a Preface, and an 'Essay, Supplementary' to it, open and close the first volume; and the poems are given the canonical treatment advertised in the Preface to *The Excursion*. (Even so, Wordsworth cannot resist raising the standard of the old dispensation: the Preface to *Lyrical Ballads* is smuggled in, at the back of Volume II.) *Poems* (1815) begins with 'My heart leaps up' and ends with the 'Ode'. A chronological arrangement would tell us that these works were being composed within days or hours of one another in March 1802; the categorical arrangement insists that they are first and last in an order which represents the shape of human life. The collection starts with 'Poems Referring to the Period of Childhood', and comes to a close with those 'Referring to the Period of Old Age'. In between these two ages of man, further categories suggest a process of mental maturation: 'Poems Founded on the Affections' lead, via 'Poems of the Fancy' and 'the Imagination', to a synthesis of thought and feeling in 'Poems Proceeding from Sentiment and Reflection'. Yet a third level of categorization matches a biological to a poetic and generic order: the 'Poems Referring to the Period of Childhood' are succeeded by 'Juvenile Pieces'; those 'Referring to the Period of Old Age' by 'Epitaphs and Elegiac Poems'. The 1815 arrangement throws one category above all into prominence. Spanning both volumes, and divided equally between them, the 'Poems of the Imagination' recognize the centrality of the imaginative faculty to the Wordsworth canon. And, as a group, it too reflects the maturing mind, opening with 'There was a Boy' and ending with 'Tintern Abbey' (where, we may recall, a transition from 'glad animal movements' to 'elevated thoughts' was first observed). A final complexity, and circularity, is implied by the fact that the 'Ode', which stands alone as an uncategorizable conclusion to the whole, has as its epigraph lines from 'My heart leaps up', the first piece in the collection.

As these multiple orderings suggest, the life of the body, the mind, and the work, all converge in the single shape of Wordsworth's new arrangement. When the rivery consciousness gets to thinking of the total effect of its meditative, meandering, overflowing courses, it does so in terms of an order of architecture. But, in the 1815 *Poems* at least, it is an order that is sympathetic to the human scale and the human lifespan. Remarkably, the architectural form retains within it a sense of the rivery process of existence, flowing from birth to death, and reflecting upon itself at every stage. Perhaps, then, it is in combining the two analogies that the shape of the career reveals itself most fully. Indeed, the 1815 edition seems to recognize as much, since, as well as categorizing the poems, its table of contents tabulates some of the dates of composition and first publication. Elsewhere, too, river and cathedral are allowed to share a common form: both *The River Duddon* (1820) and *Ecclesiastical Sketches* (1822) are groups of sonnets. Collectively speaking, each sonnet is part of a rivery sequence; individually, it is a 'narrow room', one of the church's 'little cells...and sepulchral recesses' ('Nuns fret not'; Preface to *The Excursion*).

The shape of the river has a lifelong persistence in Wordsworth, thanks to its pedestrian form, the Tour. Appropriately enough, it is in *The River Duddon* that we find the first outing, under his own name, of Wordsworth's

*Topographical Description of the Country of the Lakes*. Originally published anonymously as an introduction to Joseph Wilkinson's *Select Views in Cumberland, Westmoreland, and Lancashire* (1810), this prose work appeared in a bewildering variety of formats: it was known to the public mainly in the form of *A Guide through the District of the Lakes* (1835), though it also extends to 'An Unpublished Tour' and an incomplete essay on 'The Sublime and the Beautiful' (1811/12; available in *Prose* II). Far more than a 'Description', these writings together make up a kind of sacred text about the region in which Wordsworth had chosen to live and dedicate himself. For a man who is popularly regarded as an unbudgeable Grasmere fixture, however, Wordsworth spends a surprising amount of time away from home. The confirmed ruralist is also an avid metropolitan, making regular sorties to London throughout his life (he last visited in 1847). Quite apart from his almost daily Lakeland rambles, there is his peripatetic youth (in Cambridge, France, London, the Isle of Wight, Wales, Keswick, Racedown, Alfoxden, Goslar, and Yorkshire), and the innumerable deliberate waywardnesses of later years: the Lakes in 1799 and 1807; Calais in 1802; the Continent in 1790 and – *en famille* this time – in 1820; North Wales in 1824; Ireland in 1829; Scotland, repeatedly, from the brief trip in 1801, to the extended tours of 1803, 1814, 1831, and 1833; Belgium, Holland, and the Rhine in 1828, when Coleridge came too, and the two men were finally reconciled; and, last but not least, Italy in 1837, to which Wordsworth had been longing to return since his first glimpse in 1790, and which brings his career full circle. With impeccable symmetry, the Tour is the route taken, both by his first major publications, *An Evening Walk* (the Lakes, 1789–9) and *Descriptive Sketches* (the Continent, 1790), and by his last separate collection (1842), containing his *Memorials of a Tour in Italy, 1837*.

These journeys are best seen, perhaps, not as random holidays, but as an intrinsic element of the poetic life, and as forays into mental, quite as much as geographical, territory. Scotland, Wordsworth told Scott, 'is... the most poetical Country I ever travelled in' (7 November 1805, *WL* 1 641). One way in which it becomes poetical is that it is not only literally but imaginatively revisited. Just as *Memorials of a Tour on the Continent, 1820* (1822) retraces the steps of his ecstatic 1790 Tour, so Scotland is four times recorded, with each layer of writing referring back to earlier inscriptions. *Poems, in Two Volumes* (1807) makes muses – the Highland Girl and the Solitary Reaper, Rob Roy and Burns – of the 1803 tour, Wordsworth's first lone trip with Dorothy since his marriage; *Poems* (1815) places the unvisited Yarrow of 1803 (and 1807) alongside its visited sequel, from the 1814 tour; *Yarrow Revisited, and Other Poems* (1835) turns the

1831 Tour, during which he said a last goodbye to Scott, into his best-selling single title volume; and, finally, 1835 sees the publication of forty-odd sonnets *Composed or Suggested during a Tour in Scotland... 1833*. For the venturesome reader, each visitation yields rich and relatively neglected pickings.

Wordsworth's tourism enacts the principles of return and renewal which are embedded at the heart of his imaginative self-conception and development, in the so-called 'spots of time'. It also, more often than not, imposes a period of delay between having the experience and writing about it. In its memorializing, the Tour conforms exactly to the deep structure of Wordsworth's creative life: 'emotion recollected in tranquillity', impressions which are stored up, to lie dormant 'Until maturer seasons called them forth' (Preface to *Lyrical Ballads*, *Prose* i 148; *1805* i 623). Travel is of vital importance in prompting and inspiring new work, providing the resources for long sequences, and the occasion of many individual poems ('Tintern Abbey', notably, a tribute to the Wye, revisited in 1798, and *The White Doe of Rylstone* (1815), which came of a trip to Bolton Abbey, in 1807). The Tour is one of the most self-consciously innovative shapes of Wordsworth's career: prose Tours were commonplace in his day, poetic ones much less so. The latter first emerges as a coherent sub-genre in the 1807 volumes: a sequence of 'Poems, Composed During a Tour, Chiefly on Foot' (actually a product of several different occasions) is followed by 'Poems Written During a Tour in Scotland'. Once again, the pedestrian or linear form is brought within a defining architectonic structure.

Wordsworth's aims are at once mutual and divided. River and church coincide; but they are most vitally metaphorical in their reciprocal contradictoriness. They point to kinds of contrariness which may be seen throughout the canon. To take an example that textual scholarship has recently brought to the fore: Wordsworth toiled repeatedly to give his poems a fixed final form, both verbal and organizational; yet his doing so involved him in constant, harassing, even neurotic, revision. His last collected edition was issued only in 1849–50. There is a sense in which the poet's mind compulsively resisted the closure his professionalism tirelessly sought. When *The Prelude* welcomes the return of inspiration, it is as a marvellously 'shapeless eagerness' (*1805* ix 11); when it allegorizes the death of mental process, a self-wounding simile describes the elusive 'Tendencies to shape' as being 'Exposed and lifeless, as a written book' (viii 721–7). But fixity is by no means a consistent evil, or mobility a certain good. Wordsworth, at his most subtle, is neither dualist nor monologist. Rather, what look like the simplest and stablest of verbal structures are fraught with a destabilizing vigour. Take, for instance,

'Resolution and Independence', where the decrepit Leech-Gatherer is said to be 'Motionless as a Cloud', a comparison that only gradually yields its counter-intuitive wit – namely, the settling on a cloud, of all things, as an immovable image. Conversely, in preceding lines, the man's 'extreme old age' has been animated into an eerie half-life by the still more improbable similes of 'a huge Stone' and 'a Sea-beast' (lines 82, 64–72). All such devices, meanwhile, register the narrating eye, disconcertingly and equivocally at work on its subject. 'I have at all times endeavoured to look steadily at my subject', proclaims the realist poet of the Preface to *Lyrical Ballads* (*Prose* i 132); but that 'subject' everywhere includes the enhancing, dimming, or transforming of outward things by mind itself.

Many critics have remarked upon Wordsworth's extraordinary power of animating the world by seeing it from the perspective of our perceptions: that skater who is the centre of his own whirling universe in *The Prelude* (i 474–86); the thinker whose solitariness enables the 'cliffs' of 'Tintern Abbey' to 'impress / *Thoughts* of more deep seclusion' on an already 'secluded scene' (lines 6–7, my emphasis); the boy whose transforming receptivity is mirrored by, and yet distinct from, the tremulous instability of 'that uncertain heaven, receiv'd / Into the bosom of the steady lake' ('There Was a Boy', 24–5). From a technical point of view, there is a comparable subjectivizing of poetics: metre, diction, rhythm, are all re-conceived as being driven by 'passion', and the dramatic projections of feeling.

As a 'border' figure (a name devised by Geoffrey Hartman, in *Wordsworth's Poetry, 1787–1814* (1964), and explored by Jonathan Wordsworth, in *William Wordsworth: The Borders of Vision* (1982)), the Leech-Gatherer is emblematic of the divided impulses which shape the career. The most fundamental of these has also had the profoundest influence on the tradition: the Wordsworth who declared, disarmingly, that the poet 'is a man speaking to men' (Preface to *Lyrical Ballads, Prose* i 138), was also perceived, by Keats, as 'a thing per se' which 'stands alone' (a revealing moment, this, for showing how a Wordsworthian subjectivity is felt to acquire the hard resisting outline of an object). The advocate of a poetry whose subjects are drawn 'from common life', and whose diction approximates 'the real language of men', was also the inventor of an idiom Keats christened 'the wordsworthian or egotistical sublime' (*Prose* i 150; Keats, letter to Woodhouse, 27 October 1818). Both poetics were revolutionary, both have come to seem exemplarily modern (in *Confessions of an English Opium-Eater*, De Quincey runs away from school carrying two books: the tragedies of Euripedes for the ancients, *Lyrical Ballads* for the moderns). These split yet shared poetries are seeded as early as the first, anonymous *Lyrical Ballads* of 1798. Here, we find *both* the ballads and lyrics which anticipate the enormous profusion of Wordsworth's 'small poems' (which Coleridge despaired of as counter to *The Recluse*); *and* the 'exquisitely elaborate'[10] blank verse of 'Tintern Abbey', a work whose self-concentration and contestation look towards the epic 'Growth of a Poet's Mind'. This kind of division becomes inescapable – and, to contemporary critics, inescapably provocative – in *Poems, in Two Volumes* (1807). Looking back, the edition may be read for its incessant, if eccentric, variety; at the time, it was proof of Wordsworth's giddiness, swinging wildly 'from sublimity to silliness' (Montgomery, on *Poems in Two Volumes*).

Crucially, the division falls within poems as well as between them: Wordsworth conjures one of his greatest moments, the first of the *Prelude* 'spots of time', out of the bizarre proximity of 'ordinary sight' and 'visionary dreariness'. His 'high argument' is almost always cheek-by-jowl with 'humbler matter'. To Coleridge, this instability amounted to an illegitimate mixing of different kinds of writing, not just degrees of poetic register: his mature reservations about Wordsworth cohere around the perplexity induced by an oxymoronically 'daring humbleness' – the deflationary and inflationary antitheses and inequalities of the style (*Biographia Literaria*, ch. 22). William Hazlitt, meanwhile, diagnosed that the difficulty for readers of the *Lyrical Ballads* lay in their 'unaccountable mixture of seeming simplicity and real abstruseness' ('Mr Wordsworth', *The Spirit of the Age*); and Richard Mant turned the same mixture, in *Poems, in Two Volumes*, to parodic use: *The Simpliciad* (1808) brought Augustan standards of decorum to bear on the Romantic disproportion of 'Poets, who fix their visionary sight / On Sparrow's eggs'. With his ear for political nuance, Hazlitt detected another sort of discrepancy, identifying on separate occasions both a 'levelling Muse' and, later, deplorably, a poetry whose 'language . . . naturally falls in with the language of power'.[11]

Taking up important statements by A. C. Bradley and Matthew Arnold, M. H. Abrams has made a shape out of such divisions, in an essay called 'Two Roads to Wordsworth'. He and others have concentrated especially on the poet's joint reputation for social amicability (much enhanced by the discovery of his love letters to his wife), and for solitary and even misanthropic musings. Another – and, for my purposes, final – way of stating the fruitfulness of the problem is to say that the poet of nature and the natural man is also the mind-centred figure of whom Wilde astutely said, 'Wordsworth went to the Lakes, but he was never a Lake poet' (*The Critic as Artist*). In both these Wordsworths, the Victorians, Arnold and Mill especially, recognized a great spiritual doctor or healer of minds. But the apparently reassuring and naively continuous self, whose days are 'Bound each to each by natural piety', involves a startling and unsettling inversion of biological priority – 'The

Child is Father of the Man' ('My heart leaps up') – or requires an electrify-ing and radical purgation of experience:

> Fallings from us, vanishings;
> Blank misgivings of a Creature
> Moving about in worlds not realized...
>                         ('Ode', lines 146–8)

What both the joyous child of the lyric and the alienated figure of the 'Ode' have in common is their newness before the world. Their strength of re-sponse is owing to a paradoxical or effortful primitivism, which hopes to return the self-estranged and -forgetful adult to an uncluttered, undimin-ished version of himself. The 'spots of time', Wordsworth's core doctrine of renovation, are dated to 'our first childhood', the 'twilight of rememberable life' (1799 i 296–8); and were themselves arrived at astonishingly early, while Wordsworth was in Germany in 1798–9. In the long *Prelude*, they acquire the idealist function of illustrating that the 'mind / Is lord and master' over 'outward sense' (1805 xi 270–1). Here, the 'spots of time' serve to rescue the poet both from his own self-destructive and secondary habits of mind, and from the anarchy and ruin of the historical process he has witnessed in France (it seems no accident, then, that the *Prelude* 'spots' were being revised into their new, purgative role, in spring 1804, just as the 'Ode', including the lines quoted above, was being completed).

The principle of self-renewal radiates throughout the work: immaculate miniature versions of the 'spot'-process are available in the famous 'Daffodils' ('I wandered lonely as a Cloud') and 'The Solitary Reaper'. The 'spots of time' are also the exemplary case of those Wordsworthian anti-nomies, of shaping spirit and shapeless impulse, of spontaneity and self-control, and of the 'overflow of powerful feelings' that is produced only 'by one who has thought long and deeply'. By virtue of their combined per-manence and temporality, stasis and mobility, they are emblematic of the ambiguously insubstantial bedrock of imaginative life. That co-existence of weight, solidity, and material presence, with the impalpable, ethereal, and incorporeal – 'a real solid world / Of images' (1805 viii 604–5) – is one of Wordsworth's most suggestive, and quietly unnerving, legacies. A prime, if slightly off-beat, example occurs in the fantastic, yet somehow incontrovert-ibly realized, opening of Wordsworth's *Guide to the Lakes*. Seeking a perfect view of 'the main outlines of the country', the guide asks his reader to adopt an imaginary and ideal 'station' on a cloud:

> I know not how to give the reader a distinct image of these more readily than
> by requesting him to place himself with me, in imagination, upon some given
> point; let it be the top of either of the mountains, Great Gavel, or Scawfell;

or, rather, let us suppose our station to be a cloud hanging midway between those two mountains, at not more than half a mile's distance from the summit of each, and not many yards above their highest elevation; we shall then see stretched at our feet a number of vallies, not fewer than eight, diverging from the point, on which we are supposed to stand, like spokes from the nave of a wheel. (*Prose* ii 171)

'Hanging midway' in the sentence, the cloud-station perfectly exemplifies its ambiguous place in a Wordsworthian universe, between land and sky, real and imaginary, fixed and ephemeral, shapely and formless. Diaphanous itself, it nonetheless gives shape to the District below, which from its vantage-point gains the coherence and unity of a wheel, with spokes radiating from a substantial centre. As the 1815 Preface reveals, the verb 'hang' was fraught with complex associations for Wordsworth, both in and of itself – as registering a permanently undecided ambivalence of shape, direction, or posture – and by its appearance in *King Lear* and *Paradise Lost*, and a corresponding inclination towards or away from a Shakespearean or Miltonic order of language (*Prose* iii 31). Coleridge imagined Milton and Shakespeare as twin peaks of poetic glory; in this passage from the *Guide to the Lakes*, Wordsworth's amalgam of present-participle–adverb–preposition finds him 'hanging midway between' the rival mountains of his own region.

## NOTES

1 'Autobiographical Memoranda', 1847; *Prose* iii 372.
2 See Nicholas Roe, *Wordsworth and Coleridge: The Radical Years* (Oxford: Clarendon Press, 1988), pp. 248–62.
3 See *ibid.*, pp. 158–9, 182–7, 276–9; and Kenneth R. Johnston, *The Hidden Wordsworth: Poet, Lover, Rebel, Spy* (New York and London: W. W. Norton and Co., 1998), pp. 427–67.
4 Coleridge, letter to Thelwall, 13 May 1796; *Henry Crabb Robinson on Books and their Writers*, ed. Edith J. Morley, 3 vols. (1938), I, pp. 887, 158.
5 *Wordsworth and the Victorians* (Oxford: Clarendon Press, 1998).
6 John Taylor's gossip, as reported in Joseph Farington's *Diary* iii 249 (entry for 17 June 1806).
7 'Said Secrecy to Cowardice and Fraud', first pub. 1838 in a note to *Protest Against the Ballot* ('Forth rushed, from Envy sprung and Self-conceit, / A Power misnamed the SPIRIT OF REFORM ... ').
8 *The Faerie Queene* V ii 36, noted by Wordsworth as the model for his own line, 'Perilous is sweeping change, all chance unsound' ('Blest Stateman He', 1838).
9 Johnston, *Wordsworth and 'The Recluse'* (New Haven: Yale University Press, 1984); Jonathan Wordsworth, *William Wordsworth: The Borders of Vision* (Oxford: Clarendon Press, 1982), Epilogue.

10 James Montgomery, reviewing *Poems in Two Volumes* (1807) in the *Eclectic Review* (January 1808).

11 'Coriolanus', *Characters of Shakespear's Plays*: Hazlitt is responding to Wordsworth's 'Ode: 1815', which caused such a stir because it located God's 'pure intent' in 'Man – arrayed for mutual slaughter, / – Yea, Carnage is thy daughter' (lines 106–7).

# 2

DUNCAN WU

# Wordsworth's poetry to 1798

The 'Ode: Intimations of Immortality' was prefaced from 1815 on by an excerpt from a lyric written much earlier:

> The Child is Father of the Man;
> And I could wish my days to be
> Bound each to each by natural piety.

It would be difficult to better this as a characterization of Wordsworth's own poetic development. All the central preoccupations of his maturity are to be found in his earliest writing. It is as if he were born with his literary identity fully formed. Just how true this is has only recently been revealed, because until 1997 no comprehensive edition of the juvenilia had been published. Now, thanks to the labours of Jared Curtis and Carol Landon for the Cornell Wordsworth series edition of *Early Poems and Fragments, 1785–1797*, we can fully appreciate the achievement represented by Wordsworth's first long poem, *The Vale of Esthwaite*, completed when he was seventeen in 1787. His earliest verses, on the subject of 'The Summer Vacation', had been written three years before as a school exercise; inspiration would have come partly from his reading.

Thomas Bowman, the master of Hawkshead Grammar School, was among Wordsworth's mentors, and lent his precocious charge copies of Cowper's *The Task*, Charlotte Smith's *Elegiac Sonnets*, and Burns' *Poems* when they were first published.[1] Few facts testify so eloquently to Wordsworth's good fortune in his teachers. Contemporary poetry formed no part of the school curriculum in those days, and would not do so until the twentieth century. Virgil and Horace, on the other hand, were on the syllabus, and Bowman must have understood that their influence fed directly into the literary main-stream of his own time. In retrospect it is possible to see how significant it is that Wordsworth was early reading Cowper, Smith, and Burns. By the 1780s, with the big figures Gray, Collins, and Goldsmith gone, it must have seemed to some that poetry had lost its way: Pope's imitators thronged the periodicals and newspapers, but even the best of them lacked his originality. Ornamented and artificial in style, they imitated the Classical models, mused on abstraction, and meditated on spiritual matters. For the moment, poetry was closeted in the drawing-room, where it bore little on the outside world.

Against those conventions, such writers as Cowper, Smith, and Burns sought to explore subjects close to their own experience. The blank verse of *The Task* is a mock-epic whose playfulness masks its author's desire to redeem himself from the depressive insanity that threatened constantly to destroy him; Smith's sonnets are an attempt to enshrine in literary form their creator's response to the disasters that had befallen her and her family; while the locus of Burns' *Poems* (Kilmarnock, 1786) is the experience and language of working people. In other words, Wordsworth's early literary taste favoured poetry that bridged the gap between sentiment and confession – and his early verse bears out that preoccupation. Who, for instance, would have expected a sixteen year old to produce these lines – which display a remarkable insight into his response to his father's death three years before?

> No spot but claims the tender tear
> By joy or grief to memory dear
> One Evening when the wintry blast
> Through the sharp Hawthorn whistling pass'd
> And the poor flocks all pinch'd with cold
> Sad drooping sought the mountain fold
> Long Long upon yon steepy rock
> Alone I bore the bitter shock
> Long Long my swimming eyes did roam
> For little Horse to bear me home
> To bear me what avails my tear
> To sorrow o'er a Father's bier.
> Flow on, in vain thou hast not flow'd
> But eas'd me of a heavy load
> For much it gives my soul relief
> To pay the mighty debt of Grief
> With sighs repeated o'er and o'er
> I mourn because I mourn'd no more
> For ah! the storm was soon at rest
> Soon broke the Sun upon my breast
> Nor did my little heart foresee
> – She lost a home in losing thee.
>
> (*The Vale of Esthwaite* 272–93; *EP* 446)

Wordsworth was to revisit this early trauma twelve years later, for one of the 'spots of time' in *The Prelude* (see *Two-Part Prelude* i 327–74), where his impatience as he waited for the horses becomes the cause of John Wordsworth's death – in effect, he becomes his father's murderer.[2] This early account does not go quite that far, but Wordsworth nonetheless makes the two events sequential, as if the domestic tragedy springs out of his vigil on the 'steepy rock'. The whistling of the hawthorn and the drooping of the flocks all testify to the pervasive presence of the dead even as the poet thinks himself alone. As in the *Prelude* spot of time, the wait has somehow become the focus for displaced grief at his father's death – irrationally, as his father did not die until nearly two weeks after Wordsworth had returned to Cockermouth from Hawkshead. Something highly sophisticated is going on here, quite unlike anything to be found in published poetry at this period: it is driven by an intuitive understanding of the psychology of intense emotion. The boy's imagination has constructed a causal link between his feelings as he waited for the horses to take him home, and the death of his father. The 'poor flock' of sheep, 'Sad drooping' on the mountain side, and the 'whistling' of the hawthorn, are admonitions that he failed to understand at the time. That failure is construed as the first step in a sequence of events that leads first to his father's death in December 1783, and then to his delayed 'debt of Grief' in the present (1787).

The final step in this chronology is confirmed by Dorothy Wordsworth's letter to Jane Pollard of late July 1787, in which she reveals that the wait for the horses had just been re-enacted because the guardians of the Wordsworth children delayed sending horses to bring William back to Penrith for the last summer vacation before he went up to Cambridge: 'I was for a whole week kept in expectation of my Brothers, who staid at school all that time after the vacation begun owing to the ill-nature of my Uncle.' She goes on to reveal that the July of 1787, when Wordsworth was concluding work on *The Vale of Esthwaite*, was a highly emotional one: 'Many a time have W[illia]m, J[ohn], C[hristopher], and myself shed tears together, tears of the bitterest sorrow, we all of us, each day, feel more sensibly the loss we sustained when we were deprived of our parents...[We] always finish our conversations which generally take a melancholy turn, with wishing we had a father and a home.' Dorothy's letter is probably contemporaneous with the lines quoted from *The Vale of Esthwaite*, and the grieving she describes is almost certainly that mentioned by her brother: 'I mourn because I mourn'd no more.' The line suggests that Wordsworth's grief in the present (1787) is actuated partly by his failure fully to mourn his parents at the time of their deaths; the response is a common one, especially among children, but it often gives rise to guilt later on. And this seems to have happened to Wordsworth. Such close, accurate, and detailed psychological self-analysis is rare enough among adults; Wordsworth's ability both to comprehend and articulate his emotions at the age of sixteen testifies to an enviable sanity.

Completion of the 6,000-line *The Vale of Esthwaite* in summer 1787 was a remarkable achievement in every respect. But it was composed over a lengthy period, and sometimes appears incoherent. As we have seen, the best passages are highly personal, and that, besides anything else, would have discouraged Wordsworth from publishing it. It was not to appear in print until 1940 – and then in an unsatisfactory text. Instead, he seems at some point to have thrown it in the fire, though someone snatched the notebook from the flames before it was badly damaged (it is preserved today at the Wordsworth Library, Grasmere). Having gone up to Cambridge in October 1787, he worked up several extracts which were probably circulated among friends. But his most important poetic project there was his translation from Virgil's *Georgics*. Its extent is unknown, because only drafts survive. They were composed 1788–9, and show Wordsworth translating from all four books of the poem.[3] Among them is a sustained attempt to render Virgil's version of the Orpheus and Eurydice legend, which has particular resonance in the context of Wordsworth's grief at his parents' death. In the account of the myth followed by Virgil, the poet and lyre-singer Orpheus enters the underworld to recover Eurydice, who has been snatched by Pluto, but he loses her afresh. Orpheus is then set upon by avenging maenads. Thrown on the waves of the river Hebrus, however, Orpheus's decapitated head remains true to its owner's poetic vocation to the last:

> Ah poor Euridice it feebly cried
> All round Euridice the [moaning banks reply'd]
> From [s]till small voices heard on every side.
>
> (*EP* 644)

The last line of the quotation has no equivalent in Virgil, and is pure Wordsworth. Just as it seems that the hero is defeated, the still small voices tell us that, like the spirit of Wordsworth's father in *The Vale of Esthwaite*, Orpheus has been absorbed into the natural world that has in some way partaken of his suffering. His song is not silenced, but preserved by nature. The pantheism often detected in Wordsworth's 1798 poetry has sometimes been cited as evidence of Coleridge's influence; in fact, its traces are detectable in Wordsworth's earliest verse, and is rooted in the delayed mourning for his parents. Grief permeates many of the poems dating from Wordsworth's Hawkshead and Cambridge years – most nakedly, perhaps, in a draft fragment which the Cornell editors date to 1787–8.

Now ye meet in the cave
husband sons and all
if ye've hands oh make a grave
for she dies she dies she dies
She wishes not for a grave
bear into the salt sea, for
Where you lie there she will lie,
Oh bear her into the salt sea
If ye wish her peace [?oh] bear
Bear her to the salt sea bear
[                    ] by
The very spot where you do lie
With your [?wives] by day
In the coffins of the rock
What has she [to] do with the churchyard

(*EP* 670)

It may be incomplete, but the draft reveals Wordsworth's sense of death at its most elemental. Like the husband and sons who dig the woman's grave with their bare hands, the poet grapples with the very sense and substance of death: it's not just the practical business of laying the dead to rest, but the distinctive concern of their integration, physical and spiritual, into the natural world. Refusing to resolve that aspect of its argument, the poem shifts the place of her burial from earth to sea, and finally to 'the coffins of the rock'. Emphatically, there is no finality about the interment, as if in death the mother is ubiquitous: 'What has she [to] do with the churchyard'? The question anticipates the Lucy poems, in particular 'A slumber did my spirit seal', in which the unnamed corpse is

Roll'd round in earth's diurnal course
With rocks and stones and trees!

'Now ye meet in the cave' is concerned with the apprehension of the natural harmony, the synthesis of nature and humanity that lies beyond death. But there is that important emotional note – almost denoting guilt: '*If* ye wish her peace...' What Wordsworth seems to hope for is the shamanistic promise that grief may be exorcised by a natural order. Nature is capable of incorporating the dead and, in some sense, retrieving them: that process is held to comprise an expiation.

The Cornell Wordsworth Series edition of the juvenilia, which publishes drafts such as these for the first time, enables us to see how consistent this great poet is, from his earliest writings to his last. He was endowed with an intuitive understanding of the human mind, and from the first attempted to describe the inner truth of the emotions.

These explorations led directly to composition of Wordsworth's first two long poems. On 29 January 1793 the radical publisher Joseph Johnson published *An Evening Walk* and *Descriptive Sketches*, both written over the preceding four years. *An Evening Walk* was the crowning achievement of Wordsworth's undergraduate career, a loco-descriptive poem in the manner of Thomson's *The Seasons*, Denham's *Cooper's Hill*, Cowper's *The Task*, and Smith's *Elegiac Sonnets*. It was an extrapolation of much of the landscape poetry that had featured in *The Vale of Esthwaite*, but there was nothing about Wordsworth's father, or mother, or any of the overtly confessional material relating to them. Such concerns simmer beneath the poem's surface, emerging briefly at its culmination – a literary fantasia in which one of the Cumbrian Lakes is thronged with 'Fair spirits':

> – 'Tis restless magic all; at once the bright
> Breaks on the shade, the shade upon the light,
> Fair spirits are abroad; in sportive chase
> Brushing with lucid wands the water's face,
> While music stealing round the glimmering deeps
> Charms the tall circle of th' enchanted steeps
> (*An Evening Walk* 345–50)

The 'Fair spirits' recall Pope's sylphs in *The Rape of the Lock*, and the scene as a whole may echo the climax as evening deepens in Marvell's *Upon Appleton House*, but these lines are allusive in more than a purely literary sense. Their effect is the same as in the waiting for the horses episode in *The Vale of Esthwaite*: as the lake acquires a 'face', and 'music' drifts down the valley, Wordsworth is concerned to convey the immanent numinousness of the natural world – a quality that derives partly from the implicit presence of the dead, perhaps in the form of the 'Fair spirits'.

This notion is more explicitly revisited in *Descriptive Sketches*, another loco-descriptive poem, this time based on Wordsworth's walking tour of the Continent in 1790,[4] which he undertook with a College friend, Robert Jones. In the middle of the poem, he breaks off to contemplate the political liberties enjoyed by the inhabitants of Switzerland, as represented by an Alpine peasant:

> And as on glorious ground he draws his breath,
> With Freedom oft, with Victory and Death,
> Hath seen in grim array amid their Storms
> Mix'd with auxiliar Rocks, three hundred Forms;
> While twice ten thousand corselets at the view
> Dropp'd loud at once, Oppression shriek'd, and flew.

> Oft as those sainted Rocks before him spread,
> An unknown power connects him with the dead.
> For images of other worlds are there,
> Awful the light, and holy is the air.
> Uncertain thro' his fierce uncultur'd soul
> Like lighted tempests troubled transports roll;
> To viewless realms his Spirit towers amain,
> Beyond the senses and their little reign.
>
> *(Descriptive Sketches* 536–49)

With its cumbersome allegory, and creaking couplets, this passage is very much of its time, and may seem at first to be of scant interest to Wordsworthians; in fact, it is a vital step forward in his development. On the 'glorious ground' on which the Swiss won their freedom from tyrants, the peasant is 'connected' to his dead ancestors. Once again, nature mediates between the living and the dead, conducting him into 'other worlds' beyond the physical, the 'viewless realms' beyond the borders of life and death. This time, the poetry has an important political dimension: the vision granted the peasant is a crucial aspect of his liberty. He is fully realized, almost prelapsarian, in his engagement with the spiritual basis of his rights. The insight of these lines is that political empowerment is as important to our souls as it is to our material well-being: the same idea underlies such mature poems as 'Michael', and was evidently fostered by Wordsworth's first-hand experience of the French Revolution, during which he was at work on *Descriptive Sketches*.

It seems likely that *An Evening Walk* and *Descriptive Sketches* were meant to raise funds for their author's return to France to marry his French girlfriend, Annette Vallon, who by the time of their publication had given birth to their child, Anne-Caroline Wordsworth. Unfortunately, publication was preceded also by the execution of Louis XVI, just over a week before, which led quickly to the declaration of war between Britain and France, concluded only by Napoleon's defeat at Waterloo over two decades later. For the moment, Wordsworth was compelled to remain in Britain.

His next long poem, *Salisbury Plain*, emerged out of a walking-tour from the south of England to Wales which he undertook after the declaration of war, July–August 1793. Not surprisingly, given the circumstances, it is an anti-war poem at the centre of which Wordsworth places modern political barbarism alongside the Druid human sacrifice believed to have taken place at Stonehenge. In one of its central passages, he describes the human sacrifices supposedly consecrated by druid priests at stone circles such as Castlerigg near Keswick:

And oft a night-fire mounting to the clouds
Reveals the desert and with dismal red
Clothes the black bodies of encircling crowds.
It is the sacrificial altar fed
With living men. How deep it groans – the dead
Thrilled in their yawning tombs their helms uprear;
The sword that slept beneath the warriour's head
Thunders in fiery air: red arms appear
Uplifted thro' the gloom and shake the rattling spear.

(*Salisbury Plain* 181–9)

This hellish vision provides the obverse to the situation enjoyed by the Swiss peasant of *Descriptive Sketches*; here, the aspirations of the earlier poem are answered with a report from the front line. The burning of 'living men' is an apt metaphor for the wastefulness of modern warfare; worse still, the victims of this sacrifice have been condemned against their will, in the same way that soldiers were conscripted into service, often by press-gangs. Those who preside over these rites shadow the influence of such bishops as Richard Watson, Bishop of Llandaff, who supported the war with Revolutionary France; as Stephen Gill puts it: 'What are the Druids themselves but early practitioners of the priestly mysteries which in every age have shrouded tyranny with the mantle of religion?'[5]

The other central element of *Salisbury Plain* was the Female Vagrant, whose story, somewhat revised, would form one of the *Lyrical Ballads*. Although her narrative is geared toward the anti-war moral of the poem as a whole, it shows Wordsworth to be extending his preoccupation with human psychology. Having lost her husband, children, and father to the ravages of conflict and famine, she says that her experience has done more than condemn her to the charity of passers-by:

I lived upon the mercy of the fields,
And oft of cruelty the sky accused;
On hazard, or what general bounty yields,
Now coldly given, now utterly refused.
The fields I for my bed have often used:
But, what afflicts my peace with keenest ruth
Is, that I have my inner self abused,
Foregone the home delight of constant truth,
And clear and open soul, so prized in fearless youth.

(*Salisbury Plain* 541–9)

The female vagrant is the natural counterpart of the Swiss peasant. He is redeemed from suffering and alienation by the heroism of his ancestors in their victorious battles against tyranny. She and the other characters in *Salisbury Plain* are prisoners of a situation over which they lack influence; they are powerless, compelled to fight for a regime that discards them when they have served their purpose. Were this the full extent of Wordsworth's comment, *Salisbury Plain* would be of interest for its politics but little else. What distinguishes it as poetry is the vagrant's intuition that oppression has damaged her soul: 'what afflicts my peace with keenest ruth / Is, that I have my inner self abused'. Far from dignifying her, her experiences have led her away from 'constant truth', while the 'clear and open soul' she once had is calloused over. If liberty empowered the Swiss peasant, its denial has stunted the female vagrant. The belief that political injustice hurts the spirit is original – even, one is tempted to suggest, eccentric. It places Wordsworth at a slight remove from contemporary political comment, and reveals where his attention is focused. He is compelled by the forces that shape the mind, whether they be political, social, or religious.

The months following completion of *Salisbury Plain* represented a period of consolidation. In the spring of 1794 Wordsworth set up house with Dorothy at Windy Brow in Keswick, where he revised *An Evening Walk* (for text see Cornell Wordsworth edition, 129–56). His interest in politics did not abate; Robespierre was executed on 28 July, an event to which Wordsworth reacted with understandable pleasure, as he recalled in *The Prelude* (*1805* x 530–657). By this time he had read Godwin's *Political Justice* – a powerful influence on radicals of the day. And it's easy to see why that work would have appealed to him. Like Wordsworth, Godwin was preoccupied by the problem of why man, in his fallen state, behaved as he did, and how he might improve. Godwin's vision of a better society was based on a belief in the perfectibility of mankind, which he thought attainable through the full exercise of the reason. When all were governed exclusively by rationality, he suggested, all human institutions, including that of marriage, would wither away. Godwin regarded human beings as largely the product of the social and political forces that bore upon them. These ideas comprised the theory that, as Wordsworth recalled in *The Prelude*, 'Was flattering to the young ingenuous mind / Pleased with extremes' (*1805* XIII 815–16). Such was the perspective of an older and wiser man; in November 1795, by which time he was living with Dorothy at Racedown Lodge in Dorset, rewriting *Salisbury Plain* as *Adventures on Salisbury Plain*, Wordsworth was enough of a rationalist to illustrate Godwin's ideas in his new work. Its central character, a Sailor, becomes a murderer largely as a result of the injustices that impinge on him, and this is in line with Godwin's critique. However, Wordsworth's triumph is to transcend philosophy in his portrayal of the Sailor's inner world. Crossing Salisbury Plain, the Sailor sees a corpse hanging from a gibbet:

It was a spectacle which none might view
In spot so savage but with shuddering pain
Nor only did for him at once renew
All he had feared from man, but rouzed a train
Of the mind's phantoms, horrible as vain.
The stones, as if to sweep him from the day,
Roll'd at his back along the living plain;
He fell and without sense or motion lay,
And when the trance was gone, feebly pursued his way.
(*Adventures on Salisbury Plain* 118–26)

On a literary level, the obvious precursor is *Macbeth*, III iv 121–2: 'It will have blood, they say, blood will have blood. / Stones have been known to move and trees to speak...' But Wordsworth is not exploiting the situation for spookiness alone. The phantoms that pursue the Sailor, turning even the roadside stones into enemies, are creations of his own brain: but paradoxically, they are beyond his control. Of course, the intuition is there in Shakespeare too, but no one since had dealt so persuasively with the involuntary reflexes of the guilt-ridden conscience. Wordsworth is fascinated by the tendency of the subconscious to make manifest our innermost anxieties, even to the point of precipitating physical collapse. His own experience had taught him that our deepest emotions cannot be suppressed – a lesson that informs some of his greatest poems, including 'Goody Blake and Harry Gill', 'The Thorn', *Peter Bell*, and the spots of time in *The Prelude*.

Wordsworth's days as a Godwinian were numbered. The vision of man as a kind of automaton whose highest virtue was reason entailed a corresponding denial of passion. Godwin's perspective was a grimly materialist one that looked forward to Marxism. It was fundamentally antithetical to Wordsworth – who knew that emotional truth was the key to those questions about man and society for which he sought an answer. As dissatisfaction turned to hostility, Wordsworth must have seen that a poetic rooted in real life demanded psychological veracity. No wonder guilt crops up so frequently in his early poetry; it was something of which he had extensive first-hand experience. Besides that related to his parents' deaths, there were the feelings arising out of his enforced abandonment of Annette Vallon and their daughter. And, in the wake of Robespierre's execution, he was beginning to question his fervent support for the execution of Louis XVI (as articulated in his unpublished pamphlet, *A Letter to the Bishop of Llandaff*; *Prose* i 19–66); he may even have felt that he was in some way implicated in it.

These concerns fuel his next major work – a play, *The Borderers*, composed largely at Racedown during 1796–7. Again, the plot concerns a murder – the abandonment of an old man, Herbert, on a heath, by a young man called

Mortimer, egged on by the villainous Rivers. Rivers expounds the Godwinian denial of emotion, telling Mortimer, 'Compassion! pity! pride can do without them, / And what if you should never know them more!' (III v 74–5), but he is also aware of the nature of regret and self-blame:

> Action is transitory, a step, a blow –
> The motion of a muscle – this way or that –
> 'Tis done – and in the after vacancy
> We wonder at ourselves like men betray'd.
> Suffering is permanent, obscure and dark,
> And has the nature of infinity.
>
> (III v 60–5; 1797–9 text)

Wordsworth read these lines to William Hazlitt in 1803, and Hazlitt spent the rest of his life repeating and quoting them in his essays (*The Borderers* was not published by Wordsworth until 1842). They are indeed memorable, and are the first traces of the great poet who was to compose *The Ruined Cottage* shortly after. Their impact derives partly from the fact that Rivers is describing remorse from the inside. The point of Godwinism in *Adventures on Salisbury Plain* was that it had justified the argument that the Sailor's crime was not solely his responsibility. Although Wordsworth had rejected Godwinism, he remained intrigued by the point that people commit crimes in spite of their better natures, almost out of carelessness – that their better selves are forgotten, and, 'in the after vacancy', lamented for the rest of their lives. It was the last two lines of the quotation that left their indelible mark on Hazlitt's memory, and they comprise the most distinctive and haunting element of Rivers' speech. They affirm the enduring, formative effect of the moral choices we make: such choices are not merely an index of what we have become, but of what we are in the process of becoming. And that can't be faked. Each of us is the product of the moral decisions we have made in the past, which in turn determine our future.

In short, *The Borderers* subjects Godwin to comprehensive and drastic revision. *Adventures on Salisbury Plain*, an ostensibly Godwinite work, was designed to show how an individual could be driven to murder by political and social oppression; by contrast, *The Borderers* offers a line of thought that anticipates modern existentialism. Individuals are not compelled to murder each other, it argues; compassion and pity can detain us from bad moral choices. Guilt may exist, but is understood to have causes. By the end of the play, Mortimer perceives the errors of his ways, and vows to 'go forth a wanderer on the earth, / A shadowy thing' (v iii 265–6), in penance. It seems tragic, and to some extent it is. But the important point is that through his rejection of rationalism Wordsworth has moved towards an understanding of the human heart that is utterly original, and in its implications deeply un-tragic.

Coleridge first met Wordsworth in September 1795, but they did not become close friends until June 1797 when Coleridge visited Racedown. The first thing Wordsworth read him was *The Borderers*. His second reading was of a poem he had composed during the preceding weeks: *The Ruined Cottage*.[6] When he first wrote it, Wordsworth cannot have fully comprehended its significance in his career as a writer. It was to be his first indisputably great poem. His long apprenticeship was at an end.

*The Ruined Cottage* concerns the story of Margaret, a war-widow, whose neglect of her children in her distress leads to their deaths, her subsequent madness, and ultimate demise. This sad tale is related by her friend, the anonymous Pedlar, to the listening Poet, at the spot where she lived and died: the site of her cottage. It is simple enough, and looks back to Cowper's *The Task*, which describes a madwoman called 'Crazy Kate'.[7] The political context that provided a rationale for *Salisbury Plain*, *Adventures on Salisbury Plain*, and *The Borderers* persists in *The Ruined Cottage*, in that the story of failed harvests and high prices that entails the enlisting of Margaret's husband in the army accurately reflects conditions during the mid 1790s. But where *Salisbury Plain* was essentially an anti-war poem, *Adventures* exposed the iniquities of the world from a rationalist perspective, and *The Borderers* was geared to revising Godwinism, the new work transcends the concerns of politics and philosophy, and settles on the thing that had always fascinated Wordsworth,[8] and which would provide his central subject for the rest of his career: emotional and psychological truth. As a consequence, the narrative, though it documents Margaret's decline against a recognizably contemporary milieu, is actually driven by Wordsworth's preoccupation with her interior world. The important philosophical breakthrough of *The Borderers* – that our actions, though momentary, are of enduring significance – is integrated here into the story of a woman whose misfortune, and consequent 'abuse' of her 'inner self', leads to tragedy. Among many brilliant touches, Wordsworth's sensitive handling of the workings of the mind is illustrated by his account of her watchfulness, in the wake of her husband's desertion:

> On this old Bench
> For hours she sate, and evermore her eye
> Was busy in the distance, shaping things
> Which made her heart beat quick.
> (*Ruined Cottage* MS B 490–3)

These lines were among the first to be written for the poem: Wordsworth actually began it as an examination of the distraction and apathy arising from the pain of abandonment. There is a literary source,[9] but the psychological minutiae here are intricate, precise, and original. In an almost surreal figure of speech, Margaret's eye journeys beyond her body toward the horizon, whence her husband Robert is expected, generating shapes out of existing 'things', that give her the momentary excitement of believing that he is there. But he is not, and the hours she spends imagining his form in the distance are a self-inflicted mental torture. No wonder she goes mad. The poetry has admitted us into the deranged mind of someone powerless to save either her children or herself. As in the case of the guilty Sailor of *Adventures*, Margaret's imaginings are involuntary and beyond conscious manipulation; they compel her along the path of self-destruction.

That, at least, is the approximate shape of the poem as presented to Coleridge in June 1797: a tragic narrative alive to the social and political context of its time but driven largely by its author's interest in psychological truth. We glimpse something of it in MS B (although MS B actually dates from January–March 1798; see Butler, 42–72). Under Coleridge's influence, Wordsworth overhauled the poem in the spring of 1798, lengthening it, giving it a more formal structure, adding to the opening section, and, most importantly, composing a final exchange in which the Pedlar tells the poet not to be depressed by Margaret's story:

> Be wise and chearful, and no longer read
> The forms of things with an unworthy eye.
> She sleeps in the calm earth, and peace is here.
> I well remember that those very plumes,
> Those weeds, and the high spear-grass on that wall,
> By mist and silent rain-drops silver'd o'er,
> As once I passed did to my heart convey
> So still an image of tranquillity,
> So calm and still, and looked so beautiful
> Amid the uneasy thoughts which filled my mind,
> That what we feel of sorrow and despair
> From ruin and from change, and all the grief
> The passing shews of being leave behind,
> Appeared an ideal dream that could not live
> Where meditation was.
> (*Ruined Cottage* MS D 510–24)

In June 1797 Wordsworth had presented Coleridge with his finest work to date – a poem which told of Margaret's appalling decline precipitated by the enlistment of her husband in the army: the following spring he adds a conclusion which portrays her suffering as 'an idle dream'. What's more, the witness to her tragedy is instructed to 'Be wise and chearful', rather than empathize with her pain. It is an astonishing volte-face, and on the surface might be taken to indicate indecisiveness or, worse, incoherence. Nothing of the kind. Wordsworth has taken the final step towards realizing his genius, one he could not have made without Coleridge.

Coleridge visited Racedown in June 1797 as an aspirant writer of philosophical poetry, a mantle he quickly transferred to Wordsworth. His highest ambition had been to compose a revelatory poem that would exceed the quality of *Religious Musings*, composed 1794–6:

> Believe thou, O my soul,
> Life is a vision shadowy of Truth,
> And vice, and anguish, and the wormy grave,
> Shapes of a dream! The veiling clouds retire,
> And lo! the Throne of the redeeming God
> Forth flashing unimaginable day
> Wraps in one blaze earth, heaven, and deepest hell.
> (*Religious Musings* 421–8)[10]

As poetry these lines may not be very good, but their contention that the material world around us, that of 'vice, and anguish, and the wormy grave', is a mere shadow of the divine reality over which the enthroned deity presides, 'flashing unimaginable day', explains the 1798 conclusion to *The Ruined Cottage*. There, too, Wordsworth argues that the material world favoured by the likes of Godwin is 'a dream', an illusion. The meditation on the spear-grass in what was once Margaret's garden tells the Pedlar, and the reader of Wordsworth's poem, of tranquillity. The calmness and stillness of that moment is no mirage. It is the shadow of that higher world in which Margaret endures, relieved of the physical and mental suffering of her last months. In symbolic terms, the 'image of tranquillity' symbolizes her passage beyond the physical, into 'unimaginable day'.

In the context of Wordsworth's overall development, it is easy to understand the appeal to him of Coleridge's rather unusual ideas – heavily influenced by the philosophy of Bishop Berkeley – for they are anticipated in Wordsworth's early writing. In one way or another, the dead, from *The Vale of Esthwaite* onwards, return from the 'wormy grave' in order to affirm their continuing life. Whether Orpheus, or the Swiss soldiers who won liberty for the peasant in *Descriptive Sketches*, or even Wordsworth's father, they are forever returning. And not as ghosts, but, curiously enough, as teachers. So it is that, ultimately, Margaret's suffering is not in vain. Her death comes as a release, but also as a neccssary transition in her continuing existence. With the new conclusion, Wordsworth transforms *The Ruined Cottage* from just another pathetic tale salted with an unusually acute understanding of human nature to one in which Margaret's torment acquires purpose. Her continued influence on the Pedlar and the listening poet turns her, unexpectedly, into a spiritual guide. It is a surprising conclusion, and perhaps no one could have been more surprised by it than Wordsworth, but it possesses a logic that is the culmination of everything he had composed to date. *The Ruined Cottage* is inscribed in the twists and turns his career as a writer had taken since completing *The Vale of Esthwaite* in the summer of 1787. It is arguably the first and greatest philosophical poem Wordsworth ever wrote.[11]

## NOTES

1 See T. W. Thompson, *Wordsworth's Hawkshead*, ed. Robert Woof (Oxford, 1970), p. 344; my *Wordsworth's Reading 1770–1799* (Cambridge, 1993), pp. 23, 38, 127; and *Wordsworth's Reading 1800–1815* (Cambridge, 1995), p. 254.

2 I have compared the two versions at greater length in 'Tautology and Imaginative Vision in Wordsworth', *The Charles Lamb Bulletin*, NS 96 (October 1996), 174–84. I am indebted in general terms to the analysis offered by Jonathan Wordsworth, *William Wordsworth: The Borders of Vision* (Oxford, 1982), pp. 61–3. I have explored the work of this period in more detail than is possible here in a number of articles: 'Wordsworth's Poetry of Grief', *The Wordsworth Circle*, 21 (1990), 114–17; 'Wordsworth and Helvellyn's Womb', *Essays in Criticism*, 44 (January 1994), 6–25; and 'Navigated by Magic: Wordsworth's Cambridge Sonnets', *Review of English Studies*, 46 (August 1995), 352–65.

3 For further details see my 'Three Translations of Virgil Read by Wordsworth in 1788', *Notes and Queries*, NS 37 (December 1990), 407–9. Texts appear in Landon and Curtis, pp. 614–47.

4 For a useful account of the tour, and the resulting poem, see Stephen Gill, *William Wordsworth: A Life* (Oxford, 1989), pp. 44–9.

5 Stephen Gill, 'The Original *Salisbury Plain*', *Bicentenary Wordsworth Studies*, ed. Jonathan Wordsworth (Ithaca, NY: Cornell University Press, 1970), p. 149.

6 This early version (MS A) comprised lines 152–243 of the MS B text, and in his Cornell Wordsworth edition James A. Butler dates it to March–early June 1797. Butler reproduces the MS in facsimile, pp. 78–87.

7 Cowper, *The Task* i 534–56. The passage is extracted in my *Romanticism: An Anthology (Second Edition)* (Oxford, 1998), p. 9. Connections between Cowper and Wordsworth are discussed by Jonathan Wordsworth, *The Music of Humanity* (London, 1969), pp. 61–2 – still the best introduction to *The Ruined Cottage*.

8 Butler observes that *The Ruined Cottage* is 'the culmination of elements present in Wordsworth's poetry from the beginning. In *An Evening Walk*, for example, a female beggar – her husband killed in the American war – wanders along the road with her two babes ... The woman in *Salisbury Plain* was once living happily with her husband and children, as was Margaret in *The Ruined Cottage*' (p. 6).

9 Wordsworth goes one better than Southey's description of a war-widow in *Joan of Arc* (1796):

> At her cottage door,
> The wretched one shall sit, and with dim eye
> Gaze o'er the plain, where on his parting steps
> Her last look hung.        (vii 325–8)

Wordsworth had probably seen these lines in proof or manuscript before they were published as early as September 1795, and he certainly knew the published poem. Southey and Coleridge, during their close association in the mid-1790s, had written many political works; psychological sophistication was not, however, one of Southey's stronger suits.

10 Quoted from the text in Coleridge's *Poems* (1796).

11 It is widely discussed. Besides those already noted, analyses include Kenneth R. Johnston, *Wordsworth and The Recluse* (1984); Stephen Gill, *William Wordsworth: A Life* (1989), pp. 133–7; James H. Averill, *Wordsworth and the Poetry of Human Suffering* (1980); F. R. Leavis, *The Critic as Anti-Philosopher*, ed. G. Singh (1982), pp. 24–40; Jerome J. McGann, *The Romantic Ideology* (1983), pp. 82–6; Peter J. Manning, *Reading Romantics: Text and Context* (1990), pp. 9–34.

# 3

JAMES. A. BUTLER

# Poetry 1798–1807: *Lyrical Ballads* and *Poems, in Two Volumes*

'Wordsworth's name is nothing – to a large number of persons mine *stinks*', wrote Samuel Taylor Coleridge in 1798, urging publisher Joseph Cottle to issue the poets' co-authored *Lyrical Ballads* anonymously (*STCL* 1 412). In the ensuing decade, Wordsworth, the man with the 'nothing name', wrote many of the poems that for later generations established him as the principal poet of his age. The change is from seeing *Lyrical Ballads* as Coleridge's wife Sara early on described it – 'laughed at and disliked by all with very few excepted' – to what is the current critical consensus: 'Historically considered, it remains the most important volume of verse in English since the Renaissance, for it began modern poetry, the poetry of the growing inner self.'[1] Wordsworth's achievement is all the more remarkable because most of the chief poems published in *Lyrical Ballads* (1798 and 1800) and *Poems, in Two Volumes* (1807) came from a very few bursts of activity, first at Alfoxden in Somerset, then at Goslar in Germany, and eventually at Grasmere.

## *Lyrical Ballads* (1798)

In the aging memories of the one-time collaborators on *Lyrical Ballads*, the 1798 volume had a straightforward division of labour. Coleridge in *Biographia Literaria* (1817) recalled that he was to write on 'persons and characters supernatural', while Wordsworth would concentrate on subjects from 'ordinary life', giving 'the charm of novelty to things of every day' and showing 'the loveliness and the wonders of the world before us...' (*BL* II 5–8). The seventy-three-year-old Wordsworth, in a note dictated to Isabella Fenwick about 'We Are Seven', agreed that his task was to write about subjects from common life but to treat them imaginatively.[2] However, Wordsworth's brief critical statement, or 'Advertisement', included in *Lyrical Ballads* (1798) emphasizes stylistic matters: the majority of the poems were 'experiments' written 'to ascertain how far the language of conversation in the middle and lower classes of society is adapted to the purposes of poetic pleasure'.

As with most plans, though, what seemed so obvious to Wordsworth and Coleridge after *Lyrical Ballads* was published looks rather messy and haphazard at the start of their work on the book. In order to pay the expenses of a walking tour, the two poets began *The Rime of the Ancient Mariner* collaboratively in November 1797, but the poem soon became Coleridge's alone. As for Wordsworth's activity late in 1797 and early in 1798, he completed his play *The Borderers*, revised his tale of *The Ruined Cottage* by adding an account of the philosophic pedlar-narrator, and began an industrious programme of reading in preparation for his work on the vast philosophical poem *The Recluse*.

When plans for a trip to Germany emerged, the two poets first thought they could cover some costs by publishing a book with Coleridge's *Ancient Mariner* and some of Wordsworth's short pieces. Then they considered a volume with their two tragedies, *Osorio* and *The Borderers*. A third possibility called for a volume containing only Wordsworth's *The Ruined Cottage* and *Salisbury Plain*. They entertained still other possibilities, but what ultimately produced *Lyrical Ballads* seems less a predetermined plan and more Wordsworth's reactions to the simple, but still wondrous, change in seasons. Spring 1798 (from March to May) saw an extraordinary period of Wordsworth's creative activity on lyrics and ballads.

In March 1798, Wordsworth's first spring at Alfoxden House in a captivating rural setting overlooking the Bristol Channel, we clearly discern themes and techniques evolving toward what is now thought of as quintessentially Wordsworthian. Such accounts are sharply observed pictures of the natural world, expressed in everyday language. Many of these lyrics record the growth of the speaker's perceptions as he creates and meditates upon his view of the world. Stanzas from the first of these poems are typical:

> It is the first mild day of March:
> Each minute sweeter than before,
> The red-breast sings from the tall larch
> That stands beside our door.
>
> One moment now may give us more
> Than fifty years of reason;
> Our minds shall drink at every pore
> The spirit of the season.
>
> And from the blessed power that rolls
> About, below, above;

> We'll frame the measure of our souls,
> They shall be tuned to love.
>
> (1–4, 25–8, 33–6)

In a later poem, 'Expostulation and Reply', the 'powers' inherent in the natural world 'impress' themselves upon the mind and 'feed' it (21–3). In the companion 'The Tables Turned', the addressee is urged to quit his search for wisdom in books and to trust in the intuitive rather than in the rational: 'Come forth into the light of things, / Let Nature be your teacher' (15–16). Children's reactions, of course, are frequently emotional and intuitive, and Wordsworth's older speakers in such dramatic ballads as 'We Are Seven' and 'Anecdote for Fathers' have their irritatingly rational search for adult answers corrected, as they learn from the simply phrased perceptions of the children whom they question. With a shock, those adult speakers, and we as readers, become aware of an alternative and truer reality: 'Could I but teach the hundredth part / Of what from thee I learn' ('Anecdote for Fathers', 59–60).

Equally characteristic of Wordsworth, though, is that 'pleasant thoughts / Bring sad thoughts to the mind'. The joy of the Alfoxden spring takes place amidst the poverty and anguish of neighboring common men and women: 'Have I not', Wordsworth writes, echoing Robert Burns, 'reason to lament / What man has made of man?' ('Lines Written in Early Spring', 3–4, 23–4). A general shortage of bread in the mid-1790s is in the background of several of Wordsworth's poems, as is the destitution which caused a tripling in Alfoxden-area rates for poor relief between 1792 and 1802.[3] In that other highly influential work of 1798, Thomas Malthus' *An Essay on the Principle of Population*, the economist looked at contemporary conditions and gloomily explained why population growth would always outpace the food supply. The landscape of *Lyrical Ballads* (1798) is thus peopled not only by joyful poets of creative natural perceptions but by mad mothers, idiot boys, starving and freezing old women, terrified and despairing convicts, shepherds reduced to public relief, American Indian women abandoned to die. Some of these poems cast into ballad form, such as 'The Mad Mother' and 'The Complaint of a Forsaken Indian Woman', are unadorned, wrenching monologues portraying bleak suffering.

In the best of these poems, however, Wordsworth merges his humanitarian concerns with an interest – fostered by his recent work on *The Borderers* and on *The Ruined Cottage* – in the psychology not only of the victim but also of the poet-narrator who, interacting with the sufferer, tells the tale. In 'Simon Lee', for example, we hear of the old huntsman in a bouncing rhythm that fights with the more serious subject matter:

Full five and twenty years he lived
A running huntsman merry:
And, though he has but one eye left,
His cheek is like a cherry.   (13–16)

Before we can think too much about that one remaining eye, Wordsworth
gives us the cheerful image of Simon's ruddy cheeks. The rhythm and imagery
make the huntsman a figure of fun, perhaps even of mockery. Simon Lee,
the all-purpose picturesque peasant, seems not to be anyone for whom either
narrator or reader need feel much responsibility, especially if that reader is an
upper-class consumer of poetry. For sixty-eight increasingly dithering lines
Simon Lee is described, but we hear not a whisper of narrative, the staple of
the ballad form. Wordsworth even playfully mocks our expectations:

My gentle reader, I perceive
How patiently you've waited,
And I'm afraid that you expect
Some tale will be related.
(69–72)

What we finally reach is a brief 'tale' of Simon Lee's inability to cut out
an old tree root and of how the narrator impatiently takes the axe from
him, severing that root with a single blow. There is here hardly any story –
let alone the sensational events associated with most traditional ballads and
the revival of the genre in the eighteenth century. Wordsworth introduces
what plot there is with the comment that there is a tale in everything and
'Perhaps a tale you'll make it' (80), anticipating his remark in the 'Preface
to *Lyrical Ballads*' (1800): 'I should mention one other circumstance which
distinguishes these Poems from the popular Poetry of the day: it is this, that
the feeling therein developed gives importance to the action and situation,
and not the action and situation to the feeling' (*LB*, 746). The 'action and
situation' of the narrator's axe-wielding is in itself nothing; what gives that
incident its importance is indeed the feeling, first of Simon Lee, then of the
narrator, and finally of the reader:

The tears into his eyes were brought,
And thanks and praises seemed to run
So fast out of his heart, I thought
They never would have done.

– I've heard of hearts unkind, kind deeds
With coldness still returning.
Alas! The gratitude of men
Has oftner left me mourning.   (97–104)

Those sonorous concluding lines alter the rhythms of the poem's opening and at last establish the narrator's and reader's realization of Simon Lee's unique identity and value. The one life we share makes us all responsible for each other – even if the practical ramifications of that sometimes overwhelming obligation are frequently left unstated in *Lyrical Ballads*.

In 'Lines written a few miles above Tintern Abbey' Wordsworth changes his verse form, his use of dramatic speakers, and his diction; but in that poem he sums up many of the themes of the collection. 'Tintern Abbey' is written in the blank verse used by Milton, and like *Paradise Lost* the poem is one of belief, albeit a confession of humanistic faith without mention of a god. Setting himself outside the tradition of Christian conversion autobiographies stretching back to the fifth-century St Augustine, Wordsworth turns not to the Deity for his heart's guardian and his soul's 'moral being' but instead to nature (109–10). For Wordsworth on a walking tour taking in a Christian abbey, now in ruins, this affirmation of faith is personal and rooted in his evolving sense of self as he moved from the 'coarser pleasures' of boyhood to more 'elevated thoughts' (74, 96). The multiple dramatic speakers of some other *Lyrical Ballads* poems are gone or rather are replaced by Wordsworth's dialogue between his present and past personalities as he examines how he has changed, especially in the five years since he last visited Tintern Abbey. His sister Dorothy – not given her own voice in the poem – is suddenly addressed at the end, in part as a representative of William's former self and also as a subject of tender blessings and an embodiment of future hopes. Finally, the diction, magnificent as it is, does not sound much like the language of ordinary men and women in conversation:

> And I have felt
> A presence that disturbs me with the joy
> Of elevated thoughts; a sense sublime
> Of something far more deeply interfused,
> Whose dwelling is the light of setting suns,
> And the round ocean, and the living air,
> And the blue sky, and in the mind of man...
> (94–100)

Both the suffering and the joy detailed in *Lyrical Ballads* are acknowledged and fused by Wordsworth as he hears the 'still, sad music of humanity' and is 'A lover of the meadows and the woods / And mountains', both suffering humanity and beautiful nature parts of that 'mighty world' which we half-create and perceive (92, 104–8).

Present-day criticism of 'Tintern Abbey' has made the poem controversial. The contentious issue is not particularly to determine what Wordsworth claims in the poem but to judge how much of his past selves, particularly of his past political and revolutionary selves, he has concealed or abandoned to make those affirmations. Similarly, Wordsworth's account of the walking tour draws on eighteenth-century picturesque landscape traditions, and all but ignores the industrialization and grinding poverty of the neighbourhood. Whether the poem, written as the poet prepared to leave England for Germany, is a confident Wordsworthian re-assertion of why he is still a 'worshipper of Nature' (153) or a disingenuous masking of his doubt-riddled withdrawal from political radicalism (or, better, something in between), 'Tintern Abbey' is a pivotal work in Wordsworth's career and in the judgement of his critics.

### Lyrical Ballads (1800)

By 4 October 1798, when the first edition of *Lyrical Ballads* appeared in an edition of five hundred copies, with nineteen poems written by Wordsworth and four – including *Rime of the Ancient Mariner* – by Coleridge, the poets were in Germany hoping to improve their knowledge of German. Coleridge went to the university city of Göttingen, while the less well-funded William and Dorothy Wordsworth spent the winter at Goslar. Separated from Coleridge and isolated by language from the Goslar inhabitants, the Wordsworths weathered the coldest winter of the century in meagre accommodations, trapped in a dreary town with no library. Wordsworth turned inward and backward, writing in blank verse an autobiographical series of adult meditations on childhood episodes. Such passages in unrhymed iambic pentameter eventually contributed to *The Prelude*; and two, 'Nutting' and 'There was a Boy', appear in the added second volume of the 1800 edition of *Lyrical Ballads*.

Nearly all his rhymed poems written in that frigid winter of 1798–9 deal with death, particularly the 'Mathew' and the 'Lucy' poems. Works about 'Mathew' draw on one or more of Wordsworth's Hawkshead schoolmasters, but 'Lucy' is harder to trace to a specific source because that name for a dead lover was a commonplace in eighteenth-century literature. Coleridge speculated that Wordsworth may have 'in some gloomier moment... fancied the moment in which his Sister might die' (*STCL* I 479). In any case, the modern conception of Wordsworth's 'Lucy poems' including 'She dwelt among th'untrodden ways', 'Strange fits of passion I have known', 'A slumber did my spirit seal', 'Three years she grew in sun and shower', 'I travell'd among unknown men', probably composed later, in 1801, and sometimes a few others – owes more to the groupings of such Victorian editors as Matthew Arnold and Francis Palgrave than to Wordsworth himself. Nevertheless, those poems – often considered as a set – are among the poet's most haunting and widely read works.

In 'Strange fits of passion I have known', for example, the narrator recounts his seemingly ordinary horseback journey to Lucy's cottage. But that journey becomes increasingly mysterious and foreboding. As the moon descends toward the cottage, the speaker's consciousness gradually merges the moon with Lucy in the trance-like reverie in part produced by the rhythmic galloping of the horse. At the end of the poem, the speaker experiences a moment of pure terror:

> In one of those sweet dreams I slept,
> Kind Nature's gentlest boon!
> And, all the while, my eyes I kept
> On the descending moon.
>
> My horse mov'd on; hoof after hoof
> He rais'd and never stopp'd:
> When down behind the cottage roof
> At once the planet dropp'd.
>
> What fond and wayward thoughts will slide
> Into a Lover's head –
> 'O mercy!' to myself I cried,
> 'If Lucy should be dead!'                (17–28)

Wordsworth's later 1815 revision of the penultimate stanza makes even more shocking this precipitous disappearance of the moon, as he emphasizes its sudden drop in three stressed monosyllables: 'At once the bright Moon dropped.'

An early draft of this poem contains one additional stanza, producing a rather different conclusion:

> I told her this; her laughter light
> Is ringing in my ears;
> And when I think upon that night
> My eyes are dim with tears.[4]

With that extra stanza, we have a poem with less mystery and more of a solution. The additional lines focus on Lucy's death at some future time, and the stanza ends with the conventional tears of an age of sensibility. Wordsworth's lopping off the draft conclusion forces the reader to concentrate instead on the operation of the mind: How did the poet come to associate the moon with his lover Lucy? What psychological mechanism triggered the sudden fears of her death? How, in brief, do our minds work? When the two-volume edition of *Lyrical Ballads* (1800) appeared, Wordsworth wrote in his famous 'Preface' that the principal intent of such seemingly uneventful poems was to trace in them 'the primary laws of our nature: chiefly as far as regards the manner in which we associate ideas in a state of excitement' (p. 743).

Wordsworth returned to England from Germany in May 1799, bringing with him about half of the poems to be published in the second volume of the 1800 *Lyrical Ballads*. After visiting with their Yorkshire cousins, the Hutchinsons, William and Dorothy Wordsworth found their next home in Grasmere in the Lake District, arriving at Dove Cottage on 20 December 1799. For Wordsworth, the return to the Lakes recovered his childhood haunts, and accounts of 'homecomings' and appreciations of his new 'Home at Grasmere' (as he titled one long poem then written as part of *The Recluse*) dominate the poetry of 1800.[5]

These works written at Grasmere in 1800 differ significantly from some of what is in *Lyrical Ballads* (1798). Gone are the idiot boys, mad mothers, and despairing convicts of the 1798 volume. Nothing now written at Grasmere sounds remotely like these gothic lines from 'The Convict', a poem, in fact, dropped from the 1800 *Lyrical Ballads*:

> While the jail mastiff howls at the dull-clanking chain,
> From the roots of his hair there shall start
> A thousand sharp punctures of cold-sweating pain,
> And terror shall leap at his heart.          (37–40)

Similarly, Wordsworth abandons his psychological studies of disordered minds, as in 'The Mad Mother'. If *Lyrical Ballads* (1798) frequently laments 'what man has made of man', the poems written in the poet's first year at Grasmere sound a more hopeful strain. Those poems, no less cognizant of suffering, flow from the philosophical positions Wordsworth arrived at in 'Tintern Abbey'.

On the 1799 journey 'home' to their native Lake District, Wordsworth heard the story he recounts in 'Hart-leap Well'. That poem, one of the first written at Grasmere and the opening one in the new second volume of *Lyrical Ballads* (1800), tells of the tragic death of the hart and the remains of a pleasure-house built to mark the sad spot. On the eve of a new century, however, Wordsworth sounds almost millenarian in his belief in a better earthly world to come:

> The Being, that is in the clouds and air,
> That is in the green leaves among the groves,
> Maintains a deep and reverential care
> For them the quiet creatures whom he loves.

> She [Nature] leaves these objects to a slow decay
> That what we are, and have been, may be known;
> But at the coming of the milder day,
> These monuments shall all be overgrown.
>
> (165–8, 173–6)

In 1800 at Grasmere Wordsworth hoped that he was indeed on the cusp of 'the milder day', better – in some ways – than 'the bowers / Of blissful Eden' (*Home at Grasmere* 123–4) because the Lake District was for him a *recovered* paradise as he, like the biblical prodigal son, returned home. The Grasmere poems of 1800 mirror the aspirations of William and Dorothy, who found together at Dove Cottage their first adult home that seemed to offer the possibility of permanence.

At the start of work on Wordsworth's new second volume, Coleridge described what his friend was writing as 'Lyrical Ballads, and Pastorals' (*STCL* 1 585). Pastorals, of course, have a long and distinguished history encompassing both Greek and Roman poets, especially the originator of the form, Theocritus, and Virgil, as well as the English writers whom Wordsworth increasingly came to measure himself against – Spenser, Milton, Pope, and others. The genre's reputation as a training ground for the epic poet may also have appealed to Wordsworth, who since 1798 had thought of his assorted fragments of *The Recluse* as his epic-in-progress. Wordsworth's pastorals, however, do not contain the traditional urban poet's meditations upon simple shepherds and their bucolic life. His stance is rather as a rural man himself, one who, because he belongs to the countryside and it to him, can write truthfully about his surroundings and his neighbours. Like George Crabbe before him (*The Village* 1783), Wordsworth's depictions are realistic, but more sympathetically presented than Crabbe's. Most of these 1800 pastorals retell rural tragedies. Wordsworth's Lake District is not Shakespeare's escapist and mostly idyllic Forest of Arden, a contrast that may well have occurred to the poet himself since he refers to *As You Like It* in a verse introduction, which he did not choose to publish, to 'Nutting'.[6]

No poem in *Lyrical Ballads* (1798) is actually called a 'pastoral', and the word itself appears but twice in the volume, both times in the last-written poem, 'Tintern Abbey'. On the other hand, five titles in *Lyrical Ballads* (1800) have the word 'pastoral' in their subtitles: 'The Brothers', 'The Oak and the Broom', 'The Idle Shepherd-Boys', 'The Pet Lamb', and 'Michael'. Five additional poems record the poet's 'Naming of Places' in his new valley, christening those sacred spots after family and friends to preserve the memory of events that occurred there. In three 'Inscriptions', Wordsworth wrote about – and sometimes literally on – the pastoral landscape. Indeed, nearly every poem written at Grasmere in 1800 can be considered some version of pastoral as Wordsworth assimilates his new environment and eventually defines himself as native to it.[7]

Of the Grasmere poems published in *Lyrical Ballads* (1800), perhaps the best, 'Michael, a Pastoral Poem', concludes the second volume of new works. Like *The Ruined Cottage*, 'Michael' is a framed narrative in which the story-teller guides the reader's reactions to the distressing tale he tells. The work begins with the narrator's directions to walk 'Up the tumultuous brook of Green-head Gill' to find 'a straggling Heap of unhewn stones' (2, 17). In the poem's last two lines, the speaker again draws our attention to the heaped-up stones but now identifies them as an 'unfinished Sheepfold... / Beside the boisterous brook of Green-head Gill' (490–1). Between those paired opening and closing references to stones and stream, we find out not only what the stones are and why they are significant but also how the narrator thinks we should react to the 'history / Homely and rude' (34–5) which gives them meaning.

That story, 'ungarnish'd with events' (19) as are so many of the stories told in *Lyrical Ballads*, pushes Wordsworth's narrative technique to its limit. The climax is in fact a non-event, the moment when we hear that the old shepherd Michael 'never lifted up a single stone' (475). The history that precedes this lack of action can be simply told. Michael loves his land and his son Luke with equal intensity. Years before, Michael pledged his land as collateral for a loan to his nephew, and now 'unforeseen misfortunes' (223) mean Michael has to pay. After much anguished discussion, Michael and his wife Isabel decide not to sell any of the patrimonial lands but instead to send Luke to the city to earn the money. First, though, Michael takes Luke to a spot where the old man planned to build a sheepfold 'Near the tumultuous brook of Green-head Gill' (332). Midway through the poem, we thus get another structural repetition of the opening and closing references to a specific landscape. After hearing from his father of his love for him and of the significance of the land, Luke places the cornerstone for the sheepfold as a covenant between Luke, Michael, and the ancestral property. In only six lines, Wordsworth, his focus firmly on Michael's un-spoken feelings and not on Luke's profligate misadventures, informs us that Luke undertook unspecified 'evil courses' in the 'dissolute city' and had to flee beyond the seas (451–6). Now the reader, as in 'Simon Lee', can ap-preciate why the smallest of things, such as Michael's inability to continue work on the sheepfold, have – when properly understood – the most strik-ing import. Such tragic stories best delineate what is permanent in human nature:

There is a comfort in the strength of love;
'Twill make a thing endurable, which else
Would break the heart: – old Michael found it so.

(457–9)

Wordsworth's poems sometimes seem so plainly presented that their artistry escapes notice. Besides the poet's careful structural design in 'Michael', Wordsworth there echoes both the Bible and Virgil's *Georgics*, setting his Grasmere shepherd's tale into a timeless context that nevertheless preserves Michael's individuality. Most of the poem's readers would associate its blank verse with Milton; in 'Michael', thus, the form itself claims for this unadorned pastoral the importance of Milton's cosmic epic. The leader of the opposition party in Parliament, Charles James Fox – to whom Wordsworth sent *Lyrical Ballads* (1800) – in fact wrote back to the poet that he thought blank verse to be unsuited for ordinary subjects treated with simplicity (*STCL* II, 676n). Wordsworth's presentation letter to Fox of 14 January 1801 emphasized that this poetic artistry in 'Michael' had a political subtext: the government's policies were producing 'a rapid decay of the domestic affections among the lower orders of society'. 'Michael', and 'The Brothers', Wordsworth continued, 'were written with a view to shew that men who do not wear fine cloaths can feel deeply', a theme of most of the poems written in that first year at Grasmere.

About 25 January 1801, *Lyrical Ballads* (1800) appeared in two volumes, the first one reissuing – with revisions – *Lyrical Ballads* (1798) and the second containing a somewhat uneasy mixture of the Grasmere poems of 1800 with the Goslar ones written in 1798–9. Paramount among those changes made in the first volume of 1800 was Wordsworth's addition to it of a critical manifesto, a preface providing a lengthy theoretical justification for the works to follow. Wordsworth's unshakeable faith in his own greatness and originality created the Preface to *Lyrical Ballads* to instruct his readers how to read those poems.

## Poems, in Two Volumes (1807)

Wordsworth's lyric voice fell silent for over a year after publication of *Lyrical Ballads* (1800). By mid-1801, he had received the news that the books were nearly all sold – a welcome sign of his growing reputation – and that a new edition was called for by the publisher. No new poems were added in the edition of 1802 or in the final one of 1805, but Wordsworth in 1802 revised his already printed texts. The second volume now also acquired its own critical essay, the 'Appendix on Poetic Diction', and the Preface in the first volume gained a soaring panegyric to the role of the poet: 'He is the rock of defence of human nature; an upholder and preserver, carrying every where with him relationship and love... [T]he Poet binds together by passion and knowledge the vast empire of human society, as it is spread over the whole earth, and over all time' (*LB* 753).

If that grand pronouncement seems to have more of a self-consciously literary flavour than do many of the works in *Lyrical Ballads*, so do the poems Wordsworth wrote when he returned to composing short pieces in the startlingly creative spring and summer of 1802. He then completed about thirty lyrics; and several other poems – among them 'I wandered lonely as a cloud' and 'Ode: Intimations of Immortality' – have their roots in 1802. As Wordsworth in 1802 left behind both ballads and pastoral, new styles, forms, and subject matters found expression in the poems that dominate *Poems, in Two Volumes* (1807).

There is some carry-over from his earlier work, to be sure. The first poems written after his return to short compositions in March 1802 are similar to what is in *Lyrical Ballads*, and in some cases they may have been thought of as possible supplements to the edition of 1802. Such works – among them 'The Affliction of Mary — of — ', 'The Sailor's Mother', and 'Alice Fell' – reprise Wordsworth's psychologically complex dramatic monologues or framed narratives, again presenting speaker's tales and interlocutor's meditations to lead the reader to an imaginative confrontation with pain and loss. Verse forms of these poems vary, but the ballad stanza is usually somewhere in the background. But as the spring of 1802 progressed, many of Wordsworth's poems became more joyful, more personal, more playful, more rooted in his own and Dorothy's memories, and more varied in their lyric forms:

> Oh! pleasant, pleasant were the days,
> The time, when in our childish plays
> My sister Emmeline and I
> Together chaced the Butterfly!
>     ('To a Butterfly' ['Stay near me']
>         10–13)

One influence on Wordsworth's new style in poetry was his reading of older English writers, particularly Chaucer, some of whom he translated in December 1801, and such sixteenth- and seventeenth-century poets as Spenser, Jonson, Cowley, Herbert, and Herrick. What Wordsworth drew from these writers was not, usually, specific subjects and images but rather a more light-hearted, polished, metrically proficient, graceful style. According to Jared Curtis, one of the most acute critics of this poetry of 1802, there is within it 'a gradual movement... from the bare elements of meter and concrete image to a chaste deployment of metaphor and symbol'.[8] Wordsworth was always a careful craftsman, but in 1802 his poems became artful in a fresh way.

A comparable move to the more traditionally 'literary' occurs in metrical and stanzaic forms, some of which are drawn from the poets Wordsworth was now reading. This process continues, and accelerates, what had already happened in Wordsworth's writing from 1798 to 1800, a move from experimenting with the ballad form – because of its folk origins frequently seen as having more of the direct and simple virtues of the less literate than showing the hand of the poetic artificer – to the pastoral, a classically rooted and highly literary form in which incipient epic poets could learn their craft. Similarly, the apparently artless conversational blank verse of many poems in *Lyrical Ballads* occurs nowhere in *Poems, in Two Volumes*. No poem in *Lyrical Ballads* is entitled an ode, that elevated and elaborate classical form; two odes appear in the 1807 volumes, including the impressive final poem there titled simply 'Ode' but later expanded to 'Ode: Intimations of Immortality from Recollections of Early Childhood'.

Still another conventional literary form now also resurfaced. Wordsworth, after Dorothy read Milton's sonnets to him on 21 May 1802, had an experience analogous to Keats' in 'On First Looking into Chapman's Homer'. Wordsworth had known Milton's sonnets for many years but 'was particularly struck on that occasion with the dignified simplicity and majestic harmony that runs through most of them'. That same day in May, Wordsworth, fascinated by rediscovering a form, 'took fire' and wrote three sonnets, his first composition of that kind he recalled since he was a schoolboy.[9] Wordsworth's excitement with this demanding form continued. While there are no sonnets in *Lyrical Ballads*, fifty-six appear in *Poems, in Two Volumes*, the first explaining that ''twas pastime to be bound / Within the Sonnet's scanty plot of ground' ('Nuns fret not', 10–11). Some of these sonnets are miscellaneous in character, ones in which Wordsworth describes his personal reflections and his travels, as in 'The World is too much with us' and in the comparatively rare – for him – celebration of urban splendors in 'Composed upon Westminster Bridge' ('Earth has not anything to show more fair'). In other sonnets (see, for example, 'London, 1802': 'Milton! Thou should'st be living at this hour'), Wordsworth honours his great predecessor by likewise employing the form for explicitly political purposes. In particular, William and Dorothy's trip to Calais in August 1802 prompted such rousing protests against tyranny and oppression as 'I griev'd for Buonaparte', 'Thought of a Briton on the Subjugation of Switzerland', and 'To Toussaint L'Ouverture'.

As for the lyrics composed in 1802, they frequently focused on specific and common things: butterfly, cuckoo, rainbow, glow-worm, robin, celandine, sparrow's nest, green linnet, daisy, skylark. Here, and in many similar poems later written for *Poems, in Two Volumes*, the poet joyfully and light-heartedly records his play of emotions over these objects of the natural world. These poems, less discussed by critics today than are the experimental pieces in *Lyrical Ballads* or such longer works as *The Prelude* and the assorted fragments of *The Recluse*, were reprinted in countless anthologies and cemented Wordsworth's reputation – for good and for ill – among his contemporaries.

An ubiquitous springtime flower forms the subject of what is probably Wordsworth's most well-known work: 'I wandered lonely as a cloud', sometimes referred to as 'The Daffodils', even by the poet himself. Dorothy's Grasmere Journal for 15 April 1802 records the scene before brother and sister on their walk at Ullswater:

> I never saw daffodils so beautiful they grew among the mossy stones about & about them, some rested their heads upon these stones as on a pillow for weariness & the rest tossed & reeled & danced & seemed as if they verily laughed with the wind that blew upon them over the Lake, they looked so gay ever glancing ever changing.[10]

Unlike Dorothy's journal entry with its dazzling run-on sentence that breathlessly conveys the immediate sensation, William waited two years to write about those Ullswater daffodils, characteristically finding in his memories continuing renewal for future times. Equally distinctive of Wordsworth, unfortunately, is his elimination of Dorothy from the experience – and his appropriation of some of her language – as he concentrates solely on his own moods.

'The Daffodils' opens with the speaker remote from the natural world, as is a cloud that soars distantly above that world. Abruptly, a 'laughing company' of daffodils surrounds him. The sparkling waves of Ullswater, the daffodils 'dancing in the breeze', the surrounding trees, and even that floating cloud all fuse in a vision of unity that encompasses the poet himself. But the ultimate import of that visionary moment becomes apparent to him only years later:

> For oft when on my couch I lie
> In vacant or in pensive mood,
> They flash upon that inward eye
> Which is the bliss of solitude,
> And then my heart with pleasure feels,
> And dances with the Daffodils.
>
> (13–18)

The poem is thus a miniature *Prelude*, showing the congruence between Wordsworth's short lyrics and the mammoth blank verse poem that he was simultaneously composing. Like *The Prelude*, the lyrics of 1802 and a few years afterwards chronicle renovating 'spots of time', but in these shorter poems frequently drawing less from childhood memories than from the Grasmere poet's mature experiences. Whether those memories be in the distant or the proximate past, they bind all our days – gone, present, and to come – 'each to each by natural piety' ('My heart leaps up', 9).

  *Poems, in Two Volumes*, published on 8 May 1807, was Wordsworth's first collection of short poems to be entirely his own, since the four editions of *Lyrical Ballads* all included a few works by Coleridge. In 1807, Wordsworth carefully arranged his 115 new poems into various sections, trying to provide – sometimes successfully and sometimes not – a context in which small poems could be seen by subject, by mood, or by genre as parts of a larger conception. One such classification included pieces written during William and Dorothy's tour of Scotland in 1803; another grouping posited an imaginary 'Tour, Chiefly on Foot' in which the poet met such characters as beggars, Alice Fell, and the old leech gatherer. Sonnets had their own section, in the first part 'Miscellaneous' ones and in the second part poems 'Dedicated to Liberty'. 'Moods of My Own Mind' and two other heterogeneous sections cohere less obviously. In the first two of the volumes' final three poems, Wordsworth presents personal meditations on death. 'Lines Composed at Grasmere' and 'Elegiac Stanzas' each end with the word 'mourn' but express hope – explicitly religious in 'Lines' – as the poet memorializes first the statesman Charles James Fox to whom he had sent *Lyrical Ballads* and then John Wordsworth, who had lived with his siblings William and Dorothy at Grasmere for nine months in 1800. The final poem in 1807 and in subsequent lifetime collected editions of Wordsworth's works, 'Ode: Intimations of Immortality', presents a much more stately reflection on loss and hoped-for renewal, this time of the visionary imagination. As the poet approached his fifth decade, he placed last in *Poems, in Two Volumes* this formal ode weighing the disadvantages and advantages of growing up and growing older.

  Within a fortnight of the publication of *Poems, in Two Volumes*, Wordsworth wrote to Lady Beaumont, 21 May 1807, telling her that he expected the reviews to be unfavourable. There were those, he predicted, who might consider the subject matter of some of his new poems to be 'very trifling'. Wordsworth launched his own pre-emptive attack against such possible criticism, rhetorically asking Lady Beaumont whether the poems grouped as 'Moods of My own Mind' do not 'taken collectively, fix the attention upon a subject eminently poetical, viz., the interest which objects in nature derive from the predominance of certain affections more or less permanent, more or less capable of salutary renewal in the mind of the being contemplating these objects?' Given the confessional poetry of our own time, we are unsurprised at these personal – sometimes private – and emotionally intense 'Moods of My own Mind', taking their origin from the most commonplace of events and objects. But Wordsworth correctly anticipated criticism of this category of poems, even though it is clear he did not anticipate the firestorm of scathing ridicule.

The reviews are remarkably similar, even down to some of the descriptive adjectives criticizing Wordsworth's most personal poems: 'flimsy, puerile thoughts, expressed in such feeble halting verse we have seldom seen', 'namby-pamby' (*British Critic*); 'puerile beyond the power of imitation' (*Le Beau Monde*); 'nauseous and nauseating sensibilities to weeds and insects', 'false taste and puerile conceit' (*Critical Review*); 'a very paragon of silliness and affectation', 'an insult on the public taste', 'namby-pamby' (*Edinburgh Review*); 'calculated to excite disgust and anger in a lover of poetry' (*Poetical Register*).[11] The main problem, as Francis Jeffrey wrote in the *Edinburgh Review*, was Wordsworth's use of subjects that the 'greater part of his readers will probably persist in thinking low, silly, or uninteresting'. The reviewer in *The Satirist* wondered how anyone could think it worthwhile to write about his memories of some daffodils blowing about in the wind; similarly, the writer for the *Annual Review* excoriated Wordsworth's attaching of 'exquisite emotions' to objects in which no one else had the slightest interest. The poet, thundered Francis Jeffrey, had openly violated 'the established laws of poetry'. Clearly, the taste by which the critics could appreciate *Poems, in Two Volumes* was still in the future. In 1807, Wordsworth suffered 'the most humiliating martyrdom in his reputation as a poet' (*The Satirist*). *Lyrical Ballads* went through four editions in seven years, but after the same time span a quarter of the sole printing of *Poems, in Two Volumes* remained unsold. When Wordsworth finally did bring himself to publish another work in 1814, he did not give the reviewers any opportunity to complain about small and trivial poems: *The Excursion*, huge in itself, was announced as just a portion of *The Recluse*.

Wordsworth's life in 1807 had not yet reached its midpoint, but that year marks the last time he chose to publish an independent collection of his new and miscellaneous short poems. Henceforth, beginning with his volumes of 1815, he folded new poems into his collected editions. The poet – certainly wounded by the reviewers in 1807 – now put his faith in those with improved standards of literary taste, readers whom he hoped to educate by his poetry and critical prose: 'Every Author, as far as he is great and at the same time *original*, has had the task of *creating* the taste by which he is to be enjoyed' ('Essay, Supplementary to the Preface', 1815).[12] Even though Wordsworth continued after 1807 to write short poems and to write them well, *Lyrical Ballads* and *Poems, in Two Volumes* thus stake his claim to be a major lyric poet. Before the conclusion of the nineteenth century whose literature Wordsworth eventually so dominated, both *Lyrical Ballads* and *Poems, in Two Volumes* appeared in scholarly editions. And in our own time, astonishingly for two old collections of poetry, multiple editions of these works remain in print, preserving all the short poems – and the poet's original arrangement of them – which at last form the basis for much of Wordsworth's reputation.

## NOTES

1 *STCL* 1 489n; *The Oxford Anthology of English Literature*, ed. Harold Bloom and Lionel Trilling (New York and London: Oxford University Press, 1973), II, 125.

2 All quotations from Wordsworth's poems, 'Fenwick Notes,' and critical prose in *Lyrical Ballads* and *Poems, in Two Volumes* are from the Cornell Wordsworth Series editions: *Lyrical Ballads, and Other Poems, 1797–1800*, ed. James Butler and Karen Green (Ithaca: Cornell University Press, 1992); *Poems, in Two Volumes, and other Poems, 1800–1807*, ed. Jared Curtis (Ithaca: Cornell University Press, 1983).

3 William Greswell, 'Wordsworth's Quantock Poems', *Temple Bar*, 107 (January – April 1896), 536.

4 A complete text of this early version – titled in manuscript 'Once, when my love was strong and gay' – appears in *Lyrical Ballads*, ed. Butler and Green, pp. 293–4.

5 For a fuller discussion of these Grasmere poems of 1799–1800, see my 'Tourist or Native Son: Wordsworth's Homecomings of 1799–1800', *Nineteenth-Century Literature*, 51 (1996), 1–15.

6 This introduction to 'Nutting' from Dove Cottage Manuscript 16 is published in *Lyrical Ballads*, ed. Butler and Green, pp. 305–7.

7 Stephen Parrish provides an excellent discussion of these pastorals in *The Art of the Lyrical Ballads* (Cambridge, MA: Harvard University Press, 1973), pp. 149–87.

8 *Wordsworth's Experiments with Tradition: The Lyric Poems of 1802* (Ithaca: Cornell University Press, 1971), pp. 62–3.

9 *The Fenwick Notes of William Wordsworth*, ed. Jared Curtis (London: Bristol Classical Press, 1993), p. 19.

10 Dorothy Wordsworth, *The Grasmere Journals*, ed. Pamela Woof (Oxford: Clarendon Press, 1991), p. 85.

11 These reviews are conveniently collected in *The Romantics Reviewed: Contemporary Reviews of British Romantic Writers: Part A – The Lake Poets*, ed. Donald H. Reiman (New York and London: Garland, 1972).

12 *Prose* III 80.

# 4

LUCY NEWLYN

# 'The noble living and the noble dead': community in *The Prelude*

On his way through Westmoreland in the 1650s, the Quaker George Fox had a vision:

> Here the land opened unto me, and let me see a great people in white raiment by a river side, coming to the Lord; and the place that I saw them in was about Wensleydale and Sedbergh.[1]

Nothing so biblical appears either in Dorothy Wordsworth's *Grasmere Journals* (1800–3) or in her brother's poems. But the habit of mind shown in Fox's journal lived on in the conviction they shared with him, that epiphanies can take place by the roadside anywhere, and that they change a person's life. The traffic of that idea among what Wordsworth called 'the noble living and the noble dead' (*1805* x 969) across two centuries of English history introduces us to the community that matters most in reading *The Prelude*.

For although Wordsworth's is a secular vision, this is a deeply Protestant poem. Its roots are embedded in the dissenting tradition of confessional autobiography practised by Fox and John Wesley in their *Journals*, by John Bunyan in *Grace Abounding*, as well as by numerous authors of Methodist and Quaker conversion-narratives published throughout the eighteenth century. There are a number of important things to grasp about these narratives. First, they were written in idiomatic prose (what Wordsworth called 'the ordinary language of men'); often read aloud to a select audience, then later dictated or transcribed; sometimes published only after the author's death, with a view to converting others. Second, they concerned the private nature of conscience, whose accountability to God wasn't governed by the prescripts of the Church. And third, they really did originate from the people. In mid-eighteenth-century England they gave workers and criminals, women and dissenters, the poor, the oppressed and the homeless, a medium and a voice.[2]

According to these narratives, a religious life should be lived according to inner conviction, not theology; and often this implied rebellion against the sovereign and the law. Rebellion had its consequences. John Bunyan, who courageously declared that it was his 'Christian Profession to be villified, slandered, reproached and reviled' and that he could 'rejoyce in reproaches for Christ's sake', had been 'indicted for an Upholder and Maintainer of Unlawful Assemblies and Conventicles, and for not conforming to the National Worship of the Church of England'.[3] He was imprisoned in Bedford Gaol for twelve years. Produced in this climate of persecution, conversion narratives charted the spiritual progress of ordinary people, offering a belief in human agency alongside a literal faith in divine intervention. The hero of *Grace Abounding* is 'a lower-class itinerant whose major temptations occur when playing tipcat';[4] and many of the writers of spiritual autobiographies were either literally travellers, or portrayed on a pilgrimage, 'occasionally be-friended but ultimately alone'.[5] One need only recall that Wordsworth, cast as a traveller in *The Prelude*, was the co-author of a radical volume of ballads many of which concern the homeless; that his poem 'The Female Vagrant' is a tale in the confessional mode; that in 'Peter Bell' he produced a Methodist conversion-narrative about a potter[6] – to see the immediate relevance, political and stylistic, of these writings to his concerns. Their importance for *The Prelude* is in supplying a missing link between Wordsworth's early radical vision and his later poetry of quietism.

As he finished the poem, Wordsworth claimed of *The Prelude* in a letter (1 May 1805) that it was 'a thing unprecedented in Literary history that a man should talk so much about himself'. But self is the staple subject of all conversion-narratives from Augustine onwards. Most readers in the 1790s would have been intimate with the conventions governing that form. They understood how the authorial self tries to justify actions, to account for a sense of election, and to seek forgiveness for human frailty; how the past comes to be read as a divinely ordained plot manifesting the grace of God; and how grace can be at once intensely personal and yet shared. They knew about the intimate relationship between a convert and the scriptures. (Bunyan, in *Grace Abounding*, describes his Bible as 'so fresh, and with such comfort on my spirit that it was as if it talked with me.')[7] Above all, they grasped that spiritual autobiography is the record of a self that changes as it grows, for many of these narratives were written and revised over a period of many years.

*The Prelude* was no exception. Wordsworth began his poem in late 1798, during a short stay in Germany, but continued working on it throughout his life. Like many conversion-narratives, it remained private during that time, known by the poet and his family as 'the poem to Coleridge' – a label which neatly defined its joint functions of epistle, confession, and tribute. Only in 1850, when it was posthumously published, did 'The Prelude' appear on the title-page, at the behest of the poet's widow and executors. The poem exists in a great many versions, because each time the poet revised it he produced a new work. Nonetheless, scholars have settled on three texts – the two-book version completed in 1799, the thirteen-book version of 1805, and the fourteen-book version published in 1850 – as marking the most crucial phases of composition. Recent critical orthodoxy has favoured the text completed in 1805, and read aloud to Coleridge when Wordsworth was at the height of his powers. It makes sense, though, to think of *The Prelude*'s compositional history as reflecting the organic self which is its subject matter, and the changing circumstances under which it evolved. A long autobiography such as this is a living entity, not at any time a monolithic power.

A contemporary reader approaching the first draft of *The Prelude* (the memory-fragment composed in late 1798 while Wordsworth was in Germany, known as MS JJ) would in the first instance have been a listener; for this text, like many of its predecessors, was read aloud long before it was published. How would he or she have understood the rhetorical question, 'Was it for this?', which is repeated insistently, like a mantra, through the first seventy or so lines?[8] Surely as a signal that a confessional narrative is under way. The speaker, looking back on the progress of his life, sees it as leading to an end; and although he's unsure of his destiny, he knows himself to be chosen. Recent Wordsworth scholars have supplied a context that glosses Wordsworth's misgivings about his calling. Faced with the task of writing *The Recluse*, the great philosophical poem that Coleridge wanted him to write, would he be able to do so? What was the evidence he had the power?[9] Coleridge, hearing these lines, must have felt the full force of the generic reference that links Wordsworth back into a tradition of conversion and spiritual vocation. This was a poet who took seriously the project envisioned in a mood of radical optimism by his friend.

The account of self given in this fragment is guilty and self-justifying. The speaker confesses childhood misdemeanours, but presents these as evidence of a providential pattern: 'Though mean, / And though inglorious, were my views, the end / Was not ignoble' (lines 57–8). He prays to 'the beings of the hills', the 'voices of the clouds' and 'the familiars of the lakes and standing pools', as guardians whose ministry made nature legible to him as a growing child. And he goes on to invoke 'the eternal spirit – he that has / His life in unimaginable things' (lines 124–5) as a 'bounteous power', who has watched over his growth towards love and joy. This is poetry of self-interrogation, but also of thanksgiving. There are enough religious references to make it uncertain how far Wordsworth has shed his Puritan heritage; and more than enough to suggest that he is defining, with the excitement and commitment of a convert, the unique form of pantheism which makes sense of his life.

This fragment of 150 lines was later expanded into the *Two-Part Prelude* of 1799. Its resemblance to spiritual autobiography became clarified in the process of shaping a more finished piece of writing. Wordsworth wrote the poem for Coleridge, with whom he shared his commitment to progress, freedom, and benevolence; and whose belief in God as an energizing principle, alive in all things, had recently communicated itself powerfully to him. He structured the narrative as an account of how nature's 'ministry' led to his own calling as one of nature's prophets, and so to the 'self-same bourne' as his friend (1799 ii 499). The poem declares openly his kinship with religious non-conformism. Wordsworth shared with Thomas Paine the rational inference that God could be perceived in the patterns of nature, and with Joseph Priestley the belief that there was a divine energy, activating the material world. Paine, a deist, was the author of two radical bestselling works, *The Rights of Man* and *The Age of Reason*. Priestley, a Unitarian scientist, is now best known for his discovery of oxygen; but his notoriety in the 1790s came from the publication of radical pamphlets, and a treatise on the relation between matter and spirit that challenged the central tenets of Anglicanism. Both these writers had suffered for their convictions: we should not forget that this was a decade that saw the government-organized persecution of dissenters. Many Unitarians (including Priestley himself) emigrated from Britain to the United States. Wordsworth and Coleridge, temporary emigres at the time *The Prelude* was begun, had allegedly been followed and watched by a spy in Somerset earlier that year; and when they returned to England they were looking for a safe retreat. In an atmosphere of continuing intolerance, when religious non-conformism and inflammatory politics were seen as going hand in hand, *The Prelude* might have re-awoken suspicion had it been published. Parts of it were read aloud at various stages in Wordsworth's life, to those who shared his calling or could be trusted to sympathize. At later stages in the revision process, some of its unorthodox implications were toned down to accord with the doctrines of the Anglican church. Even so, the poem was regarded as shocking when it appeared in print: 'It is to the last degree Jacobinical, indeed socialist', wrote Thomas Macaulay on 28 July 1850, 'I understand perfectly why Wordsworth did not choose to publish it in his lifetime.'

As Wordsworth expanded *The Prelude* from the two-part version of 1799 to the thirteen-book version completed in 1805, the poem became more philosophically exploratory. In this it resembled an older, meditative tradition of autobiography going back from Rousseau to St Augustine.[10] It's not certain that Wordsworth had read Rousseau's posthumously published *Confessions* (1781), but he knew its content in the way most people know the great controversial books that are the talk of an era. There's a similarity in the way he and Rousseau handle the guilty materials of their lives – suppressing the major transgressions (in Wordsworth's case, the family he began and left in France) while bringing minor misdemeanours into the foreground.[11] Wordsworth also shared with Rousseau a fascination with the temporality of human consciousness. He wanted to prove that memory was active, not passive, and so to discredit what Coleridge called the 'sandy sophisms' of John Locke's *Essay Concerning Human Understanding*, which had for a century dominated British philosophy. He used the interaction between past and present selves (a traditional feature of confessional narrative) to show how the mind shapes the materials it absorbs, working and re-working them. The verb 'work' is an important one in his vocabulary. Along with the nouns 'effort' and 'motion' it crops up a number of times in *The Prelude* to describe imaginative process. (See *1799* i 195–8; 120–2; 370–4.) These words declare the mind to be no lazy spectator but an active participant. Through the 'work' he was himself performing, the poet might count himself one of a community, like the Cumbrian shepherds and farmers whose lives he thought of as dignified and productive.

Wordsworth always regarded *The Prelude* as preparation for writing *The Recluse*; and in this sense it was a labour of love conceived for Coleridge, who had wished the idea of a philosophical poem upon him. Although the larger work was never completed, *The Prelude* came to occupy its place as the focus for Wordsworth's abiding conviction that humankind was capable of progress. This faith had its foundations in the republican and communitarian politics of the 1790s, which he and Coleridge had shared. He refers to his friend as a collaborator in his vision, claiming that they both are 'United helpers forward of a day / Of firmer trust', 'joint labourers in a work... / Of [man's] redemption, surely yet to come' (*1805* xiii 438–41). This description acknowledges the hugely ambitious nature of Wordsworth's project, undertaken in the spirit of enquiry and experimentalism that characterised dissenting culture. The poet made himself the subject of his own 'experiment', as Coleridge did when he took nitrous oxide to test its effects on the emotions.[12] His aim was nothing less than to show how the foundations for a benevolent society might be laid, using 'the growth of a poet's mind' as his starting-point. Self, as he understood it, was best seen in terms of its responsibilities to community:

> The outermost and all-embracing circle of benevolence has inward concentric circles which, like those of the spider's web, are bound together by links, and rest upon each other; making one frame, and capable of one tremor; circles narrower and narrower, closer and closer, as they lie more near to the centre of self from which they proceeded, and which sustain the whole.[13]

Wordsworth wasn't the systematic thinker that Coleridge was, but he read voraciously; and something of Coleridge's effort to reconcile philosophy, poetry and religion can be felt in the difficult meditative texture of his verse, making the process of reading itself a kind of labour. There is, too, a powerful syncretist energy in *The Prelude*, which weaves together some of the eighteenth century's major intellectual contributions. David Hartley's *Observations on Man* (1749), a book Wordsworth had read in the early 1790s and never forgotten, gave him a scientific way of linking the theory of association with the idea of progress, by envisioning a steady improvement in man's associative capacities.[14] William Godwin's *Political Justice* (1793), a work he came to see as pernicious (because of its atheism) showed him how freedom might be built on a purely rationalist basis, without the props of religion and the law. Edmund Burke's *A Philosophical Enquiry into the Origin of our Ideas of the Sublime and the Beautiful* (1759) helped him to understand the way the mind can be pleased or shocked into an awareness of the mysterious and the vast. And Rousseau's *Emile* (1762) offered a developmental account of childhood on which to base his own reformist ideals.

The claim that mind is actively transformative is put to the proof by *The Prelude*'s handling of the intellectual materials it works upon. Influence is as much a process of revision as of absorption; and Wordsworth's eclectic methodology brings into sharp focus the vigour of his own associative processes. The integration of Burke and Rousseau into the poem's overarching design is an example. Burke had attempted to explain why terror could be pleasurable as part of aesthetic experience. He used a combination of psychological and philosophical analysis, but drew many of his examples from literature, and his essay anticipates Romanticism in its focus on imagination. Wordsworth wrote *The Prelude* under its sway, but added a spiritual-ethical dimension to the treatment of sublimity. In his poem, Burke's feminine Beauty and masculine Terror become guardian spirits, in charge of imaginative life. He transformed Burke's theory from a philosophical scheme which objectified aesthetic categories into a developmental model which intertwined the speaker's subjective experience with his moral growth. The patterning of consciousness was presented as evidence of a shaping divinity.

This Burkean narrative was grafted onto Rousseau's programme of education. Wordsworth was excited by Rousseau's radical conviction that man is innately good, but that society corrupts him. (This was the cornerstone of a progressive argument that circumstances need only to be improved for humans themselves to become more virtuous.) He borrowed from *Emile* the idea that the best education is through nature, and that the growing child can be kept in touch with goodness by protection from societal prejudices. The ultimate aim, however – to produce an adult who is truly benevolent – depended on moving the child out of his innocent safety. A difficult transition which Rousseau had scarcely negotiated became for Wordsworth his central purpose in writing the thirteen-book *Prelude*: to prove (as the subtitle of Book 8 puts it) that 'love of nature leads to love of mankind'. Under the guardianship of Terror and Beauty, implicitly likened to the watchful role of Emile's tutor, the Wordsworthian child goes through a regime of moral enlightenment. The poem is concerned with how to avoid contamination from social evils, and how to ensure that goodness spreads:

> O who is he that has his whole life long
> Preserved, enlarged, this freedom in himself?
> For this alone is genuine liberty.
>
> (*1805* xii 120–2)

Rousseau did not recommend literature in the upbringing of children. The only book Emile is allowed is Defoe's *Robinson Crusoe*, valued not for its imaginative appeal as a gripping tale of adventure and survival, but because it is a conversion narrative in the dissenting tradition. By contrast Wordsworth placed books on a par with nature in the nourishment of imaginative life, and believed the mind could become accustomed to grandeur through what Milton in *Areopagitica* called 'promiscuous' reading. Again, he put this idea to the test through his own allusive style, which suggests how experience is mediated and enhanced by literature, so that it takes on a 'texture midway betwixt life and books' (*1805* iii 614). The fabric of *The Prelude* is woven from many strands, and the voices speaking through it are multiple. On the prose side, as we've seen, are Bunyan, Paine, Burke, Godwin, Hartley, and Rousseau; among the poets, Shakespeare, Milton, Cowper, Coleridge. This intertextual fluidity reflects the collaborative nature of Wordsworth's interaction with the audiences – past, present, and future – he imagines and addresses. It makes of the poem a vast web of literary connections, expanding from the individual imagination towards an 'outermost and all-embracing circle' of precursors and readers.

Coleridge is sometimes invoked directly, as in the moving lines which conclude the poem in both 1799 and 1805.[15] On other occasions Wordsworth 'plants' him in the narrative where he doesn't chronologically belong, or speaks to him in a private language of allusion. *The Prelude* thus becomes the longest in a sequence of 'Conversation Poems' written by Coleridge and

Wordsworth to each other. Like the earlier poems in that sequence (which had included 'Frost at Midnight' and 'Tintern Abbey') it establishes a basis for benevolence in friendship, defining the ideal community as a nexus of 'domestic affections' that link family and friends into the world beyond. In this it parallels Edmund Burke's eloquent declaration in his *Reflections on the Revolution in France* (1790): 'To be attached to the subdivision, to love the little platoon we belong to in society, is the first principle (the germ, as it were) of public affections. It is the first link in the series by which we proceed towards a love to country and to mankind.'[16] But the poem is also a 'conversation' in a different sense. By juxtaposing different literary genres and influences, making them 'move / In one society' (*1805* i 354–5), it creates discussion amongst voices past and present. The Russian literary theorist, Mikhail Bakhtin, has called this kind of writing 'dialogic'. But the seventeenth-century concept of a 'republic of letters' offers a more appropriate label for the spirit of shared political and intellectual endeavour which the poem celebrates through allusion.

A key text for this communitarian poetics is *Paradise Lost* – a poem whose ending Wordsworth made the beginning of his own, as though both poets were bards in an oral culture, elaborating a traditional tale. At the opposite extreme from the 'Conversation poem' in its register, Milton's epic provided Wordsworth with the connection between his life-story and the grand narrative of mankind's fall from innocence into experience.[17] It also bonded the particular moment in history at which Wordsworth wrote with an earlier moment in the story of the English nation. For *Paradise Lost* had been dictated after the collapse of the Commonwealth and the restoration of the monarchy. In it, Milton had reflected long and deeply on the nature of freedom. Wordsworth's elective affinity with Milton came out of their shared experience of republican idealism and disillusionment. As he stood back from having witnessed the bloody aftermath of the French Revolution, Wordsworth too wondered how and where true liberty was to be found. The intricate network of allusions connecting *The Prelude*, with *Paradise Lost* shows Wordsworth looking for redemptive possibilities in the world itself, but also in the human imagination, which is 'of substance and of fabric more divine' than nature (*1805* xiii 452).

Imagination is identified in *The Prelude* with 'intellectual love' (*1805* xiii 186) and with 'reason in her most exalted mood' (*1805* xiii 170) – an allusion to Milton's 'intuitive reason', the highest human faculty (*Paradise Lost* v 467–8). Wordsworth saw it as almost synonymous with soul, and distinguished it sharply from the Godwinian reason he came to reject. In the 'Crossing of the Alps' passage in Book Six he associates imagination with spiritual hunger ('Effort, and expectation and desire / And something evermore about to be') and in the 'Climbing of Snowdon' he defines it as 'the sense of God / Or whatsoe'er is dim or vast in [the mind's] own being' (*1805* vi 541–2; xiii 72–3). These sublime moments in Wordsworth's epic envisage for the mind a transcendent possibility: discovering what Milton had called a 'paradise within', they suggest that all human beings, not just poets, can make 'communion with the invisible world' (*1805* xiii 105).

At the centre of the two-part version of *The Prelude*, and eventually providing the scaffolding for the thirteen-book version, are the 'Spots of Time'. These moments of epiphany generate the child's aesthetic, ethical, and spiritual growth. In Burkean terms, they afford him either a harmonizing and tranquillizing glimpse of beauty, or an encounter with terror, from which his own imagination emerges the stronger. But they also nourish his conscience; for in each of the darker 'Spots' there is an awareness that he himself has committed a crime (as in the woodcock-snaring, birdsnesting, and boatstealing episodes; *1799* i 30–129), or a more numinous sense that a spot is associated with guilt (as in the passages concerning the 'Woman on the Hill' or the 'Waiting for Horses'; *1799* i 302–27; 335–74). These transgressions awaken in the child a sense of the grandeur within and beyond his own mind. They introduce him to the idea of death; but they also link him with the 'Soul of things', and make up the centre of his moral being.

The 'Spots of Time' are given as momentous a significance in *The Prelude*'s plot as are the climaxes in conversion-narratives. Their structure, and the dissenting religious sensibility they evince, are strongly reminiscent of *Grace Abounding*, a book which Wordsworth surely knew. In Bunyan's story, life is understood as an internal dialogue between his conscience and the scriptures. He is accompanied everywhere by his Bible, which speaks to him directly, with the passion and urgency of a lover. The effect of each exchange upon his conscience is vividly remembered: the words 'fell with a weight upon my spirit' (p. 23); they sent 'a sweet glance'(p. 38); they 'returned upon me, as an eccho does a voice' (p. 61); they 'broke my heart, and filled me full of joy, and laid me as low as dust' (p. 67). As he reaches the single epiphany which he looks back on as his conversion, the pace slows down, and he recalls how, even then, the moment led to a process of obsessional re-visiting:

> Thorow the blessed Sentence the Lord led me over and over, first to this word, and then to that, and shewed me wonderful glory in every one of them. These words also have oft since this time been great refreshment to my Spirit. Blessed be God for having mercy on me. (p. 84)

*The Prelude* too is the journal of a spiritual renewal, in which natural forms are remembered speaking to the child and touching him with their power.

In these moments of 'ennobling interchange' (*Prel.1805* xii 306) the line between sensation and reflection becomes confused and consciousness deepens. Shelley caught this Wordsworthian process well in the phrase 'wakening a sort of thought in sense' ('Peter Bell the Third', line 312); and we can watch how a kind of arousal is achieved poetically. The river Derwent 'sent a voice / That flowed among [his] dreams' (*Prel.1799* i 5–6); a scene of beauty 'lay upon [his] mind / Even with the weight of pleasure' (*Prel.1799* ii 211–12); a 'gentle shock of mild surprise / Has carried far into his heart the voice / Of mountain torrents' (*Prel.1805* v 407–9). Notice how those simple prepositions, 'among', 'upon', 'into', ascribe depth and dimension to perceptions, just as the physical verbs 'flowed', 'lay', 'carried' make abstract feelings palpable. Shelley might well have put it the other way round: Wordsworth's poetry awakens a sort of sense in thought.

*The Prelude* shows a fascination with the way habitual impressions form identity, so that each person becomes 'a memory to himself' (*Prel.1805* iii 189). Wordsworth understood how it is through sights, sounds and sensations (not through abstract ideas) that the deep patterning of consciousness is established. This feature of his sensibility belongs unmistakeably to the dissenting culture of his day. The integration of matter and spirit was a central tenet of Unitarianism, and Coleridge (like Priestley) believed in the 'corporeality of thought' (letter 11 December 1794). Repeated throughout childhood, Wordsworthian memories make up a private associative language whose significance is realized only in retrospect. The adult, in re-visiting them as Bunyan did the words of the Scriptures, finds them refreshing to his spirit: he 'thence would drink / As at a fountain' (*Prel.1805* xi 383–4). Extraordinary experiences too are shown to have a formative power, partly because, occurring unexpectedly, they remove the 'ballast of familiar life' (*Prel.1805* vii 603), revealing an essential solitude. When separated from the forms of nature, scenes of human distress or alienation are remembered striking the narrator's conscience with the force of revelation, so that he felt 'As if admonished from another world' (*Prel.1805* vii 622). Coming face to face with a beggar in London made his mind 'turn round, / As with the might of waters' (*Prel.1805* vii 615–16); and the sight of a 'hunger-bitten' girl in France, accompanied by Beaupuy's words, went on haunting him for years: 'Tis against *that* / Which we are fighting' (*Prel.1805* ix 519–20). Wordsworth wanted to educate his readers away from gothic expectations, so the power of these moments does not derive from anything sensational. Even in the political spots of time, it's not the 'moving accidents' themselves that are crucial.[18] Wordsworth was in Paris in October 1792, a month after the uprising which had led to the 'September Massacres'. The king's deposition in

August had caused the flight of the Royal family to the Tuileries. Four hundred republican citizens and eight hundred members of the Swiss guard had been slaughtered. The king's imprisonment, and his execution in January 1793, were yet to follow. Wordsworth's guilty complicity with the forces of revolution – later regicide – makes him retrospectively identify with Macbeth. Alone at night in a Paris hotel room, he seemed 'to hear a voice that cried / To the whole city "Sleep no more!"' (*Prel.1805* x 76–7). The short interval that separated him from the bloody deeds then, and the longer interval that has since followed, have the effect for the reader of removing the immediate shock-value of the massacres themselves. But our sense of the narrator's empathy and responsibility is intensified by this awareness of the passage of time, and the reflective distance it brings.

*The Prelude* declares its deepest affinities with the medium of Puritan autobiography in these 'Spots', whose poetic language is stripped of all but the essentials. In the episode concerning the 'Woman on the Hill', the figure on the skyline, balancing her pitcher on her head while forcing her way 'with difficult steps' against the wind, is drawn from daily working life in a rural community:

> It was in truth
> An ordinary sight, but I should need
> Colours and words that are unknown to man
> To paint the visionary dreariness
> Which, while I looked all round for my lost guide,
> Did at that time invest the naked pool,
> The beacon on the lonely eminence,
> The woman and her garments vexed and tossed
> By the strong wind.        (*Prel.1805* xi 308–16)

Her nearest literary analogue is the personification of 'heavenly Truth' in Coleridge's early radical poem, 'The Destiny of Nations', described 'With gradual steps, winning her difficult way' from Bethabra northward (line 125). She also has features in common with the stylized classical figures stamped on Jacobin coins in the 1790s. But Wordsworth's scrupulous avoidance of allegory and metaphor, his almost prosaic minimalism, keep the woman firmly this side of the symbolic.

Wordsworth shared with his dissenting predecessors Bunyan and Fox a belief that the spiritual is apprehended in and through the material. His secular commitment was to 'the very world which is the world / Of all of us, the place in which, in the end, / We find our happiness, or not at all' (*Prel.1805* x 725–7). Note how verse gives way to prose here, that middle line making little pretence to iambic pentameter. A resistance to the transcendent, the allegorical, and the sacramental was part and parcel of the realist project that linked Wordsworth with later writers like George Eliot, and thus with a Protestant community that outlived him. We can see this by comparing two passages: one in typical Wordsworth blank-verse, the other in a Victorian prose-style that owes much to the deep-structure of a Wordsworthian spot of time. The first, from Book Four of the 1805 text of *The Prelude*, describes a sunrise near his home in Cumbria, and the sense of dedication which this prospect gave him:

> Magnificent
> The morning was, a memorable pomp,
> More glorious than I ever had beheld.
> The sea was laughing at a distance; all
> The solid mountains were as bright as clouds,
> Grain-tinctured, drenched in empyrean light;
> And in the meadows and the lower grounds
> Was all the sweetness of a common dawn –
> Dews, vapours, and the melody of birds,
> And labourers going forth into the fields.
> Ah, need I say, dear Friend, that to the brim
> My heart was full? I made no vows, but vows
> Were then made for me: bond unknown to me
> Was given, that I should be – else sinning greatly –
> A dedicated spirit. On I walked
> In blessedness, which even yet remains.
>
> (*Prel.1805* iv 330–45)

The verse here, sliding from the grandiloquent and the epic to the humdrum and the quotidian, matches the eye's movement from hazy distant prospect to the clearer human figures in the foreground. It takes in the full sweep of literary registers at work in *The Prelude*. A lofty, Miltonic diction, latinately polysyllabic – 'grain-tinctured, drenched in empyrean light' – gives way to the low-key, irregular, almost flatly prosaic line: 'And labourers going forth into the fields.' Then there's a pause, as the poet works over the importance of this moment to the emerging pattern of his life, relishing the sense of blessedness (it's a word that nearly, in this context, means grace) which has stayed with him.

The second passage occurs in the fictional life of Dorothea Brooke (even her name is Wordsworthian) in Eliot's *Middlemarch* (1871–2). Dorothea is seen here emerging from the selfishness of grief into a full consciousness of how little her place is in the scheme of things:

> She opened her curtains, and looked out towards the bit of road that lay in view, with fields beyond, outside the entrance-gates. On the road there was a man with a bundle on his back and a woman carrying her baby; in the field she could see figures moving – perhaps the shepherd with his dog. Far off in the bending sky was the pearly light; and she felt the largeness of the world and the manifold wakings of men to labour and endurance. She was a part of that involuntary, palpitating life, and could neither look out on it from her luxurious shelter as a mere spectator, nor hide her eyes in selfish complaining.

Again the register is mixed, moving this time from low to high, in unison with the heroine's mood. The moment of insight is led up to and framed – visually by the window, but narratorially by the slowness and deliberation of the actions. A gradual widening of perspective is accompanied by a slowing of tempo as the scene's full significance is absorbed. The powerful Wordsworthian simplicity of the human group at the centre of this scene – each figure carrying a burden – is set against the heroine's abstract ruminations, as she realizes that her own place in it is literally diminished, but spiritually enlarged.

'A man with a bundle on his back and a woman carrying a baby'; 'The woman and her garments vexed and tossed / By the strong wind'. 'Labourers going forth into the fields'; 'the manifold wakings of men to labour and endurance'. Ordinary human details in a Wordsworthian spot of time are momentous and telling, but resolutely spare, almost biblical. They accord a value to work, conscience, and the connection of self with community, which is at the heart of the English Puritan tradition. There's not a trace in them of what Keats called the 'egotistical sublime';[19] but their relation to sublimity – and specifically to the Miltonic sublime with which Wordsworth was most familiar – has a bearing on his peculiarly social and domestic version of the epic genre.

*The Prelude*, a vast multi-media collage as complex as *Paradise Lost*, links the writers of popular prose like Bunyan with those (like Milton) who chose the highest form in the hierarchy of genres. And it does so for the best of reasons. Wordsworth had come to mistrust the efficacy of revolution, and he looked elsewhere for compensatory evidence of human progress. A note of elegy can be heard in his rousing claim that 'There is one great society alone on earth / The noble living and the noble dead' (*Prel. 1805* x 968–9), with its implied admission that other forms of 'society' had failed. Nonetheless, he remained convinced that progress was possible – that there existed a pattern humanity could follow. He placed his faith in 'a spiritual community binding together the living and the dead, the good, the brave and the wise of all ages',[20] and imagined in its midst a band of prophets, writers in both poetry and prose, who were charged with the task of reminding fallen humankind of its potential for benevolence. They formed a brotherhood, 'each with each / Connected in the mighty scheme of truth', (*Prel.1805* xii 302–3) to which, as he worked on his spiritual autobiography throughout his life, Wordsworth consistently felt that he belonged. *The Prelude* is the record of his allegiance to that republic of letters.

## NOTES

1 Quoted by Frank D. McConnell, *The Confessional Imagination* (Johns Hopkins University Press, 1974), p. 85.
2 See Felicity Nussbaum, *The Autobiographical Subject: Gender and Ideology in Eighteenth Century England* (Johns Hopkins University Press, 1989), p. 86.
3 John Bunyan, *Grace Abounding to the Chief of Sinners and The Pilgrim's Progress from this World to that which is to come*, ed. with an introduction by Roger Sharrock (London: Oxford University Press, 1966), pp. 96, 97.
4 See Christopher Hill, *The World Turned Upside Down: Radical Ideas During the English Revolution* (London: Penguin, 1972), p. 408.
5 *The Autobiographical Subject*, p. 96.
6 See Mary Jacobus, *Tradition and Experiment in Wordsworth's 'Lyrical Ballads', 1798* (Oxford: Clarendon Press, 1976).
7 *Grace Abounding*, p. 23.
8 See MS JJ 'Reading Text', in Stephen Parrish, ed., *The Prelude, 1798–1799* (Ithaca: Cornell University Press, 1977), pp. 123–7.
9 The most extensive discussions of *The Recluse* can be found in Jonathan Wordsworth, *William Wordsworth: The Borders of Vision* (Oxford: Clarendon Press, 1982) and Kenneth Johnston, *Wordsworth and 'The Recluse'* (New Haven: Yale University Press, 1984).
10 For Wordsworth's debt to Rousseau and Augustine, see William Spengemann, *The Forms of Autobiography* (New Haven: Yale University Press, 1980), pp. 73–91 and W. J. T. Mitchell, 'Influence, Autobiography and Literary History: Rousseau's *Confessions* and Wordsworth's *The Prelude*'; *ELH*, 57 (1990), pp. 643–65.
11 In the 1805 version of *The Prelude*, Wordsworth's relationship with Annette Vallon, and the child (Caroline) who was conceived during their affair, are 'confessed' only at second-hand, through the fictive device of Vaudracour and Julia's romance, which is included in Book 9. In the 1850 version of the text, this section was removed altogether.
12 See Ian Wylie, *Young Coleridge and the Philosophers of Nature* (Oxford: Clarendon Press, 1989).
13 'The Convention of Cintra'; *Prose* i 340.
14 See H. W. Piper, *The Active Universe: Pantheism and the Concept of Imagination in the English Romantic Poets* (1962); Jonathan Wordsworth, *The Borders of Vision*.
15 See *Prel.1799* ii 496–514; and *Prel.1805* xiii 386–452. I have analysed Coleridge's presence in *The Prelude* at length in *Coleridge, Wordsworth, and the Language of Allusion* (Oxford: Clarendon Press, 1986), pp. 165–94. For a more recent

discussion, see Stephen Gill, *The Prelude*; Landmarks of World Literature Series (Cambridge: Cambridge University Press, 1991), pp. 14–18.

16 James Chandler has discussed the Burkean strand in Wordsworth's political thinking. See *Wordsworth's Second Nature: A Study of the Poetry and the Politics* (Chicago: Chicago University Press, 1984), esp. p. 43.

17 See M. H. Abrams, *Natural Supernaturalism: Tradition and Revolution in Romantic Literature* (New York, 1971); Jonathan Wordsworth, *The Borders of Vision*; and Lucy Newlyn, *Paradise Lost and the Romantic Reader* (Oxford: Clarendon Press, 1993).

18 Used by Wordsworth to define his anti-sensational poetics in *Lyrical Ballads*: 'The moving accident is not my trade, / To curl the blood I have no ready arts; / 'Tis my delight alone in summer shade, / To pipe a simple song to thinking hearts' ('Hart-leap Well', lines 97–100).

19 Keats referred to 'the wordsworthian or egotistical sublime, which is a thing by itself and stands alone' in a letter to Richard Woodhouse, on 27 October 1818. See *Letters of John Keats*, ed. Robert Gittings (Oxford: Oxford University Press, 1970), p. 157.

20 *The Convention of Cintra, Prose* i 339.

# 5

KENNETH R. JOHNSTON

# Wordsworth and *The Recluse*

For more than half his long life, from 1798 until he was nearly seventy, Wordsworth was writing – or thinking about writing – an immense epic poem, to be called *The Recluse*, which he intended to be his magnum opus. References to *The Recluse* occur throughout his correspondence and appear, increasingly, in modern textual, critical, and biographical writings about the poet. But since no poem with that title appears anywhere among his published works (except for a reference to it in the preface to *The Excursion*), many readers conclude that *The Recluse* does not exist, or that they, or the poet, are labouring under some kind of misconception. These suppositions are at once correct and incorrect, and both suppositions are useful.

It is true that Wordsworth never completed *The Recluse*. But he did finish, and publish, one part of it: *The Excursion* (1814), which was to be the narrative, 'Human Life' part of its projected three-part sequence, 'on Man, on Nature, and on Human Life'. Book I of Part I also exists in manuscript: the popular *Home at Grasmere*, first published posthumously in 1888, and many times since. 'The Tuft of Primroses' (1808), a long manuscript poem first published in 1949, is another instalment of *The Recluse*, conjecturally a second book of Part I. But no Part III exists, and if it was to be 'on Nature', while Part I was 'on Man', remains a mystery, not least because *The Recluse*'s three thematic terms interweave so closely throughout its extant parts – as indeed they do throughout Wordsworth's entire oeuvre.

But what about *The Prelude*? Surely this *is* Wordsworth's masterpiece, and very much a modern epic, with its emphasis on the growing self-consciousness of its hero, more central to its story than all the mighty places and events through which he passes: London, the Alps, and the French Revolution. Called simply 'the poem on the growth of my own mind' when he was writing it, is *The Prelude* part of *The Recluse*? Or is it a different poem altogether? Published posthumously, *The Prelude*'s printed title suggests a *prelusive* or preparatory relationship to something else, not clearly specified in the note accompanying its 1850 publication and, since this note is almost never reprinted, even this vague relationship was quickly lost sight of.

Approximate plan and chronology of *The Recluse*

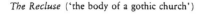

*The Recluse* ('the body of a gothic church')

| *The Prelude* or ('ante-chapel' 'portico') | Part I | Part II | Part III |
|---|---|---|---|
| (13 books in 1805; 14 in 1850) | Book I    'Home at Grasmere'<br>Book II?    'The Tuft of Primroses' (remainder never written) | *The Excursion* (9 books) | (Never written) |

| | | |
|---|---|---|
| 1797–99 | The First Drafts: 'The Ruined Cottage', 'The Old Cumberland Beggar', 'The Discharged Veteran', and 'A Night-Piece' | 1,300 lines |
| 1798–99 | The Two-Part *Prelude* | 1,000 lines |
| 1800 | The Beginning of 'Home at Grasmere' | 500 lines |
| 1800–02 | 'Prospectus' to *The Recluse* | 100 lines |
| 1803–05 | Main Composition of *The Prelude* | 8,000 lines |
| 1806 | Completion of 'Home at Grasmere' | 400 lines |
| 1808 | 'The Tuft of Primroses', 'To the Clouds', and 'St Paul's' | 700 lines |
| 1809–12 | *The Excursion*, Books II–IV | 3,200 lines |
| 1812–14 | *The Excursion*, Books V–IX | 4,700 lines |

NOTE    Line totals are very approximate, and some dates are almost equally so. 'The Ruined Cottage' became Book I ('The Wander') of *The Excursion*; 'The Discharged Veteran' concludes Book IV of *The Prelude*; the two-part *Prelude* forms the bulk of Books I and II of the finished *Prelude*; the placement of 'The Tuft of Primroses' is conjectural.

*The Prelude* also preoccupied Wordsworth throughout his creative life, even more than *The Recluse*, so it is easy to suppose that it supplanted the other, larger project. In fact, Wordsworth's own idea of *The Prelude*'s relation to *The Recluse* changed as the decades passed, making a single definitive statement of their relationship impossible. Paradoxically, it was *The Recluse*, which does not wholly exist, that was always conceived, from first to last, as a definite poem, whereas *The Prelude*, which certainly does exist, only gradually emerged in the poet's mind as a separate work of art. At first, in 1798–9, his *Prelude*-writings seemed only a 'distraction' from *The Recluse*, especially to Coleridge, who was more responsible than Wordsworth for the conception of *The Recluse* as an all-encompassing philosophic poem, and who declared himself in a letter of 12 October 1799 unable to 'hear patiently' of Wordsworth's autobiographical writing as other than 'the tail-piece of "The Recluse!"'. Still later, as years passed without *The Recluse* emerging from its hiding-place (and as both Wordsworth and Coleridge recognized what a unique poem *The Prelude* was), *The Prelude*, his unintended masterpiece, was promoted forward, in the preface to *The Excursion*, to the position of a 'portico' or 'ante-chapel' to the intended masterwork. And there it may well rest, its *pre*lusive quality always beckoning suggestively toward the mysterious *re*clusive nature of its shadowy twin, or Other.

All this is fairly clear, two hundred years after the fact, but it has taken the better part of those two centuries for generations of scholars to get the facts straight, and some of our findings still seem to be, disappointingly, non-events. Nonetheless, it is clear that *The Recluse* is something far greater, both qualitatively and quantitatively, than merely an unfinished poem. Several parts of it exist, and can profitably be read and studied, both in themselves and their relations to each other, as well as to many other parts of Wordsworth's oeuvre.

Wordsworth hinted at these relationships when, in his 1814 preface to *The Excursion*, he likened *The Recluse*'s three-part structure to 'the body of a gothic church', with his poem on 'the growth of my own mind' as its 'ante-chapel', and all his minor pieces (that is, the remainder of his poems) 'when they shall be properly arranged, will be found by the attentive Reader to have such connection with the main Work as may give them claim to be likened to the little cells, oratories, and sepulchral recesses, ordinarily included in those edifices'. This provocative suggestion remains only a hint, however, to even the most 'attentive' reader, since the very next year (1815), when Wordsworth published the first of many complete editions of his work, he arranged them not architecturally but organically, according to the life-stages, mental faculties, emotional states, and occasional events of a single individual: Poems of Childhood and Old Age, Poems of the Fancy and the Imagination, Memorials of Tours, Elegiac pieces, 'Evening Voluntaries', and the like. Hence the controlling image of his entire oeuvre shifted, very much as the titles of his intended masterworks did, from that of a clearly defined, quasi-religious monument or edifice, to that of an on-going, private, secular process of life. The difference between the two is impossible to chart exactly, but a *feeling* for it can be very useful in appreciating the tensions throughout

Wordsworth's works between those very comprehensive terms, Man, Nature, and Human Life.

All these poetic relationships are not unique to Wordsworth, however. The idea of an epic poem as the capstone of a poetic career goes back to classical antiquity, with Virgil as its great exemplar. The young poet moves upward through lyrics and other short pieces (epigrams) to more extended narrative genres (satires, *georgics*, etc.), through the various levels of impassioned odes to preparatory epics or *epyllions* (of which *The Prelude* is, technically, an example), ending with a foundational epic of his civilization. This conception of the epic, rhetorically based on the ancient models of the *Iliad* and the *Odyssey*, and consciously exemplified by the *Aeneid*, was transformed in the English Renaissance by *Paradise Lost*, as a modern (that is, Christian) subsumption of all previous mythologies. It was further re-evaluated in the Romantic era, in Coleridge's high estimation of *The Recluse* as 'the first great modern philosophic poem', by which he meant, very pointedly, that Wordsworth's achievement should outstrip Milton's, the last great *religious* poem in the language.

Here we see the Romantic transformation of the traditional epic ideal at work, in its move toward 'philosophy' and away from religion and mythology, and all the company of gods and goddesses and other supernatural machinery those older models brought with them. But what 'philosophy'? The answer to this question further clarifies what *The Recluse* was intended to be, and what it failed to be, a dilemma very much at the heart of its relation to *The Prelude*. Given its intended themes, Man, Nature, and Human Life (or Society), *The Recluse* seems to have all the makings of a systematically philosophical poem: only 'God' is omitted, and that, with reference to its modernity *vis-à-vis* tradition, is very much the point.

For Wordsworth was trying to modernize the epic tradition as he inherited it from Milton, a relationship of inheritance he took very personally (with Coleridge's encouragement), and of which he alone, of all the eighteenth century's turgid imitators of Milton, may be said to have proved himself worthy. But he only gradually came to recognize that his modern 'philosophy' lay not in the 'views' on Man, Nature, and Human Life that *The Recluse* promised, but in the attention to himself which he inserted into it as a self-protective coda: 'and if with this / I blend more lowly matter... describe the mind and man / Contemplating, and who and what he was... and when and where and how he lived, /.../ Be not this labour useless'. (1034–41). This, of course, sounds very much like *The Prelude*: not merely autobiographical, but also philosophical in its modern emphasis upon the unavoidable presence of the consciousness of the philosopher (or the scientist) in any truth-bearing statement or observation whatsoever.

Wordsworth was not alone in becoming philosophical by getting personal. For the next context in which we can understand *The Recluse* is that of other Romantic epic poems. Here, one need only remember that Whitman's 'Song of Myself' is the creative germ seeding his greater, unending poetic project, *Leaves of Grass*, to make the point. *Leaves of Grass* is about everything – views of Man, Nature, and Human Life in abundance – but it is, always and everywhere, about Walt Whitman. And it is moot whether *Leaves of Grass* is a finished poem in a traditional, or even 'organic', sense: it ended only when its creator died.

Elsewhere in England and European culture, we can easily find other examples of the same phenomenon: works of epic ambition that remain unfinished because of their unresolved tensions with their author's own story of self-creation... which in turn is inexorably caught up with his epic ambitions. Byron's *Don Juan* comes immediately to mind, and is nicely illustrative, since Byron and Wordsworth are so often understood as 'opposite' Romantic types. But in the tension between Byron's feckless young anti-hero, Don Juan, charming as he is, and his jaded, 'philosophic' narrator ('And often to myself I say, "Alas"'), we have a version of the tension between Wordsworth's philosophic views and the more 'lowly matter' of himself.

And so the roll continues, between the grandly impersonal and the lowly personal, with the frequent added interest, in these Romantic epics, of fragmentation: Keats's *Hyperion* and *The Fall of Hyperion*, Shelley's *Prometheus Unbound* (the only really finished example), Blake's *Milton* and *Jerusalem* (a relationship similar to that of *The Prelude* and *The Recluse*, but completed only at tremendous costs to readerly patience), the two parts of Goethe's *Faust*, widely separated in time and terms of composition, and others too numerous to mention.

One final context for grasping the '*Recluse*-concept' is personal in a less philosophical sense, and applies to many writers besides Wordsworth. This is simply the pressure to achieve something famously noteworthy, as in the example of The Great American Novel. Although often destructive, such a burden often has productive side effects, and so it did for Wordsworth. While his friends were worrying about his failure to get on with *The Recluse*, he was often getting quite a lot done, in the way of other 'temporary' or 'preliminary' work: finishing poems started earlier (*Peter Bell*), or writing poems that seemed easier than, and certainly provided welcome distraction from, the heavy responsibility of *The Recluse*. In this sense, *The Recluse* was like a long-term 'debt' contracted deep in the background of Wordsworth's creative economy: it was to underwrite everything else he did, but though its continuing incompleteness became more and more of an embarrassment, it nonetheless provided an impressive backdrop on which much of the rest of his work could be, as it were, sketched.

So far, I have been defining *The Recluse* extrinsically, with reference to other similar epic projects, and explaining its creative function in Wordsworth's compositional economy. But, taking up its paradoxical status as 'continually incomplete', we can look at some extant parts of the *Recluse*, and see how this same idea informs much of the intrinsic interest they have, as poems, more than as failed philosophy.

Wordsworth's first mention of *The Recluse* comes in two letters sent from Alfoxden in Somerset in early March, 1798. One to his old friend James Losh: 'I have written 1300 lines of a poem in which I contrive to convey most of the knowledge of which I am possessed. My object is to give pictures of Nature, man, and Society' (*WL* i 212). Another was to a new friend, James Tobin: '[I have been] tolerably industrious within the last few weeks. I have written 1300 lines of a poem which I hope to make of considerable utility; its title will be *The Recluse or views of Nature, Man, and Society*' (*WL* i 214). The title may have been suggested by John Thelwall, the fiery radical orator who had visited Wordsworth and Coleridge the previous summer, since Thelwall refers to himself as 'the new Recluse' in his autobiographical preface to his *Poems of 1801*, signalling his intention to remove himself from politics and devote himself to meditation.[1] Images of recluses and hermits were newly attractive in the late 1790s, as many writers opted for expressions of pastoral retreat to escape the repressive climate against free expression that Pitt's clamp-down on sedition at home had cast over the land. Or the title may have come to Wordsworth's mind from memories of more fashionable versions of retreat, in Charlotte Smith's novel *Ethelinde, or The Recluse of the Lake* (1790), which Wordsworth knew, and which features the adventures of a party of stylish London gentry in a fictitious Grasmere Abbey. In any case, by the time he announced it to the public, in his preface to *The Excursion*, he had made the title his own: 'It may be proper to state whence the poem... derives its Title of THE RECLUSE. Several years ago... the Author retired to his native mountains, with the hope of being able to construct a literary Work that might live... a philosophical Poem, containing views of Man, Nature, and Society; and to be entitled, The Recluse; as having for its principal subject the sensations and opinions of a poet living in retirement.' In this sense, the Wordsworth that we know, from his own self-creation, as the poet of the English Lake District, *is* The Recluse.

To be the Bard of *The Recluse* was the most comprehensive of Wordsworth's self-creations. The Poet of the Preface to *Lyrical Ballads* and 'the chosen Son' of *The Prelude* are versions of the same identity, only slightly less grand and heroic. In his descriptions of each of these incarnations, he uses hyperbolic language to express the existential divinity of this Poet figure and his proposed accomplishments.

To Tobin and Losh, in 1798, he was still relatively restrained: the poem will 'convey most of the knowledge of which I am possessed... I know not anything which will not come within the scope of my plan' (*WL* i 212, 214). But in the verse 'Prospectus' to *The Recluse*, composed two years later – but only published in 1814, in the preface to *The Excursion* – his ambition goes far beyond the 'considerable utility' he claimed for his poem in early 1798: 'I must tread on shadowy ground, must sink / Deep – and, aloft ascending, breathe in worlds / To which the heaven of heavens is but a veil... /... Jehovah – with his thunder, and the choir / Of shouting Angels, and the empyreal thrones – / I pass them unalarmed' ('Prospectus', 28–35). In such biblical, Miltonic language Wordsworth projects his best image of himself: a poet-prophet-philosopher, whose words will speak to people everywhere about everything: Nature, Society, and individual consciousness. The dimensions of this figure are godlike, and if Milton's more traditional epic theme – the 'ways of God to men' – seems left out of these expressions, it is because the divine role has been taken up by the poet himself: 'Not Chaos, not / The darkest pit of lowest Erebus... can breed such fear and awe / As fall upon us often when we look / Into our Minds, into the Mind of Man – / My haunt, and the main region of my song.' These dimensions are so large that they could hardly be filled by any single human being, and Wordsworth explicitly invoked his need for 'a greater Muse' than Milton's to aid him. If we recoil, as many readers do, from Wordsworth's egotism elsewhere in his work, we should keep in mind that the projected form of his ego-image, in and as The Recluse, was much larger than anything he published in his lifetime.

Coleridge was very much present at the birth of this poet-figure, partly as midwife, partly as parent. Even more than the *Lyrical Ballads*, *The Recluse* was 'half the child of [his] own brain', as he described it in a letter of 29 July 1802. He did not have even Wordsworth's comparative hesitations when he wrote Cottle the day after Wordsworth wrote to Tobin to announce the same blessed event: '– The Giant Wordsworth – God love him!... he has written near 1200 lines of a blank verse, superior, I hesitate not to aver, to any thing in our language which in any way resembles it. [It is]... likely to benefit mankind much more than any thing, Wordsworth has yet written' (*STCL* i 391). For the next seven years, Coleridge's references to *The Recluse* never fall below the level of these superlatives.

Wordsworth also took ideas from Coleridge's own epic plans, for *The Brook*, an epic of similar magnitude which he had been dreaming about for several years. 'I sought for a subject, that should give equal room and freedom for description, incident, and impassioned *reflections on men, nature, and society...*' (*BL* i 195–6). Most immediately, the idea may have come to mind when they were working very closely together from January to March of 1798, expanding and finishing 'The Ancient Mariner' and *The Ruined Cottage*. Although Coleridge's poem appeared in *Lyrical Ballads* later that year, *The Ruined Cottage* did not see light of day until 1814, when it appeared, much revised, as Book I ('The Wanderer') of *The Excursion*.

Wordsworth's difficulty in bringing *The Ruined Cottage* to a successful conclusion may well have led him, or Coleridge, to baptize it for the *Recluse*-project. Like 'The Ancient Mariner', *The Ruined Cottage* centres on an isolated figure, Margaret, a weaver's widow, who suffers the loss of her husband, her children, her livelihood, and finally her life, in a derelict structure (her cottage) in the midst of a wide surrounding natural expanse. But unlike Coleridge's poem, which could depend on both ballad and Gothic conventions to assure readers' interest, Wordsworth's poem is at once unremittingly naturalistic in detail and severely elevated in its Miltonic blank-verse diction, a combination certain to confuse contemporary readers, since the former would lead them to expect comedy or satire, while the latter prepared them for tragedy or epic heroism. What they would have found, instead, was a very uncomfortable contemporary social problem – the displacement of the rural poor by the ruinous economic consequences of Pitt's unpopular war against republican France – expressed in the context of an obscure faith in apparently indifferent natural processes as they work to promote human moral and imaginative growth. Thus both in its theme and in this unique compositional 'strategy' – that is, complete a difficult poem by incorporating it into a still larger and more difficult poem to be written later – *The Ruined Cottage* is characteristic of *The Recluse* at every point in its half-century of insubstantial existence.

In March of 1798, *The Recluse* consisted of the newly expanded *Ruined Cottage*, plus two or three other poems, which together add up to the 1300 lines Wordsworth spoke of to Tobin and Losh. The first of the others was 'The Old Cumberland Beggar', another narrative of unrelieved suffering, drafted the previous year, but now expanded with contemporary political commentary (against parish workhouses). The second was Wordsworth's description a figure very similar to Margaret and the Cumberland beggar: the Discharged Soldier he ran into near Hawkshead in 1788. This was not published until it appeared posthumously in *The Prelude* of 1850. These three narratives of suffering were originally independent poems of nearly unrelieved bleakness, but he now began to incorporate lines of explanation into them, to achieve a larger perspective of reconciliation. This effort is what made them parts of the now-christened *Recluse*: 'views of nature, man, and society', giving 'authentic comment' to the sounds of 'humanity in fields and groves / Pip[ing] solitary anguish' ('Prospectus', 76–7).

A fourth poem, rounding out the 1300 lines, was probably 'A Night-Piece', not published until Wordsworth's first collected edition in 1815. It fits the others as a prologue or coda, sketching a visionary perspective onto the landscapes through which the other three narratives move. On its open road – the inevitable Wordsworthian *mis-en-scène* – we see the naked moon, 'the glory of the heavens,' not an old beggar, a sick veteran, or a weaver's abandoned wife. Wordsworth's task in *The Recluse* was to link, somehow, that sense of natural glory to those suffering human beings.

Hence the first *Recluse* poems set human suffering down in very contemporary British landscapes, to suggest how, *in this context*, 'Human Life' might be understood, or properly cared for. They try to make sense out of suffering, but are far from 'the still, sad music of humanity' which Wordsworth had convinced himself by July of 1798 he could hear, at Tintern Abbey. They do not preach a doctrine of acceptance, their goal is more limited: simply to keep the observer (all Wordsworth-surrogates) from being overcome by despair at what he sees, and cannot help. This sense-making comfort comes in the 'image of tranquillity' the Pedlar saw in some wet weeds and spear-grass around Margaret's ruined cottage, which made him think that 'all the grief / The passing shews of being leave behind, / Appeared an idle dream that could not live / Where meditation was' (MS D 521–4; *RC* p. 75). It comes also in the Discharged Soldier's 'ghastly' trust that God will always provide a Good Samaritan on any road. In 'The Old Cumberland Beggar', Wordsworth's more provocative message is that it is better to let such old beggars die 'in the eye of Nature', on their usual rounds in neighbourhoods that know them, than make them captives in the 'HOUSE, misnamed of INDUSTRY'. Whether this life and death in nature is better than the work-house is hard to say, both as social policy and as poetic statement, and 'The Old Cumberland Beggar' has seemed to many readers a betrayal of the poor to the doctrines of Wordsworth's new religion of nature.

Considered in terms of rhetoric, however, the three *Recluse* narratives of 1798 do not come to bad ends. Rather, their conclusions are unsatisfying in the sense of philosophic conviction or political persuasion. They raise more questions than they answer. But few philosophic systems or political programmes can answer such questions satisfactorily, for they raise the problem of undeserved human suffering, which is to say, the problem of evil. This is the problem that Romanticism is always accused of slighting, and sometimes did ignore. But Wordsworth's high Romantic argument always forced him to confront this question, for it is the question that challenged his great faith in the powers of the creative human imagination. It surfaced daily in

Wordsworth's and Coleridge's conversations at this time: human suffering and, as its simultaneous companion, the question of their own guilt or remorse for it, in pulling back from their political commitments and more overtly political writings.

Facing these questions comprehensively was the task of *The Recluse* throughout its volatile existence. Wordsworth's determination to answer them led inexorably to repeated imaginative crises which kept the poem forever unfinished: but the challenge, faced so confidently in early 1798, always returned to haunt him, forbidding him from ever putting it aside. This paradoxical relation between inspiration and dejection explains better than almost any other set of Romantic texts the uncanny connection between the power of Romantic imagination and its tendency to produce magnificent fragments at least as often as it produces satisfying aesthetic wholes. The typical Romantic Ode to Dejection does not arise from cynical *weltschmerz* [literally 'world-sorrow']; it is rather the underside of all Romanticism's Odes to Joy, from Schiller to Wordsworth to Thoreau.

Given the logic of this double-bind, clear in two hundred years of hindsight but barely emerging into the light of day in the first week of March 1798, it is not surprising to learn that Wordsworth's announcements to Tobin and Losh are the last we hear of *The Recluse* at this time. Though he said all his eloquence would be devoted to it for the next year and a half, in fact nothing more of it was written for almost exactly that period of time: until he and his sister Dorothy were, after their misadventures in Germany, settled together again in a new home, at Grasmere, at the beginning of 1800.

There, with devoted friends and family around him, Wordsworth turned again to *The Recluse*. It now became the poetical justification of his career, as he recast it literally in terms of his move to Grasmere. *Home at Grasmere* is set up to show that he had reached the destination his whole life had been pointing toward. He had everything he wanted, within reason, and no more excuses. It was time to realize his genius as he defined it: the poem's manuscript sub-title is 'Book First, Part First of *The Recluse*'. But it took years to complete just one book of a poem that might have had thirty such books; Wordsworth did not finish *Home at Grasmere* until 1806, after he had completed his first full version of *The Prelude* in thirteen books.

He composed about 600 lines of the poem in 1800 before its insuperable contradictions forced him to break off composition.[2] These lines constitute a Romantic Ode to Joy in one of the highest keys ever attempted. No small part of Wordsworth's achievement was avoiding the incoherence such odes often fall into, like the youthful effusions of Shelley or Keats. His Ode to Joy launches itself over the brink of its own ecstasy into the depths of its dialectical contrary, the Ode to Dejection. Unlike the conventional pastoral poet, who writes himself into his chosen landscape as a refuge from worldly suffering and corruption, Wordsworth wrote himself out of it, as he reluctantly acknowledged the social responsibility he was shirking.

The poem opens with a 'spot of time' that may be real or imaginary: normal alternatives in any poem, but here they become matters of life and death. He remembers himself as a boy gazing down on the valley and experiencing a visionary moment of notably unboyish thoughts:

> What happy fortune were it here to live!
> And if a thought of dying, if a thought
> Of mortal separation could come in
> With paradise before me, here to die.
>
> (9–12)[3]

'Paradise before me' goes Milton one better, topping *Paradise Lost*'s final vision of 'the earth was all before them'. But Adam and Eve were leaving Paradise, while William and Dorothy are returning to it. Vaunting himself above even Milton's biblical sources, Wordsworth's thanksgiving hymn vies with *The Song of Songs*, with the striking difference that his erotic language refers not to the expectant community of believers but to the receptive natural landscape: 'Embrace me then, ye Hills, and close me in!'

The boy made a vow: 'here should be my home, this Valley be my World'. As he advanced poetically into the landscape that he and Dorothy had just entered physically, there was no expression too extreme for his joy, as he lays claim to the land in the name of his own imagination.

> The unappropriated bliss hath found
> An owner, and that owner I am he.
> The Lord of this enjoyment is on Earth
> And in my breast.             (85–8)

>       among the bowers
> Of blissful Eden this was neither given
> Nor could be given         (117–25)

This is astonishing language for even a nominally Christian writer, and one whose words, as Coleridge once said (letter, 14 August 1803) 'always *mean* the whole of their possible Meaning'. Each phrase has to be considered not only as rhetorical hyperbole but as deeply felt personal testament: 'The Lord...is on Earth.' These are the most extreme expressions of joy in Wordsworth's oeuvre, his least tranquil, most emotional mood: it is an unnerving sight, this human embracing of the divine.

The segments of *Home at Grasmere* written in 1800 advance by a series of rhetorical leaps and bounds, each exclamation more sweeping than the last.

The poem follows his and Dorothy's December walk through Wensleydale to Grasmere and the apparent confirmation of their hopes with the coming of spring and the birds' riotous pleasure in it, reflecting their own inner satisfaction. The poem works toward identification with its very moment(s) of composition, toward saying, 'here am I, writing this poem'. If all its linguistic peculiarities were compressed into a single sentence, they would collapse all tenses into one: 'Once upon a time I am living happily ever after.' It bursts into – and eventually through – its own moments of inspiration. Every aspect of it strives toward self-identification: it is full of images of reflection and circularity, tautological arguments, and redundant syntax.

It comes as no surprise that this dizzying, surreal absurdism could not be long sustained, and that the denomination of the first wild days of March 1800, as a unique imaginative entity – new century, new career, new revolutionary agenda – should falter in the face of real time. But it seems to come as an untoward shock to Wordsworth, and he registered the shock waves in the poem. At the very height of his 'O *altitudo!*' Wordsworth looks down, sees poverty, death, and evil, and plunges to the ground, not to resume the poem for over five years. Just when he seems to be parsing his poem off the page of the landscape, he reads something he doesn't like:

> But two are missing – two, a lonely pair
> Of milk-white Swans. Ah, why are they not here?
> These above all, ah, why are they not here
> To share in this day's pleasure?          (322–5)

The repetitions, the reiterated gasp, the insistent questioning – all the poem's self-reflective characteristics implode in upon it. And the reason is presented as nakedly as the ecstasy: he and Dorothy have identified themselves with these two swans to an extraordinary extent: 'to us / They were more dear than may be well believed'. But we can believe it, when we see what their disappearance does to the poem. For William and Dorothy had drastically over-invested themselves in their symbolic identification with the swans: '. . . their state so much resembled ours; . . . They strangers, and we strangers; they a pair, / And we a solitary pair like them' (338–41). The poem's extreme symbolism rebounds onto its narrator: 'Shall we behold them yet another year . . . And neither pair be broken?' (348–50). Wordsworth has pitched his claims for the special qualities of Grasmere so high that this ridiculous literalism threatens to spoil it. He goes immediately on the defensive: the bulk of the remaining lines composed in 1800 show him back-pedalling furiously to restore the damage he has done. But it was no good; he ultimately backs himself into a corner, out of the poem, and breaks off.

The extremes to which he goes to explain the swans' absence are the best guarantee of the sincerity of the joy which preceded his discovery of it. His first conjecture is that they may have been shot by the local 'dalesmen'. This was a likely reason. In her journal for 17 October 1800 Dorothy refers to 'the swan hunt,' an organized destruction of the decorative species introduced at Windermere twenty years earlier, very unpopular with the local residents because they were so noisy and aggressive. But this commonsense explanation leads Wordsworth into an even worse crisis in his poem: lack of moral confidence in Grasmere's natives. He apologizes both to the place and to his poem for even 'harbouring this thought': 'Recall, my song, the ungenerous thought; forgive, / Thrice favoured Region, the conjecture harsh.'[4]

Evidence of human frailty has introduced a complication into the argument which soon became insuperable, forcing him to break off composition. Other human beings have come on the scene, and *The Recluse*'s difficult social theme ('Human Life') disrupts the Man–Nature bonding Wordsworth loved to celebrate. Contrary to sentimental views of Wordsworth's happy return 'home' to Grasmere (he had never lived there till then), the poem of that title challenges and indeed destroys the sentimental view, showing Wordsworth's clear awareness that his greatness as a poet could never be built on Grasmere, the Lake District, or even all of Nature. No earthly place was big enough for his godlike conception of imagination. What he learned in the moments of composition in Grasmere in 1800 confirmed what he had already intuited in his delayed vision of 'Imagination!' in the Simplon Pass in 1790: the inadequacy of a literal faith in natural transcendence.

He desperately insists that Grasmere's dalesmen were not swearing, wrathful, selfish, envious people who shoot swans. They may have been poor, hungry, and ill-clothed, but 'extreme penury is here unknown . . . they who want are not too great a weight / For those who can relieve' (440–8). But this special pleading contradicts the plentiful evidence of local poverty in Dorothy's journal, and the poem's sequential composition breaks off at the interesting words, 'so here there is . . .' (457). The implied simile is intended to point a moral drawn from the geographic form of the valley: '*as* these lofty barriers break the force / Of winds – this deep vale *as* it doth in part / Conceal us from the storm – *so* here there is . . .' But nothing follows; there is no moral counter-force, equivalent to nature's mighty forms, that will protect him from society's ills and his poetic responsibility to combat them. Human passion destroys the texture of natural beauty.

Facing this impasse, Wordsworth could write only a brief coda, which in fact became the moral guarantee, in a variety of forms, of all his subsequent failed efforts on *The Recluse*. Falling back into the rhetorical habit of swerving from unstable argument to assertive personality that he had developed in 'Tintern Abbey' ('If this be but a vain belief – yet, oh!'), he projected an image of the one spiritual community he could vouch for, and one that could actually complete his interrupted simile, except that it radically reduces the extent of his claims:

> And if this
> Were not, we have enough within ourselves,
> Enough to fill the present day with joy
> And overspread the future years with hope –
> Our beautiful and quiet home, enriched
> Already with a Stranger whom we love
> Deeply, a Stranger of our Father's house,
> A never-resting Pilgrim of the Sea,
> Who finds at last an hour to his content
> Beneath our roof; and others whom we love
> Will seek us also, Sisters of our hearts,
> And one, like them, a Brother of our hearts,
> Philosopher and Poet, in whose sight
> These mountains will rejoice with open joy.
> Such is our wealth: O Vale of Peace, we are
> And must be, with God's will, a happy band!
>
> (859–74)

The unstable social dimension of his vision, exposed by the pair of missing swans, is supplied by an image of an extended family: William, Dorothy, and John Wordsworth, Mary and Sara Hutchinson, and Coleridge. This was as far as Wordsworth's social vision could extend with confidence in 1800. He set the poem aside till 1806, when he tried to generalize Grasmere's meaning in a series of tales of stoic villagers and their clever animals intended to prove 'that solitude is not where these things are'. But in the 1800 portions of *Home at Grasmere*, the identification of the master-poem with the master's life came too quickly. Having cast himself and Dorothy as the Adam and Eve of a new Eden, the strain of saving the world *from this place* proved to be too much.

Though he could not bring his *plot* to a satisfactory denouement, he did manage to leap to a conclusion: the great 'Prospectus' of *The Recluse* that he published with *The Excursion* in 1814.[5] These lines conclude *Home at Grasmere* by projecting a vision of what *could be*, to fulfil the promises made by the poem. All conclusions of any segment of *The Recluse* follow this same forward-looking pattern of deferred gratification: the difficulties of composing the current poem will be solved in the great poem yet to come. The strategy is effective to a degree, but it is also fatal, because it pays out more promissory notes to be honoured, at ever-higher rates of interest, as Wordsworth is forced to claim still more for his epic.

The 'Prospectus' begins, 'On Man, on Nature, and on Human Life', the same phrase Wordsworth used to announce *The Recluse* to Tobin and Losh in 1798. It establishes a balance between individual integrity (Man) and social responsibility (Human Life) in the world-as-given (Nature), that constitutes at once the glory and the stumbling block of Wordsworth's democratic imagination. In this vision, the individual genius is the inspirer, not the leader, of the people, singing 'Of the individual mind that keeps its own / Inviolate retirement, and consists /With being limitless the one great Life – ' (968–71). But invocations are supposed to begin, not end, poems, and Wordsworth clearly intends that his epic-to-come will surpass Milton's:

> Fit audience find though few – thus prayed the Bard,
> Holiest of Men. Urania, I shall need
> Thy guidance, or a greater Muse, if such
> Descend to earth or dwell in highest heaven!
>
> (973–6)

He justifies this out-stripping of Milton (from the invocation to Book VII of *Paradise Lost*) on the grounds that the heaven and hell of the new epic are higher and deeper than his predecessor's:

> Not Chaos, not
> The darkest pit of lowest Erebus, . . .
> . . . can breed such fear and awe
> As fall upon us often when we look
> Into our Minds, into the Mind of Man –
> My haunt, and the main region of my song.
>
> (980–90)

Wordsworth's egotism has been a stumbling block in the road of his reputation from the beginning, but it is a measure of his stature as a culture hero to reflect that millions of people now make their inner consciousness of themselves the psychic bedrock of reality, as he does here. In this sense, Wordsworth is not an egotist but a realist.

Having staked out his 'main region', Wordsworth proceeded to elaborate its two adjacent territories, Nature and Society. Natural beauty is presented as a combination of the Promised Land, the Elysian Fields, and Paradise all rolled into one:

> Beauty, whose living home is the green earth,
>
> . . .
>
> Pitches her tents before me when I move,
> An hourly Neighbour. Paradise and groves

> Elysian, fortunate islands, fields like those of old
> In the deep ocean – wherefore should they be
> A History, or but a dream, when minds
> Once wedded to this outward frame of things
> In love, find these the growth of common day?
> (991–1001)

But Human Life, or Society, is presented far more negatively, in powerful images of an implacably self-consuming – or even self-satisfying – appetite in man's inhumanity to man:

> I oft
> Must turn elsewhere, and travel near the tribes
> And fellowships of men, see ill sights
> *Of passions ravenous from each other's rage,*
> Must hear humanity in fields and groves
> Pipe solitary anguish, or must hang
> Brooding over the fierce *confederate* storm
> Of Sorrow, *barricadoed evermore*
> *Within* the walls of cities – may these sounds
> Have their authentic comment, that even these
> Hearing, I be not heartless or forlorn!
> (1015–25; italics added)

Wordsworth constantly tried, and constantly failed, to integrate a vision of imaginatively redeemed society into *The Recluse*'s epic mission. This is what halted his progress on *Home at Grasmere*, and it continued to do so in each of his efforts to move *The Recluse* forward. His determination not to neglect 'Human Life' spelled the doom of *The Recluse*, but it also gives it its fitful glory, guaranteeing that though it could not be finished, it could never be abandoned. Almost from the beginning, it has been the criticism of Wordsworth's egotism and his 'nature worship' that they lead him, in Matthew Arnold's phrase, to turn his eyes 'from half of human fate'.[6] But the manuscripts of his master-project, largely unpublished until recent times, show that he was determined to turn his vision *toward* 'the tribes and fellowships of men', to give them 'authentic comment'. He failed, not only because of the superhuman difficulty of the task, but also because of his tendency to represent general human experience in the terms of his own painful experiences. Thus the splendid egotism of his goal was undercut by the selfish egotism of his evidence.

He ended the 'Prospectus' with a fourth topic, that appears as an after-thought: himself, William Wordsworth. This shift soon led to his replacing *The Recluse* as his epic subject with a new and better one, the story of his own self-creation, *The Prelude*.

> And if with this
> I blend more lowly matter – with the thing
> Contemplated describe the mind and man
> Contemplating, and who and what he was,
> The transitory Being that beheld
> This vision, when and where and how he lived,
> With all his little realities of life –
> Be not this labour useless.          (1034–41)

However, this was not a 'labour' that in 1800 he could quite conceive of as useful. He had followed Coleridge's orders and got back to work on *The Recluse*, which as Stephen Gill wonderfully says was rapidly becoming 'Coleridge's dream and Wordsworth's secret'.[7] He had produced a mythopoeic vision of Grasmere Vale as the Garden of Eden and discovered that, like its original, it could not stand the sight of sin or evil. There was no serpent, but a new original sin, in the evidence that men could wantonly destroy Nature's beauty.

The 'Prospectus' lines leap over these difficulties by insisting that he will produce an integrated vision of Man, Nature, and Society not only in Grasmere (population 250), but throughout 'the human soul of the wide earth'. It is often easier to propose solutions for the troubles of the whole world than for one's own family and neighbourhood, but to smile at the extravagance of Wordsworth's solutions in the 'Prospectus' is to miss the point. Wordsworth's concern was whether he was being extravagant *enough*, whether his poetry would adequately reflect the goal he saw before him. As his great American disciple, Henry David Thoreau, said, 'It is a ridiculous demand which England and America make, that you shall speak so that they can understand you...I fear chiefly lest my expression may not be *extra-vagant* enough... I desire to speak somewhere *without* bounds; like a man in a waking moment, to men in their waking moments...'[8] Thoreau here echoes Wordsworth's claims for the poet of democracy ('a man speaking to men'), and his meditation on Walden Pond – which he called his 'lake country' – is so close in spirit and imagery to *Home at Grasmere* one might think he had read it, even though the publication of *Walden; or, Life in the Woods* (1854) preceded the posthumous publication of *Home at Grasmere* (1888) by over thirty years.

Every episode in *The Recluse*'s fitful existence follows a pattern like these from 1798 and 1800: energetic beginnings, followed by gradual awareness of conceptual difficulties, and finally fragmentation, compromise, and further postponement. But each collection of texts makes for interesting reading, if we can refuse the easy gesture of simply pointing out a great poet's repeated failures. In 1808, Wordsworth tried again, in 'The Tuft of Primroses', an amazing conception belied by its innocuous title. He tried to connect the

coming of spring in Grasmere (again) with the rise and fall of all of insti-
tutional Christianity, and to suggest, as in *Home at Grasmere*, that a new
imaginative dispensation for western civilization was at hand in his own
poetry – a claim at once too public and too private to be persuasive.

Persuasion is very much the issue in the next, longest, and most successful
of his efforts on *The Recluse*, the five difficult years he spent composing *The
Excursion*. It is easy to criticize *The Excursion*; indeed, some criticisms have
become almost more famous than the poem itself, from Francis Jeffrey's lead-
sentence, 'This will never do', in *The Edinburgh Review*, to Byron's dismissal
of it in *Don Juan* as 'a drowsy, frowsy poem called *The Excursion*, Writ in
a manner that is my aversion'. But only readers who have bent themselves
to the challenge of reading it all can complain, for their complaints will
inevitably combine dissatisfaction with Wordsworth's achievement and admiration for his conception. The poem's conception was exactly right for its
times, as the imminent defeat of Napoleon promised an end to a generation
of revolutionary promise and reactionary disillusion. This conception had,
presciently, been part of *The Recluse*'s mission from a very early stage, when
Coleridge told Wordsworth around 10 September 1799, 'I wish you would
write a poem, addressed to those, who, in consequence of the complete failure of the French Revolution, have thrown up all hopes of the amelioration
of mankind, and are sinking into an almost epicurean selfishness, disguising the same under the soft titles of domestic attachment and contempt for
visionary *philosophes*' (STCL i 527).

Hence, Wordsworth sets forth, as a test case for his times, a man (The
Solitary) who had thrown himself into sympathy for the ideals of the French
Revolution as enthusiastically as the young Wordsworth, only to recoil into
cynicism and quietism as the Revolution (and its enemies) turned sour and
opportunistic. He has lost his religious faith as well, and, for good (dramatic)
measure, his wife and family, and retreated into rural retirement. This hard
case, a sort of anti-recluse, is to be rescued from his *weltschmerz* by the
ministrations of a wise old pedlar (The Wanderer), whose seasonal rounds
through the countryside have transformed him into a natural philosopher –
aided by accidents of birth and early education that are clearly derived from
Wordsworth's own life, since he incorporated early drafts about the Pedlar's
childhood into the first two books of *The Prelude*. Their conversational
debate is heard by two companions, The Poet, who runs into The Wanderer
in Book I, and is escorted by him to meet The Solitary, and The Pastor,
at whose parsonage they arrive in Book VI. (In the meantime, they have
accelerated unaccountably from a West Country landscape to Langdale in
the Lake District.) Each of these characters represents transformative roles, or

challenges, Wordsworth imagined for himself as the Bard of *The Recluse*, part of its audience, and the saviour, it is hardly too much to say, of his country. (In 1845, he made additions that turn the poem's message in a much more Christian direction, in reaction to criticisms of its 'pagan' atheism. In Wordsworth's early Victorian milieu, a religious reaction against revolutionary excess had become dogmatic.)

But, after nine books and nine thousand lines of heavily slanted editorializing (two books are titled 'Despondency' and 'Despondency Corrected'), The Solitary, though shaken, remains unconvinced. There is a kind of perverse integrity in Wordsworth's failing to come to a conclusion after carrying on at such length: the poem is so undramatic as narrative (they walk here, they walk there, they walk everywhere), that many modern readers fail to notice – and more simply don't care – that Wordsworth's own nature philosophy has fallen short in its appointed task. But, in the context of the other *Recluse* fragments, we can recognize this lack of resolution as, if not exactly the 'point' of the poem, then at least its motive – *and* the freely offered point of entry that would provoke contemporary readers to decide for themselves where they would come down in the very same debate that was about to re-open in England after 1814–15: human possibility vs social stability.

Such irresolution is not the hallmark of *The Recluse* alone; it is present in Wordsworth's greatest works, from 'Tintern Abbey' onwards, where the challenge of his theme ('Nature never did betray the heart that loved her') emerges into the very texture of his verse ('If this be but a vain belief'), in ways that have led some of the most important critics of our time, such as Harold Bloom and Geoffrey Hartman, to see in Wordsworth's romanticism the beginnings of literary modernism. But in *The Recluse*, Wordsworth set himself up to deliver authoritative answers to questions that some of his contemporaries and near-contemporaries were better equipped than he to deliver, using (or modifying) traditional philosophical categories, from Hegel and Coleridge to Karl Marx and John Stuart Mill. What he did instead, or found himself doing, was to reiterate the process by which he came to find himself in that uncomfortable position of authority, in the 'poem on the growth of my own mind', that became, instead of his 'views on Man, on Nature, and on Human Life', his great philosophic poem.

## NOTES

1 Nicholas Roe, *Coleridge and Wordsworth: The Radical Years* (Oxford: Oxford University Press, 1988), p. 235.
2 Kenneth R. Johnston, *Wordsworth and 'The Recluse'* (New Haven: Yale University Press, 1984), p. 370 n10. The two textual authorities on the composition of the manuscript, Beth Darlington and Jonathan Wordsworth, differ in the amount of

composition assigned to 1800 or to 1806, though they agree that most significant work on the poem is assignable to these two years. I follow Darlington in accepting that the poem's final form was not achieved until the latter date; however, it may well be, as Jonathan Wordsworth argues, that most of its *composition* dates from 1800, albeit in fragmentary, unsequential order.

3 All line references are to MS B, unless otherwise indicated, in Darlington's edition. This is an earlier version than MS D, which is printed in *PW* v 313–39.

4 These two lines are from MS D (lines 269–70).

5 M. H. Abrams persuasively uses the 'Prospectus' as a plan to chart not only most of Wordsworth's work but also many of the main currents of European Romanticism, in *Natural Supernaturalism: Tradition and Revolution in Romantic Literature* (W. W. Norton and Co., 1971).

6 *Stanzas in Memory of the Author of 'Obermann'*, lines 53–4.

7 Stephen Gill, *William Wordsworth: A Life* (Oxford: Oxford University Press, 1989), p. 190.

8 'Conclusion', *Walden; or, Life in the Woods.*

# 6

FRANCES FERGUSON

# Wordsworth and the meaning of taste

The various essays that constitute Wordsworth's prose oeuvre bear a strange relationship to the literary marketplace. They are the work of a writer frequently interested in current issues and events (when he writes about the Convention of Cintra, for example, or the Kendal and Windermere Railway, or copyright). Yet even these, the most topical of Wordsworth's essays, also manifest his consciousness of being at some remove from those events. It was a detachment, in part, simply circumstantial. Think, for instance, of Wordsworth's political analysis of the Convention of Cintra, which concluded Napoleon's efforts to bring Portugal into the 'Continental System', his Europe-wide closure of ports to British trade, and to oust the British. Wordsworth wrote the essay on the Convention of Cintra in the Lake District, relying on British newspapers from the middle of September 1808 for news of the Convention and the complex political manoeuvring that Napoleon engaged in with the Spanish and Portuguese, and was continually adjusting his understanding of his audience. He initially planned to express his views at a County Meeting, but later sought publication for the essay as a series of entries in Daniel Stuart's daily newspaper *The Courier*, and then commissioned De Quincey to shepherd the pamphlet through publication by Longman's at the end of May 1809. Delays overtook the project. The essay that had begun as a contribution to current political debates lost most of its audience before it ever reached them. Sales were minimal, and Wordsworth's earlier plan to bring out a second edition of *Cintra* dissolved in the face of scant demand for the first.[1]

Other prose works had less ignominious publishing histories, because Wordsworth did not publish them at all. (The *Letter to the Bishop of Llandaff*, the *Essay on Morals* and two of the three *Essays upon Epitaphs*, for instance, never saw publication during Wordsworth's lifetime.) Only the prose associated with *Lyrical Ballads* could be said to have successfully created the kind of audience that Wordsworth thought that poetry – and, by extension, art of any kind – ought to be able to create for itself. It is, thus, easy enough to see Wordsworth's prose as evidence of his inability to compete very effectively in the world of reviews and reviewers that called upon the aggressive talents of a Byron.[2]

Yet Wordsworth's prose, taken as the whole that has been given to us by the fine edition that W. J. B. Owen and Jane Worthington Smyser published in 1974, enables us to make a case that Wordsworth uses his prose writings for more than elaboration on the issues better raised in his poetry. Rather, he continually tests the relationship between prose and poetry, trying, as one can see from his discussion in the Preface to *Lyrical Ballads* of poetry's need to be at least as well written as prose when prose is well written, to identify both the characteristic excellences of the two modes and also the impact that each has upon the other (*Prose* I 131–7). Part of what Wordsworth recognized in his sense that well-written prose was superior to most poetry was that the rising importance and influence of prose in British letters had contributed substantially to the rise of a poetic diction that never questioned its value because it treated itself as inevitably superior to prose.

What becomes apparent from considering the full course of development of Wordsworth's prose writings is that he moved from self-consciousness and anxiety about his skills as a writer of prose to a consciousness of the value of prose in his time. If he could write in June of 1794 that he had 'not been much used to composition of any kind particularly in prose', and that his 'style therefore [might] frequently want fluency and sometimes perhaps perspicuity', his confidence that 'these defects [would] gradually wear off' soon justified itself.[3] His prose remained complex, but it came, increasingly, to function not simply as an alternative to the poetry in which he was fluent but as a mode of expression that was interchangeable with it. Wordsworth began frequently to move directly between prose and poetry, as in his essay on the Kendal and Windermere Railway, where he drew from his own MS poem of *The Prelude* for his description of the Simplon Pass and from the sonnet *Steamboats and Railways* that he had published in 1837 (*Prose* III 354–5). Moreover, Wordsworth didn't simply alternate between poetry and prose in the same piece of writing. He also compared his poetry to novels, and suggested that their aims were similar.

From our twenty-first century vantage, Wordsworth's assimilation of poetry to prose may look like an effort to make modest adaptations in an obsolescent technology to try to gain the advantages of the technology that was replacing it. That would certainly be one way to understand what it must have felt like to be a poet experiencing the extraordinary successes of Scott's novels and the effects of the attacks of the *Edinburgh Review* on, for instance, the *Poems* of 1815.[4] Wordsworth would, on that account, be a rational actor trying to use his recognition of the rewards allocations of the literary field to win advantages for himself and his kind of work. And it is certainly easy enough to credit De Quincey's observation that Wordsworth betrayed feelings of injured merit, and to believe Owen and Smyser's suggestion that Wordsworth was at least disingenuous when he said that he never read the *Edinburgh Review*. Yet the limitation of that account is that it exaggerates the clarity of the competition for public attention. Daily events, in the last decades of the eighteenth century and the opening decades of the nineteenth, were, in and of themselves, as important in diminishing the public for particular works as hostile reviews were. Think, for instance, of the case of Jeremy Bentham. Though he went on to develop a reputation for considerable laziness in seeing his writings through publication, Bentham had just published his *Introduction to the Principles of Morals and Legislation* when the French Revolution broke out. As Elie Halevy puts it, 'in the universal upheaval the book passed unnoticed'.[5] Bentham's volume was, that is, directly engaging the questions that were animating public politics and still failed to find an immediate audience. The remarkable fact is that during much of the period in which Wordsworth was writing, one could be like Bentham, one of the most avowedly practical writers ever to hold a pen and still not achieve an audience. One could be addressing burning questions about the proper understanding of government and law, and could even be devising projects for workhouses and prisons, such as Bentham's proposed high-security prison, the Panopticon, only to feel that practical applications of one's ideas were rendered merely theoretical by neglect.

To read through all of Wordsworth's prose as a body of work, however, is to see how the various prose forms had come to exercise their influence not merely as competitors to poetry but as direct influences on it. For two distinct but related impulses had become most explicit in the novel and in the periodical literature of the eighteenth century. The novel, particularly in the line that begins in Defoe and Richardson, had made itself pre-eminently the literary form that insisted upon taking the lives of individuals as its province. The novel, in its interest in evaluating human action, was in no way unprecedented, since a great deal of writing in the epic and dramatic modes had made the recognition of the tragic or the reprehensible part of its process of judgement. Yet it placed a distinctive stress on the notions, first, that each individual has one and only one life to live and, second, that the emotional interest of the novel comes from its providing occasions for seeing motives and ends, when, as Wordsworth puts it in his Preface to *The Borderers*, 'in real life we rarely see either the one or the other; and, when the distress comes, it prevents us from attending to the cause' (*Prose* 1 80). Moreover, the novel's insistence upon the examined life related itself most naturally and directly to the examination of the larger political circumstances of that life. Fictitious though the novel might be, it lent real impetus to the expressions of opinion – the reviews of literary works and the commentaries on political events – that circulated in the periodical press. Individuals, from a novelistic perspective, needed to cultivate their opinions about their private lives and their political views.

What the novel and the periodical's expressions of opinion brought to Wordsworth's understanding of poetry was a renewed commitment to the notion of the genuineness of appearances. Thus, he could write, in the *Essay, Supplementary to the Preface* of 1815 (*Prose* III 63) that

> The appropriate business of poetry, (which, nevertheless, if genuine is as permanent as pure science), her appropriate employment, her privilege and her *duty*, is to treat things not as they *are*, but as they *appear*; not as they exist in themselves, but as they *seem* to exist to the *senses* and to the *passions*.

The concern for appearances, that is, might involve a truth somewhat at odds with available facts. Owen and Smyser for their part, and Simon Bainbridge, for his, usefully point out that Wordsworth in his *Letter to the Bishop of Llandaff* might have found his claim that the French people universally supported the Revolution embarrassed by the facts and that his accounts of Napoleon in *The Convention of Cintra* were inaccurate.[6] Yet, even in those situations in which Wordsworth was misinformed or blinded by the strength of his views, his commitment is to attend to the truth of private judgements of both private and public matters – that is, to psychology and to public opinion. His recurrent interest in what he calls the laws of human nature involves rejecting any notion that truth inevitably loses as opinion gains ground, or that opinion can never be 'mere opinion' because there is no such thing as truth and opinion is all there is.

Wordsworth's particular combination of views on aesthetic and political judgements has come to look politically retrograde to many modern commentators, as it did to the second generation of Romantic poets. Yet his positions share with many of his time a conviction in the importance of the acts of individual judgement that draw their claim to legitimacy from the simple fact of their existence. Although we have no record of his particularly endorsing specific portions of Paine's *Rights of Man*, it is easy to imagine that Paine's claim that the rights 'of thinking, of speaking, of forming and expressing opinions' are rights 'in which the *power* to execute is as perfect in the individual as the right itself'.[7] It was this general line of thought that linked them both with Rousseau and Godwin, each of whom imagined that the inalienability of individual emotions and aesthetic judgements meant that there were inevitable limitations on state power, and with a figure like Robespierre, who conducted his revolutionary politics while carrying at his breast a copy of Rousseau's *Confessions* – and not the First or Second Discourses with their explicitly political focus.[8] What looks to contemporary scholars like conservatism is a position that relinquishes the claim that a government needs to achieve full equality among individuals in favour of the insistence that men may be unalterably unequal to one another in the mental and physical powers that are ineradicably their individual identities but that this inequality is tolerable because they are, in Elie Halevy's words, 'nearly equal when all the events of their lives are considered as so many incidents in a great moral drama, equal in their obligations and in their destiny' (137).

Wordsworth's early and incompletely preserved *Letter to the Bishop of Llandaff* was written in 1793 but not published. (Owen and Smyser speculate that Wordsworth may have felt 'misgivings' about publishing the essay in the wake of the Proclamation against seditious writing of May 1792, and that Joseph Johnson, as the publisher for Wordsworth as well as for Priestley, Horne Tooke, Godwin, and other radicals, may have endorsed his more cautious stance, *Prose* 1 24–5.) Yet though it doesn't have the endorsement of publication, it provides substantial evidence of Wordsworth's interest in thinking about the relationship between morality and politics. What is, perhaps, most remarkable is the distinctness with which Wordsworth's position separates itself from those of Burke and Bentham. Both of these had sought to replace morality as an individual project – Burke by establishing the standard of social authority so strongly in his *Reflections on the Revolution in France* that all individual opinion came to look like fanaticism, Bentham by attempting to create positive law of such perspicuousness that individuals would merely need to implement their happiness and the general happiness of society. For both, then, individual judgement was a rogue faculty, one that was said to blind individuals to their own best interests and those of society more generally.

Wordsworth, by contrast, opens his essay by stressing the importance of 'reputation' in such a way as to indicate how fragile he takes reputation to be. And its fragility, in his view, is not external – as it would be if it were being assaulted from without (and could come to be treated under libel laws). Wordsworth, opening with the sentence 'Reputation may not improperly be termed the moral life of man', makes 'reputation' do the work of the notion of character, in its modern emphasis on internality. Burke had found himself defending the strongest possible account of the importance of external reputation when he appealed to the importance of traditional authority on the grounds that it was traditional authority and to the importance of aristocracy and monarchy on the grounds that the external forms rendered the personal characteristics of their bearers irrelevant; and Bentham was articulating legal and bureaucratic programmes that would enable individuals to see themselves as simply parts of a unified social field. The one might be conservative, and the other progressive, but both strongly restricted the claims of individual judgement. Wordsworth, by contrast, imagines reputation as if it were almost a private affair, in which individuals could only be betrayed by themselves. In his view, Richard Watson, Bishop of Llandaff, had earned his authority by 'continuing [his] Way for a long time, unseduced and undismayed' by the attacks on his political positions: 'The names of levelling prelate, bishop of the dissenters, which were intended as a dishonour to your character were looked upon by your friends, perhaps by yourself, as an acknowledgment of your possessing an enlarged and philosophical mind' (*Prose* I 31). It would, he thinks, have been possible for Watson, 'like the generals in a neighbouring country, if it had been equally becoming to your profession' to adopt 'as an honourable title, a denomination intended as a stigma' (*Prose* I 31).

As Watson recommends 'a servile adoption of the British constitution' to the world in preferring monarchy to a republic on the grounds that a republic pretends to offer liberty but in fact merely enables individuals to be tyrannized 'by their equals' (*Prose* I 35), Wordsworth replies by carving out a common ground for them by imagining Watson's views. He insists that they must agree that 'the great evils which desolate states proceed from the governors' having an interest distinct from that of the governed (*Prose* I 36–7), and proceeds to make the balance of the essay revolve around the question of what the best means are for eliminating the differences between the interests of the governed and those of the governors. He defends republicanism, arguing that it involves less violence to our understanding of what people are and can be than monarchy does: 'The office of king is a trial to which human virtue is not equal', because an individual is asked to become and remain as enlightened as if he could personally sustain the responsibility for representing the interests of the governed (*Prose* I 41). Thus, while Watson argues that the office can make the man, Wordsworth responds that no amount of reverence for office can enable a man to override 'the eternal nature of man' (*Prose* I 41). Instead, he insists that government itself involves inequality, that the 'end of government cannot be attained without authorizing some members of the society to command, and, of course, without imposing on the rest the necessity of obedience' (*Prose* I 42). The best governments are those that restrict the length of time in which that inequality attaches to particular individuals and that give the governors a stake in the justice of the laws they enact by returning them to the position of the citizen, so that they see themselves less as governors than as persons who are about to become the governed. In adopting that view, Wordsworth rests his argument on the question of respect and self-respect that he introduced at the essay's opening. There should be limitations on the terms of the governors, just as there should be limitations on hereditary authority, because it compromises the self-respect of the governed – and, ultimately, the self-respect of the governors – to proceed in any other fashion.

In the *Letter to the Bishop of Llandaff*, Wordsworth produces arguments that take the general lines of arguments to be found in Rousseau, Paine, and Godwin. Without trying to establish the degree and the importance of the originality of Wordsworth's views, we should note that it represents important evidence of Wordsworth's contribution to a republican rhetoric that characterizes the principal aim of government as the achievement of self-respect for all its citizens and that introduces a strongly *generationalized* view of the importance of the contemporaneity of governmental legitimacy. He sees government as most legitimate when it needs to exercise the least force to compel obedience to its laws; and argues that such government draws its strength from seeing fathers as in the position of republican governors – 'only enfranchised', and not guaranteed permanent authority by virtue of the authority they had exercised (*Prose* I 34).

The utilitarian conviction that happiness provided the only true measure of the value of actions was one that Wordsworth shared with a host of writers from Adam Smith through Bentham and Malthus and Godwin. The chief differences of opinion revolved around whether there was a natural identity of interests among individuals (as Smith and Godwin thought) or whether one needed to have a government that would actively function to enable persons to recognize their own interests accurately (as Bentham and Malthus thought). Those who favoured more active roles for government – through bureaucratic structures or education or both – were essentially claiming that morality and government could become interchangeable – that individuals would do things that were good and happiness-promoting if they knew enough to see that they were happiness-promoting things. And it was in the context of such views that essays like Wordsworth's Preface to his tragedy *The Borderers* (1797) or his fragmentary essay on morals (1798) have their particular force. In the Preface Wordsworth considers at length the potential for evil of great intellectual powers not grounded in 'any solid principles of benevolence'. As Wordsworth describes Rivers (called Oswald in the version of the play finally published in 1842) going into the world and being 'betrayed into a great crime', his discussion centres on the kind of threat that efforts to translate happiness and good action into a rational language encounter from the possibility of self-deception. It becomes difficult to return 'bad men to virtue' because, he says, good actions speak more softly than evil ones and also because actions lose their uniform appearance outside of artificially constructed moral and legal schemata. Such uniformity is the first illusion: 'we insensibly suppose that a criminal action assumes the same form to the agent as to ourselves', and 'we forget that his feelings and his reason are equally busy in contracting its dimensions and pleading for its necessity' (*Prose* I 77, 80). In the Preface, Wordsworth even goes so far as to treat moral self-deception as 'superstition', as if to endorse the basic view that goodness and rationality are ultimately identical, but in both the Preface and the fragment on morals he casts doubt upon the efficacy of resolving the problem of self-deception with positive law, saying, 'I think publications in which we formally and systematically lay down rules for the actions of Men cannot be too long delayed' (*Prose* I 103–4).

One can see in these early writings the basis for Wordsworth's efforts to make a poetry that both committed itself to the production of happiness by imparting 'that sort of pleasure and that quantity of pleasure... which a Poet may rationally endeavour to impart' (Preface to *Lyrical Ballads*, *Prose* I 118) and also recognized the kinds of self-deception and superstition that made it difficult for pleasure simply to make its way directly and uncomplicatedly in the world. Indeed, his account of 'habit' in relation to poetry is a particularly important element of this project. Given, as he says in the fragment on morals that 'we do not *argue* in defence of our *good* actions... [but rather] feel internally their beneficent effect', happiness is incompletely external in its manifestations. It assumes the forms of habit rather than that of more conspicuous rules and arguments. Moreover, the Preface to *Lyrical Ballads* suggests that 'Poetry is the most philosophic of all writing' because it does not stand 'upon external testimony' but rather gives external form to the habitual, 'truth which is its own testimony', the language of the 'fluxes and refluxes of the mind when agitated by the great and simple affections of our nature (*Prose* I 139; I 126).

Wordsworth thus insists upon poetry as a moral enterprise, and describes his friends as seeing his poetry as part of 'a class of Poetry... not unimportant in the multiplicity and in the quality of its moral relations' (*Prose* I 120). Yet the peculiarity of Wordsworth's position is that he scarcely concerns himself with describing these moral relations in terms of the subject matter of the poems or recommendations of specific moral actions. Rather, the morality of poetry develops, in his view, from the promulgation of sympathy by pleasure, for which metrical language is a crucial element. Meter does not simply adorn thought but makes it possible to think about – and even dwell upon – distressful things, since metrical language (with its power to generate pleasure in the perception of similitude in dissimilitude) produces 'excitement in coexistence with an overbalance of pleasure' (*Prose* I 146). Wordsworth, insisting upon 'the grand elementary principle of pleasure', argues that all understanding is 'propagated by pleasure' and that every occasion in which we sympathize with pain 'is produced and carried on by subtle combinations with pleasure' (*Prose* I 140). Moreover, the importance of plea-sure holds even for apparently dry or distasteful varieties of knowledge – that of the 'Man of Science, the Chemist and Mathematician,' and the 'Anatomist' (*Prose* I 140). It is, however, the poet's distinctive mission to supplement the scientific knowledge that is 'a personal and individual acquisition' that does not 'connect us with our fellow-beings' with the knowledge of 'a nec-essary part of our existence, our natural and unalienable inheritance' of emotional and moral understanding (*Prose* I 141). Scientific knowledge may be universalizable, but it is remarkably dependent upon individuals. Poetic knowledge, by contrast, involves us in recognizing the commonality of the inalienability of individual emotion – the way in which the 'primary laws of our nature' express themselves in emotional connections (*Prose* I 122).

Two particularly important themes converge in Wordsworth's discussion in the Preface to *Lyrical Ballads*. The first involves the statement of an es-sentially liberal position, in the form of a view that there is no possibility of finding one all-encompassing language or representational scheme in which to evaluate all of human experience. The persistence of poetry and science thus comes to be a version of the persistence of various different religious views. The differences between the two do not resolve themselves into doc-trinal disputes in the way that religious differences do; and they therefore do not open the same lines of argument that developed in conjunction with religious toleration. No one feels obliged to contend that it is only practical to argue for toleration because the costs of war are too high, because poetry and science do not prompt wars with anything more than metaphor-ical casualties. Yet Wordsworth essentially adopts the liberal position that fundamental differences in the basic views of the various persons in his soci-ety can never be completely resolved. Neither poetry nor science will ever be able to replace the other, because the pleasures that each affords are not com-parable. Moreover, his anticipation of C. P. Snow's mid-twentieth-century identification of the 'two cultures' of poetry and science starts to mark out some of the crucial questions of modern political culture, in which the theo-retically universalizable (the scientific) is, in practice, the world of experts and individualized knowledge while the theoretically private (the poetic, the emotional) is, in practice, the arena of common experience. Indeed, the very strengths of each mode are precisely what call the other mode into being: the advances that scientific progress achieves becoming available to a smaller and smaller portion of the population, the commonality of experience that obtains for poetic and psychological life tending toward homogenization and uniformity.

The second issue that develops particular force – as a direct consequence of the inevitable persistence of different intellectual modes – is that of taste.

From Wordsworth's earliest pronouncements on taste in the materials surrounding *Lyrical Ballads* through the Preface to the edition of 1815 and the *Essay Supplementary to the Preface*, he outlined a position that would seem at least in part self-contradictory. Individuals should, on the one hand, be receptive to the appeal of new kinds of writing (of the kind that Wordsworth announced himself to be presenting in *Lyrical Ballads*), but this receptivity to new objects did not, in his view, really amount to an abandonment of one's earlier taste. Indeed, he thought it entirely right that 'all men feel an habitual gratitude, and something of an honorable bigotry for the objects which have long continued to please them: we not only wish to be pleased, but to be pleased in that particular way in which we have been accustomed to be pleased' (*Prose* 1 156). Yet the claim that he held out for the individual faculty of taste was that it represented what we might think of as the liberal capacity in its essence: it represented appreciation without exclusivity. Just as his poem 'Anecdote for Fathers: How the Art of Lying Might be Taught' dramatized the mistakenness of asking a child to compare his pleasures – to choose between Kilve and Liswyn, so his claim for taste imagined in the first place that part of what was important about taste was that it did not establish the same kind of competition between choices that many other kinds of experience did. By contrast, many utilitarian social systems (such as the classrooms that Bell, Lancaster, and Bentham devised) were committed to establishing comparability – in different students' performances in spelling or maths – that would make it possible to choose and choose until one had arrived at a recognition of 'the best' in a particular category.[9] Wordsworth's approach was distinctly different, in that he treated taste as a fundamentally emotional faculty that, also and importantly, saw the emotions as their own justification and saw them as open to different kinds of uncompared objects (parents *and* siblings, brothers *and* sisters, children *and* spouses). In affectionate attachments and objects of taste, he might have said, one doesn't love one's mother or father for being the best mother or father; one takes them to be the best mother or father because one loves them. One doesn't select the best family member, but loves a mother or a brother without treating them as comparable.

To put it in this way may seem, however, to countenance the view that the affections involve their own kind of ineluctable fatality – that, as Stephen Guest would put it in *The Mill on the Floss* (1860) or Emma Bovary would put it in *Madame Bovary* (1857), one's love is one's destiny. Morality would, on this account, be as irrelevant as in any description of the ancients that emphasized their fatedness. So the puzzle that we are left to resolve is why Wordsworth thinks that there is any need to account for tastes, and it is perfectly clear that he takes the project of accounting for tastes to be central and necessary. We may begin to develop an answer by noting how feelings, in his view, are not circumstantial, as he emphasizes in talking about how the poems of *Lyrical Ballads* differ from 'the popular poetry of the day' in that 'the feeling... developed [in them] gives importance to the action and situation and not the action and situation to the feeling' (*Prose* I 128). If feelings could be derived or inferred from circumstances, they would be completely determined and would, thus, never call on any capacity for judgement at all. Because there would be no alternatives among feelings dictated by circumstances, there would never be any possibility that circumstances would produce a variety of feelings. There would be nothing to choose.

Yet Wordsworth, in claiming that his poems may place his 'Reader in the way of receiving from ordinary moral sensations another and more salutary impression than we are accustomed to receive from them' (*Prose* I 128) is already stressing the importance of the moral judgement and the aesthetic judgement. These are capacities that neither eliminate choice nor suggest the irrelevance of what one chooses. And it is this combination of claims about judgement that fuels his remarkable survey of the vagaries of literary taste in the Preface to the *Poems of 1815* and the *Essay, Supplementary to the Preface* and that continues his earlier discussion of taste in the Preface to *Lyrical Ballads*. From the moment that Wordsworth produces an account of what the poet ought to be doing in his discussion 'What is a Poet?' in the Preface (*Prose* I 138–43), he announces an understanding of poetic duty – or, more modestly – a job description. The immediate consequence of ascertaining what is involved in a poet's duty is to exert pressure on any account of poetic history that is purely historical – based, that is, on a chronological and precedential order. A chronological order need not meet with any questions, because it merely reports on two largely unrelated things – that certain poems were written in a particular time and that those poems met with a particular kind of reception. The notion of a mistake has no place in an historical account. What Wordsworth provides in his account of poetic duty and in his elaboration in the *Essay, Supplementary to the Preface* of 1815 is, by contrast, a standard by which to judge poetry that does not rest simply on the available examples. The fact that a poem was the best poem there was would, in this view, be insufficient justification of it and of poetry. Whether current popular taste or past popular taste ratifies it or not, Wordsworth asserts that 'the only infallible sign' of genius in the fine arts is 'the widening the sphere of human sensibility, for the delight, honour, and benefit of human nature (*Prose* III 82).

Wordsworth's examples of the poets who have widened human sensibility are now uncontroversial: Shakespeare and Milton are chief among them.

Yet what Wordsworth stresses in his description of their reception is the discrepancy between the nineteenth-century estimation of them and the reception of their contemporaries. Shakespeare, he claims, 'stooped to accommodate himself to the People', but never made enough 'impression upon the ruling Intellects of the time' to have been alluded to by Lord Bacon; and he says that Dryden reports of his era that Beaumont and Fletcher's plays were twice as likely to be acted as Shakespeare's (*Prose* III 68). He asserts that Milton provides another example of the divergence of a poet's contemporaries and his subsequent readers. Milton's poems 'are now much read, and loudly praised; yet were they little heard of till more than 150 years after their publication', and cites Boswell testifying to Dr Johnson's repeated expressions of contempt for them (*Prose* III 70). The principle that Wordsworth enunciates is not, however, that poets are always without proper honour in their own time. He argues, rather, that poetry creates the taste by which it is to be appreciated in its own time and that that taste has cumulative effect. Poetry like Shakespeare's that speaks with the logic of the emotions proves its worth by producing a taste that will enable it to become progenitive. While Wordsworth does not exactly argue that the justice of critical judgements of poetry will emerge with time, he does produce an account of critical justice that closely approaches T. S. Eliot's position in *Tradition and the Individual Talent* in arguing that the most significant poetry gets its due eventually by virtue of subtly but inexorably transforming the critical understanding of the entire literary tradition. The interplay between a larger tradition of influence and individual poems and poets finally means that taste is not at all an individual or merely personal matter. People may take themselves to love Ossian and to have nothing but scorn for Percy's *Reliques of Ancient English Poetry*, and it may seem as if one must trust their reports since individuals would seem to be the best informants about their preferences. Yet Wordsworth thinks that the fact of their being mistaken in these impressions will emerge as the ballads that Percy catalogued make their influence felt while Ossian's poetry turns out to have been a mule, work of no generative power.

Wordsworth's description of taste foregrounds a preference for poetry of psychological depth (of the kind that Shakespeare so abundantly produced) but also suggests that poetry is itself a testimony to the psychological depth of individuals and societies, to the ways in which people respond differently and more deeply than they themselves are always conscious of. It is easy to see why Wordsworth thinks that poetry's 'obligation' to present things 'as they *seem* to exist to the *senses* and to the *passions*' prepares 'a world of delusion ... for the inexperienced', because only experience can balance an appropriate confidence in one's appreciative responses with an appropriate mistrust of one's own capacity for self-delusion (*Prose* III 63).

Clearly, experience is a help in predicting 'the destiny of a new work', as Wordsworth puts it in the *Essay, Supplementary…*, in talking about how the most dependable critics are those who have continued to comprehend poetry *as a study* (*Prose* III 63). Yet it is worth noticing that he does not go so far as to argue that the most experienced students of poetry always have the best taste. (Indeed, he produces a catalogue of possible ways in which a critic might confuse his judgement of a work's merit with a judgement of the excellence of its particular ideas and words, and particularly instances the 'misconceptions and mistakes peculiar to themselves' that 'men who read from religious or moral inclinations' may make.) Wordsworth's consciousness of the difficulties of judgement does not simply resolve itself into a claim that greater experience will automatically produce better judgement – that all mature judgements will automatically be more accurate than those of younger people. For 'the mind grows serious from the weight of life', and 'the range of its passions is contracted accordingly; and its sympathies become so exclusive, that many species of high excellence wholly escape' (*Prose* III 64).

With this last remark, which suggests the limitations of the experience that had earlier made taste look reliable, Wordsworth might seem to have arrived at what he elsewhere calls 'unmanly despair' on the subject of taste. Developing the knowledge that makes taste informed and informative also carries with it a kind of constriction. Yet this apparent inadequacy turns out to be the aspect of taste that most clearly indicates the distinctive nature of its contribution. For taste parallels a crucial understanding of the liberal tradition as Rousseau and Kant had been developing it – that the general will both acknowledges the legitimacy of virtually all positions and also has a humbling effect on its individual representatives. In so far as they have views, they are to be respected and taken into consideration; in so far as they claim to represent the general will themselves, they will reveal themselves as pretenders. For the key issue at stake in the notion of the general will is that it requires individuals to imagine an ideal that includes differences from their own particular situations and that recognizes the limitations of even their own strengths.

Wordsworth had in his early *Letter to the Bishop of Llandaff* applied this logic to the situation of the monarch who is pitiable because he is forced into impersonating an unavailable ideal, but he works out the force of its logic most clearly in his classification of his poems and his elaboration on it in the Preface of 1815. Wordsworth's classification is indeed complicated. He begins by enumerating the 'powers requisite for the production of poetry' (Observation and Description, Sensibility, Reflection, Imagination and Fancy, Invention, and Judgement), and then proceeds to a list of poetic forms (*Prose* III 27–8). As if these lists were insufficient, however, Wordsworth proceeds to explain that he has arranged his 'apparently miscellaneous' poems 'either with reference to the powers of mind *predominant* in the production of them' or to form, or to subject; and he complicates even this remark about the various classificatory arrangements by saying that he has arranged them 'as far as it was possible, according to an order of time, commencing with Childhood, and terminating with Old Age, Death, and Immortality' (*Prose* III 28). Wordsworth's taxonomizing impulses seem to have run away with him, and led him to produce classes of poetic faculties, genres, and reception *before* having talked about the question of the stages of human life. Yet this last classification – according to the stages of life – is particularly revelatory, in that it enables Wordsworth to describe the faculties and subject matters that 'predominate' in the various different poems while implicitly arguing how distinct and distinctive these faculties and concerns will be. In other words, his classification establishes the same kind of categorization of experience that he elaborates on in his remarks on taste in the *Essay, Supplementary*... Individual poems thus enter their claims to attention under certain obvious implicit restrictions, and no poem is asked to play the role of monarch to the rest. Each poem gains value from its association with the whole collection, but each poem is also allowed a kind of specialization. The faculties and characteristic intensities also appear as constrictions and restrictions in the passions of poet, the dramatic characters in the poems, and the reader. Wordsworth's classification of his poems thus participates in a liberal understanding of the role of poetry: rather than involving a sympathetic identification between any reader and any poetic emotion as expressed in a poem or by a poetic character, the classification asks readers to accept and respect emotions and perspectives that they themselves do not share, to see children or elderly people – without imagining that they can be those persons.

The three *Essays upon Epitaphs* constitute something like an epitome of the logic of argument that I have been tracing. (Only the first of them appeared during Wordsworth's lifetime, after having been used to fill some space in the 22 February 1810 number of Coleridge's journal *The Friend*, when Coleridge was in low spirits and 'utterly unprovided' with material.) Although the other two were held in reserve for possible later publication in *The Friend*, Coleridge ceased publishing his journal before they could appear; Wordsworth revised the first essay and reprinted it (in revised form as a note to *The Excursion* in 1814) without ever bringing the other two to the light of day. In their parts and as a whole, the *Essays upon Epitaphs* represent a remarkable statement of Wordsworth's poetic faith. Indeed, they have an eerie affinity with the Profession of Faith of Rousseau's Savoyard Vicar, in that they attempt to determine what an individual finds it necessary to believe even if – and especially because – he has distanced himself from the doctrines on offer.[10]

Various social influences and historical developments had caused funeral monuments and memorials to become increasingly important artifacts. The importance that Protestantism placed on an individual sense of an eternal account of one's actions, the particular emphasis that certain dissenting sects placed on the body and its handling in preparation for eventual reunion with the soul contributed to their prominence – as did the rise of modern armies that led soldiers to die in another country in the service of one's own. In that sense, funeral monuments and epitaphs would seem to have begun to come into their own – before reaching intense popularity in Queen Victoria's widowhood. Yet Wordsworth's attention to epitaphs is peculiarly keen. He treats the epitaph as the poetic genre in which one must seek the causes of poetry, an answer to the question 'Why write poetry?' that had perennially occupied him from the time of his early work on the *Prelude*. In the *Prelude*, the question seems to have an answer from affection – the commitment that the poet has to his family and close friends and, finally, to a larger and more abstract sense of humanity. In the *Essays upon Epitaphs*, however, he selects a poetic form that is, of all forms, the one most commonly prompted by affectionate grief and argues, improbably enough, for the insufficiency of affection as an explanation of the form:

> And, verily, without the consciousness of a principle of immortality in the human soul, Man could never have awakened in him the desire to live in the remembrance of his fellows: mere love, of the yearning of kind towards kind could not have produced it. (*Prose* II 50)

A conviction of human immortality emerges, that is, from no framework of religious doctrine but rather as a necessary hypothesis underlying the fact that people do write epitaphs. For Wordsworth's central assertion is that the affections could never unfold themselves 'in a creature endowed with the faculties of foresight and reason' if he took death at face value. 'The individual dying could not have had a desire to survive in the remembrance of his fellows, nor on their side could they have felt a wish to preserve for future times' tokens of the departed unless a belief in the immortality of the human soul operated as a practical belief (*Prose* II 52).

Even if individual humans never spoke of either God or immortality, then, the belief in immortality is carried by the epitaphs that they utter. Moreover,

Wordsworth's insistence upon the epitaph's credence in an immortality has at least three important consequences for poetry and the proper understanding of it. First, it establishes a transcendental perspective – albeit, a negative one – that evaluates lives in the light of immortality, past the perspective of any one individual. In that, it provides reasons for criticizing not just specific epitaphs and remarks of Pope and Johnson but their basic presuppositions and procedures. Wordsworth criticizes their interest in discrimination – their cultivation of observation and the appreciation of characters distinctive enough to call observation forth. In his view, the difficulty of the epitaph is not due, as Dr Johnson remarked, to 'the scantiness of the objects of human praise' or 'the want of variety in the characters of men'. It lies, rather, in minimizing the importance of the fact that epitaphs are 'records placed in the bosom of the all-uniting and equalising receptacle of the dead' (*Prose* II 57).

Thus, Wordsworth asserts that 'the affections are their own justification', that the writers of epitaphs do not need to provide any credentials for the persons whom they mourn, because the very fact that they are moved to write an epitaph is the only relevant justification (*Prose* II 57). Yet the second consequence of Wordsworth's insistence upon the epitaph's involvement with a transcendental perspective is that the affections may always justify an epitaph without making all epitaphs equal. One may judge them and criticize them – not for falling short in minute observation but rather for emphasizing what is personal in grief. Although the affections of particular persons for the person they lament may motivate the epitaph, the epitaph should not fall into the circumstantial. Even if it were proper for us to analyse those we love, it would none the less mean nothing to the reader to have a detailed picture of the exact nature of the relationships between mourned and mourners.

The third consequence of Wordsworth's treatment of the epitaph is that it becomes the emblem of a poetry that aspires to counteract the increasing segmentation of the literary marketplace. Against the factionalism of the reviews, with their commitment to deriving identity for themselves from their opposition to others, Wordsworth presents the epitaph as the very obverse to 'proud writing'. The epitaph, he says, is not 'shut up for the studious: it is exposed to all – to the wise and the most ignorant; ... the stooping old man cons the engraven record like a second horn-book; – the child is proud that he can read it; ... it is concerning all, and for all ...' (*Prose* II 59). Wordsworth had, we saw in his *Letter to the Bishop of Llandaff*, raised the question of authority and its generational reach, and had argued for a limitation on paternal authority much like the limitation he proposed for political representatives. Yet in his discussions of the epitaph, he prizes it as the literary form that most completely escapes the partiality of political and literary party and the more abstract but real partiality of poetic genre and subject (exemplified in the appeal of religious subjects to elderly readers of poetry that Wordsworth had mentioned in his *Essay Supplementary to the Preface*).

What draws Wordsworth to the epitaph as he describes it is that it epitomizes the urgency of questions of autonomy to his understanding of the poetic mission. For the epitaph identifies death as one of the few experiences that all humans face, and attempts to accommodate that universality to a series of individual perspectives that can retain their autonomous value and accord it to other perspectives. (The stooping old man and the child 'proud that he can read it' are not trying to debate with one another over who has the superior interpretation or evaluation.) With Wordsworth's emphasis on the epitaph's importance, his commitment to an essentiallly liberal version of what poetry can do is complete. The disagreement between the views of the child and the stooping old man cannot be remedied by discussion, because their views are importantly part of who they are. Yet the epitaph registers an insistence that human attachment – to friends, family, and country – continues in the absence of agreement.

## NOTES

1 See Owen and Smyser's discussion, *Prose* I 193–220. For a sustained analysis, see Margaret Russet, *De Quincey's Romanticism: Canonical Minority and the Forms of Transmission* (Cambridge: Cambridge University Press, 1997).
2 Wordsworth's only commercially successful prose was his *A Guide through the District of the Lakes in the North of England*, which appeared in various editions from 1810 through 1835 during his lifetime. Although this essay scants *A Guide*, its basic argument – that Wordsworth evolves a strong claim for the importance of judgement rather than reliance on the existence of objects – could be extended to *A Guide*. Wordsworth's distinctive treatment of the guidebook involves treating it as an occasion for explaining how one should see particular views rather than for an inventory of the important sites of the Lake District.
3 *WL* I 123–9.
4 See *Prose* III 23–4. See also Jon Klancher, *The Making of English Reading Audiences, 1790–1832* (Madison: University of Wisconsin Press, 1987); and Kevin Gilmartin, *Print Politics: The Press and Radical Opposition in Early Nineteenth-Century England* (Cambridge: Cambridge University Press, 1996).
5 Elie Halevy, *The Growth of Philosophic Radicalism*, trans. Mary Morris (Boston: The Beacon Press, 1955), p. 153.
6 *Prose* I 24; and Bainbridge, *Napoleon and English Romanticism* (Cambridge: Cambridge University Press, 1995), pp. 95–133.
7 Paine, *Rights of Man* (1791–2), cited Halevy, *Philosophical Radicalism*, p. 187.
8 Gregory Dart, *Rousseau, Robespierre and Romanticism* (Cambridge: Cambridge University Press, 1999).

9 Andrew Bell's school in Madras and Joseph Lancaster's in London were proto-types of a new systematized classroom that developed around 1800; Jeremy Bentham elaborated on their schemes in his *Chrestomathia* of 1817. These schools harnessed mutual instruction – which involved scrutiny and competition among students – so as to make mass education financially practicable.

10 The Savoyard Vicar makes his profession of faith in Rousseau's prose discourse on education, *Emile* (1762). It caused outrage because it is a negative defence of religion, which replaces claims that the existence of the world is evidence of the existence of God with the argument that individual conscience and moral capacity provide a model for the possibility of a divine being. Kant's *Critique of Judgment* of 1790 pursues a similar line of argument.

# 7

SUSAN J. WOLFSON

# Wordsworth's craft

## Composition and craft

If you consult 'craft' in a Wordsworth concordance or a database, the report is not often cheering. There is much to do with contrivance, debased art, suspect artfulness: the 'dangerous craft of picking phrases out / From languages that want the living voice / To make of them a nature to the heart' (*Prel.1805* vi 130–2), the 'craft' of 'gilded sympathies' in affected 'dreams and fictions' (vi 481–3), 'the marvellous craft / Of modern Merlins' (vii 686–7), 'the Wizard's craft' ('The Egyptian Maid' 44), modern 'Life' decked out by 'the mean handywork of craftsman' ('London 1802' 4), assassins led by those 'whose craft holds no consent / With aught that breathes the ethereal element' (*Dion* 54–5), the 'craft of age, seducing reason' (*Borderers* 363) or 'the craft / Of a shrewd Counsellor' ('Wars of York and Lancaster' 1–2). About as good as it gets is a rare reverence for 'the painter's true Promethean craft' ('Lines suggested' 24) or the poet's hope that his own 'Imagination' has 'learn'd to ply her craft / By judgement steadied' (*Prel.1805* xiii 290–4). Making rigorous inquisition into Wordsworth and poetic craft might even seem perversity, for he is, legendarily, the antithesis. What care for craft can there be in his praise for 'Poets... sown / By Nature; Men endowed with highest gifts, / The vision and the faculty divine, / Yet wanting the accomplishment of Verse' (*The Excursion* i 81–4) – 'wanting' signifying no urgent desire but an unimportant, accidental lack?

It was Wordsworth, after all, who prompted Hazlitt's wry lecture on the 'new school' of poetry (1818), a few years after *The Excursion* (1814) and twenty years after the debut of *Lyrical Ballads*. With a principle of 'pure nature void of art', this school (said Hazlitt) had expelled traditions of craft as surely as the French Revolution had expelled the monarchy:

According to the prevailing notions, all was to be natural and new. Nothing that was established was to be tolerated. [...] rhyme was looked upon as a relic of the feudal system, and regular metre was abolished along with regular government.[1]

This is burlesque, but Hazlitt is taking his cue from such manifestos as the Preface to *Lyrical Ballads*, in which Wordsworth rejected neoclassical tenets to declare that 'all good poetry is the spontaneous overflow of powerful feelings' *LB* 744). So convinced was the poet of this sweeping equation that he called it back, some pages on, to elaborate:

> I have said that Poetry is the spontaneous overflow of powerful feelings: it takes its origin from emotion recollected in tranquillity: the emotion is contemplated till by a species of reaction the tranquillity gradually disappears, and an emotion, similar to that which was before the subject of contemplation, is gradually produced, and does itself actually exist in the mind. In this mood successful composition generally begins, and in a mood similar to this it is carried on. (*LB* 756)

No utterance in Wordsworth's critical writing, remarks Stephen Parrish, 'has taken on the historical significance of [this] one' (*The Art of the 'Lyrical Ballads'* (Cambridge: Harvard University Press, 1973), p. 4). If the 'Poet' (as Wordsworth knew) is a crafter by etymology (Greek for *maker*), what sort of poetic 'making' is a 'spontaneous overflow'?

Out of the phase of recollection at least, William Wimsatt (writing at the high tide of New Criticism's concern with poetic structure and form) hoped to tease craftwork: Reading the Wordsworthian formula 'emotion recollected in tranquillity', he proposed 'that "emotion" refers to a kind of poetic content, and tranquil "recollection" to the control or shaping of this content – the formal poetic principle' (*Literary Criticism: A Short History* (New York, 1957), p. 408). Wimsatt hoped thereby to extricate Wordsworth from any theorizing (in some Coleridgean formulas) of emotion 'as the organizing principle'. 'The difference is crucial', he insists; 'As organization is a form of intelligibility, it is a basic question of poetic theory whether in fact emotion as such can become the formal or organizing principle of a poem without the disappearance of the principle' (408–9). But as Wimsatt's prompting to defence may suggest, Wordsworth's Preface flagrantly courts this question, not the least because of a crucial absence in its account: namely, any scene of the poet at his craft, in control of, or shaping emotion. This is Wimsatt's supplement. Even the interval of 'contemplation', when such craftwork might be expected to have entertainment, offers no such project. 'Obeying blindly and mechanically' feeling-informed habits of mind (*LB* 745), contemplation works chiefly to reanimate those powerful feelings that are the mood and muse of poetry.

About half way between the moment of Wordsworth's Preface and that of Wimsatt's follow-up question, Matthew Arnold conjured Wimsatt's worry. In his own preface to a carefully sifted anthology of Wordsworth's poetry (1879), he proposed that

> Wordsworth's poetry, when he is at his best, is inevitable, as inevitable as Nature herself. It might seem that Nature not only gave him the matter for his poem, but wrote his poem for him. He has no style.
>
> (*Poems of Wordsworth* xxii)

Matching Wordsworth's twice-told definition of good poetry, Arnold repeats: 'Nature herself seems, I say, to take the pen out of his hand, to write for him with her own bare, sheer, penetrating power' (xxiv). Sharpening the convention whereby Nature and Muse are gendered as female, Arnold pointedly uncrafts the agency of Wordsworth himself: the poet claiming to be 'a man [...] possessed of more than usual organic sensibility' (*LB* 744) turns out to be a man unpossessed of poetic craft. His feelings may be 'powerful', but Nature is the 'power'. More than a muse, she takes 'the pen out of his hand' to take over the work of the poet unmanned in default, writing 'for him with her own [...] penetrating power'. Whatever the hyperbole, Arnold succeeded (remarks Christopher Ricks) 'in limning the poet with intense recognisability'. The scandal played well into the twentieth century. 'The Preface unfolds a dangerously simplistic concept of language', reported another critic in 1969 (although he saw the instabilities): 'By inflating the role of natural response in the exercise of imaginative power', such theory 'forces the poet to give up virtually all of the conscious control over his poem'; 'consciousness plays no part in the creative act itself'; 'the poet abdicates his responsibility to shape and mold the materials of his poem'.[2]

The illusion of poetic passivity under the force of natural inevitability has prompted a critique in recent decades of what might be termed a 'craft of spontaneity', analogous to the insinuation of ideology under the guise of 'organic' origination and value. Anthony Easthope, for one, indicts the Wordsworthian formula with leaving 'unproblematized as aesthetic, formal and natural' the constructedness of 'poetic discourse'.[3] Well before him, Coleridge (collaborator on the first edition of *Lyrical Ballads*) thought the Wordsworthian conception at least contradictory, and so begged to differ. Poetic imagination, he proposes in *Biographia Literaria* (1817), is a balancing act of 'a more than usual state of emotion, with more than usual order; judgement ever awake and steady self-possession, with enthusiasm and feeling profound or vehement'(*BL* ii 17). Yet Wordsworth's own practice (if not always theorizing) has a way of making Coleridge's case (and unmaking Easthope's). Even poems seemingly staged to show how 'emotion recollected in tranquillity' may turn into a 'spontaneous overflow of powerful feelings' give deliberate craft an important role in the drama.

Take, for example, the paradigmatic lyric of after-reflection in *Poems, in Two Volumes* (1807) that concludes:

> For oft when on my couch I lie
> In vacant or in pensive mood,
> They flash upon that inward eye
> Which is the bliss of solitude
> And then my heart with pleasure fills,
> And dances with the Daffodils.
>
> (13–18)

Walter Pater admired the way this poetic 'dance' uses craft to produce pleasure: 'prompted by a sort of half-playful mysticism', the poem indulges 'a certain quaint gaiety of metre' (1874; *Appreciations* (1879) 57–8). Indeed, it's an old form, an octosyllabic sestet, here so metrically regular as to suggest an incantation of verse. This effect is neither a symptom of ambivalence nor a sign of contradiction, but an intelligent collation of craft and poetic power.

It is with semantically rich craft that Wordsworth shapes the end of the first stanza of another poem in these volumes, 'The Solitary Reaper':

> Alone she cuts, and binds the grain,
> And sings a melancholy strain;
> O listen! for the Vale profound
> Is overflowing with the sound.
>
> (5–8)

The theme is the Wordsworthian myth of poetry, doubled in poet and Maid. To her emotive overflowing (her sound pure song, the import evocatively mysterious), he matches a deftly crafted song. Note how the enjambment (overflowing) of lines 7–8 performs what it describes: 7 halts in a pause of deep silence, then the syntax flows over to 8, where the sound runs softly through the stresses and slips of 'overflowing *with the*' toward the rhyme. Listen, too, to how beautifully this rhyme has 'sound' echo, as if returning from, 'Vale profound' (how much duller would be 'the sound / Is overflowing the Vale profound'). To the power of this sound, Dorothy Wordsworth could attest: 'There is something inexpressibly soothing to me in the sound of those two Lines', she wrote, listening to and then renewing them with her own echo: 'I often catch myself repeating them' (*WL* i 649–50).

The prototype of this catching is the poem itself. At its conclusion, Wordsworth crafts his lines not only to recall but also to catch its inspiration:

> Whate'er the theme, the Maiden sang
> As if her song could have no ending;
> I saw her singing at her work,
> And o'er the sickle bending;
> I listen'd till I had my fill:
> And, as I mounted up the hill,
> The music in my heart I bore,
> Long after it was heard no more.
>
> (25–32)

Theme shapes poetry, not only in the lilting measures linking Maiden's song to poet's but also in the semantics of rhyme and non-rhyme. In this craft and subtle art, the poet's rhymes are not of her actions (*work* and *sang* are unrhymed) but his. Murmuring through *sang, song, ending, singing*, the stanza's first rhyme chimes at the falling feminine-measured *bending*, the word literally resounding *ending*, as if to signify how the impression of a song with 'no ending' were to be (and now is) realized in the rhyme of recollection. The 1815 version of the daffodil poem added a stanza that capitalizes on this sense of an ending:

> They stretched in never-ending line
> Along the margin of the bay.

The first line pauses at the verbal margin of 'line', where, without terminal punctuation, it seems to stretch its claims emblematically into the page's open space – an effect that superimposes on the illusion of the flowers' never-ending line their continuation into the poet's open-ended line.[4] Wordsworth's craft at once evokes this suggestion and gives it a poetic correlative.

*Ending* and *bending* play in the stanza from 'The Solitary Reaper' as similar tropes of poetic craft: *ending* ends the verse line, and *bending* coincides with the bending of the verse line into the poet's listening. Wordsworth intensifies this experiential shift from seeing to pre-poetic listening with the rhyme that rings through *till / fill / hill* ('I listen'd till I had my fill' is a wonderful little self-listening couplet). He lost this chord when (in 1820) he revised 'till I had my fill' to 'motionless and still', but it was to gain a rich mine in the multiple and interrelated senses of 'still': arrested motion and hushed sound; the counter-pulse (even so) and duration (even yet) in which successful composition begins. In the wake of these vibrations, even as the final lines describe a parting of poet and Maid, the craft of couplets keeps them coupled, and show the shadow of no parting from her. The music 'heard no more' is borne in the 'heart' ('heard' shifted only by a letter) and then, as after-effect and in imagination, reborn in poetic craft.

This textual transformation may be what licensed Wordsworth to place this poem, in 1807, in the subgroup *Poems Written During a Tour in Scotland*

and, simultaneously, to append a potentially contradictory note: 'This Poem was suggested by a beautiful sentence in a MS. Tour in Scotland written by a Friend, the last line being taken from it *verbatim*.'[5] He retained this note of influence in 1815, even as he assigned the lyric to his own *Poems of the Imagination*. This is the sentence (to which he alludes but stops short of quoting) from his friend's 1789 journal:

> Passed a female who was reaping alone: she sung in Erse as she bended over her sickle; the sweetest human voice I ever heard: her strains were tenderly melancholy, and felt delicious, long after they were heard no more.[6]

Until 1824, when Thomas Wilkinson's *Tours to the British Mountains* was finally published, a general reader had to take Wordsworth's word for his debts and their limit to the last phrase (its perfect iambic tetrameter predicting the poem's measure). When in November 1806 he told Wilkinson, 'your Journal [...] is locked up with my manuscripts' (*WL* iii 104), he meant its whereabouts while on loan to him, but the verb 'locked up' uncannily intimates a textual association.

The linked and imported material does not belie Wordsworth's mythology of recollection so much as collate poetic craft with an already textualized memory. Wordsworth has not simply fabricated history (a fiction of 'written during' denying pre-reading and after-writing), nor has he simply lifted and shifted Wilkinson's prose into his rhymes and metres, nor, in a similar textual influence, blithely plucked his sister's journal-prose about the golden daffodils (15 April 1802) for transplant into his own garden of verses. Recollecting these texts in imagination-as-text is the forge of a poetic craft that keeps visible the workmanship exercised to shape 'emotion recollected' into 'successful composition'.

## Crafted measures

The slipperiest issue in this success is metre, the radical distinction of verse from conversation or prose. Is poetic metre spontaneous and organic? Or is it supplementary, super-added, even wrought in opposition to, the pulse of spontaneity? As M. H. Abrams remarked (at about the time Wimsatt was worrying the question of emotion as the muse of poetic craft), 'the justification of poetic meter' was 'particularly troublesome' to Wordsworth, for 'although the natural language of feeling may be broadly rhythmical, the use in poetry of highly regular stress and stanza patterns would seem a matter not of nature, but of artifice and convention' (*The Mirror and the Lamp* (1953; 1958), p. 116). 'I write in metre', Coleridge says with no apology, 'because I am about to use a language different from that of prose' (*BL* ii 69). His critique in *Biographia* (ch. 18) of the Wordsworthian mythology of composition is particularly tuned to the advent of metre, which he ascribes to a 'balance in the mind effected by that spontaneous effort which strives to hold in check the workings of passion'. Revising Wordsworth's equation of poetry to a spontaneous overflow of passion, Coleridge theorizes a spontaneous countercheck, a 'balance of antagonists [...] organized into *metre*' (ii 64). Yet, as we shall see, Wordsworth sometimes agrees, and over the course of his theory (even in the Preface[s] to *Lyrical Ballads*) and his practice, metre plays as a sliding signifier. It shuttles and shifts between nature and culture, passion and restraint, text and intertexture – oppositions which themselves may reverse polarity, depending on the pressure of the moment. Caught in the labyrinth of metre, Wordsworth maps a deeper, more self-conscious commitment to poetic craft than some readers recognize.

The most radical metre is blank verse, 'blank' of rhyme – and thus to some, blank as versecraft. For Wordsworth as for everyone, the romance was the trope of blank-verse 'liberty', and its primer was Milton's note on 'The Verse' of *Paradise Lost*, which announced 'an example set, the first in English, of ancient liberty recovered' from 'the modern bondage of rhyming'. Dr. Johnson worried that such verse was nearly self-cancelling, 'verse only to the eye' (*Life of Milton* (1783)). Coleridge echoed him: when metre – 'the sole acknowledged difference' between prose and verse – becomes 'metre to the eye only', the craft of verse, 'even to the most delicate ear', may be 'unrecognisable'. For proof, he prosed part of Wordsworth's 'The Brothers' (*Lyrical Ballads* 1800) to show that (save a few phrases) no 'ear *could* suspect, that these sentences were ever printed as metre' (*BL* i 79–80). To interrogators such as Easthope, this effect is culpably crafty: 'pentameter would disavow its own metricality' (74), 'would render poetic discourse transparent' (75), would suppress 'recognition of the work of metric *production* – and so of the poem as constructed artifice' in order to foist the illusion of a 'spontaneously generated *product*' (67).

Yet this critique elides an effect not lost on Wordsworth's contemporary, Charles James Fox, then Whig leader in Parliament: the democratizing of blank verse in *Lyrical Ballads*. If we expect Whig politics to pattern Whig poetics, it is a sign of how ingrained conventions of craft were that Fox felt able to complain to Wordsworth about seeing the measure of lofty contemplation in 'Tintern Abbey' deployed for the humble tales 'Michael' and 'The Brothers': 'I am no great friend to blank verse for subjects which are to be treated of with simplicity' (Christopher Wordsworth, *Memoirs of William Wordsworth* (2 vols.; 1851) i 172). Wordsworth's challenge was calculated: he had begun 'Michael' as a pastoral ballad (*LB* 319–20), a 'low' form, then decided to give the shepherd's story a claim to blank verse. This is a move that reverses Easthope's claims: far from disavowing poetic craft, Wordsworth visibly motivates it to confront what his 1798 'Advertisement' called 'that most dreadful enemy to our pleasures, our own pre-established codes of decision' (*LB* 739).

In these codes, the craft of the measure was not in dispute: 'no man in ordinary conversation [. . .] speak[s] in blank verse', remarks a conversant in Dryden's essay on *Dramatick Poesie* (1668). Many agreed well into the eighteenth century. Wordsworth makes the case in reverse at the outset of *The Prelude* in a patently extraordinary moment of happily 'pour[ing] out' his 'soul in measur'd strains' (*Prel.1805* i 57): the measure is metre as well as the Miltonic ideal of unstrained, easy inspiration into 'unpremeditated verse' (*Paradise Lost* ix 23–4). When he said 'poetic numbers [metre] came / Spontaneously' (i 60–1), he understood the extravagance. Years later, in 1829, he remarked that the technical demands made blank verse 'infinitely the most difficult metre to manage (*WL* v 58), and in 1831 he would conflate his language and Milton's to critique the illusion of any poet's 'pouring easy his unpremeditated verse', contending 'that the composition of verse is infinitely more of an art than Men are prepared to believe' (*WL* v 454). *Contra* Easthope (and Dr Johnson), Wordsworth insisted even on the verbal marking of metric production, of measured strain: 'as long as blank verse shall be printed in lines', he wrote in 1804, 'it will be Physically impossible to pronounce the last word or syllable of the lines' without 'an intonation of one kind or an other, or to follow them with a pause, not called out for by the passion of the subject, but by the passion of the metre merely' (*WL* i 434).[7]

The attachment of passion to versification involves central questions of poetic origin and agency, ones not easily reduced to critical measures that discern only mystificatory device. At times, metre seems to matter as an art that is the antithesis of artifice. A note Wordsworth added in the 1800 *Lyrical Ballads* to one of his most famous poems in blank verse points this way as it speaks of the 'impassioned [. . .] versification' (*LB* 357). Years later he told this story of its crafting:

> I began it upon leaving Tintern, after crossing the Wye, and concluded it just as I was entering Bristol in the evening. [. . .] Not a line of it was altered, and not any part of written down till I reached Bristol. It was published almost immediately after. (*LB* 357)

A recollection of poetic passion is synonymous with a passion for poetry. 'I have not ventured to call this Poem an Ode', he said in his note of 1800 to 'Lines written a few miles above Tintern Abbey, on Revisiting the Banks of the Wye during a Tour, July 13, 1798'; but venture he does: 'it was written

with a hope that in the transitions, and the impassioned music of the versification would be found the principal requisites of that species of composition'
(*LB* 357). The transitions and the versification are the workings of passion
through craft, the verse not just conveying but turning (Latin *versus*: *turning*) the feelings – in a form informed almost instinctively (Geoffrey Hartman
suggests) by the generic structuring of the ode through turn and counterturn
(*Wordsworth's Poetry, 1787–1814*, 27). It's a Latin pun Wordsworth liked;
see, for example, 'the turnings intricate of Verse' (*Prel.1805* v 627).

Yet for all this passion of versification, metre persists as a critical problem,
and does so less for the incidental reason Hazlitt suggests, the poetical reforms associated with Wordsworth and the 'Lake School', than for its durable
mark of distinction from other modes of language. For liberal poetics, this effect was an embarrassment both to myths of spontaneous origination and to
any insistence on the common language of poetry, prose, and conversation –
the other big claim of the Preface of 1800, also in the teeth of neoclassical
consensus. In *Elements of Elocution* (1781), for example, John Walker described prose as 'common, familiar and practical [in] nature', and verse as
'beautiful, elevated, and ideal [...] the latter as different from the former as
the elegant step of a minuet is from the common motions of walking' (239).
Metrical feet are art, not nature, ideal not familiar, elegant and elevated,
not common and pedestrian, practised and courtly, not just practical: class
difference is the elementary code in this description. So when Wordsworth,
theorizing a common language of common values, raised the question in
his Preface to *Lyrical Ballads* – 'Is there then, it will be asked, no essential
difference between the language of prose and metrical composition?' – and
stayed to answer, 'there neither is nor can be any essential difference' (*LB*
749), he knew he was putting his feet in his mouth. In the opening paragraph
he referred to his 'experiment' in 'fitting to metrical arrangement a selection
of the real language of men in a state of vivid sensation' (*LB* 741) without
pausing over the work of 'fitting', as though there were no ultimate contradiction between fit and feel, arranged and real. But a few paragraphs on,
the poet (parenthetically) concedes a bit of craft: 'the real language' he has
been advertising has actually been 'purified' from 'its real defects, from all
lasting and rational causes of dislike or disgust'; a poetic 'real' has replaced
the socially 'real' (744).

Subtracting defects, the poet also adds elements of craft. Can he distinguish these from the artifices he is at pains to reject, but which traditionally
accompany 'the act of writing in verse' (*LB* 742)? Having just married the
languages of prose and poetic composition, Wordsworth admits impedi-
ments, hoping to rein them in: 'If it be affirmed that rhyme and metrical
arrangement of themselves constitute a distinction which overturns what I

have been saying on the strict affinity of metrical language with that of prose, and paves the way for other distinctions', he is armed with a rejoinder: the crucial distinction is between a language of the 'passions' and the artifice of 'poetic diction' (*LB* 750, 754). Still refusing to view metre as a 'foreign splendour' incongruous with what 'passion naturally suggests' (he adds in 1802; *LB* 750), he treats with it as a natural ally. Poetic diction is 'arbitrary, and subject to infinite caprices', but metre 'is regular and uniform' and 'obeys certain laws' – ones to which, moreover, 'Poet and Reader both willingly submit', because far from 'interference', metre has long been 'shewn to heighten and improve [poetic] pleasure'. This is a custom sufficiently naturalized as to seem natural: 'I have endeavoured to superadd the charm which by the consent of all nations is acknowledged to exist in metrical language' (754). Even so, Wordsworth knows that what he calls a 'charm' may be a forgery, and that metre may be as much a fetter as Milton ever thought rhyme was. Thus he writes to John Scott in 1816: 'if you have not practised metre in youth, I should apprehend that your thoughts would not easily accommodate themselves to those chains, so as to give you a consciousness that you were moving under them and with them, gracefully and with spirit' (*WL* iii 284).

This shift from 'charms' to 'chains', from practice to 'accommodation' (literally, a fitting), and then to the illusion of spirit and grace, sets the stage for what seems (but ultimately is not) a new defence: 'I might point out various causes why, when the style is manly, and the subject of some importance, words metrically arranged will long continue to impart such a pleasure' (*LB* 755). In 'an unusual and irregular state of the mind', in which 'ideas and feelings do not [...] succeed each other in accustomed order', and words involve images and feelings 'connected' with an 'undue proportion of pain', Wordsworth says, there is a 'danger that the excitement may be carried beyond its proper bounds'. This is why metre matters, as a welcome chain: 'the co-presence of something regular, something to which the mind has been accustomed when in an unexcited or a less excited state, cannot but have great efficacy in tempering and restraining the passion by an intertexture of ordinary feeling' (755). Redeemed from alienated craft, metre returns on behalf of 'accustomed order as a bearer of ordinary feeling'. 'So feeling comes in aid / Of feeling, and diversity of strength / Attends us, if but once we have been strong', Wordsworth writes of a recovery from trauma in *The Prelude* (1805 xi 326–8).

Pater discerned this intertexture at exactly those moments of 'highest poetical expression,' when Wordsworthian craft seems most invisible: when, in a 'fusion of matter and form', 'his words are themselves thought and feeling' (57) – or, in Wordsworth's terms, those phases of composition when 'the

words by which [...] excitement is produced are in themselves powerful'
(*LB* 755). In this 'fusion', Pater suggests, 'the music of metre performs but a
limited, yet a very peculiar and subtly ascertained function':

> It is a sedative to that excitement, an excitement sometimes almost painful,
> under which the language, alike of poetry and prose, attains a rhythmical
> power, independent of metrical combination, and dependent rather on some
> subtle adjustment of the elementary sounds of words themselves to the image
> or feeling they convey. (57)

As Pater recognizes, Wordsworth's question about the origin of metre – craft
or natural impulse? – also involves a question of effect: is metre the charming
enhancement of poetic passion, or its desired regulator? A reconciliation
might be tendered: as a craft cultivated by and identified with the culture of
'poetry', metre assists passion into capable expression, and a sense of this
dynamic infuses the 'natural' pleasure of reading. But this effect is strained
by the way, even in the theorizing of the Preface, the force of metre as a
regulator becomes increasingly entrammelled in what it is supposed to be
regulating. We sense this convergence in Wordsworth's comment on reciting
blank verse (in the letter quoted above): the terminal pause is 'not called out
for by the passion of the subject, but by the passion of the metre merely'
(*WL* i 434). Here, metre is passion, possessed by and possessing it.

### Fits of passion

In more than a few lyrical ballads, the efficacy of metre 'in tempering and
restraining the passion' that produces poetry (Preface *LB* 755) is under stress.
The untitled ballad that opens with the spondee 'Strange fits of passion' is
just such a meta-metrical crisis. It recounts what Wordsworth (with another
referent) calls a 'fit of imagination' (*LB* 398): a poet is on a nocturnal trek
to his beloved's cottage, towards which the moon appeared to descend; as it
'dropp'd' below the roof, he had a vivid sensation that she might be dead. He
would convey this fit, as the Preface says, 'fitting [it] to metrical arrangement'
(*LB* 741) – a fitting that presumably contrasts 'fits of passion'. But the archaic
sense of *fits* as poetic craft (*OED*, 'Fit, fytte': 'A part or section of a poem or
song, a canto'), observes Hartman, leaves its sense 'unsettled' (*Wordsworth's
Poetry* xix).

From its start, the ballad is haunted by an uncertain relation between psychic and poetic fits. For all its speaker's irony about the shaping fantasies of
which the lunatic, the lover, and the poet are compact ('What fond and wayward thoughts will slide / Into a Lover's head – ' (25–6)), his ballad cannot

defuse a sense that this too-knowing 'will slide' is not just diagnostic, but helplessly predictive. In its present-progressive inception, the poet's confession seems compelled as well as rehearsed:

> Strange fits of passion I have known,
> And I will dare to tell,
> But in the lover's ear alone,
> What once to me befel.          (1–4)

Is the event at hand extraordinary ('once') or habitual ('fits')?

As metre enters this question, the ballad shimmers into a counter-Preface. Metre may promise to fit passion to 'continual and regular impulses' (*LB* 756) but in this poem its pulsation seems less to restrain than to revive the original compulsion, giving a sensation of a fated sequence, of a consciousness continually possessed:

> Upon the moon I fix'd my eye,
> All over the wide lea;
> My horse trudg'd on, and we drew nigh
> Those paths so dear to me.
>
> And now we reach'd the orchard-plot,
> And, as we climb'd the hill,
> Towards the roof of Lucy's cot
> The moon descended still.          (9–16)

A present progressive tense in a draft, 'And now I've reached the orchard-plot' (*LB* 294), predicts the first line's strange-familiar 'I have known', while the punctuated acceleration from *and* to *and* spells a hypnotic (re)possession. Telling his wayward thoughts in an ambiguously situated 'now,' this balladeer is more than recollecting them: he is reliving them. His lines, tightly (almost over-) rhymed, reined into prescribed iambic tetrameter and trimeter, seem as fixed as his moonstruck eye:

> And, all the while, my eyes I kept
> On the descending moon.
>
> My horse mov'd on; hoof after hoof
> He rais'd and never stopp'd:
> (19–22)

Telling seems to have become another fit of passion, induced by a metrical repetition of the paces that first led helplessly wayward; mania as metre. But are we sure of this pathology, or might there be a metrical plot? Might the metre have been crafted to induce our sympathy with a strange case? To lead us to expect disaster, and thus to endorse the lunatic surmise?

> 'O mercy!' to myself I cried,
> 'If Lucy should be dead!'
> (27–28)

By this point, we probably think so, too (this climax is an anti-climax).[8]

In this strange fit, metre produces passion even as it fits it out. Sometimes Wordsworth strips his verse to an almost radical metrical punctuation of passion:

> 'O misery! oh misery!
> O woe is me! oh misery!'
> ('The Thorn' 252–3)

> Oh! what's the matter? what's the matter?
> What is't that ails young Harry Gill?
> That evermore his teeth they chatter,
> Chatter, chatter, chatter still.
> ('Goody Blake, and Harry Gill' 1–4)

> The owlets hoot, the owlets curr,
> And Johnny's lips they burr, burr, burr.
>
> . . .
>
> 'The cocks did crow to-whoo, to-whoo.'
> ('The Idiot Boy' 114–15, 460)

'The Idiot Boy' is the lightest case, uttering a little ode to joy in rhyme with nature's sounds. But the others, fraught with that 'undue proportion of pain' for which metre is the recommended antidote (*LB* 755), convey more ambiguous effects. The metrics of 'Goody Blake', 'rather than converting pain into pleasure by reducing excitement to a regular level', Adela Pinch argues, convey anarchy, 'a painful disintegration of a man into a chattering old woman'.[9] As in 'Strange fits', metre is not just mimetic of passion but symptomatic of diseased poetic craft. And more: a betrayal of Wordsworth's hint in the Preface of maintaining a 'manly' style with 'words metrically arranged' (*LB* 755) – no small concern to Coleridge when he described 'Tintern Abbey', a poem by virtue of metre only, as a 'manly reflection' on 'passion and appetite' (*BL* i 79).

Passion intensified by feminine incursion (whether from female suffering or a passion-prone literary culture) saturates the controversial metres of 'The Thorn'. The poem ends with a male balladeer's repetition of, and seeming possession by, a woman's repeated cry, in metrically punctuated sounds: 'O misery! oh misery! / O woe is me! oh misery!' In his ground-breaking reading of this ballad as a manic monologue, Stephen Parrish proposes that the force of Wordsworth's craft is to make us wonder whether the balladeer has heard any woman at all – or whether, in a moment of panic and its aftermath, he has (mis)taken the sound of the wind for her cry (100–1; 105). In all these ballads of passion, Wordsworth crafts the mimetic metres to signal literary as well as natural inspirations. 'O woe is me! oh misery!' has legible textual lineage, as if from a handbook of pathetic expressions. The metrics of chatter in 'Goody Blake, and Harry Gill' not only employ onomatopoeia but draw attention to the device itself.

Commenting on both these ballads in his Preface, Wordsworth argues for a pleasure principle in the alliance of 'elementary' passion and a craft that solicits interest. The effect of metre, he says, depends both on 'the pleasure [...] derive[d] from the perception of similitude in dissimilitude' and on 'the blind association of pleasure [...] previously received from works of rhyme or metre of the same or similar construction' (*LB* 756, 757). He is willing to guess that even if a poet's words fail to grab a reader – that is, seem 'incommensurate with the passion' – metre may supply the needed measure:

> in the feelings of pleasure which the Reader has been accustomed to connect with metre in general, and in the feeling, whether chearful or melancholy, which he has been accustomed to connect with that particular movement of metre, there will be found something which will greatly contribute to impart passion to the words, and to effect the complex end which the poet proposes to himself. (*LB* 756)

In line with this value-added custom, the long note he appended to 'The Thorn' in 1800 explains metre as an antidote to his other risky poetic experiment, 'the repetition of words' in the poem 'not only as symbols of the passion, but as *things*, active and efficient, which are of themselves part of the passion'. For those not 'accustomed to sympathize with men feeling in that manner or using such language', Wordsworth hopes for 'the assistance of Lyrical and rapid Metre'. To the potentially alien(ating) spectacle of how 'superstition acts upon the mind', he 'superadd[s] the charm' of metre (*LB* 351, 754); one *super*-meets another. Likewise, 'Goody Blake, and Harry Gill', he says in the Preface, is 'related in metre' in hopes of 'draw[ing] attention to the truth' of its tale of hysteric possession, aiding its communication to 'many hundreds of people who would never have heard of it' had it not been versed as 'a Ballad, and in a more impressive metre than is usual in Ballads' (*LB* 757).

Yet metre crafted to facilitate a reader's sympathy might be fabricating it, as an immediately preceding remark concedes: 'We see that Pope by the power of verse alone, has contrived to render the plainest common sense interesting, and even frequently to invest it with the appearance of passion' (*LB* 757). Pope's metres seem to manufacture interest, as a mnemonic aid or artifice of investment yielding a dubious return, a contrived appearance.

This yoking of contradictory interests – whether metre evokes natural expression or just shams a passion; whether it aids common sympathy or serves a contrived common sense – is sufficiently strained to prompt Wordsworth to revise the Preface in 1802. Reassigning metre to a poetics of estrangement and defamiliarization, he now argues that the 'complex feeling of delight' in poetic pleasure (so described in 1800) involves 'an indistinct perception perpetually renewed of language closely resembling that of real life, and yet, in the circumstance of metre, differing from it so widely' (757). In this difference, metre is effective not because it doesn't interfere with passion, but because it does. Correspondingly, he revises the paragraph about the effect of 'tempering and restraining' passion to say that 'the tendency of metre to divest language in a certain degree of its reality, and thus to throw a sort of half consciousness of unsubstantial existence over the whole composition', makes it easier to endure 'pathetic situations and sentiments' which 'have a greater proportion of pain connected with them' (755). The conscious craft and its derealizing effect are now essential.

## The crafted Poet

Even with this revision, Wordsworth does not ultimately unravel the issue of circular and reciprocal causes and consequences. Its very irresolution keeps the matter active in the meta-poetry of poetic craft. The metrical poetry that became his greatest devotion was his perpetually revised autobiography (later called *The Prelude*), a work whose craft does not just organize recollection but also produces it. In writing as a poet about becoming a poet, Wordsworth stages the autobiographical subject as both constituted and made legible by its affinity for poetic craft. An early draft displays just this self-reading, as the autobiographer ponders the import of several immediately previous recollections of boyhood thefts. Each event had recoiled in an arrest of the self by what seems to be external craftwork, a formative intention:

> The mind of man is fashioned & built up
> Even as a strain of music: I believe
> That there are spirits, which, when they would form
> A favored being, from his very dawn
> Of infancy do open out the clouds
> As at the touch of lightning, seeking him
> With gentle visitation[.] quiet Powers!
> Retired and seldom recognized, yet kind,
> And to the very meanest not unknown;
> With me, though rarely,
> They communed: others too there are who use,

> Yet haply aiming at the selfsame end,
> Severer interventions, ministry
> More palpable, and of their school was I.
>
> (*Prel.1799* 232)

Ministry, intervention, design toward an end – all this is but another name for craft. The hero 'I' comes into the verse as fashioned, built up, shaped, even as the poetic 'I' ('I believe') shapes a verse that crafts memory into argument. Such reflexivity informs many sophisticated autobiographies; what distinguishes Wordsworth's is the way his verse becomes a trope for craft: the lines above appear in MS v as a sonnet-stanza, its summary couplet sight-rhyming 'I' with 'ministry'.

Wordsworth liked discovering such forms in *Paradise Lost*, marvelling at some 'fine fourteen lines' as 'a perfect sonnet without rhyme' (so reports his friend Henry Crabb Robinson). To craft this form in the flow of autobiographical verse is to acknowledge that he is reading the history of 'the Poet' into a poetic craft with a history. Indeed, no poetic craft is more self-reflexive about its history than the sonnet, as the performative meta-genre of 'sonnets on the sonnet' makes clear. Wordsworth himself contributed with a 'Prefatory Sonnet' to the section of 'Sonnets' in the 1807 *Poems* (that is, 'Nuns fret not at their Convent's narrow room'), and 'Scorn not the Sonnet' (1827). While his revisions of his autobiography do not preserve its evocative sonnet stanza, the textual archaeology is telling, for it shows how deeply embedded is Wordsworth's poetic self-composition with intuitive commitments to poetic craft.

Wordsworth's perpetual revisions of this and other poems have had debatable effects on theme and argument, but he was always motivated by a craftsman's attention.[10] Advising an aspiring poet in 1824, he stressed the importance of 'the logical faculty': 'the materials upon which that faculty is exercised in poetry are so subtle, so plastic, so complex, the application of it requires an adroitness which can proceed from nothing but practice'. In this practised craftwork, 'emotion is so far from bestowing' any help (he went on to add) that 'at first it is ever in the way of it' (*WL* iv 546).

This was no late-developing news. Arguing in 1814 with a correspondent about whether 'such thoughts as arise in the progress of composition should be expressed in the first words that offer themselves, as being likely to be most energetic and natural', Wordsworth countered, 'My first expressions I often find detestable; and it is frequently true of second words as of second thoughts, that they are the best' (*WL* iii 179). The poet who became famous for equating the best poetry with a spontaneous overflow of feeling turns out to have had second thoughts about this expression as well.

NOTES

1 'On the Living Poets', *The Complete Works of William Hazlitt*, ed. P. P. Howe (21 vols.; 1930–4), V, pp. 161–2.

2 James Heffernan, *Wordsworth's Theory of Poetry: The Transforming Imagination* (Ithaca: Cornell University Press, 1969), pp. 37, 43, 48; Christopher Ricks, *The Force of Poetry* (1984; Oxford: Oxford University Press, 1987), p. 117.

3 Anthony Easthope, *Poetry as Discourse* (London: Methuen, 1983), p. 23.

4 'The use of line-endings can be a type or symbol or emblem of what the poet values, as well as the instrument by which his values are expressed', proposes Christopher Ricks (91). For his brilliant discussion of Wordsworth's performance with terms of poetic form, including this instance, see 'A Pure Organic Pleasure from the Lines', in *The Force of Poetry*, pp. 91–116.

5 *P2V* 415. Peter Manning comments that Wordsworth's placement of the poem in 1807 in the subgroup advertised as 'Written During' belies the craft of recollection by 'presenting as a spontaneous record a subsequent, carefully ordered collection' ('"Will No One Tell Me What She Sings?": "The Solitary Reaper" and the Contexts of Criticism', in *Reading Romantics: Text and Context* (New York and Oxford: Oxford University Press, 1990) p. 258.

6 *P2V* 415. Observing that Wordsworth wrote his poem in 1805, two years after the tour on which he took Wilkinson's *Tours* as a guide, Manning reads the note as an originary rather than an intermediary text – less significant, however, as a verbal source than as a reflection of Wordsworth's composition of the poem within 'a specific historic matrix' (the domestic situations and international events of 1805–7) even as the poem itself, in a mode of polemically conservative nostalgia, invests the reaper 'with the aura of mythic timelessness' (*ibid.* 254–5, 267–8).

7 For related discussion, see David Perkins's capacious investigation, 'How the Romantics Recited Poetry', *Studies in English Literature*, 31 (1991), 655–71; and for the complex involvement of Wordsworth and others with the question of metre, my own 'Romanticism and the Measures of Meter', *Eighteenth Century Life* (1992), 162–80.

8 In the key phrase 'Strange fits of passion' Barbara Johnson sees 'Wordsworth's poetic project' summarized: 'poetry is a fit, an outburst, an overflow, of feeling; and poetry is an attempt to fit, to arrange, feeling into form' ('Strange Fits: Poe and Wordsworth on the Nature of Poetic Language,' in *A World of Difference* (Baltimore, Johns Hopkins University Press, 1989) p. 95).

9 *Strange Fits of Passion: Etymologies of Emotion, Hume to Austen* (Stanford University Press, 1996), pp. 90–1.

10 See my discussion and relevant bibliography in *Formal Charges: The Shaping of Poetry in British Romanticism* (Stanford: Stanford University Press, 1997).

# 8

JUDITH W. PAGE

# Gender and domesticity

> She was totally ignorant of housewifery & could as easily have managed the
> spear of Minerva as her needle. It was from observing these deficiencies that
> one day, while she was under my roof, I *purposely* directed her attention to
> household economy & told her I had purchased *Scales* wh. I intended to present
> to a young lady as a wedding present, pointed out their utility, (for her especial
> benefit) & said that no ménage ought to be without them.[1]

Readers who think of Wordsworth as a visionary poet with his head in the
clouds would be surprised to discover that these were his words. Such concern with the minutiae of domestic life as getting, spending, and weighing
might not seem Wordsworthian. But these thoughts were on the seventy-
three-year-old poet's mind when he dictated notes on his poetry to his friend
Isabella Fenwick. Ah, the puzzled reader might now say, these are the concerns of the stodgy old poet, not the fiery young man of the 1790s. But
I will argue here that from an early age Wordsworth was concerned with
*home-making* and with the dynamics of gender within 'household economy'. While we do see a shift in emphasis from the early to later years (an
embracing of Victorian domesticity), the idea of domesticity as the source
of family, love, and stability remains a constant in Wordsworth's life and
work.

Paradoxically, too, Wordsworth's critique of housewifery in the quoted
passage referred to the popular poet Felicia Hemans, a woman who did not
find the kind of domestic happiness in her own life that she praised in her
poetry. Hemans might not have managed Minerva's spear or a nineteenth-
century lady's needle, but she certainly used her pen to praise the idea of
domesticity. In fact, she helped usher in the Victorian view of Wordsworth
as soother of the soul and family poet: 'Thine is the strain to read among
the hills /... Or by some happy hearth where faces meet.'[2] While the tenor
of Hemans' praise would please Wordsworth, it masks the difficulties of
achieving and sustaining domestic happiness, a theme that is either on the

surface of Wordsworth's elegiac poetry or thinly veiled below. Because in his poetry the greatest celebrations derive from the deepest losses, balance is always tenuous. Domestic tranquillity is no exception.

I shall divide my essay into three sections: First, I argue that Wordsworth was interested in domesticity as a real value in his *life* and as an idea in his *art*. His notion of domestic life as the source of human affection and community is central to the poetry and political ideas of the poet who found 'patriotic and domestic love' intimately related (*1805* ii 195). Domestic happiness is dependent on political and economic stability, as we see in *The Ruined Cottage*, and in Wordsworth's own struggle for such security. The second and longest section of the essay focuses on the two places most associated with the idea of home in Wordsworth: Dove Cottage and Rydal Mount. Each place represents a phase in the life of the Wordsworth family, with particular attitudes toward home-making, and with particular poems. How does Wordsworth move from Dorothy Wordsworth's Grasmere journals and *Home at Grasmere*, we might ask, to the world of keepsakes and *The Triad*? Finally, I consider the question of Wordsworth's dependence on women for his domestic happiness, and, increasingly, on conventional ideas of womanhood in his poetry.

## Patriotic and domestic love

Where does this yearning for domestic happiness begin? In Wordsworth's imagination, it begins at the moment it is lost. The details of Wordsworth's childhood are well known: the deaths of both parents, the scattering of the five children (Richard, William, Dorothy, John, and Christopher), the financial woes. While the boys were sent to school, Dorothy began a semi-nomadic existence, shuttled from one set of relatives to another. Although the children struggled to keep in touch, there were long periods of separation. At one point, Dorothy did not see William for nine years. Throughout this time, Dorothy in particular nurtured the idea of setting up a home, of finding both love and happiness in this imagined order. As she writes to her friend Jane Pollard, 16 February 1793,

> I look forward with full confidence to the Happiness of receiving you in my little Parsonage, I hope you will spend at least a year with me. I have laid the particular scheme of happiness for each Season. When I think of Winter I hasten to furnish our little Parlour, I close the Shutters, set out the Tea-table, brighten the Fire. When our Refreshment is ended I produce our Work, and William brings his book to our Table and contributes at once to our Instruction and amusement, and at Intervals we lay aside the Book and each hazard our

observations upon what has been read without the fear of Ridicule or Censure.
We talk over past days, we do not sigh for any Pleasures beyond our humble
Habitation 'The central point of all our joys.'                    (*WL* i 88)

This might seem like an intimate girlish fantasy, but its valuing of a secure
home and its gender-based distinction between *their* [needle]work and *his*
'instruction' seems prophetic of the Wordsworthian households to come.
Most important, though, is Dorothy's conviction that home is the source of
happiness and pleasure, as well as the site of knowledge and work. From
young Dorothy's point of view, it is also the place where her own intellectual
discovery and speculation will be taken seriously.

William's desire for this kind of home increased during the troubling
decade of the 1790s when, for a few years, he found himself wandering from
place to place, depending on the kindness of friends and increasingly judge-
mental relatives. William's wandering, his flight from the personal and political turmoil he experienced in revolutionary France, coincided with Dorothy's
desperate desire for a home. As war and distance made an immediate household with his French lover Annette Vallon and their daughter Caroline seem
impossible, Wordsworth apparently found in his renewed relationship with
Dorothy a domestic refuge. Beginning in 1794 they lived together in a series
of places in the Lake District, the West Country, and in Germany before
settling in Grasmere in December of 1799.

The months spent with Dorothy in Germany during 1798–9 were particularly important in Wordsworth's rediscovery of the meaning of his
Englishness. In a pattern typical of his career and imaginative life, Wordsworth renewed this identity while separated from England, isolated with
Dorothy in the town of Goslar during the coldest winter of the century.
Dorothy records in her Hamburg journal and in her letters home during
this time their intense alienation from their surroundings. In a letter to their
brother Christopher Wordsworth, Dorothy confides that 'Goslar is not a
place where it is possible to see any thing of the manners of the more cultivated Germans, or of the higher classes. Its inhabitants are all petty trades-
people; in general a low and selfish race; intent upon gain, and perpetually of
course disappointed' (*WL* i 245). Likewise, William writes to Josiah Wedg-
wood that Goslar 'was once the residence of Emperors, and it is now the
residence of Grocers and Linen-drapers who are, I say it with a feeling of sorrow, a wretched race; the flesh, blood, and bone of their minds being nothing
but knavery and low falshood [sic]' (*WL* i 249). For their part, the locals
distrusted the Wordsworths. In fact, Coleridge surmised that the towns-
people assumed that Dorothy was William's lover and shunned the supposed

impropriety of the relationship. Wordsworth's recent biographer Kenneth Johnston follows others in speculating that this unacknowledged tension was behind William's composition of the Lucy poems and fragmentary 'spots of time' for *The Prelude*.[3]

This period of German isolation and alienation influenced Wordsworth not only in reformulating his English identity but in embracing the conviction that his only *home* could be in England, thus the merging of patriotic and domestic love. This identification of patriotic and domestic love is best exemplified in the Lucy poem that he wrote in early 1801 when settled in Grasmere:

> I travelled among unknown Men,
> In Lands beyond the Sea;
> Nor England! Did I know till then
> What love I bore to thee.

The poem goes on to celebrate an image of domesticity that combines the speaker's love for Lucy and her English home, her spinning wheel serving as a metonymy for this mingling of domestic and patriotic love:

> Among the mountains did I feel
> The joy of my desire;
> And she I cherished turned her wheel
> Beside an English fire.

The implicit death of Lucy in this poem (as in all of the poems of the Lucy cycle) serves as a reminder of the fragility of happiness in face of mortality or loss of hope. But the death of Lucy ('the last green field / Which Lucy's eyes surveyed!') does not diminish the power of the speaker's attachment to her *English* hearth.

The years preceding Goslar had also been formative in Wordsworth's creative life, and it is not surprising that his poetry of this period often focuses on the possibilities of domestic happiness and community, and on the relationship between domestic and political economies. Perhaps Wordsworth's first great poem, *The Ruined Cottage*, best illustrates this dynamic. Like so many of Wordsworth's poems, this one begins with an image or images and then weaves the narrative around them. The images refer to the ruin: the 'four naked walls' (31) of the cottage, the overgrown garden emblematic of human loss and decay, or the 'useless fragment of a wooden bowl' (91). While all of the images reveal the transformation of a productive cottage into a ruin, this last one especially moves the Pedlar's heart because it represents a particular domestic detail and as such carries metonymic significance for all of the losses suffered. The cluster of images reminds that not only things have been ruined, but human lives: the 'useless fragment', once a part of a working household, now represents its destruction.

Furthermore, Wordsworth implies in *The Ruined Cottage* that domestic happiness and security depend on economic and political stability. For a while, Margaret and her husband Robert, a weaver, lived hardworking and productive lives with their two children. But as the Pedlar explains to his young friend,

> You may remember, now some ten years gone,
> Two blighting seasons when the fields were left
> With half a harvest. It pleased heaven to add
> A worse affliction in the plague of war
>
> (134–7)

> As I have said, 'twas now
> A time of trouble; shoals of artisans
> Were from their daily labour turned away
> To hang for bread on parish charity
>
> (153–6).

Wordsworth traces the effects of these ills on the family, at first focusing particularly on the effect on Robert. He becomes idle and loses his will to survive. The Pedlar explains that 'poverty brought on a petted mood / And a sore temper' (174–5), and finally to the destruction of domestic calm. Although this poem is linked to a particular working class family, like so many of Wordsworth's poems it focuses on loss and what can be made of it – in this case for those who tell or hear the sad tale, not the protagonists themselves.

Wordsworth echoes the same theme when he writes to Whig leader Charles James Fox in a letter dated 14 January 1801, in recommending 'The Brothers' and 'Michael' from the second volume of *Lyrical Ballads*:

> It appears to me that the most calamitous effect, which has followed the measures which have lately been pursued in this country, is a rapid decay of the domestic affections among the lower orders of society. This effect the present Rulers of this country are not conscious of, or they disregard it. For many years past, the tendency of society amongst almost all the nations of Europe has been to produce it. But recently by the spreading of manufactures through every part of the country, by the heavy taxes upon postage, by workhouses, Houses of Industry, and the invention of Soup-shops &c. &c. superadded to the encreasing disproportion between the price of labor and that of the necessaries of life, the bonds of domestic feeling among the poor, as far as the influence of these things has extended, have been weakened, and in innumerable instances entirely destroyed.

Throughout the letter, Wordsworth maintains that these social conditions are destroying 'independent domestic life' and the happiness associated with it. Wordsworth argues here and elsewhere that these affections are the moral backbone of England, an island of stability in a sea of change. And yet the poems themselves chronicle the collapse of this life that Wordsworth wants so urgently to preserve.

If the domestic affections are the backbone of the country, the family is the microcosm of the larger world. Wordsworth shared with writers on both the right (Edmund Burke) and the left (Mary Wollstonecraft) an interest in the family as the stage where dramas of power, authority, passion, and independence are acted out. The family both represents (on a smaller scale) and is analogous to the society. Certainly the drama of Wordsworth's own family life in the 1790s represented many of these conflicts as he struggled to find his place in the world in both the literal and figurative senses. After the tense and alienating season in Germany, the search for this domestic security became even more urgent.

## Home at Grasmere, home at Rydal Mount

By the time William and Dorothy Wordsworth arrived in Grasmere a few days before Christmas in 1799, they viewed this leg of their journey as a homecoming and Grasmere as home – 'our little domestic slip of mountain' (24 and 27 December 1799; *WL* 1 274–5). During the early years at Grasmere, the Wordsworths also recreated the *meaning* of domesticity within their own lives, even as William continued to document the failures of domestic stability in his poetry. But at Grasmere he and Dorothy, as well as their expanding circle with their brother John and their friends the Hutchinsons, define a domestic life that is intellectually self-conscious and centred around creative work.

Anyone who visits what is now known as Dove Cottage must be surprised to see the cramped living space – small, dark rooms with ceilings so low that Wordsworth had to watch his head while moving about. In some ways though, as others have suggested, this spatial constraint paradoxically inspired imaginative leaps in creative life. John Murdoch has argued, in fact, that the Wordsworths were highly original in transforming a cottage on a public road: 'the deliberate construction of a cottage and garden adapted to the existence of scholar-gentleman was a characteristic development of the early 19th century'.[4] Perhaps this explains Dorothy's recognition in her journal at one point that their endeavours were a matter of special interest: 'A coronetted Landau went by when we were sitting upon the sodded wall. The ladies (evidently Tourists) turned an eye of interest upon our little garden

& cottage' (9 June 1800).[5] In order to extend their domestic space, William and Dorothy (and to a certain extent their brother John) collaborated on gardens surrounding the cottage and 'on the construction of sheltered secreted places' on the property, so that the garden became an extension of the household, garden 'rooms' that for a time made up for the constraints within. In fact, gardening became a lifelong pursuit of William's, and remained linked to his idea of promoting 'the affections' by connecting human life to nature (WL 1 627; 17 and 24 October 1805) – to one's plot of ground. But if gardens would become more aesthetic pleasure grounds at Rydal Mount, at Dove Cottage the garden's main function was practical and immediate: nourishment.

To a certain extent, domestic life at Grasmere was a collaboration, although I would not go as far as claiming, as some have done, that there was not a gendered division of labour at Grasmere.[6] While it is true that gardening was truly collaborative, the work associated with the interior household – cooking, baking, washing, copying – seems to have been Dorothy and her female servant's responsibility. Both Dorothy and William were, however, engaged in creative work – Dorothy on her journals and William on his poetry. But Dorothy was the glue holding their domestic life together, and her journals brim with endless cycles of housework and kitchen gardening, all of which she engages in with tremendous energy. This energetic work seems to have intensified Dorothy's consciousness of the value of life at Dove Cottage: 'Grasmere was very solemn in the last glimpse of twilight it calls home the heart to quietness' (Journals, p. 17).

We might also say that Home at Grasmere is William's attempt – not entirely successful – to call home the heart to quietness. For while Home at Grasmere is a celebratory poem that commemorates this homecoming and new life, it also reveals the anxieties of domesticity, no doubt reflecting William's own conflicted emotions over his relationships with Dorothy, Mary Hutchinson, and Annette Vallon, not to mention his anxiety about his career and his capacity to earn money. The narrator of Home at Grasmere celebrates his happiness with Emma [Dorothy], but the joy is qualified. In appreciating the spring and flocks of birds, the narrator must acknowledge:

> But two are missing – two, a lonely pair
> Of milk-white Swans – ah, why are they not here?
> These above all, ah, why are they not here
> To share in this day's pleasure? From afar
> They came, like Emma and myself, to live
> Together here in peace and solitude
> Choosing this Valley, they who had the choice
> Of the whole world.                    (322–9)

Although the speaker muses that 'They should not have departed' (342), he senses that they will not return. Their absence highlights the fragility of the 'placid way of life' (336) that he and 'Emma' have chosen in Grasmere, that their peace and happiness may also be difficult to sustain.

Other vignettes and images of domesticity support this tenuousness, although there is yearning for hope. First there is the story of the man who became a 'lawless Suitor' (506) to a girl working within his household. Wracked by guilt and shame, the man cannot speak his shame and becomes alienated from his home and family: 'he died of his own grief, / He could not bear the weight of his own shame' (531–2). The other story is more hopeful, although it is tinged with sadness because it tells of six motherless daughters and their father. The narrator focuses on one of the daughters, who

> Companion of her Father, does for him
> Where'er he wanders in his pastoral course
> The service of a Boy, and with delight
> More keen and prouder daring: yet hath She
> Within the garden, like the rest, a bed
> For her own flowers, or favorite Herbs, a space
> Holden by sacred charter; and I guess
> She also helped to frame that tiny Plot
> Of garden ground which one day 'twas my chance
> To find among the woody rocks that rise
> Above the House, a Slip of smoother earth...
>
> (575–86)

As in the Wordsworths' letters and journals of the period, the garden becomes an emblem both of the human connection to nature and of domestic order. The very language echoes other writing: plot of ground, slip of earth. In addition, the political resonance of 'sacred charter' suggests that this garden links domestic and patriotic affections, a Wordsworthian ideal.

During this period of settling into Grasmere, Coleridge had begun to urge Wordsworth to write the great philosophical poem of the age: *The Recluse*. Although Wordsworth wrote portions of what was to have become this poem, he also (and more happily) focused on shorter pieces. Just as the cramped interiors of Dove Cottage inspired improvements in the landscape and bursts of creativity, Wordsworth found the less daunting structures of the shorter genres liberating. As one writer has ingeniously noted, Wordsworth uses the 'very language that describes the Grasmere property' in the sonnet that 'speaks of "the Sonnet's scanty plot of ground" ('Nuns fret not'). The sonnet, in short, epitomizes the domestic space that William celebrated at Grasmere and bestows upon that space an aesthetic analogue' (Heinzelman, 'Cult of Domesticity', p. 63). This is especially interesting because Wordsworth thought of gardening as a liberal art bound by the same formal concerns and affective possibilities as poetry.[7] Furthermore, the poem turns with this thought:

> In truth, the prison, unto which we doom
> Ourselves, no prison is: and hence to me,
> In sundry moods, 'twas pastime to be bound
> Within the Sonnet's scanty plot of ground:
> Pleased if some Souls (for such there needs must be)
> Who have felt the weight of too much liberty,
> Should find short solace there, as I have found.

These lines are also interesting in terms of Wordsworth's life in and preceding Grasmere. We can interpret 'the weight of too much liberty' as referring both to the *Recluse* project and to Wordsworth's own emotional life before Grasmere – his time in France, his wandering. The 'prison' of Grasmere and domesticity must have been a welcome antidote to this homelessness, wandering, and alienation.

With Wordsworth's marriage to Mary Hutchinson and the growing family at Grasmere (which, at different times, included Sara Hutchinson, Coleridge, and others, as well as Dorothy and eventually five children), Dove Cottage became too scanty even for the most imaginative homemakers. The ménage moved through several unsatisfactory homes and sustained the tragic loss of two of the children – Thomas and Catherine – before they became tenants of Rydal Mount, Wordsworth's home for the rest of his life and the place most associated with the idea of 'Wordsworth'. Although Rydal is only about a mile from Dove Cottage, in some ways it could be a world away. Comparatively spacious and beautifully situated, the house became another kind of home, one suitable to Turkish carpets, tea urns, keepsakes, and landscaped lawns. Paintings of the Wordsworths during this period represent Rydal Mount as an idealized retreat with both elegant interiors and terraced exterior spaces. But despite these contemporary images, we should keep in mind that although Rydal Mount was comfortable, it was in reality never luxuriously furnished or excessively decorated. Furthermore, luxury was never the issue: for Wordsworth, Rydal Mount became a domestic anchor and spiritual home. When Lady le Fleming, the owner of Rydal Mount, seemed ready to evict the Wordsworths in favour of her aunt in 1825, Wordsworth quickly bought a field adjoining her property and commissioned plans for a grand villa next to Lady le Fleming's own home. Wordsworth's ploy was successful. Lady le Fleming backed off and never again tried to evict her poetic tenant.

During the Rydal years, the idea of domesticity is both highly idealized in Wordsworth's poetry and very practical in his prose – letters, notes, reported comments. His prefatory poem to *The White Doe of Rylstone*, for instance, celebrates the power of domestic affections and of poetry to console the wounded spirit. Having just lost two beloved children, Wordsworth begins the poem by addressing his wife:

> In trellis'd shed with clustering roses gay,
> And, MARY! Oft beside our blazing fire,
> When years of wedded life were as a day
> Whose current answers to the heart's desire,
> Did we together read in Spenser's Lay
> How Una, sad of soul – in sad attire,
> The gentle Una, born of heavenly birth,
> To seek her Knight went wandering o'er the earth.
>
> (1–8)

Here two emblems of domestic life – the garden refuge and the hearth – become perfect spots for reading Spenser and finding 'recompense' (51). Through the years, Rydal also nurtured Wordsworth's practical side – his concern with how actual domestic life can be maintained through certain economies. As Harriet Martineau recounts in her *Autobiography*, Wordsworth (even in 1845) remained concerned with this practical side. After planting a tree on her property, Wordsworth advised the eccentric and unpredictable Martineau: ' "When you have a visitor", said he, "you must do as we did; – you must say 'if you like to have a cup of tea with us, you are very welcome: but if you want any meat, – you must pay for your board' "... The mixture of odd economies and neighborly generosity was one of the most striking things in the old poet.'[8] Perhaps Wordsworth's economy was not as odd as Martineau implies, especially if he was thinking back on his years at Dove Cottage and the struggle to support his young family.

So what was Rydal Mount really like? To a certain extent, we can reconstruct the home by reading the poetry and letters of the period and by reading what such friends as Martineau, as well as Henry Crabb Robinson, Isabella Fenwick, and Hartley Coleridge say about it. While Rydal Mount has been rightly associated in recent years with Victorian interiority and a 'cult of domesticity' (Heinzelman's term), I do not think we can view Rydal Mount as simply representing a Victorian separation of spheres. For while Wordsworth certainly saw women and 'womanly virtues' (*WL* vii 235) as closely associated with home, the division of the domestic and the public spheres was not absolute. The home was more than just a refuge from the world: it was also a well-situated and protected vantage point from which to view the larger world. And, furthermore, because the home was the site of work for the poet and increasingly a tourist destination in itself, it was not 'separate' from the larger world.

But a new emphasis in the poetry from the 1820s onward reveals that Wordsworth accepted and contributed to emerging Victorian ideas of femininity and the domestic sphere. At the same time, the elegiac sense that pervades the earlier poetry and its hope for the 'domestic affections' are replaced by a more light and playful approach that belies continuing tensions in the Wordsworths' family romance. *The Triad*, written for the 1828 gift annual *The Keepsake*, best exemplifies this new emphasis. This poem, like other contributions, was written for the marketplace – quite literally. Including a medley of selections in prose and verse as well as engraved plates, *The Keepsake* and other gift annuals were designed more to be seen than read. They were the nineteenth-century equivalent of our decorative coffee table books. Following years of resisting and balking, Wordsworth stooped to conquer, and as Peter Manning has suggested, 'After a career-long suspicion of popular narrative, the almost sixty-year-old poet was learning new tricks.'[9] What especially interests me here is not just this new engagement with the literary marketplace, but the fact that the marketplace was calling for poems that embraced a particular ideology of feminine beauty and virtue centred on domesticity and domestic accomplishments. As the unsophisticated worker Bob Jakin exclaims over the illustrations in a *Keepsake* in George Eliot's *The Mill on the Floss*, published in 1860 but set in the 1820s, ' "here's ladies for you, some wi' curly hair and some wi' smooth, an' some a-smiling wi' their heads o' one side, an' some as if they were goin' to cry – look here – a-sittin' on the ground out o' door, dressed like the ladies I'n seen get out o' carriages at the balls in th' Old Hall there" ' (Book IV, chapter III).

Eliot's description of the *Keepsake* leads us to Wordsworth's playful comment to a correspondent in 1826 – 'My Daughter, Dora by name, is now installed in my House in the office of regular tea maker, why cannot you come and swell the chorus of praises she draws forth for her performance of that important part of feminine duty?' – and to the world of *The Triad* and keepsakes. In *The Triad*, Wordsworth celebrates the kind of feminine beauty that Eliot's character catalogues. Although the poem imagines a youth from 'Olympian clime' – a proto-Victorian judgement of Paris – who has come to select a wife from among the 'Phantasms' of three young women, Edith Southey, Dora Wordsworth, and Sara Coleridge, there is no real drama. Instead, the poem uses this fiction to create a tableau of ideal womanhood from the male poet's point of view. Sara Coleridge later asserted that 'There is no truth in it [the poem] as a whole, although bits of truth, glazed and magnified, are embodied in it' (*LP* 439). This glazing is an apt metaphor for Wordsworth's technique, and I think it is Sara Coleridge's way of resisting the unnatural lustre and display in which she and the other women are turned into chaste art objects. Her comment gives the 'mute Phantoms' (212) imagined by the poet a say in how we remember them.

All three of the portraits link the women to images of domesticity, and in fact see women as responsible for creating domestic calm. The speaker first describes Edith Southey:

> O Lady, worthy of earth's proudest throne!
> Nor less, by excellence of nature, fit
> Beside an unambitious hearth to sit
> Domestic queen, where grandeur is unknown;
> What living man could fear
> The worst of Fortune's malice, wert Thou near,
> Humbling that lily-stem, thy sceptre meek,
> That its fair flowers may from his cheek
> Brush the too happy tear?                    (52–60)

Wordsworth's 'Domestic queen' fits well into this idealized world, as does the picture of Dora as a damsel of romance who 'bears the stringed lute of old romance, / That cheered the trellised arbour's privacy, / And soothed war-wearied knights in raftered hall' (101–3). The speaker praises Dora's 'self-forgetfulness' (160), reminding us of the virtue of self-sacrifice often associated with Victorian womanhood. Even Sara Coleridge, who was the most intellectually accomplished of the three, must fit into the context of domestic life so the youth does not 'dread the depth of meditative eye' (193).

These formal descriptions connecting women to chivalrous notions and genres as well as Victorian interiors carry us away from the Grasmere and pre-Grasmere days, when Dorothy Wordsworth went hiking through the countryside like Austen's Elizabeth Bennet and her wild eyes reflected the poet's own passions. After Dorothy's Aunt (Mrs Christopher) Crackanthorpe criticized her for 'rambling about the country on foot', Dorothy defended herself in a letter from Windy Brow in April of 1794. But in *The Triad* the narrator urges the daughters of the poets to embrace propriety and sit before the paternal tea urn dispensing tea and sympathy to weary knights. Unlike Tennyson in *Mariana* or *The Lady of Shalott*, Wordsworth does not intuit the dark side of these gilded cages or the possibility that this domestic ideal has its price.

Actual life at Rydal Mount was certainly not as idealized as this portrait. As we have seen in Wordsworth's comments about Hemans, the poet had a very practical and prosaic sense of 'housewifery' to go with his idealized views of femininity. Furthermore, even amidst a close family, numerous tensions will surface. Wordsworth's relationships with his three children were not always easy. Both John and William, Jr were disappointments intellectually, and Wordsworth worried much about their futures. And as we shall see, his intense and loving relationship with Dora was not without pain on both sides. Furthermore, Dorothy, who for years was a mainstay of the household, went into a mental and physical decline after 1829. In her own words:

> When shall I tread your garden path?
> Or climb your sheltering hill?
> When shall I wander, free as air,
> And track the foaming rill?
>
> A prisoner on my pillowed couch
> Five years in feebleness I've lain,
> Oh! shall I e'er with vigorous step
> Travel the hills again?
>
> To Mr Carter DW<br>Novr 11–1835[10]

The sad answer to this question for Dorothy Wordsworth is 'no'; her condition as an invalid also meant a changed domestic life for her and for the family circle. She who had been the caregiver now became totally dependent on others for her life and care – imprisoned on her couch in a cruel parody both of her former self and of positive poetic images of domestic entrapment.

## The company of women

Viewing Dorothy Wordsworth's life more than two centuries after her birth, it is tempting to find a medical diagnosis or to blame her ruined health on frustrated personal desires and years of self-sacrifice. To this latter reading, her long illness inflicted a kind of poetic justice on the household that had accepted those sacrifices for so long. But the fate of Dorothy Wordsworth raises additional and more complicated questions about Wordsworth's different relationships with the many women in his life and their role in making both Grasmere and Rydal Mount home.

The early feminist critique of Wordsworth interprets William as a patriarchal villain who took advantage of the women in his household, especially Dorothy.[11] The criticism of Wordsworth's dependence on women did not originate in the last twenty or so years, however. In the autumn of 1803 Coleridge complained that Wordsworth was 'hypocondriacal' from 'living wholly among *Devotees* – having every the [sic] minutest Thing, almost his very Eating & Drinking done for him by his Sister, or Wife' (*STCL* ii, 1013). Although Coleridge's comments are tainted by his own envy and wish that *he* could be surrounded by devotees, his comments are nonetheless perceptive. After Wordsworth's marriage to Mary Hutchinson in 1802, Wordsworth and his career became increasingly the focal point. It was no longer just William and Dorothy, sharing and collaborating, but a whole household of (mostly) women who revolved around William.

But it would be inaccurate to say that the other members of the household were ever held hostage to William's demands. This view overlooks the fact that Dorothy Wordsworth, Mary Wordsworth, and Sara Hutchinson had minds and wills of their own. It denies the value that they themselves placed on their home-making and on the choices they made. It also overlooks their irreverent attitude toward some of William's concerns. For instance, Wordsworth was afraid of publishing *The Convention of Cintra* because it was politically controversial. Following William's serious worry about 'Prosecution in any of the courts of law', Sara adds to the letter: 'We Females shall be very sorry to find that the pamphlet is not published for we have not the least fear of Newgate – if there was but a Garden to walk in we think we should do very nicely – and a Gaol in the Country would be quite pleasant' (*WL* ii 330). Sara's letter not only reveals her own sardonic wit, but also suggests that there is a female solidarity in this household for whom she speaks. She certainly does not fit the pattern of a woman oppressed and beaten down by the forces of male ego, and she herself sees the sly humour in portraying home life as analogous to prison in the country. Nor was she afraid to smuggle *Blackwood's* into the house to read hostile reviews of her brother-in-law's poetry.

Much of the specific criticism of Wordsworth has focused on Dorothy and her long life with William and his family. The case of Dorothy *is* more complicated because her fate is so much more closely linked with William's from the beginning. Some feminist criticism has focused on William's alleged theft of Dorothy's ideas and images from the journals and on his preventing her own career as a writer. Kenneth Johnston's analysis is more on the mark when he writes that Dorothy 'knew by now [1799] that she would never marry and that she was in a real sense wedded to him for life. It is hard to argue that Dorothy missed out on a writing career for her devotion, but it is certainly true that she sacrificed herself *as a woman* to William's (vocational) desires' (*The Hidden Wordsworth*, p. 651). From this perspective, it is less William's overriding selfishness in appropriating Dorothy to his household than it is Dorothy's circumstances as an unmarried sister without a fortune – a prerequisite in her culture to either independence or marriage – that led to her casting her lot for home and happiness with her favourite brother.

I do suggest, however, that we view Dorothy's transformation over the years from a passionate and energetic young woman to a ruin of her former self in the context of the life that she embraced. For her life at Grasmere and Rydal required a constant sublimation of her own individual desires in favour of the good of the household and the need to serve others. And we must remember that in one sense Dorothy bore the responsibilities of a wife without the benefit of having a husband with whom she could share her deepest passions. For as her behaviour at the time of William's marriage to her good friend Mary reveals, Dorothy knew that this marriage would break the particular intimacy that she and William had established in the early days at Grasmere when William was *her* beloved.

Nor can Wordsworth be said to have been tyrannical with his wife, to whom he was married for almost fifty years. Mary Wordsworth apparently did not share her sister Sara's sharp wit, but she was a strong woman, passionately attached to her family. She was not a pushover. Although she often served as her husband's amanuensis, she sometimes refused to work with him until his mood improved. Wordsworth was a relentless reviser who depended on various members of the household (usually female) to carry out the arduous task of taking dictation and copying manuscripts. He did not take this work lightly or for granted. In a letter on 5 July 1837 written from abroad, he pleads: 'Dearest Mary, when I have felt how harshly I often demeaned myself to you, my inestimable fellow-labourer, while correcting the last Edition of my poems, I often pray to God that He would grant us both life, that I may make some amends to you for that, and all my unworthiness.' Wordsworth was aware of his own shortcomings. When Crabb Robinson told him that De Quincey had said that he had a better wife than he deserved, Wordsworth reportedly agreed.[12] While this may be the case, Wordsworth did see Mary as his 'inestimable fellow-labourer', his partner in the whole Wordsworthian enterprise.

With all of the women who were his contemporaries – Dorothy, Mary, Sara – it is fair to say that their role in Wordsworthian domesticity was to a large extent *by choice*. The same cannot be said for his daughter Dorothy, or Dora, as she was known. Wordsworth's only surviving legitimate daughter, Dora was much beloved by her father – a feeling that she reciprocated. But this love carried with it a burden, especially as Dora matured. Dora, this second Dorothy, was groomed for her role as her father's amanuensis, companion, and 'regular tea maker' – a Victorian angel with editorial responsibilities. From the outside, others saw that Dora's responsibilities placed a constraint on her life, particularly on her making a life for herself independent of Rydal Mount. Dora's friend Sara Coleridge (and one of the three Graces from *The Triad*) commented that 'The Rydal Mount career frustrated a real talent',[13] referring to her travel journal on Spain and Portugal. In 1830, Sara's brother Hartley had written that 'Dora, as sweet a creature as ever breath'd, suffers sadly from debility. I have my suspicions that she would be a healthier matron than she is a Virgin, but strong indeed must be the love that could induce her to leave her father, whom she adores and who quite doats upon her' (30 August 1830).[14]

After a too-long courtship, Dora married Edward Quillinan when she was thirty-seven – with her father's grudging consent, gained after years of painful intransigence on Wordsworth's part. Dora's difficult time separating herself from home – and her father's long refusal to let her go – both reveal the darker side of Rydal Mount and family relations (as does Dorothy Wordsworth's sad fate). While in earlier years Wordsworth felt the weight of too much liberty and thrived on the scanty plot at Grasmere, Dora felt the weight of too much control.

And yet these tensions only strengthened the fabric of domestic attachments at Rydal Mount. Dora returned home in 1847 to be nursed in her final illness by her parents. According to various accounts, including that of Crabb Robinson, vitality and happiness never returned to the Mount after Dora's death, but the home remained a focal point for affection and memory during the Wordsworths' last years, an emblem of both loss and hope.[15] Even after the poet stopped writing about this or any subject, he was sustained and comforted by the home and the *idea of home* that they had all worked so long and hard to create. In the end, Rydal called the heart home to quietness too.

## NOTES

1 Jared Curtis (ed.), *The Fenwick Notes of William Wordsworth* (London: Bristol Classical Press 1993), p. 60.
2 From 'To Wordsworth', in William M. Rossetti (ed.), *The Poetical Works of Felicia Hemans* (London: Ward Lock and Co., 1878).
3 Kenneth R. Johnston, *The Hidden Wordsworth: Poet, Lover, Rebel, Spy* (New York: Norton, 1998), p. 635.
4 John Murdoch, *The Discovery of the Lake District* (London: The Victoria and Albert Museum, 1984), p. 81.
5 Dorothy Wordsworth, *The Grasmere Journals*, ed. Pamela Woof (Oxford, 1991), p. 9.
6 Kurt Heinzelman, 'The Cult of Domesticity: Dorothy and William Wordsworth at Grasmere', in Anne K. Mellor (ed.), *Romanticism and Feminism* (Bloomington: University of Indiana Press, 1988), p. 53 and *passim*. Despite some differences, I am indebted to the insights of this important essay.
7 For the best developed analysis of this topic, see Russell Noyes, *Wordsworth and the Art of Landscape* (1968 rpt. New York: Haskell House, 1973).
8 Harriet Martineau, *Autobiography*, 3rd edn 2 vols. (London: Smith, Elder, 1877), vol. 2, p. 235.

9 Peter J. Manning, 'Wordsworth in the *Keepsake*, 1829', in John O. Jordan and Robert L. Patten (eds.), *Literature in the Marketplace* (Cambridge: Cambridge University Press, 1995).

10 Quoted in Susan M. Levin, *Dorothy Wordsworth and Romanticism* (New Brunswick: Rutgers University Press, 1987), p. 231.

11 For instance, see Margaret Homans, *Women Writers and Poetic Identity* (Princeton: Princeton University Press, 1980). For an extended analysis of the feminist critique of Wordsworth, see my *Wordsworth and the Cultivation of Women* (University of California Press, 1994).

12 Edith C. Batho, *The Later Wordsworth* (Cambridge: Cambridge University Press, 1933), p. 90.

13 Howard P. Vincent (ed.), *The Letters of Dora Wordsworth* (Chicago: Packard, 1944), 'Introduction', p. 11.

14 *The Letters of Hartley Coleridge*, ed. Grace Evelyn Griggs and Earl Leslie Griggs (New York: Oxford University Press, 1936), p. 112.

15 See Edith J. Morley (ed.), *The Correspondence of Henry Crabb Robinson with the Wordsworth Circle (1808–66)*, 2 vols. (Oxford: Clarendon Press, 1927), including 'Introduction', vol. 1, pp. 1–27. Also corroborating this is Stephen Gill's conclusion in *William Wordsworth: A Life* (Oxford: Clarendon Press, 1989); I have relied on Gill throughout.

# 9

STEPHEN GILL

# The philosophic poet

When the Victorian novelist Elizabeth Gaskell learnt that a friend was planning to visit the Lake District, she urged him to pack something by Wordsworth, not, as one might expect, his *Guide to the Lakes*, but the long,
philosophical work in blank verse, *The Excursion*.[1] The poem is set in the
heart of the Lake District and its scenes and characters could have been
of interest to any tourist going there; but Gaskell is not recommending *The
Excursion* just for this reason. It is rather that to her mind Wordsworth is the
prophet of the mountains and valleys, the best tutor and guide to the spiritual
nourishment available from natural beauty, and *The Excursion* is his inspired
word. Four figures occupy the ground of the poem, supposedly in dramatic
interaction, but few readers have ever doubted that the most important of
them is the Wanderer and that through him speaks Wordsworth the Sage.
When the Wanderer declares that 'To every Form of being is assigned.../
An *active* Principle' (*Excursion* IX 1–3), his confession of faith recalls
'Tintern Abbey' and the early *Prelude* and it is no surprise to learn that
the discourse of the Wanderer first published in 1814 was actually drafted
in the year of 'Tintern Abbey', 1798.[2]

Whether or not Gaskell's friend, Charles Bosanquet, was uplifted by the
Wanderer's sermon among the mountains is not known, but it is unlikely
that a student nowadays will be moved by the passage, simply because it is
not likely to be read. *The Prelude* offers much greater pleasure and interest
than *The Excursion* and even the most assiduous student can only take so
many thousand blank-verse lines before wilting. But though the '*active* principle' passage may escape the notice of most readers nowadays, there are
many others like it in Wordsworth's most studied poems, equally difficult
and equally challenging. For example: 'Wisdom and spirit of the universe, /
Thou soul that art the eternity of thought, / That giv'st to forms and images a
breath / And everlasting motion' (now recognized as *Prelude*, 1805 1 428–31,
but published in Wordsworth's lifetime as a discrete poem, 'Influence of
Natural Objects in Calling Forth and Strengthening the Imagination in

Boyhood and Early Youth'); the Pedlar's exhortation to the Poet at the close of *The Ruined Cottage*, that he must no longer question the 'purposes of wisdom', reading the 'forms of things with an unworthy eye' (MS D 509–10); the final lines of *The Prelude* which mystifyingly declare that it will be Wordsworth's and Coleridge's task as 'Prophets of Nature' to teach how 'the mind of man becomes / A thousand times more beautiful than the earth / On which he dwells'. The list could be greatly extended. In Wordsworth's body of work there are many passages which, from the strangeness of their vocabulary and conceptual frame and often from the complexity of their syntax, are difficult to understand in themselves and very difficult to know what to make of as a body of poetic utterance once one starts linking them up. Wallace Stevens was unspecific when he alluded to 'those pages of Wordsworth, which have done so much to strengthen the critics of poetry in their attacks on the poetry of thought', but it was surely such passages he had in mind.[3]

Growing awareness of philosophical aspiration was integral to Wordsworth's discovery of his poetic vocation, the discovery, as Kenneth Johnston's chapter in this volume explains, that was inextricable from Wordsworth's conceiving the scope of his planned great work, *The Recluse*, from 1798 onwards. This chapter proposes simply to highlight some of the problems this fact poses for the modern reader, especially for one coming to Wordsworth's poetry for the first time. I will waste no time asking 'Is Wordsworth a philosophical poet?', since this is invariably the prelude to pointless manoeuvres aimed at redefining the word 'philosophical' to ensure that the answer is Yes. A glance at the poetry discussed in this chapter will show that it is at least what Stevens calls 'poetry of thought', and familiarity with Wordsworth's poetic forebears will indicate how securely he was working within a tradition of meditative verse. Nor will I offer a summary of 'Wordsworth's Thought', believing this to be a wholly reductive and useless exercise applied to Wordsworth or any other poet, nor a survey of what other scholars have written about Wordsworth and Hartley, Wordsworth and Kant, and so on. To repeat: the aim of the chapter is modest. It is to play light on the assertion that philosophical aspiration was integral to Wordsworth's sense of his poetic vocation and to bring into focus some questions about the poetry.

Wordsworth the Sage of Rydal Mount was a Victorian construction, but the real beginning of Wordsworth as philosophic poet was in the year when almost every aspect of his life took on a new complexion, the *annus mirabilis* of 1797–8. In 1794 he had introduced into revision of *An Evening Walk* (published 1793) a striking passage on the Life in (or to be perceived in) Nature:

> A heart that vibrates evermore, awake
> To feeling for all forms that Life can take;
> That wider still its sympathy extends
> And sees not any line where being ends;
> Sees sense, through Nature's rudest forms betrayed,
> Tremble obscure in fountain rock and shade,
> And while a secret power those forms endears
> Their social accents never vainly hears.
>                    (*An Evening Walk*, ed. Averill, p. 135)

The meditation, sustained over many lines, undoubtedly enlarges the intellectual field of the poem, but not markedly beyond that already traversed by earlier eighteenth-century poets of meditation, notably James Thomson in *The Seasons* (1726–30), Mark Akenside in *The Pleasures of Imagination* (1744), and William Cowper in *The Task* (1785).[4] Wordsworth's work of 1797–8 was of quite another order. Confident in a steadily growing self-assurance, hard-won over the previous few years, Wordsworth was sure at last that he was destined to be a poet. Coleridge was sure that he was to be a certain kind of poet: 'I dare affirm that he will hereafter be admitted as the first & greatest philosophical Poet' (letter 15 January 1804). That assertion may date from a few years on, but it expresses what Coleridge had believed ever since his intimate knowledge of Wordsworth began. It underpinned Wordsworth's declaration in the summer of 1798 that he was starting work on a poem so ambitious that 'I know not anything which will not come within the scope of my plan' (letter 6 March 1798) and the vauntingly ambitious 'Prospectus' he drafted to the whole project two years or so later (for reference and discussion see Johnston's essay in the present volume).

From the outset, however, insofar as the two poets had any clear conception of what a philosophical poem should be, they differed without knowing how crucially they differed. Coleridge looked for Wordsworth to pronounce 'upon authority' a 'system of philosophy', whereas Wordsworth had declared only that his 'object' was 'to give pictures of Nature, Man, and Society' (6 March 1798) and in the only part of the poem he published, *The Excursion*, he pointedly disavowed in a preface any intention 'formally to announce a system'.[5] Inevitably Coleridge was disappointed. When Wordsworth heard of this he asked Coleridge to send his 'remarks' on the poem and added that, 'One of my principal aims in the Ex[cursion] has been to put the commonplace truths, of the human affections especially, in an interesting point of view; and rather to remind men of their knowledge, as it lurks inoperative and unvalued in their own minds, than to attempt to convey recondite or refined truths' (22 May 1815). But Coleridge was not disarmed by this defensive manoeuvre and how deeply disappointed he was is evident in his long, careful, and devastating letter to Wordsworth of 30 May 1815, in which he explained what kind of philosophic poem he had imagined him to be writing for so many years. Coleridge looked for a survey of 'the faculties of Man in the abstract' and of the 'Human Race in the concrete' from origins to the present, orchestrated to 'conclude by a grand didactic swell on the necessary identity of a true Philosophy with true Religion' – and a great deal more. The letter is too long to quote and resists excerpting. Coleridge's vision could not be more different from what *The Excursion* is and his delineation of it effectively killed the project of which he had been the joint begetter.[6]

Wordsworth's description of his aim in *The Excursion* is a brilliantly perceptive characterization of the bed-rock of his achievement and he made many similar observations over his lifetime. Repeatedly he emphasized that his poetry rests on fundamentals, on the shared. 'If my writings are to last', he declared in late life, 'it will I myself believe, be mainly owing to this characteristic. They will please for the single cause, "That we have all of us one human heart!" '[7] Just though it is, however, Wordsworth's 1815 letter to Coleridge is disingenuous. Yes, he wanted to be (and surely is) the poet of the naked, simple, elemental, but there is also abundant evidence that his most creative period began with struggles in poetry with matters which were not at all simple, or rather, matters which defied simple formulation.

In a letter on 3 February 1801 Coleridge reported:

> I have been *thinking* vigorously during my Illness – so that I cannot say that my long, long wakeful nights have all been lost to me. The subject of my meditations has been the Relation of Thoughts to Things, in the language of Hume, of Ideas to Impressions.

This quintessentially Coleridgean utterance finely catches the difference between the two poets. It is impossible to imagine Wordsworth passing wakeful nights *thinking* in the language of Hume or of any other philosopher. Nowhere in his letters is there a statement at all like this, whereas Coleridge's letters and notebooks are full of them. But it does not follow from the overall flatness of Wordsworth's letters that such matters as the 'Relation of... Ideas to Impressions' were of no interest to him. They were, but his way of actively thinking about them was through poetry – literally, through writing in metre.

Over the period 1798–1800 Wordsworth drafted hundreds of lines of poetry, some in short passages, some for longer stretches of consecutive explication. These manuscript workings were plundered for *The Prelude* (not published in Wordsworth's lifetime) and *The Excursion* (published 1814), but much of the drafting was not used in completed and published poems and awaited transcription and dissemination by Wordsworth's later editors. It is a fascinating body of work, in which Wordsworth grapples with the main questions of epistemology as they presented themselves in the century after John Locke and Isaac Newton ('epistemology: the theory of knowledge, esp. with regard to its methods and validation', *OED*): (a) how do we know the world – that is, what is the relation between what we think of as our independent minds and the world 'out there'; (b) can perception of the world out there give knowledge of the world's creator – that is, of a transcendent power; (c) what is the relation between our sensory being, that which perceives, knows, learns, and our moral being?

Coarsened by reduction into a textbook list, of course, this body of work sounds anything but inviting, save perhaps mildy to a historically minded philosopher curious about what poetic concerns were in the late eighteenth century. Looked at from the opposite direction, however, from the point of view of someone primarily interested in Wordsworth, the poetry in these notebooks beckons precisely because it so evidently issues from personal experience and not from an attempt to think through, point by point, topics listed in a philosophical primer.

'Axioms in philosophy are not axioms until they are proved upon our pulses', declared Keats (letter, 3 May 1818). A human pulse beats in these drafts. Formulations which verge upon becoming philosophical questions take shape as if they are being insisted on by the uncertainty of the personal experience from which they arise and which, reciprocally, they seem to help the poet grasp. Here, for example, is one draft passage not introduced elsewhere into a published poem:

> Oh 'tis a joy divine on summer days
> When not a breeze is stirring, not a cloud,
> To sit within some solitary wood,
> Far in some lonely wood, and hear no so[und]
> Which the heart does not make, or else so fit[s]
> To its own temper that in external things
> No longer seem internal difference:
> All melts away, and things that are without
> Live in our minds as in their native home.
> (*Lyrical Ballads*, ed. Butler and Green,
> p. 322)

This is a very characteristic utterance from the period of *Lyrical Ballads*. 'Solitary . . . lonely', the mystery of perception is felt profoundly in alone-ness.

But the 1794 revisions to *An Evening Walk* had introduced the concept of the 'social accents' inherent in perception of the forms of life and pursuing it becomes the motor force of the later drafting. Through one line can be traced Wordsworth's growing absorption in memories of sensory experience, which culminated soon after in the first part of the two-part *Prelude*. But inextricable from it also is the verse which continually touches on and slowly brings into definition questions about the moral power, and spiritual value, of yielding as 'free gift' our 'whole being' to 'Nature and her impulses' (*Lyrical Ballads*, ed. Butler and Green, p. 324). In mid-summer 1798 the poet of 'Lines ... Tintern Abbey' was ready to honour 'nature and the language of the sense' as 'The guide, the guardian of my heart, and soul / Of all my moral being.' The confidence, the note of exultation, rests in part on his having as it were taken possession of his own convictions in the struggle with a long and demanding passage which begins:

> Not useless do I deem
> These quiet sympathies with things that hold
> An inarticulate language, for the man
> Once taught to love such objects as excite
> No morbid passions no disquietude,
> No vengeance and no hatred needs must feel
> The joy of that pure principle of love
> So deeply that unsatisfied with aught
> Less pure and exquisite he cannot chuse
> But seek for objects of a kindred love
> In fellow-natures and a kindred joy.
> (*The Ruined Cottage*, ed. Butler, p. 372)

Wordsworth never published this exposition – which continues for another 100 lines – in its entirety, but it was for him what certain lines in *Endymion* were for Keats, 'a regular stepping of the Imagination towards a Truth' (letter 30 January 1818). They appeared in part in *The Excursion*, but it would be true to say that even without appearing they are everywhere in Wordsworth. The poet's sense of how the mind's relation to the external world might best be understood was continually to change during his poetically most creative years and so was his understanding of 'the one/Surpassing Life, which out of space and time, / Nor touched by welterings of passion, is / And hath the name of God' (*Prelude* VI 54–7), but what remained constant was the conviction – even if the language of that conviction could alter – that love of nature's 'beauteous and majestic' scenes (*Prelude* I 636) was inseparable from, in a mysterious but absolutely certain way, moral growth, knowledge of the divine, and acceptance of the nature of human life.

The exchange between Wordsworth and Coleridge in 1815 may serve to highlight the fact that from its very inception the idea of Wordsworth as philosophical poet had a question mark over it – what *kind* of poet is that? It was a question that nagged at many of his great contemporaries, Keats, perhaps most of all. Throughout his short writing life Keats was uncertain about the relative worth of poetry and philosophy and his estimation of Wordsworth correspondingly wavered. *The Excursion* was one of the things in the age to rejoice at (letter, 10 January 1818) and Wordsworth was a greater poet than Milton because of his greater human sympathy – he thought more deeply 'into the human heart' (letter 3 May 1818). But Wordsworth's grandeur could also overwhelm and oppress: '... for the sake of a few fine imaginative or domestic passages, are we to be bullied into a certain Philosophy engendered in the whims of an Egotist – Every man has his speculations, but every man does not brood and peacock over them till he makes a false coinage and deceives himself... We hate poetry that has a palpable design upon us' (letter 3 February 1818).

The opposition which troubled Keats ('fine imaginative or domestic passages... certain Philosophy') reached an advanced point of definition later in the Victorian era in opposed essays by Leslie Stephen and Matthew Arnold. Both profoundly sympathetic critics of Wordsworth, they agreed that he was a great poet but disagreed sharply as to why one might think so. In 1876 Stephen argued that Wordsworth's poetry retained its capacity to inspire and console, and 'wears well' because it is solidly based on ethics capable of 'systematic exposition'.[8] This was not its only appeal, of course, but it was the virtue without which all other attractions must ultimately fade. Not so, Arnold demurred three years later. This is the kind of claim no 'disinterested lover of poetry' could make, but which is made with deep and complacent satisfaction by Wordsworthians, disciples of the Sage of Rydal Mount, whose yearning for spiritual counsel renders them incapable of recognising that Wordsworth's 'poetry is the reality... his philosophy is the illusion'.[9]

Arnold's essay is one of his most attractive and its culminating affirmation of what really does matter in the poetry, Wordsworthian in its directness and simplicity, is more heart-stirring than anything in Leslie Stephen. But Arnold's no-nonsense clearing of the decks is too thorough. In Wordsworth's case, he insists, 'we cannot do him justice until we dismiss his formal philosophy'. Reviewing a *Primer of English Literature* (1876) by Stopford Brooke, himself a passionate Wordsworthian, Arnold had made a much more nuanced observation on this point: 'No one will be much helped by Wordsworth's philosophy of Nature, as a scheme in itself and disjoined from his poems.

Nor shall we be led to enjoy the poems the more for having a philosophy of Nature abstracted from them and presented to us in its nakedness.'[10] But this is not how he put it in the clinching declaration in the wittiest and most persuasive part of his essay. Here there is no middle ground: Wordsworth's *philosophy* is in contradistinction to his *poetry*. We cannot do justice to the one without *dismissing* the other.

In an important sense Arnold is surely right. No one could put together a treatise called *The Philosophy of William Wordsworth* that would satisfy professional philosophers, and a little red book, *The Sayings of William Wordsworth*, would change no one's life. But in a more important way Arnold is wrong, in that he drives a wedge between philosophy and poetry, where what is needed in Wordsworth's case is a bridge. For the philosophical poetry underpins everything else. *The Ruined Cottage* and 'Tintern Abbey'; much, perhaps most, of *The Prelude*, especially Books II, IV, VI, VIII, X, XII, and XIII; the conclusion to *Home at Grasmere*, later printed as the 'Prospectus' to *The Recluse*; the re-written 'Pedlar' of 1802; 'Ode to Duty'; 'Ode: Intimations of Immortality'; much of *The Excursion*, notably Books IV and IX; and all of the manuscript drafting not finally incorporated in published poems. This wonderful body of meditative, discursive, expository poetry is not *opposed* to 'pure' lyric poems such as 'The Solitary Reaper'; nor is it the setting against which jewels such as the 'Lucy' poems sparkle more brightly; nor is it, to anticipate another much used figure, the ore which when refined yields gold. To 'do justice' to all of Wordsworth's poetry, the challenge of the philosophic verse must be embraced.

What problems face readers fresh to Wordsworth who try to follow that injunction? One is I think easily resolved. Much of the verse is difficult to follow. The explication of a point is often sustained over many lines and the concentration required to keep eye and attention on the syntax of the developing argument is enormous (I am not, of course, suggesting that Wordsworth is alone in making such demands). Read out loud, however, many a difficult passage will yield itself up because the rhythm will make the emphases and supply the punctuation. Never were Hopkins's words more applicable, that 'the true nature of poetry' is as 'the darling child of speech, of lips and spoken utterance: it must be spoken'.[11]

Three problems at least, though, will remain. The first is vocabulary (leaving aside the issue of familiar words such as 'plastic' and 'vulgar', which have simply shifted in meaning). When Wordsworth describes childhood experiences the language is usually accessible, as in, for example, *Prelude* II 176–80:

> oh, then the calm
> And dead still water lay upon my mind
> Even with a weight of pleasure, and the sky,
> Never before so beautiful, sank down
> Into my heart and held me like a dream.

But when meditating on these experiences Wordsworth habitually employs the language of eighteenth-century philosophical discourse, not with the professional's concern about terminological niceties, but not casually either. And this language is not readily accessible; if it seems so on occasion it is probably treacherous. Take 'sense'.[12] 'Tintern Abbey''s 'language of the sense' and *Prelude*, I's 'hallowed and pure motions of the sense' should not cause too much difficulty, but one might begin to struggle with the cluster of affirmations which contrast worlds of life and death:

> They need not extraordinary calls
> To rouze them – in a world of life they live,
> By sensible impressions not enthralled,
> But quickened, rouzed, and made thereby more fit
> To hold communion with the invisible world.
>                     I mean
> Oppress it by the laws of vulgar sense,
> And substitute a universe of death,
> The falsest of all worlds, in place of that
> Which is divine and true.

> I, long before the blissful hour arrives
> Would chant, in lonely peace, the spousal verse
> Of this great consummation: – and, by words
> Which speak of nothing more that what we are,
> Would I arouse the sensual from their sleep
> Of Death, and win the vacant and the vain
> To noble raptures...

These three quotations, it should be noted, are taken not from manuscript drafts familiar only to a few scholars, but from key canonical texts: the climax of Wordsworth's greatest poem, *The Prelude* XIII 101–5; 139–43; and the manifesto to what he hoped would be his greatest work, *The Recluse*.

The second is that the poetry appears to entertain a variety of views, whose apparent chafing would not discompose a trained philosopher or an eighteenth-century historian, but which probably will the late twentieth-century reader who is neither. Within the two poems just mentioned, Wordsworth avers, for example, that Paradise can be the produce of the common day, but also that our home is with infinitude and only there; that our dignity originates and is maintained by an interchange of action from within and from without, but also that it is from within ourselves that we must give or else we never can receive; that his calling with Coleridge is to be a prophet of Nature, but also that his high argument is how much more beautiful than the earth on which he dwells is the mind of Man.

These two difficulties are obvious – they will strike any serious reader at once. What makes the third difficulty so troublesome is that it is not obvious enough. It is that much of Wordsworth's meditative verse explores ideas which have become – in part from his influence – such half-accepted commonplaces of nineteenth and twentieth-century western culture that they no longer stand out as needing inspection. Consider by contrast a moment in Milton's *Lycidas*. At its climax the elegy for the drowned Edward King insists that grief must ultimately be assuaged by the assurance that Lycidas,

<blockquote>
is not dead<br>
Sunk though he be beneath the watery floor;<br>
...<br>
but mounted high,<br>
Through the dear might of him that walked the waves.
</blockquote>

These lines are either understood or they are not. A note that 'him that walked the waves' refers to Jesus Christ will be of no help to a reader who has no idea about Christian doctrine. In what way does Christ's power 'raise' King? Unless we *know* or *learn* the answer, the turn of the poem's argument will be baffling. In other words, it is obvious that here is a mystery which must be attended to. Many passages of Wordsworth's poetry, on the other hand, which ought similarly to signal the need for close attention, don't any longer. Whereas what was once the intellectual core of western culture – specific Christian doctrine – has been marginalized to the point where it is all but invisible, Wordsworth's ideas about 'Nature, Man, and Society' occupy the ground of what is now matter of everyday discussion and debate. They are part of the cultural furniture of our lives. In one form they survive in the ideals of the emerging ecological movement, but at the other extreme they underpin copy from advertising agencies and the pitch of tour operators who specialize in transporting clients to 'unspoilt Nature'. In short, the third difficulty about Wordsworth's philosophical verse about the relation between human beings and the natural world is that its drift is now too familiar to shock and challenge readers into the kind of alertness which poetry demands.

How then might the student best approach Wordsworth's philosophical poetry? Not, I suggest, *at first* through scholarly investigations into his intellectual indebtednesses. In 1881 J. H. Shorthouse lectured members of the Wordsworth Society on 'The Platonism of Wordsworth' and he was harbinger of many others who have sought to establish the poet's philosophical affiliations: for example, Arthur Beatty, *Wordsworth's Doctrine and Art in their Historical Relations* (1922), Newton P. Stallknecht, *Strange Seas of Thought: Studies in William Wordsworth's Philosophy of Man and Nature* (1945), John A. Hodgson, *Wordsworth's Philosophical Poetry 1797–1814* (1980), Keith G. Thomas, *Wordsworth and Philosophy: Empiricism and Transcendentalism in the Poetry* (1989), Melvin Rader, *Wordsworth: A Philosophical Approach* (1967). Books of this kind tend to over-emphasize the degree of Wordsworth's indebtedness to a particular figure or school of thought, but they mostly contain much fascinating historical material, which illuminates the verse by placing words such as 'impressions' and 'plastic', and allied concepts, within the philosophical lexicon available to the poet. To follow up all these leads, however, in a study such as Rader's (which remains the best starting-point) serves primarily to establish that Wordsworth was not a zany; that his thought was within the expected parameters of an intelligent, Cambridge-educated, and enquiring man of his time. And the downside to this historical approach (again I stress *at first*) is that tracing Wordsworth's use of a word or concept back to Hartley, or Locke, or Spinoza, or Boehme, or the Cambridge Platonists (which any advanced student is going eventually to enjoy doing), encourages a way of looking through the verse to something beyond, rather than at it.

As verse, what are the most striking characteristics of this body of writing? When Arnold notoriously pronounced that Wordsworth had no style, his verbal flourish was meant to reinforce an argument about the simplicity of the poetry being like the grand simplicities of Nature, but it licensed the idea that Wordsworth's poetic technique does not repay close attention as Keats's, for example, clearly does. Disputing Arnold, a number of excellent critics have highlighted the unobtrusive but highly effective function of certain elements in Wordsworth's verse. In his classic essay already mentioned William Empson demonstrated Wordsworth's subtlety in exploitation of the potential of one word. Donald Davie has emphasized the distinctiveness of the syntax of the *Prelude*'s blank verse and in a much-admired essay Christopher Ricks has examined Wordsworth's sense of the dynamics of balance and rhythm in verse lines. More recently Susan Wolfson has initiated an overdue attempt to redirect critical attention to the specifics of Wordsworth's metrics and language use.[13]

The word-limit on this chapter leaves too little space for mention of other aspects of poetic craft which make Wordsworth's poetry at its strongest so alive. So I want to emphasize what continues to strike me as as the dominant characteristic of Wordsworth's philosophic verse overall, its signature. It is that the poetry shifts continually on the axis between the exultantly affirmative and the hesitantly exploratory. Keats's remark that Wordsworth's was the 'egotistical sublime' (letter 27 October 1818) and Hazlitt's, that Wordsworth seems to exist 'as if there were nothing but himself and the universe',[14] both profound comments, acknowledge the poet's self-confidence, but the poetry also registers other tones. In the drafting touched on earlier, uncertainty, equivocation, opacity even, are present in varying degrees, as might be expected, for these drafts are as near as one gets in Wordsworth's manuscripts to sensing poetry as what Byron termed it – 'lava of the imagination' (letter 29 November 1813). The poet's thought is visibly taking shape under pressure. The pressure is the resistance of language itself:

> nor had my voice
> Been silent often times had I burst forth
> In verse which with a strong and random light
> Touching an object in its prominent parts
> Created a memorial which to me
> Was all sufficient and to my own mind
> Recalling the whole picture, seemed to speak
> An universal language: Scattering thus
> In passion many a desultory sound,
> I deemed that I had adequately cloathed
> Meanings at which I hardly hinted[, ] thoughts
> And forms of which I scarcely had produced
> A monument and arbitrary sign.
>
> (*The Prelude, 1798–1799*, ed. Parrish,
> p. 163)

As Kenneth Johnston has recently pointed out, however, the exploratory–affirmative tension is evident not just in drafting but in finished and highly wrought verse, such as that of 'Tintern Abbey', whose triumph, he suggests, is its 'awareness of its own weakness and proximity to failure'. Though the poem 'is usually read as a deeply affirmative statement of secular or existential faith, it achieves its affirmation', Johnston declares, 'in ways that are shot through with signs of their own deconstruction'.[15] The observation could be extended to include, for example, the comparably 'deeply affirmative' climax to the two-part *Prelude*, which, even as it unfolds to a majestic hymn of gratitude and indebtedness, insists, with a sort of dogged honesty, that viewed sceptically Wordsworth's experiences might be susceptible to various interpretations (II 426–96). It may be, says the poet, that my sense of life in Nature was entirely self-created, but it may be, on the contrary, that I was being granted a glimpse of divine truth 'in revelation'. Either way, 'I at this time / Saw blessings spread around me like a sea.' A crucial philosophical distinction is paraded, as if to demonstrate the poet's intellectual *bona fides*, before being swept aside with an assertion of what he *knows* for certain:

> I was only then
> Contented when with bliss ineffable
> I felt the sentiment of being spread
> O'er all that moves, and all that seemeth still,
> O'er all that, lost beyond the reach of thought
> And human knowledge, to the human eye
> Invisible, yet liveth to the heart,
> O'er all that leaps, and runs, and shouts, and sings
> Or beats the gladsome air, o'er all that glides
> Beneath the wave, yea, in the wave itself
> And mighty depth of waters: wonder not
> If such my transports were, for in all things
> I saw one life and felt that it was joy.

'Saw', 'felt', 'transports' – these are the key words. The immediate sensation of the 'most despotic of the senses' (*Prelude* XI 173) is diffused into feeling, conviction, and an overflowing sense of joy, 'transports'. Yet within a few lines Wordsworth concedes that this 'might be error, and another faith / Find easier access to the pious mind', only to use the concession as introduction to a still more vehement affirmation that everything that is best in his nature, everything that has supported him through an iron time, all his gifts, in short, are Nature's:

> Thou hast fed
> My lofty speculations, and in thee
> For this uneasy heart of ours, I find
> A never-failing principle of joy
> And purest passion.

Despite all the exploratory gestures, the rhetorical hesitancies of 'yet', 'but', 'if' and so on, the affirmatory note is clearly the dominant and its best known and most easily memorable formulations have become the identifiers of Wordsworthian faith: 'I saw one life, and felt that it was joy', 'A never-failing principle of joy / And purest passion', 'Nature never did betray / The heart that loved her'. There is another element to the affirmation, however, quite as important as Wordsworth's ability to recall the profoundest moments of his experience or his ability to place them within philosophical discourse. It is that he is doing both of these things *in poetry*.

This obvious point is one that is often overlooked in discussions of Wordsworth's discovery of his vocation. In the 'Prospectus' to *The Recluse*, in *Home at Grasmere*, in the 'Preamble' to *The Prelude*, Wordsworth reveals that he is a man who bears what is both a burden and a mark of divine election, as when in *Home at Grasmere* 897–902, he declares,

> Possessions have I wholly, solely, mine,
> Something within, which yet is shared by none,
> Not even the nearest to me and most dear,
> Something which power and effort may impart.
> I would impart it; I would spread it wide,
> Immortal in the world which is to come.

What this 'something' consists of is an important question. But equally so is the question, 'Why impart it in a difficult, minority art form, Poetry?'

The answer is that by the summer of 1798 Wordsworth had come to entertain a sublime vision of Poetry which was to underpin the whole of his life's effort, to affect Keats and Shelley deeply, and to help shape the history of poetry and the criticism of it ever since. It was a vision of Poetry as both a species of knowledge *and* a vehicle for knowledge of the profoundest kind, which in its operation brings into unity mind and heart. 'Aristotle . . . hath said, that Poetry is the most philosophic of all writing: it is so', Wordsworth averred in the 1802 additions to the Preface to *Lyrical Ballads* and much of this manifesto is given over to making good such an inordinate claim by indicating the scope of poetry's engagement with human life. It is central because it deals with central things, the great, elemental passions of our existence. But it is equally important for Wordsworth to stress, immediately following the words just quoted, that Poetry's especial claim is that, to put it crudely, it works. This most philosophic of all writing carries Truth 'alive into the heart by passion'. A year or two earlier Wordsworth, who by his own account in *The Prelude* had once devoured books and pamphlets on topics such as political justice, rounded on the author of one of the most famous of them all, William Godwin, and others like him, declaring their work 'impotent [to] all their intended good purposes'. All attempts 'formally & systematically [to] lay down rules for the actions of Man' are misguided, because they cannot reach the human heart: 'I know of no book or system of moral philosophy written with sufficient power to melt into our affection[?s], to incorporate itself with the blood & vital juices of our minds' (*Prose* I 103).

Wordsworth and Coleridge jointly hammered out the ideas which appeared in the Preface to *Lyrical Ballads* 1800 and 1802 and their later discovery of how widely they differed about *The Excursion* makes it all the more poignant that it should be Coleridge's formulations about philosophical poetry which are the really memorable ones and deservedly well known. As in every aspect of his thought, Coleridge sought to unify and his quest inevitably determined his vision of the ideal poet: 'a great Poet must be, implicité if not explicité, a profound Metaphysician. He may not have it in logical coherence, in his Brain & Tongue; but he must have it by *Tact* / for all sounds, & forms of human nature he must have the *ear* of wild Arab listening in the silent Desart, the eye of a North American Indian tracing the footsteps of an Enemy upon the Leaves that strew the Forest –; the *Touch* of a Blind Man feeling the face of a darling Child' (letter 13 July 1802).

Coleridge had at one time believed that he was such a poet: 'I feel strongly, and I think strongly; but I seldom feel without thinking, or think without feeling. Hence tho' my poetry has in general a *hue* of tenderness, or Passion over it, yet it seldom exhibits unmixed & simple tenderness or Passion. My philosophical opinions are blended with, or deduced from, my feelings: & this, I think, peculiarizes my style of Writing' (letter 17 December 1796). Once convinced that it was Wordsworth who possessed the powers exactly suited to what the age (and Poetry) most needed, Coleridge transferred to him all claim to the ambition he had himself cherished to effect 'a compleat and constant synthesis of Thought & Feeling' (letter 15 January 1804). Addressing Wordsworth in a letter of [23 July 1803], Coleridge reported that he had told Sir George and Lady Beaumont exactly what to believe: 'that you were a great Poet by inspirations, & in the Moments of revelation, but that you were a thinking feeling Philosopher habitually – that your Poetry was your Philosophy under the action of strong winds of Feeling – a sea rolling high'.

However, though Coleridge's definitions of the capacity of Poetry may be the more memorable, they are only marginally more so than Wordsworth's in the Preface to *Lyrical Ballads*, and it is important to recognize that Wordsworth's sense of Poetry was no less exalted than Coleridge's and that his personal ambition was commensurate. It is Wordsworth who confesses in *The Prelude* (XII 307–12) to an early hope,

> That unto me had also been vouchsafed
> An influx, that in some sort I possessed
> A privilege, and that a work of mine,
> Proceeding from the depth of untaught things,
> Enduring and creative, might become
> A power like one of Nature's.

Annotating his copies of *The Excursion* and Wordsworth's 1815 two-volume collection Blake furiously registered his disagreement with what Wordsworth was saying about the 'fitting' of the Mind and Nature, about Memory and Imagination, and about the influence of natural objects in fostering Imagination. His anger at some lines was so hot that it brought on a bowel complaint he feared would kill him. Wordsworth might have been shocked at Blake's repudiation of his ideas, but he would, I think, have approved the nature of the response in itself, becaue it demonstrated just how seriously Blake was reading his poetry. This observation may serve to introduce the coda to this essay. I stated earlier that three difficulties face us in Wordsworth's philosophic verse. There is, I believe, a fourth, but it is less a difficulty than one of those potential embarrassments which are handled by not being talked about. It is that much of Wordsworth's poetry requires you to ask whether or not it is true.

For all that Wordsworth struck Carlyle as 'essentially a cold, hard, silent, practical man, who, if he had not fallen into poetry, would have done effectual work of some sort in the world',[16] he was not literal-minded and on occasion defended his work, against literal-minded Christians especially, by stressing the licence of Poetry's domain. In 1815, for example, he insisted that a passage in *The Excursion* of seemingly straight Spinoza must be read with a sense of its '*dramatic* propriety' (letter (January 1815)). The 1843 Fenwick note to the *Ode: Intimations* explains that the notion of preexistence appears in the poem not in order to promote it as a doctrine, but because Wordsworth felt that its long acceptance in various cultures authorized him 'to make for my purpose the best use of it I could as a Poet'.[17] Most of Wordsworth's poetry, however, is not fenced round by such protestations. It does not invite us to consider the nature of the truth claims made by Poetry as the Supreme Fiction: it asks us to consider its claim to truth.

Across his creative lifetime Wordsworth returned repeatedly to meditations on such topics as the relation of human beings to their world, the formation of moral development, and the core values which give life its worth. Of course the emphasis and tone of the poetry changes, but there is much continuity between early and late. In 1798 in 'Not useless do I deem' Wordsworth was exploring convictions about the moral value of looking 'with feelings of fraternal love / Upon those unassuming things that hold / A silent station in this beauteous world' (*Prelude* XII 50–2). Six years later he was drafting over two hundred lines about the foundations of moral growth, beginning, 'We live by admiration and by love, / And even as these are well and wisely fixed, / In dignity of being we ascend' (see *The Thirteen-Book Prelude*, ed. Mark L. Reed, vol. II, 378–88). Nearly forty years later he composed this beautiful lyric:

Glad sight wherever new with old
Is joined through some dear homeborn tie;
The life of all that we behold
Depends upon that mystery.
Vain is the glory of the sky,
The beauty vain of field and grove,
Unless, while with admiring eye
We gaze, we also learn to love.

This is a poetry of conviction and what needs to be emphasized about it is that Wordsworth was invariably direct about his stance towards his readers. His declaration to Sir George Beaumont that he wished 'to be considered as a Teacher, or as nothing' (letter (February 1808)) is much quoted, as is the claim he made to Lady Beaumont that there is 'scarcely one of my Poems which does not aim to direct the attention to some moral sentiment, or to some general principle, or law of thought, or of our intellectual constitution' (21 May 1807). But Wordsworth did not reserve such comments only for private letters. He alerted his readers to his demands upon them in 1802, in the Preface to *Lyrical Ballads*, and what he maintained then was his blazon for the rest of his life:

> And if, in what I am about to say, it shall appear to some that my labour is unnecessary, and that I am like a man fighting a battle without enemies, I would remind such persons that, whatever may be the language outwardly holden by men, a practical faith in the opinions which I am wishing to establish is almost unknown.

Such a 'palpable design', as Keats termed it, has always divided readers. Early on, when Wordsworth was failing to make any impact at all nationally, his reputation was fostered by a coterie of devotees, who were jibed at as 'disciples' or 'worshippers'. Later they were referred to more respectfully as 'Wordsworthians', members of a growing sect, and until very recently the term was still in use. Fine scholars such as Ernest de Selincourt, Helen Darbishire, Mary Moorman, Basil Willey, and many others counted themselves as Wordsworthians in a line stretching back to the poet's most ardent nineteenth-century scholar-proselytizers, William Knight, Edward Dowden, Stopford Brooke. Today, in academic circles, the term means only, 'someone who works on Wordsworth'.

This essay is not an attempt to revive its older meaning, but it is worth dwelling briefly on what a strange but very instructive usage it was, for to lose entirely the fuller connotation of the term is to diminish what is absolutely central to Wordsworth's work. Has any other poet's name been used in this way, to denote both the characteristics of the poetry ('what a

Wordsworthian use of the preposition!') and the characteristics of its readers ('I am a Wordsworthian' – Matthew Arnold)? To describe oneself in the 1870s, say, as a Keatsian would imply that one was steeped in his poetry, that one revelled in his imagination, but not that one necessarily shared his views about Beauty, Truth, Christianity and the Pagan World. When Gerard Manley Hopkins explained in a wonderfully inventive letter to Alexander Baillie (10–11 September 1864) why he has 'begun to *doubt* Tennyson', his trouble of mind concerns the signs that the Poet Laureate is becoming, paradoxically, 'what we used to call Tennysonian' and has nothing to do with losing faith in a Tennysonian creed. With Wordsworth it is different. His poetry asks us to become Wordsworthians, and that means not that we are required to 'believe' this poet's philosophical utterances, but, at the very least, that we acknowledge that his poetry is the way it is because he wants us to.

## NOTES

1 For references and a fuller account see my *Wordsworth and the Victorians* (Oxford: Clarendon Press, 1988), p. 129.

2 Full information and a reading text are presented in *Lyrical Ballads and Other Poems*, ed. Butler and Green, pp. 309–10.

3 Wallace Stevens, 'A Collect of Philosophy', *Opus Posthumous*, ed. Samuel French Morse (London, 1959), p. 187.

4 Mary Jacobus, *Tradition and Experiment in Wordsworth's Lyrical Ballads 1798* (Oxford, 1976) remains the best starting-point for work on Wordsworth's relation to eighteenth-century poets.

5 Samuel Taylor Coleridge, *Table Talk*, ed. Carl Woodring, 2 vols. (Princeton: Princeton University Press, 1990), I, p. 307. Entry for 21 July 1832. Recalling the 'plan' of *The Recluse* even after such a long time Coleridge strikingly echoes his letter of 30 May 1815.

6 It is one more of the sad ironies of the *Recluse* project that shortly after he had unwittingly doomed it, Coleridge made public in chapter 22 of *Biographia Literaria* (1817) his continuing faith in what Wordsworth *might* do: 'What Mr Wordsworth *will* produce, it is not for me to prophesy: but I could pronounce with the liveliest convictions what he is capable of producing. It is the FIRST GENUINE PHILOSOPHIC POEM.'

7 Letter [*c.* 27 April 1835]. The quoted line is from Wordsworth's own poem, 'The Old Cumberland Beggar'.

8 Leslie Stephen, 'Wordsworth's Ethics', *Cornhill Magazine* 34 (1876), 206–26; reprinted *Hours in a Library. Third Series* (London, 1879).

9 Matthew Arnold, 'Wordsworth', *Macmillan's Magazine*, 40 (July 1879), 193–204; reprinted as the introduction to Arnold's *Poems of Wordsworth* (1879).

10 Matthew Arnold, *Essays Religious and Mixed*, ed. R. H. Super (1972), p. 250.

11 Gerard Manley Hopkins to Everard Hopkins, 5/8 November 1885. *Gerard Manley Hopkins: Selected Prose*, ed. Gerald Roberts (Oxford: Oxford University Press, 1980), p. 137.

12 William Empson's classic essay 'Sense in *The Prelude*' in his *The Structure of Complex Words* (1951) remains essential reading.

13 Donald Davie, *Articulate Energy: An Inquiry into the Syntax of English Poetry* (1955); Christopher Ricks, *The Force of Poetry* (1987); Susan J. Wolfson, *Formal Charges: The Shaping of Poetry in British Romanticism* (1997). For a good discussion of poetic language see also Michael Baron, *Language and Relationship in Wordsworth's Writing* (1995), esp. pp. 119–25.

14 William Hazlitt, 'Character of Mr Wordsworth's New Poem, The Excursion', *Examiner*, 21 August 1814. *The Complete Works*, ed. P. P. Howe, 21 vols. (1930–4), XIX, p. 11.

15 Kenneth R. Johnston, *The Hidden Wordsworth: Poet. Lover. Rebel. Spy* (1998), p. 595.

16 Sir Charles Gavan Duffy, *Conversations with Carlyle* (1892), p. 55.

17 *The Fenwick Notes of William Wordsworth*, ed. Jared Curtis (1993), pp. 61–2.

# 10

SEAMUS PERRY

# Wordsworth and Coleridge

So many of Coleridge's most fundamental poetic convictions converge on the figure of Wordsworth that, you feel, had he not existed, Coleridge would have had to invent him – which, in a manner of speaking, is what he did. Coleridge's Wordsworth – the great philosophical poet, divinely endowed with 'THE VISION AND THE FACULTY DIVINE' (*The Excursion* I 79, as quoted by Coleridge, *BL* ii 60), sublimely solitary inhabitant of '[t]he dread Watch-Tower of man's absolute Self' (*To William Wordsworth*) – is one of the great creations of the age, one which affected the way Wordsworth's contemporaries perceived him, and continues to influence modern criticism. More importantly for us here, this idea of the poet decisively shaped Wordsworth's conception of himself too: it confirmed in him a colossal awareness of poetic vocation, and established in his mind the shape of that career which would testify to the vocation's successful fulfilment. But Wordsworth, and this Coleridgean figure of Wordsworth, are not a perfect fit; and the visionary ideal to which both men subscribed became increasingly the standard by which they could assess Wordsworth's failure, not his triumph. This sense of a discrepancy between the poet and Coleridge's invention of the poet was personally tragic, instilling in Wordsworth a conviction that, despite some of the language's greatest verse, his poetic life had somehow failed. At the same time, paradoxically, the sense of discrepancy proved thoroughly enabling: Wordsworth absorbed the gap between vocation and achievement and made of it some of his very greatest and most characteristic poetry – a poetry of embarrassed expectations which, if not precisely Coleridgean in its triumphs, still could hardly have achieved the kinds of triumph it did without a Coleridgean calling to frustrate. But then, to complicate the picture a little more, speaking of 'a Coleridgean calling' may imply too single-minded a conception of the poetic good life. For Wordsworth doesn't turn away from Coleridge's visionary portrait of genius into a kind of imagination that is uniquely his own: on the contrary, the alternative style of genius he then becomes is one that Coleridge himself enthusiastically celebrated from time to time, and announced excitedly as an eminent Wordsworthian virtue. So, the divisive internal life of Wordsworth's imagination is not only a personal response to Coleridge's ideas of poethood, but, in a way, the fullest enactment of them, in all their fertile contrariness. After an intense, but relatively brief, period of collaboration, each poet persisted in the consciousness of the other as a reminder of promises, a warning example, an ideal to emulate – no wonder, then, Wordsworth stood at the centre of Coleridge's greatest single piece of criticism (*Biographia Literaria*), or that Coleridge was the addressee of Wordsworth's greatest poem (*The Prelude*): for if Wordsworth's career and ambition as a poet are simply unthinkable without Coleridge, then Coleridge's thinking about literature and the imagination is similarly inconceivable without the provocative example of Wordsworth's genius.

At their first acquaintance, however, in Bristol in September 1795, they met not as poet and critic, nor even as two poets exactly, but rather as two friends of liberty, caught up in the continuing ideological excitement that followed the revolution in France. Coleridge was prominent on the radical scene, delivering lectures that propounded his own highly personal mixture of Unitarianism and political activism. Wordsworth in 1795 was a member of Godwin's circle; and *Adventures on Salisbury Plain*, which he worked on toward the end of the year, reproduced Godwin's line on the evils of social inequity: it was a Godwinian Wordsworth who first met Coleridge. When, however, in the Spring of 1796, Wordsworth read *Political Justice* in its recent second edition, he was profoundly disappointed: in letters, he criticised the 'barbarous' prose style (21 March 1796), but his repugnance went much deeper, for Godwin's confidence seemed suddenly specious, and its consequences pernicious. Wordsworth seems to have suffered some kind of mental crisis, later described in *The Prelude* (x 888–904), and implicitly registered at the time in *The Borderers*, an impracticable tragedy which he began in the Autumn. In the 1805 *Prelude* Wordsworth casts Coleridge as a personal saviour whose intervention corrected this post-revolutionary despair: 'Ah, then it was / That thou, most precious friend, about this time / First known to me, didst lend a living help / To regulate my soul' (x 904–7). But 'about this time' is tellingly vague, for Wordsworth is rejigging the chronology: the Godwinian crisis occurred in the spring of 1796, some six months or so after the two poets became '[f]irst known', but a year or so before their full intimacy. They had certainly impressed one another at their original meeting, and it seems likely that they met again a few times more, and corresponded afterwards;[1] but that was the limit of their contact, and a scrupulous Wordsworth later cut the lines. Nevertheless, they contain a broad truth: Wordsworth's restoration was largely a matter of him becoming, at least for a time and however equivocally, a Coleridgean.

In the spring of 1797, travelling home from Bristol to Racedown in Dorset, Wordsworth dropped in on Coleridge, now living in bruised retirement in Nether Stowey in Somerset. Wordsworth was still busy with his play just as Coleridge was dallying with one of his own, so they found a new ground for friendship in poetry: they agreed on the shortcomings of Southey as a poet, which must have been cheering for them both, and their talk set Coleridge thinking about epic (see Coleridge's letter of early April 1797; *STCL* i 320). Their conversations ran as well (if the re-appearance of an 'answer to Godwin' in Coleridge's letters is a clue) on the shortcomings of Godwinianism: Coleridge had never sympathized much with its atheism, and his suspicions of its unconsoling rationality would have found confirming testimony in Wordsworth's experience. When, in early June, Coleridge paid a return visit, Wordsworth was occupied with *The Ruined Cottage*, which he read to Coleridge at once; the next day, he read *The Borderers*, and Coleridge responded with what was done of his own tragedy (as Dorothy's letter recorded, June 1797). It was a sensationally successful visit; both Wordsworths were bowled over by their charismatic friend: 'He is a wonderful man', wrote Dorothy. Coleridge was no less ecstatic: 'She is a woman indeed!' he told a friend, and of Wordsworth, 'I feel myself *a little man by his* side'; 'Wordsworth is a great man' (*c.* 3 July, 8 June, and 10 June, 1797; *STCL* i 330; 325; 327). In a few weeks, he had transplanted the Wordsworths to Alfoxden, an ample house at a surprisingly low rent, a short way from his cottage in Stowey.

Coleridge was at first especially impressed by Wordsworth's tragedy, whose young intellectual hero is tricked into murderous complicity by the spurious authority of a Godwinian rhetoric: an allegory of their radical generation, as it must have seemed. The wisdom that would have saved them from this, and which might save them now from despondency, rejected revolutionary rationalism for the kind of epiphanic nature-mysticism that Coleridge had been expounding in lectures and poems. His Unitarianism denied most of the normal Christian dogmas, including the Incarnation: instead of the unique Revelation of God in Christ, it described a perpetual revelation of God in nature. This renders the cosmos, not the atomistic machine envisaged by Newtonian materialism, but rather an immense organic unity, brought to divine oneness by the ubiquitously animating life of God, 'Nature's Essence, Mind, and Energy!' (*Religious Musings*, line 55), the diffuse vitality of 'one Life' (as Coleridge called it in a revision of *The Eolian Harp*), into which the individual lives of creation, including man's, were dissolved. The theology has an inevitable impact on the way you regard sensory experience: it ennobles nature by endowing its objects with a positively religious authority, and makes the whole tactile world immanently symbolical. 'In

Earth or Air the meadow's purple stores, the Moons mild radiance, or the Virgins form Blooming with rosy smiles, we see pourtrayed the bright Impressions of the eternal Mind', as Coleridge put it, a little cloyingly, to his lecture audience in 1795 (*Lectures 1795*, ed. Lewis Patton and Peter Mann, 1971, p. 94). One emotive corollary of a belief in 'the wisdom & goodness of Nature' (10 March 1798; *STCL* i 396) is an enlivened pastoralism: a life led in unspoiled scenery would be necessarily improving, in a way that life amid urban scenes (such as Coleridge had experienced as a child) could never be. The position is strictly illogical: city squalor must be as much a part of the life of God as anything else; but it was under the influence of such intoxicating visions that Coleridge, his brother-in-law Southey, and others, had planned in 1795 to found a commune, 'Pantisocracy', in (allegedly) untouched America.

By 1797, Pantisocracy was long dead; but something of the same Utopian temper now filled the partnership with Wordsworth. They attempted to co-author a ballad, although Wordsworth soon discovered (as he later recalled) that their styles 'would not assimilate', and other attempts at collaboration, including the prose poem 'The Wanderings of Cain', similarly foundered.[2] Coleridge took up the ballad on his own: it became 'The Ancient Mariner' (a first version was complete by November 1797), which revealingly, like much of his other great poetry of the year – 'Kubla Khan' and the first part of 'Christabel' – approached the central theme of natural piety negatively, through powerful but flawed figures (compelling solitaries, like Mortimer at the end of *The Borderers*), mysteriously dead to natural influence, or destructively subversive of its divine unity. More positively, other Coleridge poems from this period, like 'This Lime-Tree Bower My Prison' and 'Frost at Midnight', while couched in an habitual idiom of self-doubt, raised themselves to the momentary heights of a credal confidence that Wordsworth evidently found infectious:

> So my friend
> Struck with deep joy may stand, as I have stood,
> Silent with swimming sense; yea, gazing round
> On the wide landscape, gaze till all doth seem
> Less gross than bodily; and of such hues
> As veil the Almighty Spirit, when yet he makes
> Spirits perceive his presence.

This intoxicating nature-vision, imagined in the solitude of Coleridge's Lime-Tree Bower, silently corrects a Wordsworthian despondency: the misanthropic solitary of 'Lines left upon a Seat in a Yew-Tree', would similarly 'gaze / On the more distant scene', and gaze 'till it became / Far lovelier', but only to intensify his feelings of lofty isolation. Wordsworth's moralizing conclusion criticizes such moping self-absorption and counsels his reader to avoid it; but Coleridge announces grounds for disapproval much more ambitiously metaphysical: 'No sound is dissonant which tells of Life.' As well as this message of universal fraternity, Coleridge's meditative, blank-verse landscape poems (the 'conversation' poems) provided a poetic form, at once naturalistic and visionary, that Wordsworth was quickly to make his own. Set in a natural scene of observed specifics, the conversation poem enacts the process of the mind, prompted by that initial physical reality into an inward exploration of the self and its history; rising to some kind of revelatory climax; and then returning, self-educated and self-confirmed, to the external scene again, a scene of particulars that is now silently but unmistakably informed by a visionary potential which the course of the poem has discovered.

After witnessing Coleridge's extraordinary out-pouring, and himself barely writing for six months, Wordsworth stirred again in February 1798. Wordsworth had found in Coleridge what he hadn't found in Godwin: an emotional repertoire of hope, one which re-established the philosophical respectability of feeling, and a poetic language of optimism, which rehabilitated intimations of the numinous by rooting them in particular experience of the natural world. The new idiom is startlingly registered in the alterations made to *The Ruined Cottage*. The poem Coleridge heard in June 1797 was a story of personal suffering, a study in the psycho-pathology of mental decline played out against a background of engulfing political crisis, which ended with the bleakly epitaphic lines: 'and here she died, / Last human tenant of these ruined walls' (as Coleridge had it copied in a letter of 10 June 1797: *STCL* i 328). The new tenants are animals, and their presence is transgressive and terrible: non-human nature here is *in*human, the intrusive bindweed that strangles the garden, or the shockingly creaturely worm on dead Margaret's cheek. But in the poem's revised Coleridgean ending, written in the spring of 1798, nature assumes a quite different aspect: the invasive speargrass, which the metaphorical life of the original poem identifies as undermining and brutally disruptive, finds itself conjured into an emblem of natural religious feeling, 'an image of tranquillity' to ease from the meditative mind 'what we feel of sorrow and despair / From ruin and from change' (lines 517; 520–1). It is an extraordinary shift into a wholly different kind of world, which the verse scarcely owns up to, and that creates a curiously double-minded poem, the new Wordsworth (as it were) writing alongside the pre-Coleridgean one: such inconsistencies, the result of Wordsworth's instinctively accretive method, characterize a good deal of his intently philosophical verse.

If Wordsworth found in Coleridge a vision and an idiom to exploit, then in Wordsworth, Coleridge found nothing less than 'the best poet of the age' (13 May 1796; *STCL* i 215); and he identified him very quickly. While still at Cambridge he had already spotted Wordsworth's genius in *Descriptive Sketches*, which was certainly astute (*BL* i 77–8); and he had quoted a vivid phrase from *An Evening Walk* in one of his own poems ('Lines written at Shurton Bars'), written about the time of their first meeting in Bristol. Now in Wordsworth's daily company, Coleridge's perpetual tendency to hero-worship found its most irresistible (and unresisting) object; and during the spring, Coleridge's conviction of his friend's immense vocation gathered itself into a plan for a Wordsworthian epic, a life-work which would prove and exemplify that greatness. An enormous philosophical poem in several parts to be entitled *The Recluse*, this Coleridgean commission would establish Wordsworth as successor to Milton – as 'the first & greatest philosophical Poet' (letter, 15 January 1804; *STCL* ii 1034) – in a poem telling, not of man's fall from God, but of God's persistent and informing presence in an unfallen nature, itself always and already paradisal when viewed by a worthy eye ('in the end / All gratulant if rightly understood', as Wordsworth was to put it in *The Prelude*: XIII 384–5). Over a year later, when progress on the great work was already stalled, Coleridge reminded his friend of the historical importance of the poem, at least of that major part of it 'addressed to those, who, in consequence of the complete failure of the French Revolution, have thrown up all hopes of the amelioration of mankind, and are sinking into an almost epicurean selfishness' (*c.* 10 September 1799; *STCL* i 527): *The Recluse*, then, like the failed Pantisocratic scheme, was to 'remove the *Selfish* Principle from ourselves' (13 November 1795; *STCL* i 163).

Coleridge had himself toyed unproductively with the idea of a philosophical epic called *The Brook*, a large-scale conversation poem set to combine meditative reflections and natural description, all organized by the governing trope of a river's course from spring to sea (see *BL* i 196); so, *The Recluse* was in some measure a displacement of Coleridgean ambitions, and Coleridge continued to regard the project with an almost proprietorial interest which inevitably complicated its progress – especially as, while his own philosophical ambitions shifted over the years, he continued to look expectantly for the great epic to capture them in verse. (Coleridge explicitly makes the parallel between his own metaphysical system and the unfinished *Recluse* in his table talk for 21 July 1832: *TT* i 307–9). In the meantime, however, Wordsworth seized eagerly on a philosophical optimism beside which the most vehement apostles of imminent political revolution must have seemed hesitant:

> There is an active principle alive in all things;
> In all things, in all natures, in the flowers
> And in the trees, in every pebbly stone
> That paves the brooks, the stationary rocks,
> The moving waters and the invisible air.
>
> (see *LB* 309–10)

Not the least appeal of such emotive monism was its connective inclusiveness: 'My object is to give pictures of Nature, Man, and Society', Wordsworth wrote, 'Indeed I know not any thing which will not come within the scope of my plan' (6 March 1798). The sense of comprehensiveness was also, in the short term at least, practically enabling: it meant that existing works, however apparently incongruous their meanings, could be conscripted within the emergent masterpiece in good faith (no sound is dissonant which tells of life); and this is what happened to *The Ruined Cottage*, to which Wordsworth now returned, making (as we've seen) alterations to the main narrative, and also adding a lengthy biographical account of the poem's visionary Pedlar, whose instinctive expertise in the One Life empowers him to discern the encompassing natural piety symbolized by the speargrass. This shift of attention – from an epiphanic awareness of natural religion, to the quality of mind necessary to *experience* such epiphanies – is a crucial Wordsworthian variation on Coleridgean doctrine, a subjective turn of the imagination which was to determine the nature of the Wordsworthian epic which, as by default, began to emerge from beneath the shadow of the doomed *Recluse*.

But that puts things too starkly, as discussions of the relationship which speak of its 'conversation' or 'dialogue' often do: for, in fact, this 'Wordsworthian' turn to the self was already anticipated by important elements in Coleridge's thinking. The most obvious implication of the One Life theology was the reduction of the self's independence to merely devoted passivity; but the self's intrinsic interest dies hard in Coleridge (and in the end became his major theme). In a lecture on the slave trade in 1795, for instance, he had spoken eloquently of the God-given imagination; and his conversation poems, in practice, throw quite as much weight on the vividly lived experience of the individual self, moving towards illumination and returning to solitariness, as they do on the blissful dissolution of identity that spiritual success is meant to entail. A second look at the lines from 'This Lime-Tree Bower' that I quoted earlier emphasizes the point: the spiritual climax in that poem (as contrasted with, say, 'Frost at Midnight') involves a *transcending* of nature's sensory specifics, brought about by the quality of the perceiver's 'gaze'. This sense of the mind's elevation above its worldly circumstances features importantly in many of Coleridge's descriptions of the spiritual life – even though the emphasis which such neo-Platonic transcendence throws upon the disembodied self is quite at odds with the ideas of natural 'oneness' that otherwise excited him, in which the self is abnegated for the whole. As we shall presently see, a good deal of Coleridge's most pointed criticism would arise when he saw Wordsworth replicating this formative irresolution of his own, between the rival claims of spirit and nature.

But, in the heady spring of 1798, any sense of undermining intellectual discrepancy was quite subdued, with no thoughts of anything except complete success. As a sign of this long-term confidence, perhaps, short-term energies were largely directed to a different project: a co-authored volume of verse, primarily intended to cash in on the vogue for balladry. Coleridge already had 'The Ancient Mariner'; and now, beginning in March 1798, Wordsworth completed new poems at an extraordinary pace – 'Goody Blake and Harry Gill', 'The Idiot Boy', 'The Thorn', and others – in a way which ominously anticipated the imaginative fertility that would repeatedly arise when *The Recluse* was put to one side. Wordsworth's ballads were written in a colloquial vernacular that was subsequently announced (in the 'Advertisement' to *Lyrical Ballads* (1798)) as the programme for both men, although, actually, it hadn't much in common with the zealously cultivated historicism of Coleridge's pseudo-medieval 'Mariner'. Several of Wordsworth's spring ballads bear obvious Coleridgean credentials of a different kind – rather too obvious, perhaps, when their lyrical statement of doctrine teeters on the merely sing-song: 'One impulse from a vernal wood / May teach you more of man; / Of moral evil and of good, / Than all the sages can' ('The Tables Turned'). But the most powerful of the ballads are much more tangential to the putative *Recluse*-wisdom, and some even covertly parody the symbolical potential which the two poets attributed to natural objects. The narrator of 'The Thorn', for instance, scrutinizes objects with obsessional interest, not to detect God's presence, but to persuade himself of his leering fantasies of infanticide; and in 'The Idiot Boy', Johnny Foy, whose surname might promise a person of natural faith, certainly responds to nature's influences spontaneously enough, but within a story of gabbling comedy that hardly grants him a solemn authority. Many of the most striking of these Wordsworthian ballads are dramatic: the speaker of 'The Thorn' anticipates the poisonous, self-deluding narrators of Browning's monologues; and the lasting effect of such poems is to stress, not a loss of individuality in the common life of the universe, but rather the recalcitrant individuality of the point of view – the ego's insistent creation of its own experience, rising to the extreme cases of monomania and psychosomatic disease. Hazlitt, who encountered the two poets at the peak of their *annus mirabilis*, recalled Coleridge criticising Wordsworth's scepticism about local superstitions;[3]

and a fundamentally 'enlightenment' impulse to psychologize supposedly supernatural experience underlies many of Wordsworth's ballads. 'The Ancient Mariner', while not positively insisting on the objective reality of its supernatural events, nevertheless allows them to exceed the likelihood of a strictly rational explanation; Wordsworth's *Peter Bell*, by contrast, while replaying Coleridge's plot of a crime against nature and subsequent redemption, makes no bones about the self-created character of Peter's salvation. (A more general equivocation over the strict objectivity of religious feeling also crops up in compulsive 'or's of the philosophical verse – 'I saw them feel, / Or linked them to some feeling' (*Prel.1805* III 126–7) – so foreshadowing the fruitful disregard for conceptual exactitude that Coleridge, keen for a vicarious systematic rigour, came to regard as slippery incoherence.) Wordsworth can hardly have been aware of the counter-voice the best of his ballads raised against the prophetic universalism of his planned epic: the sprightly individuality that underwrites the 1798 ballads is doubtless simply evidence of good spirits and ease, Wordsworth's especially (one imagines) after so fraught and unsettled a time. Later critics, however, have seen in the diversity of Wordsworth's voices – the Wordsworth of the 'ordinary language' ballads, and the vatic Wordsworth of the philosophic mind – the symptom of a fundamental and (as far as *The Recluse* was concerned anyway) disabling heterogeneity. (Coleridge certainly came to think so, as we shall see presently.)

Having deposited *Lyrical Ballads* with the publisher, Wordsworth and Dorothy went on to tour the Wye valley, in the course of which he composed 'Lines written a few miles above Tintern Abbey', holding it in his head until they reached Bristol and a pen and paper. It is the high-water mark of Wordsworth's Coleridgean nature-vision, a poem which could never have existed without Coleridge's Unitarian enthusiasm, yet a poem which subtly revises that theological perspective, as Wordsworth's winding verse discovers an alternative poetic mythology: himself. In 'Frost at Midnight', Coleridge had lamented his own city-bound childhood, and wished tenderly for his baby son the rural upbringing appropriate for an apprenticeship in the One Life; in 'Tintern Abbey', Wordsworth claimed such a childhood as his own, reworking the religious language of Coleridgean revelation into a description of psychological experience:

> I have felt
> A presence that disturbs me with the joy
> Of elevated thoughts; a sense sublime
> Of something far more deeply interfused...

'Interfused' is a quasi-technical term from Coleridge's *Religious Musings* (line 423), where it appears in a passage describing God's presence in the objects of nature; Wordsworth gratefully accepts the rhetoric, but uses it as a metaphor to describe an internal 'sense', and replaces the doctrinal assertiveness of Coleridge's God ("'tis *God* / Diffused through all, that doth make all one whole': lines 139–40; my italics), with his own brand of the numinously non-specific ('something'), exchanging religious claim for psychological implication. Religion was always the point at which the poets' common cause silently unravelled: they seem to have avoided the subject ('we found our data dissimilar, & never renewed the subject', Coleridge explained stiffly: 18 May 1798; *STCL* i 410). Coleridge had long recognized Wordsworth to be 'at least a *Semi*-atheist' (13 May 1796; *STCL* i 216), and even that was probably hedging: Wordsworth once announced himself free of the need for a redeemer, a thoroughly anti-Coleridgean sentiment;[4] and even when, in later life, Wordsworth embraced a solid form of Anglicanism, Coleridge remained unimpressed by his theological subtlety (8 August 1820; *STCL* v 95).

With *Lyrical Ballads* in press, the group travelled to Germany, where they separated, the Wordsworths settling in the small town of Goslar. Wordsworth's Coleridgean project was very clear, but progress stalled, apparently at once; and instead of *The Recluse* appeared the first uncertain lines of what would later become 'The Poem to Coleridge', or (posthumously) *The Prelude*. The poem seems originally to have been an exercise in confidence-building, a summoning of memories of the rural childhood that Coleridgean theory had recently been insisting made him uniquely suited for the task ahead. The contours of a One Life childhood were well-established: Coleridge had described them, wishfully, in 'Frost at Midnight', even placing little Hartley in a mock-up of Cumbria ('*thou*, my babe! shalt wander like a breeze / By lakes and sandy shores, beneath the crags / Of ancient mountain'). But instead, in the 'spots of time' Wordsworth discovered the formative powers of individualizing pain: childhood trauma, guilt, self-reproach. Like the most striking of his ballads, the 'spots of time' are exemplary episodes of creative misapprehension, though now told in the first person; and their impact does not feel part of nature's providential education, but more like evidence of the singular mind's awful capacity to create its own private realities. The poem discovers alternative sources of power, that is to say: internal ones; and they are associated with suffering and disquiet. A few slightly strained transitional passages acknowledge the discrepancy between Wordsworthian material and Coleridgean occasion, while trying to manage it: introducing, at length, the 'quiet powers, / Retired, and seldom recognized, yet kind', and wholly appropriate to a nurturing natural benevolence, Wordsworth is forced to concede other powers, 'who use, / Yet haply aiming at the self-same end, / Severer interventions,' and to confess himself rather one of *their* school (*Prel.1799* i 74–5; 77–9). So, a counter-voice to Coleridge's optimistic determinism immediately makes itself felt, and that places at the very origins of the poem one of its greatest strengths: an openness to disruptive details that spoil a Coleridgean thesis. (The rural idyll required by the stucture of the argument in *Home at Grasmere* (1800), a fragment of *The Recluse*, is similarly checked by insistent intimations of death and destruction.)

Coleridge belatedly followed the Wordsworths back to England in July 1799; in October he travelled with them in the Lake District, finally initiated into Wordsworthian territory. Learning that he was the dedicatee of *The Recluse*, Coleridge wrote encouragingly (*STCL* i 538); but Wordsworth's energies were devoted to a second edition of *Lyrical Ballads*, which Coleridge saw through the press in late 1800. The addition to the book which would eventually cause the greatest controversy was in prose: the lengthy 'Preface', which Coleridge pressed upon Wordsworth. Coleridge later called it 'half a child of my own Brain', and claimed at the time that it contained 'our joint opinions on poetry' (29 July 1802, *c.* 30 September 1800; *STCL* ii 830; i 627), which there seems no reason to doubt: a conviction of a division in their opinions only arose later. The 'Preface' is not a One Life manifesto, but it does celebrate, like that theology, the criterion of 'naturalness', while distrusting urbanity, mannerism, and artifice. The position is not without its paradoxes; but its emotive bias – toward the pastoral ('[l]ow and rustic life') and truth to nature ('I hope that there is in these Poems little falsehood of description'), against the intrusions of the poetic ego ('[the] incongruity which would shock the intelligent Reader, should the Poet interweave any foreign splendour of his own'), and for a minute attentiveness toward the world ('I have at all times endeavoured to look steadily at my subject') – is eminently clear. The 'Preface' seems to confirm that it was Wordsworth's excellence as a poet of nature (as in *Descriptive Sketches*) that first appealed to Coleridge; his other early enthusiasm for Bowles and Cowper, who offered 'natural thoughts with natural diction' (*BL* i 25), bear out the point; and some of his own early verses similarly seek to shrug off artistic afflatus for a 'natural' idiom (one early poem was subtitled, 'A Poem which affects not to be Poetry').[5]

Besides the new 'Preface', the book was greatly changed, and the alterations all imply Wordsworth's new dominance in their creative partnership: where the first edition had been anonymous, the new title page carried Wordsworth's name alone; a second volume consisted entirely of new poems by Wordsworth (very few showing much trace of the philosophical enthusiasms of 1797–8); 'The Ancient Mariner', first in the 1798 text, was now tucked into a quiet corner just before 'Tintern Abbey' at the end of volume one, in a revised version that muted its medievalisms (Wordsworth thought their prominent eccentricity had damaged sales, as he explained to the publisher: 24 June 1799); and a bizarre note to 'The Ancient Mariner', by Wordsworth, listed its comparative virtues and several faults. Perhaps the most significant element of the 1800 collection from Coleridge's point of view was, to most readers, invisible: 'Christabel', meant for the new volume two, but never completed, was dropped at the last minute – largely, it seems, at the instigation of Wordsworth, who replaced it with 'Michael'. Biographers have often seen the abandonment of 'Christabel' as marking the end of Coleridge the poet, though there actually isn't much sign of humiliation in the contemporary records that survive. Nevertheless, there is no doubt that, for whatever reason, Coleridge began to see his future less in poetry, and more in philosophy, especially when he compared himself with his one-time collaborator: 'He is a great, a true Poet', he wrote in December 1800, 'I am only a kind of Metaphysician' (19 December 1800; *STCL* i 658). In fact, Coleridge continued to write verses all his life; but the task of epic greatness was now, unequivocally, Wordsworth's to fulfil: 'If I die', Coleridge wrote self-dramatizingly, 'and the Booksellers will give you any thing for my Life, be sure to say – "Wordsworth descended on him, like the Γνῶθι σεαυτόν [Know Thyself] from Heaven; by shewing him what true Poetry was, he made him know, that he himself was no Poet"' (25 March 1801; *STCL* ii 714).

Wordsworth's descent from heaven there is comic and rueful, but taps into a perfectly serious aspect of Coleridge's literary theory: that the poet emulates, in a small way, the creative activity of God; and this conception gathered strength as Coleridge's thought began to redirect itself in the first years of the century. As I have already mentioned, one important element in his religious sensibility was always disposed to value the mind or spirit as a sovereign power above the contingencies of the natural world, stressing the transcendence of the divine rather than its immanence; and now this side of his thought came increasingly to overshadow its One Life alternative. Where once the creativity of God was innate in things at large, and the appearance of the individual mind happily subsumed into it, now Coleridge came more and more consistently to attribute that creativity to the independent mind, which did not partake of a generally ubiquitous vitality but projected one onto the world about it. This seems a complete turn-about, as indeed it is; but the two positions have an odd kind of interchangeability: if you detect divinity in everything you see, this may well be because you are truly discerning the divine lurking in everything; but then it may equally be because divinity somehow lurks inherently within the act of you seeing. This second position makes the mind something like God in Genesis, gathering the sensory provisions of nature, and creating imaginative order out of their given incoherence. We can see this doctrine of creation beginning to stir most vividly in Coleridge's own verse in 'Dejection: an Ode', in which our erstwhile One-Lifer hero turns away in despair from the puzzlingly unconsoling beauties of nature, and relocates the Godly power of life instead in the individual self: 'I may not hope from outward forms to win / The passion and the life, whose fountains are within'. Those same 'outward Forms' were what, in the 1799 *Prelude*, Wordsworth had found charged with deity: 'bliss ineffable... of being spread / O'er all that moves, and all that seemeth still' (II 449; 450–1); now the position was quite inverted. Coleridge later reminded himself

> [t]o write to the Recluse that he may insert something concerning *Ego* / its metaphysical Sublimity – & intimate Synthesis with the principle of Co-adunation – without *it* every where all things were a waste – nothing, &c.
>
> (*Nbks* ii, 2057)

'Co-adunation' is the synthesizing activity of the 'I' – the imagination, which was now set to displace nature as the principal subject for Wordsworth's philosophizing verse to celebrate. It is present in every act of perception, but self-consciously manifest in poetry, where it reveals itself as the power that 'diffuses a tone, and spirit of unity, that blends, and (as it were) *fuses*, each into each' (*BL* ii 16). The overriding sense of unity is still the same, but now it is subjectively achieved, its source not an interfused deity but the God-like mind: 'a repetition in the finite mind of the eternal act of creation in the infinite I AM' (*BL* i 304), as Coleridge put it in a famous passage. Such God-like poethood was later exemplified in Coleridge's aesthetics by the idealizing genius of Milton, who 'attracts all forms and things to himself, into the unity of his own IDEAL' (*BL* ii 27–8): Wordsworth's sublime egotism made him Milton's heir apparent.

Wordsworth, as we have seen, was already stirred by the creative mind as a poetic subject, though often in the form of diseased or neurotic misapprehension. Coleridge was evidently haunted by the lines from the dramatic monologue of the 'Mad Mother', whose deranged egocentrism pathetically attributes a benevolent influence to nature which it does not properly have: 'The breeze I see is in the tree! / It comes to cool my babe and me' (*BL* i 150–1). His developing theology of the imagination redeemed such self-centring creativity, instilling the figure of the poet with divine awe; and, as he revised *The Prelude* in the first few years of the century, Wordsworth eagerly seized upon this new source of sublimity, and took its opportunity for religiose self-aggrandisement: 'Of genius, power, / Creation, and divinity itself, / I have been speaking, for my theme has been / What passed within me' (III 171–4). Lines added to the 'spots of time' passage describe how imagination

> chiefly lurks
> Among those passages of life in which
> We have had deepest feeling that the mind
> Is lord and master, and that outward sense
> Is but the obedient servant of her will.
>
> (XI 268–72)

And that seems emphatic enough (although the mind's shifting gender might imply a subconscious uncertainty of purpose). But in the same poem, Wordsworth tells us, 'in all things / I saw one life, and felt that it was joy' (II 429–30) – lines appropriated from his account of the One Life Pedlar. Nearing its end, the poem announces Wordsworth and Coleridge 'Prophets of Nature', yet its very last lines describe 'the mind of man' exalted above nature and 'itself / Of substance and of fabric more divine' (XIII 442; 451–2). This kind of contradictoriness, and the resultant uncertainty about the place of Wordsworth's innate 'plastic power' (II 381), characterizes the poem at large. The ambiguous portrayal of Coleridge in the poem enforces much the same indecision: at times, he is pitied for enduring the 'self-created sustenance of a mind / Debarred from Nature's living images' (VI 312–13), while at other times he is celebrated as 'one / The most intense of Nature's worshippers' (II 476–7). This sort of double-focus, while hardly what Coleridge could have wanted, is what makes the poem so eminently Coleridgean an achievement; and, despite Wordsworth's attempts, in *Home at Grasmere*, to tie together the alternative agencies of mind and nature in the hopeful metaphor of a marriage (lines 1006–14), such inconsistency didn't promise to ease progress. When, sick of opium and unhappiness, Coleridge sailed for Malta in 1804, and seemed likely never to return, Wordsworth wrote frantically asking for notes on *The Recluse* (29 March 1804), eloquently implying the fatal uncertainty of purpose that took over the poem as its Coleridgean milieu shifted.

'The history of Wordsworth's later philosophical poetry', Jonathan Wordsworth justly remarks, 'is one of declining belief in the One Life, bolstered by greater and greater claims made for the Imagination and "the Mind of Man" '.[6] That places it in approximate parallel to Coleridge's own career. Coleridge's One Life inclinations had once worked to ensure 'the World our Home' ('Lines Written in the Album at Elbingerode, in the Hartz Forest', line 39), and Wordsworth instinctively responded to this noble resignation of other-worldliness, celebrating in *The Prelude* 'the very world which is the world / Of all of us, the place in which, in the end, / We find our happiness, or not at all' (X 725–7). But, at the same time, a developing anti-sensuousness in Wordsworth lamented (in the words of a sonnet of 1802–4) that 'The world is too much with us'; and, in the explicitly Platonic 'Ode: Intimations of Immortality', in part an answer to Coleridge's 'Dejection', the world of sensory nature, to which Coleridge had forlornly turned in his poem, is re-figured as a 'prison-house', the shadows of which close remorselessly upon the sadly embodied human. In the poem he wrote after hearing *The Prelude*, Coleridge praised Wordsworth for his depiction of moments when 'Power stream'd from thee, and thy soul received / The light reflected, as a light bestow'd' (lines 19–20) – a triumphant restatement of the idealist position he had announced in 'Dejection', and would later repeat as a philosophical fundamental: 'We behold our own light reflected from the object as light bestowed *by* it' (12 August 1829; *STCL* vi 813).

The sublime self-dependence of Wordsworth's imagination became a recurrent object of Coleridge's wonder ('the dread Watch-Tower of man's absolute Self'), and Wordsworth's own extraordinary emphasis upon the authority of the self (a theme that much modern criticism has also dwelt upon) clearly satisfied much in the new Coleridgean dispensation. But it was also – especially alongside his experience of Wordsworth as a person – the subject of some powerfully mixed feelings. These doubts about '*Self*-ness' (*Nbks* iii 4243) would find their fullest expression in the criticisms of *Biographia Literaria* (published in 1817), an autobiography-cum-philosophical-treatise, on which Coleridge had begun to meditate in 1803 (*Nbks* i 1515), very possibly on the model of *The Prelude*. Coleridge had nursed reservations about the direction Wordsworth's genius was taking as early as 1802, when he wrote a series of letters worrying about the implications of Wordsworth's latest poems: little poems, as Coleridge complained, not the unified magnificence of *The Recluse*. Coleridge's unease about them – they include 'Resolution and Independence', 'To a Daisy', and others – rests on what kind of relationship poetry should maintain with natural truth; and Wordsworth's failings, as Coleridge sees them, are revealingly diverse. On the one hand, Wordsworth is guilty of 'a daring Humbleness of Language & Versification, and a strict adherence to matter of fact, even to prolixity' (29 July 1802; *STCL* ii 830) – the charge of 'prosaisms' that Wordsworth had nervously defended himself against in the 'Preface' to *Lyrical Ballads*, and which would reappear in *Biographia*, illustrated there by passages from Wordsworth like 'I've measured it from side to side; / 'Tis three feet long, and two feet wide' (*BL* ii 79; 50n.). Such poetry, it seems, fulfils a 'natural' aesthetic all too completely, isn't imaginative *enough*: Wordsworth's vehemently naturalistic axioms in the 'Preface' to *Lyrical Ballads* came under sustained attack in *Biographia* (quite disguising the fact that Coleridge himself had once subscribed to them) and the whole project was dismissed as a false start. But that aspect of Wordsworth's genius lingered tenaciously, alongside the more visionary excellences, which is the complaint Coleridge makes about 'Resolution and

Independence', where the prosaic descriptions of the leechgather are juxtaposed unforgivingly with the properly imaginative vision of that magnificent figure as he appears to Wordsworth's 'mind's eye' (*BL* ii 125).

But, on the other hand, several of the small poems Coleridge criticizes in the Summer of 1802 exemplify quite another kind of failing, which he is beginning to diagnose as 'but Fancy, or the aggregating Faculty of the mind' (10 September 1802; *STCL* ii 865), a fault that *Biographia* will call '*mental* bombast', and characterize by its imposition of 'thoughts and images too great for the subject' (*BL* ii 136). Not, that is, keeping one's eye steadily on the subject, but flying off into the mind's private associations: 'A Nun demure of lowly port, / Or sprightly Maiden of Love's Court', for instance, as Wordsworth addressed a daisy. *Resolution and Independence*, too, might as well be read (if we were to take the leechgatherer as its hero, rather than the poet) as exemplifying the mind's excessively appropriative ambitions: Wordsworth conjures the raw material of the actual man into haunting vision, but he politely, yet tenaciously, resists his idealization into Wordsworth's mind – 'He with a smile did then his words repeat' (line 127). The appropriative creativity the leechgatherer there resists amounts to a kind of egotism, and, by 1802, Coleridge had begun to suspect that Wordsworth's egotistic self-reliance might be as much a limitation as an empowering autonomy: 'I trembled, lest a Film should rise, and thicken on his moral Eye' – the magnificence of the sublime ego now tipping into the humane shortcomings of 'self-involution' (14 October 1803; *STCL* ii 1013). Coleridge certainly came to feel that his treatment by Wordsworth exemplified a failure of sympathy or love (although he would have proved a taxing enough friend for anyone); and this personal conviction corresponds to a voice in the literary criticism *opposed* to Wordsworth's otherwise splendid egotism, in which Coleridge repeatedly insists on the objective pleasures of nature all over again, against the broadly idealist temper of his thought. When the limitations of that kind of egotistic creativity are contrasted (in a letter of 1802, as later they are in *Biographia*) with full imagination, 'the *modifying*, and *co-adunating* Faculty', the theological origins of the superior activity become immediately recognizable: 'Nature has her proper interest; & he will know what it is, who believes & feels, that every Thing has a Life of it's own, & that we are all *one Life*' (10 September 1802; *STCL* ii 866; 864).

Coleridge would continue to attribute Wordsworth's genius, at times, to his 'Community with nature...the Eye & Heart intuitive of *all* living yet *One* Life in all', while distrusting his excessive 'self-concentration' (*Nbks* iii 4243) as an obstacle to that imagination's free expression. But then again, at other times, scorning Wordsworth's lingering pantheist regard for nature in her own right ('Nature-worship': 8 August 1820; *STCL* v 95), it is the *inadequacy* of his idealizing imagination that causes the problem: prosaic blots on his poems, at which 'we seem to sink most abruptly, not to say burlesquely, and almost as in a *medly*' (*BL* ii 137). To speak of a '*medly*', or to find an 'incongruity' at the heart of 'Resolution and Independence', is to discern in Wordsworth a deep-seated heterogeneity; but while this is recurrently the subject of attack, it is, at some of the most glowing moments of *Biographia*, reconceived as a triumphant reconcilation of opposites within the one genius. Then we meet a more notional Wordsworth, the very idea of genius, uniting the idealizing power of the sublime ego with the steady eye of a nature poet; and so exemplifying

> the union of deep feeling with profound thought; the fine balance of truth in observing with the imaginative faculty in modifying the objects observed; and above all the original gift of spreading the tone, the *atmosphere*, and with it the depth and height of the ideal world around forms, incidents, and situations, of which, for the common view, custom had bedimmed all the lustre, had dried up the sparkle and the dew drops.
>
> (*BL* i 80)

But such balancing acts are a tall order: you feel the praise occasionally lavished on Wordsworth in *Biographia* was at least as uncomfortable for its subject as the protracted fault-finding. (Wordsworth implies as much; but he took the book enough to heart to revise several of his poems in response to Coleridge's account.)[7] Wordsworth, the ultimate poet, is meant to combine what Coleridge calls the 'two cardinal points of poetry, the power of exciting the sympathy of the reader by a faithful adherence to the truth of nature, and the power of giving the interest of novelty by the modifying colours of imagination' (*BL* ii 5); and *Biographia* sporadically announces his success while, sometimes subtly, sometimes harshly, tracing his inability to do so. The twin 'points of poetry' appear again, in chapter fifteen of *Biographia*, as the division of labour originally intended in *Lyrical Ballads*: Wordsworth's poetry is to reawaken his readers to the 'inexhaustible treasure' of the ordinary things of nature, Coleridge's to treat the imagination's more 'romantic' subjects. Together, this belated scheme of perfect collaboration implies, they would have been capable of reconciling the diverse types of poetry into a single work, at once natural and idealizing – what Wordsworth on his own has subsequently proved sadly unable to pull off. But Coleridge's contributions (he says) came to seem a clog on the enterprise, and so he withdrew (*BL* ii 6; 8). It is almost certainly untrue as an historical account of the book;[8] but it has the profundity of a Coleridgean myth of genius, and its failure, focused upon Wordsworth in a way at once poignant and reproachful.

The differences animating *Biographia* were personal as well as literary, for the poets' intimacy had waned by the time of its writing:[9] the unhappy biographical details lie beyond the scope of this essay, but the change in their personal relationship is worth noticing because it helps explain the occasionally unforgiving sharpness of tone in *Biographia*. The friendship was patched up, but never returned to its original intensity; and mutual disappointment replaced expectation as its main emotion. When *The Excursion*, a book of narrative relief from the philosophical rigours of the unwritten *Recluse*, appeared in 1814, Coleridge wrote at length expressing his immense disappointment that Wordsworth had still not managed to synthesize the recalcitrant ingredients of his philosophy (30 May 1815; *STCL* iv 574–5). Wordsworth, meanwhile, came increasingly to lament Coleridge's abstracted absorption in those same metaphysical concerns: 'He is now too often dreamy', he told Coleridge's nephew, 'he rarely comes into contact with popular feelings & modes of thought' (15 October 1829; *TT* i 546). One has the sad sense of two minds, once deeply congenial, becoming increasingly alien. '[D]id you understand it?' the poet Rogers asked Wordsworth after Coleridge had talked philosophy at them for two hours. ' "Not one syllable of it", was Wordsworth's reply.'[10]

Yet traces of the old admiration persisted, poignantly. In conversation in 1828, Crabb Robinson called Coleridge 'Southey' by mistake: ' "Pray do not make such a blunder again"', Coleridge responded, adding, ' "I should have no objection to your doing it with him." (Pointing to Wordsworth)';[11] and when Coleridge died, prematurely aged in 1834, Wordsworth found himself drawn to the same epithet that Dorothy had used almost forty years before: 'He . . . called him the most *wonderful* man that he had ever known', as though involuntarily returning in memory to the first hopeful days of their partnership.[12] His public monument was some lines elegizing 'the rapt One, of the godlike forehead' in 'Extempore Effusion Upon the Death of James Hogg'. Privately, Wordsworth's sense of continuity with an earlier self, and a sense too perhaps of his indebtedness to Coleridgean gifts, manifested itself in his lasting kindness towards Hartley Coleridge, who dissipated his unmistakeable genius in a wandering, dissolute life amid the Cumbrian mountains, as if in a cruel parody of the idealized Wordsworthian destiny his father had envisaged for him in 'Frost at Midnight'. When Hartley died in 1849, he was buried in the Wordsworth plot in Grasmere churchyard.

## NOTES

1 See Robert Woof, 'Wordsworth and Coleridge: Some Early Matters', in Jonathan Wordsworth (ed.), *Bicentenary Wordsworth Studies* (Ithaca, NY: 1970), pp. 76–91.

2 Quoted in Michael Mason (ed.), *Lyrical Ballads* (London, 1992), p. 367. The failure of 'The Wanderings of Cain' is described in Coleridge's preface of 1828: Beer, p. 172.

3 'My First Acquaintance with Poets', in Howe, P. P. (ed.), *The Complete Works of William Hazlitt* (London, 1930–4), XVII, p. 117.

4 Edith J. Morley (ed.), *Henry Crabb Robinson on Books and their Writers* (3 vols.; London, 1938), I, p. 158.

5 *Complete Poetical Works*, ed. E. H. Coleridge (2 vols.; Oxford, 1912), I, 106n.

6 Jonathan Wordsworth, *The Music of Humanity* (1969), p. 212.

7 'The praise is extravagant and the censure inconsiderate' (Crabb Robinson, I: 213). For Wordsworth's revisions, see Eric C. Walker, '*Biographia Literaria* and Wordsworth's Revisions', *Studies in English Literature*, 28 (1988), 569–88.

8 See Mark L. Reed, 'Wordsworth, Coleridge, and the "Plan" of the *Lyrical Ballads*', *University of Toronto Quarterly*, 34 (1964–5), 238–53.

9 See Stephen Gill, *William Wordsworth: A Life* (Oxford, 1989), pp. 288–9.

10 Richard W. Armour and Raymond F. Howes (eds.), *Coleridge the Talker. A Series of Contemporary Descriptions and Comments* (Ithaca, NY, 1940), p. 336.

11 Crabb Robinson, I, p. 360.

12 Armour and Howes, *Coleridge*, p. 378.

# 11

RALPH PITE

# Wordsworth and the natural world

In 1921, David Nichol Smith described Wordsworth as 'our greatest nature poet' and it is a judgement many would still accept. The poem generally called 'Daffodils' ('I wandered lonely as a cloud'), like Kipling's 'It', is one of the last remaining genuinely popular poems. From it, one gains an image of Wordsworth as someone sustained and cheered by the flowers he finds when walking among the dales and hills. In other words, Wordsworth's natural world seems to be restricted to the country – implicitly denying that urban life is 'natural' – and, secondly, Wordsworth is seen as emotionally nourished by attractive, rural objects. This example of his nature poetry is easily aligned with pastoral and, at the same time, it seems to support a tourist's or holidaymaker's experience of the countryside.

'Nature' in this context means, roughly speaking, the non-urban or rural and this meaning of the word now predominates (partly because of the way in which Wordsworth was understood by his Victorian readers). When celebrating Wordsworth as a nature poet, it is easy to assume he is no more than a spokesperson for rural values or for the National Trust, the society established in the late nineteenth century for the preservation of the finest of the English landscape, amongst the founders of which were many admirers of his poetry. It is easy, in other words, to forget that in Wordsworth's day 'Nature' was a term continuously employed in profound theological, philosophical, and political debates. Nature could be seen as brutal or as a harmonious system reflecting the perfect order of its creator or as the world of the heart not the head – as a realm of intuitions and affections which counterbalanced the overly strict dictates of reason. Each of these readings could be employed in support of different political positions: natural brutality justifies an oppressive tyranny, natural harmony reflects not only God's order but the settled order of the established state, and natural feeling encourages the rebel to believe that his or her impulse of defiance is right. If Wordsworth is 'our greatest nature poet' we need to decide to what extent his writing contributes to these larger questions, inevitably raised by the word.

Our modern assumptions, then, about what nature means may distort our understanding of Wordsworth, turning him into a great *pastoral* poet whose work defends rural life against the invading corruptions of the city. If the natural is considered to be the same as the rural, then nature will, like pastoral, provide a refuge from the afflictions of everyday life and the opportunity to leave behind philosophical uncertainties and political difficulties. The following essay argues that Wordsworth's position is more complex because, for him, nature involves community. In Wordsworth's work 'the natural world' is always social, both in itself and in its relation to man. Consequently, nature does not offer an escape from other people so much as express an alternative mode of relating to them. As he says in *The Excursion*, it is not 'a refuge from distress or pain, / A breathing-time, vacation, or a truce' but, potentially at least, nature will provide 'a life of peace, / Stability without regret or fear'. Moreover, Wordsworth's writings about nature are often strangely jarring. It can be difficult to read them with any confidence that you are reading them correctly. In my view, they employ their oddity to provoke in their readers what Wordsworth sees as nature's social relations. His writings aim to awaken in us what he called, in *Home at Grasmere*, the 'kindred independence' shown and shared by natural things.[1]

The 1798 *Lyrical Ballads* begins with two poems by Coleridge, 'The Rime of the Ancyent Marinere', followed by 'The Foster Mother's Tale'. The first poem by Wordsworth in the collection, and hence the first poem he had published for five years or more, is the clumsily entitled, 'Lines left upon a Seat in a Yew-Tree Which Stands near the Lake of Esthwaite, On a Desolate Part of the Shore, Yet Commanding a Beautiful Prospect'. Several such titles interrupt the collection at regular intervals: 'Lines written at a small distance from my House, and sent by my little Boy to the Person to whom they are addressed', 'Lines written near Richmond, upon the Thames, at Evening'. These titles stand in contrast to the abrupt terseness of 'We are Seven', 'The Thorn', 'The Last of the Flock'. They run like a thread through the book, from Wordsworth's first contribution to his last (which ends the volume): 'Lines Written a Few Miles above Tintern Abbey, on Revisiting the Banks of the Wye during a Tour, July 13, 1798'. Notably, the longer titles Wordsworth gives all refer, with extreme specificity, to time and place, especially place. By emphasizing the circumstances of these poems, Wordsworth makes them appear occasional – prompted by a moment in time and place, and to be understood by keeping that situation in mind. Conversely, his shorter titles lend 'The Thorn', 'The Mad Mother', 'The Idiot Boy' a representative and universal quality. These poems are displaced from the circumstances which, in the case of Wordsworth's

poems called 'Lines', both engender his writing and threaten to limit its applicability.

Wordsworth uses these extremely long and very short titles to draw attention to personhood (the person writing or reading at one, particular moment) and, on the other hand, to its opposite – a world quite different from, indifferent to and unconfined by the character of the poet or speaker. In the various titles, as in the title of the collection, 'lyrical' is paired with and opposed to 'ballad' – the lyrical repose of his 'Lines' with their expansive titles contrasts with the brisk, ballad-like crispness of his other titles. Both in the book and in its separate poems, then, Wordsworth is probing the relation between 'lyrical' and 'ballad', between personal feeling and given world, between, in philosophical terms, subjective and objective.

This is confirmed by the fact that the poems called 'Lines', which seem more subjective, are also those situated most exactly within nature. At the opening of 'Tintern Abbey', for example, Wordsworth attends to the natural world in a verse-paragraph which catalogues 'steep and lofty cliffs', 'plots of cottage-ground', 'woods and copses'. Similarly, in 'Lines left upon a Seat in a Yew-Tree', the reader is urged first of all to stop and take in 'the barren boughs' and 'the curling waves, / That break against the shore'. Personal history and its configuration through poetry seem to arise out of and be dependent upon precise self-location. Yet, at the same time, the natural world apparently declines at moments into mere context. All the objects mentioned at the beginning of 'Tintern Abbey' are being seen 'Once again'. 'Again' is used four times in the first fifteen lines, on each occasion linked to Wordsworth's actions: 'again I hear', 'again / Do I behold', 'I again repose', 'again I see'. Objects do not provoke particular recollections, in a Proustian way; rather, and more introvertedly, Wordsworth's seeing and hearing is suffused with his personal feelings. More important than what he sees is the fact that he is seeing these things again, with an overwhelming sense of relief and release.

Some of Wordsworth's earliest readers objected to this intrusion of private feelings into his landscapes. Francis Jeffrey, who was in his contributions to the *Edinburgh Review* Wordsworth's most influential assailant, contrasts him unfavourably with the poet Crabbe, who 'delights us by the truth, and vivid and picturesque beauty of his representations' while 'Mr Wordsworth and his associates':

> introduce us to beings whose existence was not previously suspected by the acutest observers of nature: and excite an interest for them – where they do excite any interest – more by an eloquent and refined analysis of their own capricious feelings, than by any obvious or intelligible ground of sympathy in their situation.[2]

For Jeffrey, Wordsworth's 1807 poems are unlikely and boring – they excite little interest and their subject-matter is so out-of-the-way as to stretch credibility. Furthermore, he says, Wordsworth tries to make the subjects of his poems interesting by an analysis of his own 'capricious feelings' about them, instead of by providing reasons for his (and his readers') 'sympathy in their situation'. The two projects – of observation and self-analysis – are in clear and unavoidable conflict, as far as Jeffrey is concerned, and this has moral consequences. Better, more acute observation would produce greater sympathy, while Wordsworth's self-concern produces instead 'an eloquent and refined analysis'. All the terms Jeffrey employs here are loaded: Wordsworth appears scientifically heartless ('analysis' instead of 'sympathy'), snobbishly condescending ('refined' instead of 'obvious') and impressive but deceitful ('eloquent', by contrast with 'intelligible'). His self-involvement hampers his perception of the world around and, for Jeffrey, it makes him cruel.

By abandoning Crabbe's 'vivid [...] representations', Wordsworth has replaced truth with the analysis of capricious feelings, an exercise which is pointless because it attempts to find a pattern in the merely transitory moods of a single mind. Wordsworth's cruelty and his self-deception, however, are less important for Jeffrey than his interference with 'picturesque representations' – that is, with a consensual mode of perception and depiction in which, theoretically, the nature of things is made available to all, without fear or favour. By imbuing his landscapes with personal feeling, Wordsworth puts himself first and this suggests (among other things) that it may be difficult to find an 'intelligible ground of sympathy' between his readers and the landscape or between his readers and the 'beings' whose situation he presents. Epistemological confidence and the access which it gives to social sympathies are both overturned by Wordsworth's writing. It is in response to this extremely disturbing challenge that Jeffrey deploys his highly charged vocabulary and accusations of egoism.[3]

'We are Seven' supports the idea that what Jeffrey noticed in Wordsworth's poetry and condemned as vulgar egotism may have been a purposeful disruption of 'picturesque' certainties. The poem stages a confrontation between its presumptuous speaker and the resisting distinctiveness of a little girl's perceptions. Despite the adult's arguments to the contrary, she will not concede that her two dead siblings are no longer part of her family, insisting repeatedly that, nevertheless, 'We are seven'. One can see in this disagreement an educative disruption of the speaker's belief that the world conforms to his idea of it and, equally, that there is one idea of the world which everyone shares. Instead, the little girl's world seems utterly separate from his own and from what he assumes to be everyone else's. The speaker is brought abruptly into contact with something external to himself and his response is obstinately to regard it as nonsensical. There is a comic self-importance to his manner throughout this undignified squabble. There is also an ungenerous disregard for what one might read as the child's griefwork. Wordsworth presents the poem without comment or explication so that his readers cannot help but see the clash between two stoutly defended and incompatible points of view. It is not really a question of who one sides with in this poem. Rather, 'We are Seven' suggests that sympathy for others needs to countenance (more than Jeffrey is willing to do and more than picturesque assumptions allow) the radical differences between people's points of view. To Wordsworth's mind, there is no one landscape which poets observe and represent; there are as many as there are people whose lives are structured and made meaningful through their love for that landscape. Likewise, for Wordsworth, society is 'seven' – seventy times seven, even – and not one. Yet, at the same time, he regards it as meaningful and as vitally important to think in terms of 'We', to remember 'That we have all of us one human heart' ('The Old Cumberland Beggar', line 146).[4]

It has been usual to think of Wordsworth's relation to the natural world either as separate from politics or as a 'displacement' of politics. Both accounts have tended to underestimate the sociality of Wordsworth's natural world. For M. H. Abrams, and Geoffrey Hartman as well, Wordsworth's writing is understood by reference to the starkly dichotomous epistemologies of the Enlightenment. His project is seen as, fundamentally, a reunification of subjective and objective. Wordsworth's fusion of personal feelings and external objects is treated as predominantly perceptual – as the resolution of dilemmas produced by the eighteenth-century scientific world-view (the idea that objects are seen truthfully when seen in terms of their constituent elements and under the light of universal laws.)[5] Subsequently, New Historicist accounts of Romanticism have followed this reading and found its seeds in Wordsworth himself. His works – 'Tintern Abbey' and the 'Ode: Intimations of Immortality', in particular – are regarded as disguising political quietism and defeated radicalism by elevating the speaker above the worldly and political. Wordsworth's spiritualizing of the material world, which Abrams celebrates, is re-read as his pretending to escape the immediate concerns of his historical moment. Wordsworth's set of fraudulent moves in this area conform to and help produce 'The Romantic Ideology' which is perpetuated by the 'romantic' critical readings of his work, such as those by Abrams and Hartman. New Historicism criticizes Wordsworth's treatment of the natural world in terms reminiscent of Jeffrey: in the famous poems, Jerome McGann believes, the 'light and appearances of sense fade into [...] the landscape of Wordsworth's emotional needs'.[6] Jeffrey opposed 'Acutest observers' to 'capricious feelings'; this is repeated in McGann's opposition between 'sense' and 'emotional needs'; in both, it is assumed that the truth lies in externals and that perception is, at best, impersonal; sensation can and should occur without the distorting influence of personal feeling.

Influential readings of Wordsworth, then, either make his treatment of nature central to his achievement of 'the philosophic mind' or they condemn it as a pre-eminent area of deceit. Either way, however, emphasis is laid on Wordsworth's concept of 'Nature' and little attention is paid to the interaction in his work between 'Nature' and 'natural objects'. Secondly, 'Nature' is allegorized: in Abrams, it is synonymous with 'the Other' to the Self; in McGann, 'Nature' means 'the immaterial plane of reality' where particulars are replaced with 'a record of pure consciousness' (McGann, *Romantic Ideology*, p. 90); in other words, it is the falsified version of Wordsworth's experience. There are other consequences too: firstly, Wordsworth is made into a sublime egoist, in the tradition of romantic idealist philosophy; his selfhood is either glorious or reprehensible; it's rarely doubted. *The Prelude* is read as a story of self-realization and his withdrawals from the proclamation of his own centrality are seen as self-protective strategies (by Hartman) or a drift towards sympathy instead of political agitation (by McGann).

Secondly, Wordsworth's relation to particular places is not discussed very much and when discussed, it is treated as merely intriguing. Recently, Jonathan Bate's reading of Wordsworth as an early environmentalist has brought with it a renewed attention to the poetry's embeddedness in identifiable, specific locations. Similarly, Stephen Gill has shown Wordsworth's considerable influence over late nineteenth-century conservationism and the beginnings of the National Trust.[7]

These related emphases are both valuable, not least for suggesting that Wordsworth's sense of nature arises out of and depicts a particular group of places with which he feels himself irremovably bound up. The fact and form of his involvement is as important as the particularity. Wordsworth's explorations of nature are constantly inquiries into social relations. Neither apolitical nor anti-radical, they continue to seek a form of social life which allows personhood and community to coexist.

This, lastly, implies that Wordsworth is more than just an early conservationist. Modern ecology is divided between 'deep' greens and environmentalists; these groups differ radically on the question of humanity's status within the natural world and, therefore, on the proper relations which should exist between the two. 'Deep' ecologists maintain, broadly speaking, that human beings can re-enter a state of union with nature, through what Arne Naess has called 'identification' – 'One experiences oneself to be a genuine part of all life'.[8] Mainstream conservationists, on the other hand, propose only to change man's treatment of nature and not his fundamental relation to it. They argue for better management – for the more enlightened stewardship of an environment in which man is the possessor and from which he remains separate. These disagreements imply that human personhood is either lost in nature (through 'identification') or exists strictly independent of it. Ecological arguments are repeating, in other words, Wordsworth's preoccupation with how people emerge from and are tied into the natural world. Moreover, some of the most insightful ecological writing (such as that by the major American conservationist Aldo Leopold, 1887–1948) reaches towards a more social understanding of humanity's relations with nature – an understanding similar to Wordsworth's.[9]

'Lines left upon a Seat in a Yew-Tree' is very helpful in considering how Wordsworth thinks about the natural world and people's relations to it. The piece describes a 'youth, by genius nurs'd' who 'to the world / Went forth, pure in his heart' and returned, disappointed by the world's neglect of his 'lofty views', by its indifference to his war against 'dissolute tongues [...] jealousy, and hate'. The yew-tree seat is his refuge, where 'he loved to sit', 'And with the food of pride sustained his soul / In solitude'. This life-history presents in miniature that of 'the Solitary' in *The Excursion*; indeed, the poem puts in a nutshell the central issue of books three and four of the longer work: how can one move beyond 'Despondency' to the state where 'Despondency [is] Corrected'? 'Lines left upon a Seat in a Yew-Tree' shows two relations to natural objects which offer comfort to dejection – the first is a glance downwards:

> on these barren rocks, with juniper,
> And heath, and thistle, thinly sprinkled o'er,
> Fixing his downward eye, he many an hour
> A morbid pleasure nourished, tracing here
> An emblem of his own unfruitful life

Wordsworth changed 'downward' to 'downcast' in 1800 as if to stress the connection, which he also makes in several other places, between gazing fixedly on the ground and unhealthy depression. Interestingly, too, Wordsworth seems to be agreeing with the likes of Francis Jeffrey when he says that it is a 'morbid pleasure' which looks for and discovers traces and emblems of oneself in the world around.

The alternative is more elevated, both literally and metaphorically. '[L]ifting up his head,' Wordsworth says, 'he then would gaze / On the more distant scene; how lovely 'tis / Thou seest, and he would gaze till it became /

Far lovelier'. Wordsworth is apparently following a fairly conventional pattern here, which contrasts melancholy self-involvement with 'the labours of benevolence' – the first is confined to narrow views while the second is evoked by a view of distant, beautiful prospects. To Wordsworth's youthful recluse this traditional narrative is ineffective, however; although he accepts that the world seems a kindly place to kindly people he cannot share their experience.

> Nor, that time,
> Would he forget those beings, to whose minds,
> Warm from the labours of benevolence,
> The world, and man himself, appeared a scene
> Of kindred loveliness: then he would sigh
> With mournful joy, to think that others felt
> What he must never feel: and so, lost man!
> On visionary views would fancy feed,
> Till his eye streamed with tears.        (34–42)

Rejection by the world gives rise to a despondent isolation, in which self-certainty comes at the price of losing kinship with others. What Francis Jeffrey condemned as an indulgence is here regarded as a plight: once one begins to trace emblems of oneself in the surrounding world, it becomes almost impossible to recover benevolent feelings of social sympathy. Wordsworth's account of the better state, which his protagonist has lost, is, however, already different from Jeffrey's: the minds of the benevolent perceive a 'scene / Of kindred loveliness' and 'kindred' applies to the relation between mind and world and similarly to that between world and man. Benevolence seems not so much to reveal grounds of sympathy between viewer and object as, instead, to produce the perception that mind and world replicate each other because they are *kin* to one another. The 'individual Mind [...] to the external World / Is Fitted' and 'The external World is fitted to the Mind', Wordsworth wrote around the same time in a section of *Home at Grasmere* which he presented as a Prospectus to *The Recluse* in the preface to *The Excursion* sixteen years later. 'Lines left upon a Seat' shares this conviction and represents it poetically – the lines contrast the stable variety of the section describing benevolence and the tightened alliterativeness, a minute later, of 'visionary views' and 'fancy feed'. The feeling of over-rigid concentration is continued by the assonance of 'feed' and 'streamed' (the second word made more prominent by the rhythm of this line) and when 'feed' nearly repeats 'feel'. The obsessiveness of the hermit-figure's self-involvement is reproduced by the sounds of Wordsworth's language. Furthermore, his final position seems an echo and a worsening of his situation earlier when looking fixedly down. Then the near-rhymes and half-rhymes of 'sand-piper', 'juniper', 'o'er' and 'hour' culminate in the word 'here', as if to raise the suspicion that his gaze downward is becoming a fixation. Both extremes of attention – which are customarily seen sequentially as disease and cure – are shown to lead to the same condition of morbid self-attention, the last more extreme and desolate than the first.[10]

The resolution offered by 'Lines left upon a Seat' is humility, the 'lowliness of heart' which engenders a temperate sense of one's own relative insignificance. Editors have suggested the closing verse-paragraph (lines 44–60) may be influenced by Coleridge and manuscript evidence suggests that the lines were certainly an afterthought.[11] Whatever their origin, they downplay 'kindred loveliness' in favour of submission – a more orthodox Christian view in which the individual is placed within a natural order, which is greater and more valuable than he or she can ever be. However moving and impressive (which I think they are), the lines seem less to resolve the poem than to redirect it.

In *The Excursion*, Wordsworth treats the whole issue once again. In book 4, the Solitary's despondency is 'corrected' by the long speeches of the Wanderer, who argues that 'living things, and things inanimate, / Do speak, at Heaven's command, to eye and ear, / And speak to social reason's inner sense, / With inarticulate language'. The man, he goes on, who communes with nature, who knows and loves its forms and objects:

> needs must feel
> The joy of that pure principle of love
> So deeply, that, unsatisfied with aught
> Less pure and exquisite, he cannot choose
> But seek for objects of a kindred love
> In fellow-natures and a kindred joy.

His discontent and self-involvement no longer need to be condemned or warned against because they disappear: 'he looks round / And seeks for good; and finds the good he seeks: / Until abhorrence and contempt are things / He only knows by name' (*The Excursion*, book 4, lines 1204–7, 1212–17, 1223–6).[12]

The living and the inanimate things of nature all 'speak to social reason's inner sense' because they exhibit sociality themselves, at all levels from the smallest to the largest, from the 'craggy regions' to 'The tiny creatures strong by social league', to 'the mute company of changeful clouds' and as high as 'The mild assemblage of the starry heavens'. Furthermore, these 'Creatures that in communities exist' do so less 'through dependence upon mutual aid / Than by participation in delight'.[13] Avoiding 'dependence' is, curiously, essential to Wordsworth's idea of 'kindred' and hence to his concept of our proper relationship to the natural world. Resisting 'dependence' is motivated in part by his aim of ensuring that nature's laws are authoritative without becoming absolute: the right-thinking and right-feeling person, Wordsworth says, 'needs must feel' and 'cannot choose/But seek'. This sounds dangerously like a determinist point of view in which nature is thought to condition people, programming them with reflex preferences. Wordsworth, however much he wishes to credit nature with an influence over our hearts and minds, dislikes the idea that our responses are automatic. He would not deny that nature has formed him but wants to preserve a full sense of what it is that nature has formed: an independent being who repeats, freely and with delight, the loving behaviour which fashioned his independence originally. Equally, that independent self naturally seeks 'objects of a kindred love/In fellow-natures'; it seeks a community of fellows comparable to the one it finds. Consequently, instead of the ardent, overwrought vision of nature, in 'Lines left upon a Seat in a Yew-Tree', which moves from 'lovely' to 'lovelier', from 'beauty' to something 'still more beauteous' beyond it, Wordsworth now recommends a more prosaic reciprocity: the man properly attuned, the Wanderer says, 'seeks for good; and finds the good he seeks'. This phrasing verges on suggesting the delusional or solipsistic; Wordsworth accepts that danger because anything less risky would diminish a person's equality with what he or she sees and hears.

The account of 'independence' is so precise because it takes part in an effort to redefine the word. In *The Borderers*, his play composed 1796–7, Wordsworth considers intellectual independence as a terrifying and self-destructive claim to pure rationality. His target is the thought of William Godwin (whose influence he had recently thrown off) and more generally the ideas of those who advocated the French Revolution as the triumph of reason. His villain in the play urges obedience to 'the only law that wisdom/Can ever recognize: the immediate law / Flashed from the light of circumstances/Upon an independent intellect.' This law offers freedom from 'the tyranny / Of moralists and saints and lawgivers'. When, in *The Prelude*, Wordsworth returns to the same concerns and quotes these lines from *The Borderers*, he sees the 'independent intellect' as dismissing not only received morality but, in addition, 'with a resolute mastery shaking off / The accidents of nature, time, and place'. So the independence he wants to defend must be prevented from turning back into this Godwinian disregard for precedent and the consequent deracination of self from context – this treatment of circumstances as mere 'accidents' or as only a mirror of the 'immediate law'.[14]

At the same time, Wordsworth is writing in the knowledge that, for some opponents of the revolution, its disastrous consequences proved the absolute and necessary authority of precedent, confirming that the self must acknowledge its dependence on 'nature, time and place'. Burke's *Reflections on the Revolution in France* recommends following 'our nature rather than our speculations, our breasts rather than our inventions, for the great conservatories and magazines of our rights and privileges'. The application of speculative, philosophical ideas to the practical matter of political life has led, Burke believes, to insurrection and carnage. Hence, nature 'rather than' reflection must be our guide – nature which is, Burke says, 'wisdom without reflection' and obliges us to observe 'the great primaeval contract of eternal society [...] which holds all physical and all moral natures, each in their appointed place'.[15] Notoriously, Wordsworth showed increasing admiration for Burke as he grew older. *The Prelude*, however, wrestles with a paradox that Burke would not have recognized: that the reliance on nature which defends us against the inhumanity of untrammelled reason, produces in turn an inhumanity of its own. Subjects who act 'without reflection' may be content and it may even be that nature is guiding them aright, yet they are not practising full humanity. The danger of Godwinian 'independence' provokes an opposite reaction – Burke's advocacy of willing, submissive dependency, with the paternalistic politics that it entails.

If nature can neither be passively relied upon nor safely ignored, its position in relation to us becomes difficult to grasp, particularly when one moves from speaking dogmatically, as in *The Excursion*, towards personal testimony, as in *The Prelude*. Early on in his autobiography, Wordsworth is keen to establish that his response to nature was initially untaught and spontaneous, unprompted by others, by books or by convention. This experience confirms the existence of and helped create the 'independent musings [which] pleased me so / That spells seemed on me when I was alone' (*Prel.1805* iii 231–2). Even London, in some respects threatening to this sense of himself, reveals itself to be 'thronged with impregnations, like those wilds / In which my early feelings had been nursed'. Wordsworth is able to perceive around him in the city things that are 'like the enduring majesty and power / Of independent nature'. Human-kind, the 'individual sights / Of courage, and integrity, and truth' which he comes across, nurse him rather as nature had done before, sustaining his confidence in himself, in his own convictions and in 'the unity of man' (*Prel.1805* viii 791–2, 785–6, 839–40, 827). He finds in the city – at least at times – an equivalent to the balance between kinship and independence which characterizes the natural world and man's relationship to it. For Wordsworth, the brotherhood of man is born out of this perception that others are autonomous and, at the same time, united to oneself.

An autobiographical poem such as *The Prelude* is based, however, on giving oneself disproportionate centrality. Arguably, it is an exercise in vanity.

Wordsworth pursues the project not only to vindicate himself as a poetic authority (his publicly avowed reason for composing the poem). He writes *The Prelude* also to defend egoism, seeing it as a true component of the independence in which full humanity consists. Brotherhood – revolutionary *fraternité* – will decay without our insistence that each person is, from one perspective, a world unto themselves. Without this counterweight, ideas of 'the unity of man' will produce either the Terror's totalitarian devotion to the state or Godwin's unacknowledged will to power over one's fellows or Burke's insistence on natural hierarchy. Consequently, the poem has two apparently conflicting purposes: the first, to elevate Wordsworth into authority over the world of his experience and, the second, to place him amidst it. In Book Eight, for example, he writes that at 'a time of greater dignity' when:

> the pulse of being everywhere was felt,
> When all the several frames of things, like stars
> Through every magnitude distinguishable,
> Were half confounded in each other's blaze,
> One galaxy of life and joy. Then rose
> Man, inwardly contemplated, and present
> In my own being, to a loftier height [...]
> Acknowledging dependency sublime.

In this argument – more like Coleridge's ideas of 'One Life' than the community everywhere present in *The Excursion* – 'Man' becomes pre-eminent, 'first / In capability of feeling what / Was to be felt'. The 1850 version of the poem tones down this portrait: 'In the midst stood Man', still first but nonetheless 'kindred to the worm'. As has been noted, Wordsworth displays here his anxiety about keeping himself within the bounds of Christian orthodoxy. His use of 'kindred', however, also marries with his rewriting of the lines about the stars; instead of being 'half confounded', it is now stated that they 'Shone mutually indebted, or half lost / Each in the other's blaze, a galaxy / Of life and glory' (*Prel.1850* viii 483–5). This revision is clearer than before, less rapturous and more considered in its portrayal of a society based upon reciprocity. Man's being 'kindred' to the worm consequently appears another instance of being 'mutually indebted' so that our 'dependency sublime' upon God stands alongside a humbler involvement with 'the several frames of things'. The 1850 version is more consistent with *The Excursion* but as a result it deflects *The Prelude* from its real aim, not only removing the poem's possible heresy but obscuring its energizing paradox as well. How individuality, seen from the inside, is both all-embracing and confronted by the indisputably separate to which it is also joined – this is, perhaps, the central issue of the poem and the concept of 'mutual indebtedness' cannot do justice to it.

Later poems by Wordsworth continue to engage with the paradoxical relations between consciousness and object, man and nature and do so in ways that still register the paradox. Less abrupt than the clashes between lyric and ballad forms in *Lyrical Ballads* and less grandiloquent than *The Prelude* in addressing the perplexity, his later work (at its best) hints at the irresolvable curiosity of the mind's place in the world.

The tenth sonnet in Part 2 of the *Miscellaneous Sonnets*, for example, first published in 1815, begins, 'Mark the concentred hazels that enclose / Yon old grey Stone, protected from the ray / Of noontide suns'. It ends, 'Solitary nature condescends / To mimic Time's forlorn humanities.'[16] The hazels gather round and enclose the spot, making the stone into 'the pensive likeness' of a grave and themselves into natural mourners. They mimic human sympathy and Wordsworth feels this imitation not as a parody or cruel irony but as a sign of nature's condescension to man. Solitary nature does not suffer itself. It is, however, generous enough to recognize how mankind suffers and to respond with kindness. This is a curious idea and one that Wordsworth slips into the sonnet almost unnoticed. The complication of the relation between nature, time, and humanity (meaning here 'humane behaviour') is presented so rapidly that it sounds like an enigma and, not quite understanding him perhaps, we may pass on to the next poem in the series. Wordsworth's thinking is so strange because it reverses usual expectations. We would not be surprised to be told that churchyards were laid out like a natural feature, in this case like a grove of hazels, but Wordsworth says it is the other way round; that the hazels have grown in imitation of churchyards. They reveal the willingness of nature to go along with his impulses of sympathy.

Wordsworth personifies nature here as a regal figure, unmoved yet sympathetic, who is literally *benevolent* – nature desires our welfare even though our harm would do it no harm. Such regality 'condescends' to our weaknesses, yet also mimics our acts of sympathy. Nature's imitation of the graveyard looks, on the one hand, like a disinterested, supportive gesture and, on the other, like a spontaneous repetition. The sonnet, then, first reverses our expected understanding of the relation between man and nature. It then unbalances the new relation which has been set up. Nature is first our imitator (where usually we are its imitator), then our kindly ruler, and finally our mimic.

Two points arise from the sonnet, I think: firstly, Wordsworth presents human behaviour as appropriate when nature imitates it. Taken literally, this sounds untenable. It is difficult to imagine hazel trees checking out the latest in churchyard design before deciding where to grow. Wordsworth wants, however, to say something of this kind in order to preserve the separateness and the co-existence of 'humanities' and natural things. Human behaviour should not be judged appropriate when it is found in nature, nor should we think that the two spheres are convergent. Rather, the enterprise of 'humanity' continues as best it can, independently, and suddenly finds itself reflected in nature in unexpected ways. These reflections back are not replications of human sympathy but likenesses to it. (One is reminded of the emphasis he lays on 'like' in *The Prelude* book xviii: the city is '*like* those wilds' and '*like* the enduring majesty and power / Of independent nature' [my emphasis].) Similarly, the hazels resemble the owls who hoot when Wordsworth's boy impersonates them.[17]

Secondly, the sonnet is dependent on something counter-intuitive, which if expressed directly would have to sound fanciful to be heard at all. The density and sudden complication of the sonnet's last lines enclose the kernel of the poem as if it needed protection. They preserve an imaginative perception from being exposed as a mere fancy while, at the same time, they leave the attentive reader the chance to understand properly. And, for Wordsworth, this proper understanding is not confined by the normal categories of reason nor is it entirely mystical. The imaginative perception is continuous with the exercise of mind that reading the poem demands. Yet, on the other hand, the sonnet is decorous and standard so that its deep insight may be passed over by those who do not (or would not) understand it.

In Wordsworth's *The River Duddon: A Series of Sonnets* (1820), the speaker is again drawn to the thought that nature actively protects – as the stream descends from bare upland, 'to form a shade / For Thee, green alders have together wound / Their foliage; ashes flung their arms around; / And birch-trees risen in silver colonnade'. In the sequence, individual sonnets present different parts of the landscape, often raising the possibility of an allegorical meaning for them, sometimes making it unmistakable. In this case, the trees are like parents watching over and nurturing the young stream; the course of a life, charted by the stream, has reached childhood and nature's nursing of the human soul is visible in the trees' protective efforts and again, a moment later, in the cottage nearby where a 'mother's eyes / Carelessly watched' her children at play (Sonnet 5). This movement of thought is typical of the sonnets and, as here, the fancifulness of Wordsworth's language draws attention to the mind creating the allegorical sense at the same time as it claims that that sense is genuinely present.

These delicate, modest allegorical suggestions are a mode of kinship and independence between man and nature. Wordsworth's speaker at times yearns after a more intimate communion, asking in 'The Faery Chasm', 'where / Is traceable a vestige of the notes' that were once immediately audible – where, in other words, can one recapture an immediate experience of natural things? 'On, loitering Muse – the swift Stream chides us – on!' the next in the sequence promptly begins (Sonnet 12, 'Hints for the Fancy'). The old relationship cannot be re-entered (except, perhaps, by going on); nature, in the stream's onward flow, proves it is natural to leave childhood behind and enter adulthood, to leave union with nature and enter allegory's kindred independence. The 'River Duddon' sequence, then, follows in thought and idea the pattern of 'Tintern Abbey' or *The Prelude*. In the jolting shifts from one sonnet to the next, however, Wordsworth keeps us alert to the complications of his position: as each sonnet's achieved stability vanishes, sometimes abruptly, Wordsworth creates the sense of kinship being thrown back into independence, so that in the next sonnet it has to be rediscovered again. Likewise, in tracking the course of the river, Wordsworth repeatedly finds calm stretches between a rapid descent earlier and turbulence to come. The sonnets are equivalents to these calms and the transitions of mind are pictured in the structure of the landscape. Moreover, the sonnets were first published in one volume with *A Topographical Description of the Country of the Lakes, in the North of England*, a version of what later became Wordsworth's *Guide Through the District of the Lakes*. They suggest a mode of visiting landscapes which the *Guide* recommends as well: one in which the visitor adopts neither a serenely picturesque attitude towards the objects around nor a position of sublime command over them. Instead, the Lake District offers to engender 'pleased attention'. This formulation parallels 'kindred independence'. Such attention, Wordsworth says in the introductory poem to the River Duddon sequence, promises to 'fill the hollow vale with joy' ('To the Revd Dr Wordsworth'). The 'hollow vale' refers to the Lake District, whose dells and recesses are described in the *Guide* and the sonnets. It refers, at the same time, to human life, the 'vale of tears'. As always in his poetry, the natural world and the person experiencing it are understood as quite separate and as inseparable.

## NOTES

1 Wordsworth, *Poetry and Prose*, with an introduction by David Nichol Smith (Oxford: Clarendon Press, 1921, repr. 1969); *The Excursion*, book 3, lines 383–6; Wordsworth, *Home at Grasmere*, MS B, line 461, *Home at Grasmere: Part First, Book First of 'The Recluse'*, ed. Beth Darlington, The Cornell Wordsworth (Ithaca and London: Cornell University Press, 1977), p. 68.

2 Francis Jeffrey, writing in the *Edinburgh Review*, April 1808; quoted in Geoffrey Hartman, *Wordsworth's Poetry, 1787–1814* (New Haven and London: Yale University Press, 1964), p. 5.

3 Wordsworth's relation to picturesque representations has been discussed frequently, most recently in Tim Fulford, *Landscape, Liberty and Authority: Poetry, Criticism and Politics from Thomson to Wordsworth* (Cambridge: Cambridge University Press, 1996).

4 Wordsworth remarked in a letter (*c.* 27 April 1835) that he regarded this as one of the key lines of his whole life-work. See Stephen Gill, *Wordsworth and the Victorians* (Oxford: Clarendon Press, 1998), p. 121.

5 See Jonathan Bate, *Romantic Ecology: Wordsworth and the Environmental Tradition* (London and New York: Routledge, 1991), pp. 1–11.

6 Jerome McGann, *The Romantic Ideology: A Critical Investigation* (Chicago and London: University of Chicago Press, 1983), p. 87; see also pp. 90–1.

7 Gill, *Wordsworth and the Victorians*, pp. 235–60.

8 Arne Naess, *Ecology, Community and Lifestyle: Outline of an Ecosophy*, translated and revised by David Rothenberg (Cambridge: Cambridge University Press, 1989), p. 174.

9 I discuss Wordsworth's relation to ecology more fully in 'How Green Were the Romantics?', *Studies in Romanticism*, 35: 3 (Fall 1996), 357–73.

10 Margaret in 'The Ruined Cottage' is similar: 'her eyes were downward cast; / And when she at her table gave me food / She did not look at me', MS B, lines 416–18, *RC*, p. 66.

11 *LB*, pp. 341–3, and Jonathan Wordsworth, *The Music of Humanity: A Critical Study of Wordsworth's 'Ruined Cottage'* (London: Thomas Nelson, 1969), pp. 206–7.

12 *The Excursion*, book 4, lines 1207–98 were originally drafted in 1798–9 as part of 'The Ruined Cottage'. See *RC*, pp. 121, 261–71, 372–5.

13 From one verse-paragraph (*The Excursion*, book 4, lines 427–65) which is worth consulting as a whole.

14 Wordsworth, *Borderers*, pp. 210–11; *1805 Prelude*, X, 821–2, 828–9.

15 Edmund Burke, *Reflections on the Revolution in France* (1790), *The Writings and Speeches of Edmund Burke*, gen. ed. Paul Langford, vol. VIII (Oxford: Clarendon Press, 1989), pp. 85, 83, 147.

16 *PW* III 24–5.

17 'There was a Boy, ye knew him well, ye Cliffs / And Islands of Winander!...'. *LB* 139. The Winander boy passage was incorporated in *The Prelude*, 1805, V, 389–422.

# 12

## NICHOLAS ROE

# Politics, history, and Wordsworth's poems

We know more about Wordsworth than before. The Cornell Wordsworth Series and new biographies – Gill, Johnston, Barker, Wu – have enhanced understanding of the poems and the life. And there have been startling discoveries. The National Library of Scotland yielded a manuscript of Wordsworth's *Imitation of Juvenal*, a satire on government and aristocracy dating from 1795 which the poet had determined should be suppressed. The Public Record Office, London, disclosed correspondence between the Home Office and their agent James Walsh who in August 1797 was sent to spy on Coleridge and the Wordsworths at Nether Stowey. Wordsworth's letters to Mary Hutchinson, found in 1977 among scrap paper at Carlisle, offered unprecedented insight into their marriage. So we do know more about Wordsworth, but not all about Wordsworth. Gaps and silences in *The Prelude*, and the conjectured career of the 'hidden Wordsworth', now seem as significant as the documented life. Emile Legouis's pioneering *Early Life of William Wordsworth, 1770–1798*, first published in 1896, announced its source and subject as 'A Study of *The Prelude*'. One hundred years later Kenneth Johnston's *The Hidden Wordsworth* (1998) set out to dispel the 'Wordsworthian cover-up' by revealing how what 'seem to be metaphors' in the poetry 'often turn out to have a literal correspondence to the life'.

Wordsworth invites speculation and provokes questions, in that his innate reserve as a person was deepened by the politically reactionary mood of an age when 'most people who wrote autobiographies drastically played down any involvement they might have had in the Jacobinism of the 1790s'.[1] In his essay 'Wordsworth's Crisis', E. P. Thompson remarked that there was 'something secretive about Wordsworth through much of the 1790s, and secretive in more than the matter of Annette Vallon (which was so successfully hushed up)'.[2] Wordsworth's love affair with Annette Vallon was indirectly noticed in the passage in *The Prelude*, Book IX (published separately as *Vaudracour and Julia* in 1820) and – as Stephen Gill has observed – it was strongly hinted at in Christopher Wordsworth's otherwise discreet *Memoirs of William Wordsworth* published in 1851:

> Wordsworth's condition in France was a very critical one: he was an orphan, young, inexperienced, impetuous, enthusiastic, with no friendly voice to guide him, in a foreign country, and that country in a state of revolution . . . The most licentious theories were propounded; all restraints were broken; libertinism was the law. He was encompassed with strong temptations; and although it is not the design of the present work to chronicle the events of his life except so far as they illustrate his writings, yet I could not pass over this period of it without noticing the dangers which surround those who in an ardent emotion of enthusiasm put themselves in a position of peril without due consideration of the circumstances which ought to regulate their practice.[3]

Given this 'authorized' account of Wordsworth in licentious, libertine France, 'encompassed with strong temptations' and 'dangers', it's all the more surprising that Annette's existence was indeed 'hushed up' until revealed in 1916 (as 'an unfortunate attachment') by the American scholar George McLean Harper.[4] Wordsworth had arrived at Orléans in December 1791, and lodged in 'a very handsome appartment' on Rue Royale belonging to a milliner named Jean-Henri Gellet-Duvivier. In a letter to his brother Richard on the 19th he describes his life in Orléans as 'comfortable', says that he has 'every prospect of liking this place extremely well' and has already noted that 'all the people of any opulen[ce are] aristocrates and all the others democrates'. '[T]wo or three officers of the Cavalry' boarded in the house too, and Wordsworth joined their 'routs' and 'card-tables' at which, he remembered,

> through punctilios of elegance
> And deeper causes, all discourse, alike
> Of good and evil in the time, was shunned
> (*Prel. 1805* IX 119–21)

In this fashionable royalist society Wordsworth met a 'very agreeable' family, most likely Annette's (*WL* i 70). When she returned to her home town Blois further down the Loire valley, Wordsworth followed and settled there for the spring and summer of 1792. In September they returned to Orléans, and Wordsworth went on to Paris where he lingered for two months before heading back across the Channel to England and London. Their daughter Caroline was baptized on 15 December at the cathedral of Sainte Croix, Orléans, with Annette's brother Paul standing as godfather to the child.[5] It's likely that Wordsworth intended to return to France once he had raised money for their support, but the outbreak of war between England and France in February 1793 made the journey hazardous.[6]

Wordsworth's memory in 'Tintern Abbey' of his first visit to the Wye, July 1793, evokes the yearning of 'one / Who sought the thing he loved', and the poem identifies 'the thing loved' as a most fortunate attachment: 'nature then... / To me was all in all' (73, 76). Yet in recalling more fully 'what I was, when first / I came among these hills' (67–8) loving quest is overlaid by a fearful reactive impulse,

> more like a man
> Flying from something that he dreads, than one
> Who sought the thing he loved.        (71–3)

I argue in this essay that Wordsworth's haunted intertwining of 'dread' and 'love' arose from tragic revolutionary events in which the Vallon family and others known to Wordsworth were ensnared. In relating 'dread' in the poetry to the revolution, the essay responds to recent studies which identify from *The Borderers*, 'Tintern Abbey', and *The Prelude* some kind of 'crisis' in Wordsworth during the 1790s. Rather than seeking literal correspondences between poetry and history, I want to suggest how recovery of personal and public contexts for the poetry may refresh readings of otherwise familiar passages. More specifically I want to argue that those contexts allow us to see how Wordsworth's most transcendental claims reflect back upon the life out of which they emerged.

From reading *The Prelude* Book x, the Marxist historian E. P. Thompson detected a 'climactic crisis' in Wordsworth's early life 'giving rise to a flight from its temptations and to a decade of arduous self-reflection' ('Wordsworth's Crisis', 84). He located the crisis in 1795 when Wordsworth was captivated by the philosophic rationalism of William Godwin's *Political Justice*. The violence of the French Terror (1793–4) had shown how revolutionary action betrayed otherwise humane motives; the attraction of *Political Justice* was its argument for social progress – and ultimately human perfectibility – through the power of reason alone. For a time, Wordsworth was won-over by 'the philosophy / That promised to abstract the hopes of man / Out of his feelings' (x 806–8). In London during summer 1795 he sought out William Godwin, and met reformers and radicals such as Thomas Holcroft, novelist and dramatist; William Frend, Fellow of Jesus College, Cambridge, a unitarian and leader of the reformist London Corresponding Society; George Dyer, poet, scholar, and pamphleteer; and John Thelwall, poet, journalist, political lecturer, also a leader of the Corresponding Society.[7] These were turbulent, unsettled, exciting times in Britain when the threat of revolution and a French invasion seemed likely to provoke the violent reaction of a 'British Terror'. And Wordsworth was at the heart of it all, keeping company with the most controversial radical thinkers and 'jacobin' activists of the day. It would be fascinating to know all that he did at this moment but, apart from brief entries in Godwin's *Diary*, material for recreating this period of the poet's life is hard to come by. As a result, Wordsworth's 'Godwinian phase' has been recounted in terms of his enthusiasm for and subsequent disappointment with Godwin's 'false philosophy' rather than through his lived experience of the noisy, argumentative world of advanced radicalism.

It is possible to show, as Thompson does, that *Political Justice* encouraged quite outlandish behaviour in Wordsworth's circle of friends and acquaintances. The artist Joseph Farington recorded a dinner at which Wordsworth's friend Basil Montagu suddenly sprang to his feet and announced his 'violent' conversion to 'the speculative principles of the new Philosophers' (in other words, the 'speculative principles' of *Political Justice*). Montagu tried to persuade the party around the table

> against the existence of *Instinct* . . . [saying] that Poets are made by *education*. – That a Parent should not love his Child better than the Child of another, but in proportion as the Child might possess better qualities and endowments.[8]

This anecdote agrees with the diarist Henry Crabb Robinson's remark that *Political Justice* 'produced a powerful effect on the youth of that generation', and Robinson goes on to claim that by encouraging disinterestedness Godwin's book made him 'feel more *generously*': 'I had never before, nor, I am afraid, have I ever since felt so strongly the duty of not living to one's self, but of having for one's sole object the good of the community'.[9] Wordsworth too recalled in *The Prelude* that Godwin's appeal had been principally to young enthusiasts who were '[p]leased with extremes' and 'flattered' in as much as the new philosophy enabled them to

> look through all the frailties of the world,
> And, with a resolute mastery shaking off
> The accidents of nature, time, and place,
> That make up the weak being of the past,
> Build social freedom on its only basis:
> The freedom of the individual mind,
> Which, to the blind restraint of general laws
> Superior, magisterially adopts
> One guide, the light of circumstances, flashed
> Upon an independent intellect.     (x 820–9)

Wordsworth's poetry recreates the superficial command of *Political Justice*, its assertion of a Godwinian 'mastery' confidently abstracted from the realities of life. Two lines at the centre of the passage above encapsulate Godwin's philosophy, which based social improvement on the seemingly boundless speculative freedom of the 'individual mind'. But the lines are separated by a colon, marking the point from which *Political Justice* collapsed back into the world it seemed so compellingly to have 'shaken off'. Rather than opening a thrilling prospect in which 'social freedom' meant 'the good of the community', the Godwinian enlightenment dwindled into a consideration of how 'circumstances' or 'accidents of nature, time, and place' appear to 'independent intellect'. The superior vision of *Political Justice* disclosed only 'things as they are', a phrase Godwin incorporated in the title of his novel *Caleb Williams* (1794) to point to the oppressiveness of contemporary English society.

Given the extremity *Political Justice* encouraged it isn't surprising that E. P. Thompson should have located Wordsworth's crisis in the speculative terrain inhabited by the book's admirers rather than in the world of actions and events. Thompson suggests that the crisis was precipitated by Wordsworth's recognition of Godwin's duplicity: '[Wordsworth] had found self-interest in the mask of reason', Thompson writes, 'and self-love masked as philanthropy. There was a sudden motion of recoil, which took him from London to Racedown, Stowey and Goslar, and . . . from the "Descriptive Sketches" to "Salisbury Plain" and *The Borderers*' ('Wordsworth's Crisis', 93). *The Prelude* records Wordsworth's 'despair' about Godwin (see especially x 878–900) although as the impulse for a prolonged 'recoil' it is unconvincing and especially so when read in relation to 'Tintern Abbey'. Because philosopher Godwin proved as selfish as Basil Montagu did Wordsworth exile himself to the English west country (1795–8) and then to freezing Goslar in Germany (1798–9)? I doubt it. The Wordsworthian 'recoil' described by Thompson needs the compelling motives of 'betrayal' and 'dread' which surface in 'Tintern Abbey'.

'Tintern Abbey''s introspective and universalizing language invites and resists speculation about how the poem may or may not draw upon and reconfigure lived experiences. Throughout the poem a mournful undersong tells of 'the heavy and the weary weight / Of all this unintelligible world' (40–1) until a more uplifting claim supervenes,

> And this prayer I make,
> Knowing that Nature never did betray
> The heart that loved her . . .    (122–4)

– a claim which folds the knowledge of betrayal into the heart of prayer, rather as the pursuit of nature as loving quest glanced back to acknowledge 'something' dreaded (71–3). There need be no exact biographical referents for 'betray' and 'dread' in 'Tintern Abbey' but if Wordsworth's 'knowing' was the growth of five years' reflection (as the poem tells us) then any original experience, whether first-hand or otherwise, was a comparatively recent one – perhaps at some point during the poet's residence in France in 1792, or following his return to England in December of that year. This possibility has gained on me in the course of writing this essay, and was reinforced by David Bromwich's remark that he 'became convinced (while thinking and writing) that [Wordsworth's] Salisbury Plain mood of early 1794 holds a real panic under self-repression. The poem and the letters around it, the action and inaction, have to do with a feeling not only of things wrongly left undone but with things terribly and actually done.'[10] If Bromwich is right, those terrible things, done and/or undone, must have dated from 1793 or a little earlier.

Wordsworth was an 'inveterate coverer of traces', David Bromwich says, 'for prudential reasons, and in politics most of all'. So rather than attempting to identify 'what Wordsworth may have done (or crucially failed to do)', he attends to the evidence of the imagination arguing that by interpreting *The Borderers*, which he reads as a 'personal allegory', one can offer informed speculation about otherwise irretrievable history.[11] The argument cannot be rehearsed step by step here, but Bromwich's conclusions must be paused over, for they are extraordinary. Bromwich reads the play as 'the outcome of Wordsworth's hopes and fears reacting upon the impersonal principles of the philosophic radicalism of the 1790s'.[12] Many commentators have found in *The Borderers* a disillusioned response to *Political Justice*, but Bromwich finds Godwin contributing to a more disturbing Wordsworthian insight about action and guilt. For him the story of Rivers and Mortimer, both of whom are persuaded or reasoned into committing murder, implies 'the necessity of murder, exile, and self-reflection in the making of an individual mind'. In one of many brilliant juxtapositions, Bromwich relates Rivers's central speech on what it feels like to have committed murder, 'Action is transitory... Suffering is permanent, obscure and dark' (III v 60–5)[13] to the situation and mood of Wordsworth in 'Tintern Abbey', suggesting the affinity between all that is 'permanent, obscure and dark' and 'Tintern Abbey''s 'burthen of the mystery'. 'And if that is so', Bromwich continues, 'how different are the situations of Wordsworth in "Tintern Abbey", with his "many recognitions dim and faint", and Mortimer reflecting on his murderous crime in *The Borderers*? "Deep, deep and vast, vast beyond human thought, / Yet calm... In terror, / Remembered terror, there is peace and rest"' (*Disowned by Memory* 49–50). Mortimer's 'mighty burden' of guilt (v iii 100), his knowledge that human nature is 'decoyed, betrayed' (v iii 59), casts a murderous implication across 'Tintern Abbey' and 'the heavy and the weary weight / Of all this unintelligible world'.

The eerie similarities between *The Borderers* and 'Tintern Abbey' give imaginative shape to Bromwich's 'hunch that [Wordsworth] had once been in the thick of a conspiracy and seen someone badly hurt or killed on information from himself' (*Disowned by Memory* 17). Rather than arising from the inadequacy of Godwin's 'false philosophy', or its potential to release violence like Robespierre's terror (1793–4),[14] betrayal and dread in Wordsworth were apparently connected with events in France. When John Keats read 'Tintern Abbey' he came to something like the same conclusion. In his letter to John Hamilton Reynolds, 3 May 1818, Keats describes life as 'a large Mansion of Many Apartments' – an image for which one source was the large mansion at Enfield where Keats had attended school. In it the 'infant or thoughtless Chamber' opens, as consciousness awakens, into a second which Keats calls 'the Chamber of Maiden-Thought'. Here 'light... atmosphere... [and] pleasant wonders' are concentrated in an 'intoxicating' experience, the 'effects' of which according to Keats include

> that tremendous one of sharpening one's vision into the [head: *deleted*] heart and nature of Man – of convincing ones nerves that the World is full of Misery and Heratbreak [sic], Pain, Sickness and oppression – whereby This Chamber of Maiden Thought becomes gradually darken'd and at the same time on all sides of it many doors are set open – but all dark – all leading to dark passages... To this point was Wordsworth come, as far as I can conceive when he wrote 'Tintern Abbey' and it seems to me that his Genius is explorative of those dark Passages.[15]

At the darkling existential 'point' represented by 'Tintern Abbey' '[w]e see not the ballance of good and evil. We are in a Mist – *We* are now in that state – We feel the "burden of the Mystery"' (*Keats Letters* i 281). Keats says that Wordsworth's genius is explorative of the 'dark passages' of life, and capable of 'discoveries'; in this respect Wordsworth 'is deeper than Milton' (who for Keats as for Blake was 'content' with Reformation religion) and 'proves there is really a grand march of intellect... proves that a mighty providence subdues the mightiest Minds to the service of the time being, whether it be in human Knowledge or Religion' (*Keats Letters* i 281–2). The sharpening, chastening power was associated in Wordsworth's life experience with a period of the French Revolution Keats believed had put a 'temporry stop' to the 'march of intellect' and 'the rapid progress of free sentiments': the Terror (*Keats Letters* ii 193–4). Betrayal and dread in Wordsworth were associated with revolutionary events that have long been known about, and which draw together his residence in France, his love affair with Annette Vallon, the Terror, and the poetry. More than this, the career of one revolutionary involved in these events dramatized the 'stop' to enlightened progress noted by Keats – and in doing so offered a compelling pattern for *The Borderers* as well as the recovery signalled by 'Tintern Abbey'.

In 1842, having revised *The Borderers* for publication, Wordsworth recalled what had prompted him to write the play:

> The study of human nature suggests this awful truth, that, as in the trials to which life subjects us, sin and crime are apt to start from their very opposite qualities, so are there no limits to the hardening of the heart, and the perversion of the understanding to which they may carry their slaves. During my long residence in France, while the Revolution was rapidly advancing to its extreme of wickedness, I had frequent opportunities of being an eye-witness of this process, and it was while that knowledge was fresh upon my memory, that the Tragedy of 'The Borderers' was composed.      (*Borderers* 813)

This tantalizing recollection explains what went into the creation of the character Rivers, but the occasions of Wordsworth's 'eye-witness' observations in France are seemingly left unspecified. Seemingly, that is, unless one understands a more-or-less distinct reference for the otherwise commonplace analogy 'as in the trials to which life subjects us'. Trials. Wordsworth had concluded his earlier 'Preface' to the play (written *c.* 1797) with 'one word more' on 'motives' in law-suits, reflecting on how 'utter ruin' and 'deadly feuds' may proceed from 'trifling and apparently inadequate sources' (*Borderers* 68). The Wordsworth family's quarrel with the Earl of Lonsdale was one such legal suit, and while the effort to recover John Wordsworth's estate wasn't an 'inadequate source' it doesn't explain the extremity of Wordsworth's remarks about 'deadly feuds in families'. Godwin's novel *Caleb Williams* dissected legal and psychological tyranny, and we know that Wordsworth read and was influenced by the book.[16] Still, this does not account for experiences of 'hardening of the heart' and 'perversion of the understanding'.

The legal 'process' to which I believe Wordsworth was a horrified spectator was notorious. It was reported in *The Times* on 4 September 1793 as an instance of the 'despotism of [the] anarchic faction' in control of the Revolutionary Tribunal at Paris. And it was noticed prominently in the five-volume *Histoire Générale et Impartiale des Erreurs, des Fautes et des Crimes Commis Pendant le Révolution Française*. The 'contrast between the alleged deed and the punishment which followed' was recalled in 1880 as 'one of the most shocking proceedings' of the Revolutionary Tribunal at Paris. The case featured in Edmond Biré's imaginary *Diary of a Citizen of Paris During the Terror*, where the verdict of the jury was described as having created a 'tremendous sensation' in the courtroom. In 1909 it was invoked as an example of the 'implacable severity' of the Revolutionary Tribunal; in 1965 it was described as 'the outrageous Bourdon case'.[17]

Léonard Bourdon (1754–1807) was a native of Orléans, where he was educated at the College d'Orléans before going to Paris where he founded a successful school for boys. In the early years of the revolution he was a leading activist in the Cercle Social and the Paris Jacobin club, advocating international revolution and 'an ideal community of all free peoples'. Bourdon was one of the organizers of 'the glorious day' of 10 August 1792 when Louis XVI was deposed, thus opening the way for the Republic, and he was elected to the National Convention by the Department of the Loiret.[18] As David Erdman has shown, it was Léonard Bourdon who in 1791 crystallized the enlightened, universalist ideals of the Revolution in a ceremonial *commerce des lumières* between the French, British, and Americans – an image which Erdman says allowed a blend of meanings: 'the meeting of luminaries, by mutual recognition of one another's auras; exchanges of bright ideas, insight, wisdom; with a suggestion of aural – even mesmeric – contact'.[19]

Such lively exchanges did indeed take place between the Jacobin club at Paris and reformist associations like the London Revolution Society in Britain. One such occurred during the visit of Jérome Pétion to London, 30 October–8 November 1791. Pétion had been a member of the Constituent Assembly at Paris, and on 4 November he was guest of honour at the Revolution Society's anniversary dinner in the London Tavern where he met Joseph Priestley, Tom Paine, and Thomas Walker, founder in 1790 of the Manchester Constitutional Society, one of the most important of the many such groups nationwide calling for political reform. There were some 350 guests at this dinner, and the event developed into a remarkable celebration of Anglo-French solidarity. Pétion's diary noted that the royal toast was drunk 'in gloomy silence', and that support for France was demonstrated by tricoloured cockades, by display of the national flags intertwined, and in spirited singing of the revolutionary anthem *Ça ira*. Pétion responded proposing a toast to the unity of England and France; Paine upped the stakes by giving 'The Revolution of the World'.[20] Back again at Paris Pétion was elected mayor on 16 November; he addressed the Jacobin club two days later, describing the Revolution Society dinner and remarking on how the toast to the French Revolution and his own to Anglo-French union had been received 'with transport'. Immediately after Pétion's address Léonard Bourdon came to the tribune and evoked the spirit of universal patriotism as a 'commerce des lumières'.

Another instance of electrifying *commerce* between London and Paris was the presence of 'Citizen' Charles Stanhope – 'le Whig constitutionel' – at the Jacobin Club, Paris, on Sunday 18 December 1791. Here Stanhope witnessed in a pageant suffused with light and atmosphere the ceremonial alliance of

America, England, and France: '*Vivent les trois nations! Vive la liberté!*'[21] On this occasion Léonard Bourdon spoke again, congratulating the Jacobins and the 'incorruptible' Pétion on having 'brought about the ceremony which unites us today' and moving that busts of Price and Franklin should be purchased by 'voluntary subscription' for display in the Jacobin Club (see Erdman, 146–7).

All that we know of his actions and sentiments shows that up until December 1791 Léonard Bourdon was one of the most prominent advocates of universal peace and liberty, embodying the ardent spirit in which revolutionaries at Paris reached out to Britain and America in a *commerce des lumières*. Bourdon was evidently well known to the many international visitors like 'Citizen' Stanhope who made their way to Paris, and he can scarcely have escaped Wordsworth's attention. Wordsworth and Bourdon had mutual acquaintances among the English Jacobins at Paris and it's no exaggeration to claim that, at the close of 1791, as Wordsworth followed 'Citizen Stanhope' across the Channel for a longer sojourn in France, Bourdon's ideals represented everything Wordsworth hoped the revolution might achieve. But, as Wordsworth was soon to learn, 'sin and crime are apt to start from their very opposite qualities'.

Léonard Bourdon arrived at his native city, Orléans, 16 March 1793, *en route* for the south.[22] This was his second visit in recent months. Back in September 1792, when Wordsworth may well have been in Orléans, Bourdon as a Deputy of the Convention had assisted in the despatch of some fifty state prisoners to Paris where they were massacred. Now he attended and harangued a meeting of the jacobin 'société populaire', joined a patriotic banquet, and then prepared to continue on his journey. No doubt the patriots were excited; probably they were drunk. Meanwhile, resentment among royalists in the city was running high. Bourdon himself takes up the story in a letter to the National Convention:

> More than thirty counter-revolutionaries with bayonets set upon me in front of the Town Hall. They flung me to the ground, battering me with kicks and blows; as soon as I went down all bayonets were readied – one of the bastards stabbed me in the belly, others in my arms and head. I managed to fend them off – only just, mind – and staggered and stumbled into the Town Hall where commandant Dulac separated us . . . I'm told that my wounds aren't dangerous; my overcoat was some protection, and my hat so firmly stuck on my head that the bayonet only grazed skin-deep.

Bourdon goes on to notice several pistol shots aimed at him (they missed) and concludes his letter by mentioning to the Convention his 'sense of exquisite satisfaction' in being 'a martyr for liberty'.[23]

But Léonard Bourdon wasn't dead. Nor was he severely wounded in the brawl, since he was sufficiently recovered by 3 o'clock the following morning to write his letter to the National Convention. At Paris word about the attack on Bourdon arrived along with news of an uprising in the Vendée. Together these events appeared like a concerted insurrection, 'links in a grand conspiracy forged by the enemies of liberty'; two Representatives of the Convention reported that 'the assassination of our colleague Bourdon at Orléans, along with insults and provocations directed at several others, are all connected with the same plot'.[24] The Convention acted immediately. At Orléans the mayor and civic officers were arrested, along with those guarding the Town Hall on 16 March (Aulard ii 390–1). Among the arrested was Jean-Henri Gellet-Duvivier, formerly Wordsworth's landlord, who had been in the forefront of the scuffle with Bourdon. Legouis (*Wordsworth and Annette Vallon* 43) describes him grabbing Bourdon by the throat, knocking him down and striking him with his sword. Annette Vallon's brother Paul was implicated too, although he seems to have tried to get away from the scene using 'every means to tear himself out of the hands of the patriots who held him' (*Wordsworth and Annette Vallon* 43). By 24 April when the warrant for his arrest was produced, Paul Vallon had gone into hiding. Unquestionably this saved his life, for he was listed among the twenty-six indicted for the 'assassination' of Bourdon, imprisoned in the Conciergerie at Paris, and committed to appear before the Revolutionary Tribunal on a charge of murder.

What made the ensuing trial sensational, notorious, sickening was Léonard Bourdon's presence at the Tribunal, ready to testify against the so-called assassins from his native city (see Loomis, *Paris in the Terror*, 122). No longer the prophet of a benign *commerce des lumières*, he now prowled the courtroom 'dans l'attitude d'un tigre' (*Histoire* v 201). The trial began on 28 June and finished on 12 July when nine of the defendants, including Gellet-Duvivier, were found guilty of a murder that never happened. As soon as the verdict was announced, 'there was a tremendous uproar in court. Everyone was grief-stricken; the accused fell to their knees, raised their hands protesting their innocence to God, swearing they didn't know and had never even seen Léonard Bourdon' (Wallon 1 184–5). When sentence of death was pronounced the whole court, except for Bourdon, was in tears. Next day the court reconvened, and was confronted with a petition from relatives of the condemned: 'We appeal for our fathers, brothers, children ... We trust to Léonard Bourdon's humanity in helping us find some way, any way of proving the innocence of our unfortunate relatives' (Wallon 1 185). Duvivier's eldest daughter pleaded for her father's life: 'just ten years old, her bravery and persistence sustained her over three long months of petitioning the judges and Deputies of the Convention; all to whom she spoke were moved to tears. She called on Léonard Bourdon at least twenty times, but a man with no humanity wasn't to be moved to pity' (*Histoire* v 200). Bourdon, one-time advocate of enlightened humanity, now sat silent, inexorable, '*impassible*' (Wallon I 186). That afternoon the nine condemned men were dressed in red shirts to identify them as murderers, taken to the scaffold in the Place de la Révolution, and guillotined. The date was 13 July 1793.

Émile Legouis wrote about the Bourdon trial and executions in his book *Wordsworth and Annette Vallon*, but he did so as a tragic episode in the life of the Vallon family. Coming right up to the present Kenneth Johnston's *Hidden Wordsworth* gives us Bourdon as the 'petty dictator of Orléans' and 'mortal enemy' of Paul Vallon, describing the trial but I think under-estimating its impact on Wordsworth for contributing merely a 'share of pathos' to the 'unjust tribunals' passage in *Prelude* Book X (Johnston, *Hidden Wordsworth*, 290, 374). The change in Bourdon himself is sharply disturbing: formerly the advocate of revolutionary enlightenment and community, by 1793 Bourdon had become a kind of specimen example for Wordsworth's claim that 'there no limits to the hardening of the heart, and the perversion of the understanding'. Sure, the Bourdon trial and its consequences were 'important to Wordsworth privately' (Johnston 373) – but we need to re-spond more adequately to the horror of what had happened to Bourdon and to individuals well known to, some of them intimately acquainted with, Wordsworth: Gellet-Duvivier and his daughter, the Vallons, perhaps others who were on trial too. Much research has been undertaken to identify per-sons Wordsworth may have known in revolutionary France, and to make a case for him revisiting France in 1793 when he might have witnessed the execution of his acquaintance the journalist Gorsas.[25] But these studies have overlooked the traumatic effect of the Bourdon case on Wordsworth, who saw his attachments as a lover, a father, and as a partisan of the revolution betrayed by a *lumière* in the name of revolutionary 'justice' and 'national honour'. The psychic fall-out from this shock emerged in nightmares:

> Through months, through years, long after the last beat
> Of those atrocities...
> Such ghastly visions had I of despair
> And tyranny, and implements of death,
> And long orations which in dreams I pleaded
> Before unjust tribunals, with a voice
> Labouring, a brain confounded, and a sense
> Of treachery and desertion...       (X 370–9)

This agonized passage from *Prelude* Book x is so placed in the narrative as to identify 'those atrocities', and the 'beat' of the blade on the scaffold, with July 1793.[26] Of course the lines don't have to apply to the Bourdon case: there were many other such 'tribunals' during the Terror, but none so grotesquely unjust as the capital charge for murder of a man present in court watching the proceedings. And no tribunal that highlighted so powerfully the dreadful miscarriage of the Revolution.

In July 1793 Wordsworth spent some weeks in the Isle of Wight (see Reed, 144) although what he was doing there remains one of the mysterious 'gaps' in his early life. Could he have crossed the Channel, made his way to Paris, and sat in the Tribunal as a helpless 'eye-witness of the process' – an eye-witness who for years afterwards would plead in his dreams on behalf of the accused? It hardly matters. This outrage, one of many reported in London newspapers, was (and is) so uniquely dismaying that we can understand how for anyone sympathetic to France news of it would have stirred feelings of 'treachery and desertion', as Wordsworth tells us of himself, 'in the place / The holiest that I knew of, my own soul' (x 379–80). Perhaps it's not too far-fetched to consider how Mortimer's words to Matilda in *The Borderers* might stand for Wordsworth's confounding discovery about human nature and about himself:

> Now mark this world of ours:
> A man may be a murderer and his hand
> Shall tell no tales, nay, the first brook he meets
> Shall wash it clean...
> Thou must be wise as I am, thou must know
> What human nature is, decoyed, betrayed –
> I have the proofs.                   (v iii 50–3; 58–60)

Mortimer's confession follows some forty lines later, 'I am the murderer of thy father', followed by his (self-deluding) reflection: 'Three words have such a power! This mighty burden / All off at once! 'Tis done...' (v iii 100–1).

'This mighty burden': the knowledge of murderous guilt but also perhaps a transliteration and, wishfully, a riddance of 'Bourdon'? *The Oxford English Dictionary* identifies 'bourdon' as a variant form of English 'burden' (in *OED* sense 2. a., meaning a 'load of...blame, sin, sorrow'), and English 'bourdon', meaning a bass accompaniment or undersong, was adopted from the French 'bourdon'.[27] Maybe the burden/Bourdon pun is too slender a link from which to make the case that Mortimer's 'mighty burden' may refer darkly to that damaged *lumière*, Léonard Bourdon. But Wordsworth liked quibbling[28] and there may be a second, more uncanny recall of Bourdon in *The Borderers* too. Mortimer's burden is not so readily 'off at once', for he is confronted by a weird hallucinatory barrier which seemingly projects his guilt and reminds us once again of 'bourdon'. When Mortimer 'hysterically' sets out in quest of an 'executioner' to 'do the business' and purge his guilt, he finds himself baffled: 'There is something / That must be cleared away – / ... That staff / Which bars the road before me there. – 'Tis there, / 'Tis there breast-high and will not let me pass' (v iii 197–200). *Macbeth* is in the background here, although the 'staff' that seemingly 'bars the road' bizarrely, but literally, invokes Léonard Bourdon through the sense of 'bourdon' as a 'stout staff'.[29]

In the Bourdon tribunal and executions, which drew in the Duvivier and Vallon families, we can see how close Wordsworth was to the Terror and to the actuality of heart-hardening that he recreates in *The Borderers*. That proximity helps explain his distracted mood of 1793, and the obsession with guilt and treachery in poems like *Salisbury Plain*, *The Borderers* and, later still, *The Prelude*. You may think I'm going to suggest now that the 'burden of the mystery' in 'Tintern Abbey', which so powerfully affected Keats, was a skewed literalism relating 'decoyed' perplexity at an 'unintelligible world' specifically to Léonard Bourdon. It does seem to me most likely that the five-year anniversary signalled by the poem's date, 'July 13, 1798', and the opening of the poem, do indeed mark the executions at Paris on that day in 1793. But when Keats wrote 'We are in a Mist... We feel the "burden of the Mystery"' (*Keats Letters* i 281) he was misquoting the poem, which says nothing about a 'burden'. The lines run,

> that blessed mood,
> In which the burthen of the mystery,
> In which the heavy and the weary weight
> Of all this unintelligible world
> Is lightened...                    (38–42)

Even supposing that there is indeed a punning acquaintance between 'burden' and 'Bourdon', the slippage from 'burden' (a word used only four times by Wordsworth) to 'burthen' would be an exemplary instance of 'Tintern Abbey''s universalizing – or canny obscuring – of historical reference.

No. The poem says nothing about Léonard Bourdon. Nothing about the events of 13 July 1793, nothing about poor Gellet-Duvivier and his daughter, nothing about Paul Vallon, nothing at all about Godwin or about *Political Justice* and its disappointments. But just as there are dark affinities between the poetry in *The Borderers* and 'Tintern Abbey', so too are there aspects of 'Tintern Abbey' which seem to hark back to the brighter temper of earlier years. Mortimer's rash and self-deceiving assumption in *The Borderers* – 'This mighty burden / All off at once!' – 'Tintern Abbey' steadies into a slow-growing awareness that through human relationship and glimpses of universal greeting the 'burthen of the mystery, / ... Is lightened'. Wordsworth's 'lightening' is a gradual clearing of 'mist', an easing of the spirit. 'The setting sun will always set me to rights', Keats said (*Letters* i 186), cheerily echoing the lines in 'Tintern Abbey' which report upon an omnipresence

> Whose dwelling is the light of setting suns,
> And the round ocean, and the living air,
> And the blue sky, and in the mind of man,
> A motion and a spirit, that impels
> All thinking things ...          (98–102)

The participation here 'felt' or 'sensed' is seemingly little akin to the 'commerce des lumières' between France, Britain, and America, or to the benevolent impulse that brought together citizens Wordsworth and Pétion, Paine, Stanhope and, yes, Léonard Bourdon. It took an instinctive lumière like John Keats to intuit that these famous lines about 'the light of setting suns' might indeed embrace a universal 'setting to rights', that Wordsworth's most transcendental claim in 'Tintern Abbey' reflects back upon a world burdened by things that think and the mystery of 'things as they are'.

## NOTES

1 Kenneth Johnston, *The Hidden Wordsworth: Poet, Lover, Rebel, Spy* (New York and London, 1998), pp. 6–9.
2 See 'Wordsworth's Crisis', *London Review of Books* (8 December 1988), rpt in E. P. Thompson, *The Romantics: England in a Revolutionary Age: Wordsworth, Coleridge, Thelwall* (Woodbridge, Suffolk, 1997), p. 77.
3 See *Memoirs of William Wordsworth, Poet-Laureate, DCL* (2 vols., London, 1851), I, p. 74, and Stephen Gill, *Wordsworth and the Victorians* (Oxford, 1998), p. 35.
4 See George McLean Harper, *William Wordsworth: His Life, Works, and Influence* (2 vols., London, 1916), I, pp. 141–2, and for further comment Gill, *Wordsworth and the Victorians*, pp. 233–4.
5 See Émile Legouis, *William Wordsworth and Annette Vallon* (London and Toronto, 1922), p. 25. Caroline's certificate of baptism is reproduced in George McLean Harper, *Wordsworth's French Daughter. The Story of her Birth, with the Certificates of her Baptism and Marriage* (Princeton and Oxford, 1921), pp. 28–30.
6 Compare Wordsworth's memory in *Prelude* x 190–1, that he had left France in December 1792, 'Compelled by nothing less than absolute want / Of funds'.
7 For Wordsworth in London radical circles in 1795, see my *Wordsworth and Coleridge: The Radical Years* (Oxford, 1988), pp. 186–98.
8 *The Diary of Joseph Farington*, ed. Kenneth Garlick, Angus Macintyre and Kathryn Cave (17 vols., New Haven and London, 1978–98), III, pp. 700–1. Entry of 22 November 1796. One consequence of Basil Montagu's philosophically independent attitude to parenthood was that from September 1795 the Wordsworths acted as

guardians of his son – a role they maintained for some three years until August 1798.

9 See *Henry Crabb Robinson's Diary*, ed. Thomas Sadler (3 vols., London, 1869), I, pp. 31–2.

10 Personal correspondence, 22 October 1999. I am grateful to David Bromwich for responding to my questions about the 'terrible things' which might lie behind Wordsworth's poetry of the 1790s.

11 David Bromwich, *Disowned by Memory. Wordsworth's Poetry of the 1790s* (Chicago, 1998), p. 46.

12 *Disowned by Memory*, p. 44.

13 Quoted from the 1797–9 text of *The Borderers*. David Bromwich quotes from the 1842 text of *The Borderers* in which, he argues, Wordsworth near the end of his life was able to recover 'the heat and danger of the longest poem of his radical years' (*Disowned by Memory*, p. 46). There are alterations in punctuation between 1797–9 and 1842, but the substance of the passage is the same.

14 For Godwin's 'abstract and unprincipled philosophy' leading to 'violence like that witnessed in France', see *Wordsworth and Coleridge: The Radical Years*, p. 219.

15 *The Letters of John Keats 1814–1821*, ed. Hyder E. Rollins (2 vols., Cambridge, Mass., 1958), I, pp. 280–1.

16 See Duncan Wu, *Wordsworth's Reading 1770–1799* (Cambridge, 1993), pp. 66–7.

17 See *The Times* (4 September 1793); H. Wallon, *Histoire du Tribunal Révolutionnaire de Paris* (6 vols., Paris, 1880–2), I, p. 181; Edmond Biré, *The Diary of a Citizen of Paris During 'The Terror'*, trans. John de Villiers (2 vols., London, 1896), II, p. 188; G. Lenôtre, *The Tribunal of the Terror. A Study of Paris in 1793–1795*, tr. Frederic Lees (London, 1909), p. 69; Stanley Loomis, *Paris in the Terror, June 1793–July 1794* (London, 1965), p. 122.

18 See H. Morse Stephens, *The Principal Speeches of the Statesmen and Orators of the French Revolution, 1789–1795* (2 vols., Oxford 1892), II, pp. 230–1 n, for details of Bourdon's life. The Scottish radical John Oswald spoke at the Jacobin Club at Paris, 22 August 1792, on the need 'to undeceive the British nation' about the 'glorious day of 10 August'; see David Erdman's brilliant recovery of Oswald's life and times in *Commerce des Lumières: John Oswald and the British in Paris, 1790–1793* (Columbia, Missouri, 1986), pp. 202–3.

19 See Erdman, 139, 143, and the epigraph to the whole book.

20 For a full account of the London Revolution Society dinner, see Albert Goodwin, *The Friends of Liberty: The English Democratic Movement in the Age of the French Revolution* (London, 1979), pp. 187–8.

21 See 'London Embraces Paris' in Erdman, 143–7, and Erdman's earlier account of Stanhope's visit, 'Citizen Stanhope and the French Revolution' in *The Wordsworth Circle*, 15, 1 (Winter 1984): 8–15.

22 'Deuxième Voyage Sanguinaire à Orléans, le 15 Mars 1793, par Léonard Bourdon, Représentant du Peuple', in *Histoire Générale et Impartiale des Erreurs, des Fautes et des Crimes Commis Pendant le Révolution Française* (5 vols., Paris, 1797), V, pp. 191–203, 192.

23 F. A. Aulard, *Receuil des Actes du Comité de Salut Public* (Paris, 1789–1964), II, pp. 382–3.

24 See Aulard, *Receuil*, II, p. 381 for this letter linking the Bourdon case with a wider counter-revolutionary conspiracy.

25 See for example my *Politics of Nature: William Wordsworth and some Contemporaries* (Basingstoke, 2002), pp. 143–58, and Johnston, 358–400.

26 *Prelude* x 290–306 recalls Wordsworth's sojourn in the Isle of Wight, July 1793, and x 307–80 the beginning of the Terror in France, July 1793, and Wordsworth's 'melancholy at that time' leading into the 'unjust tribunals' passage.

27 See *The Oxford English Dictionary. Second Edition* (20 vols., Oxford, 1989), 'burden' form ß. 6 and sense IV 9; etymology of the English 'bourdon'.

28 Wordsworth's first published poem was 'Sonnet on seeing Miss Helen Maria Williams weep at a Tale of Distress' in the *European Magazine*, 11 (March 1787), p. 202. It appeared over the signature 'Axiologus', a Graeco-Latin transliteration of 'Wordsworth'.

29 See *OED* 'bourdon', sense 2.

# 13

PAUL HAMILTON

# Wordsworth and Romanticism

William Wordsworth's centrality to any review of English Romantic period writing continues fundamentally undisturbed. Critical fashions and methodologies change, but as regards English Romanticism they are tested against a canonical core of writers. Of those, Wordsworth almost always takes centre stage either as the best support of the new theories, or as the writer whose authority they must displace in order to show their innovative power and originality. One might risk saying that, for good or ill, Arnold has proved right in his predictions and Swinburne wrong: it is Wordsworth and Byron, not Coleridge and Shelley, who have remained the touchstones of canonical English poetry of the romantic age.[1] In Wordsworth and Byron inhere the definitive contrasts of the period's sensibility and style, the consistent Englishness of the former and the cosmopolitan inconsistency of the latter. But the recognition Wordsworth received in his own lifetime was not so straightforward.

Many major works routinely used in his critical evaluation now – the 'Salisbury Plain' poems, *The Borderers*, *The Prelude* in its several versions – remained unpublished while Wordswsorth was alive and largely unknown to his contemporaries. The depth of his immersion in republican thinking and radicalism generally during the Revolutionary period, the formative stress which must have been occasioned by his enforced abandonment of Annette Vallon and their daughter, Caroline (a connection itself politically fraught because of the mother's staunchly Royalist persuasion), now seem crucial to the interpretation of his work. His writings successfully displace both these commitments, historical and personal, on to the *distraits*, indigent characters typical of his early poetry, and on to the communitarianism he found exemplified by Lakeland society, charging his poetry with the same compensatory energies which the childhood fragmentation of his own family must have inspired. Yet such involvements appear to be what had to be overlooked by his critics or suppressed by him for his reputation to flourish. Yet it is because he is so implicated intellectually and humanly in his age that Wordsworth can articulate most comprehensively that passage through revolution to restoration which is commonly taken to identify the Romantic dilemma.

Official recognition of his literary pre-eminence, though, came in Victoria's reign rather than in the heyday of Romanticism, and it is uncertain that by then a romantic poet was being honoured. Wordsworth was laden with doctorates from the University of Durham in 1838 and Oxford in 1839, awarded a pension from the Civil List in 1842, and created Poet Laureate in 1843 after Robert Southey's death. Thomas De Quincey's history of Wordsworth's critical reception in his *Recollections* as if it might properly be couched in the language of a Church history is still plausible: 'up to 1820, the name of Wordsworth was trampled under foot; from 1820 to 1830 it was militant; from 1830 to 1835 it has been triumphant'.[2] And, one should add, from here the royal progress begins. After his death, the battles over his reputation were conducted in terms he might not himself have invited, especially in his writings up to 1814. As Stephen Gill records in *Wordsworth and the Victorians* (1998), protagonists as varied as John Stuart Mill, Matthew Arnold, Walter Pater, Leslie Stephen, Edward Caird, William Hale White, and Thomas Hardy debated Wordsworth's entitlement to cultural veneration in arguments which invoked a contradictory range of criteria – religious, moral, aesthetic, and political – clearly orientated towards mid and late-Victorian needs rather than towards those which had driven the poet himself at the time of writing the disputed works. No doubt this is quite proper, and Wordsworth's translatability into a figure of contemporary debate is always going to be a sign of his enduring literary merit. But what gets left out, and what certainly became muted in Victorian discussion, was the sense that he might be located in a period rightly called romantic amongst writers sharing peculiarly romantic premises for writing and thinking. His home in the Lake District became not only a shrine for the faithful but an occasional salon for all sorts of thinkers, geologists, and mathematicians as well as critics and writers.[3] Wordsworth produced Wordsworthians, intellectuals redeemed from the abstraction or dissociation incurred by scientific advance at the expense of religious belief, or by utilitarianism in public policy and private morality. Those not satisfied by the doctrinally unspecific religiosity of his poetry could be affected by the comprehensiveness of his ethical vision, in both cases enjoying an unprecedented expansion of sympathies too large to be housed within one church or a single practical social programme. To them, Wordsworth demonstrated that culture might be separated from action, and this contemplative ethos (which nevertheless produced action to safeguard it) sets the tone for a recognizably modern sequestration of the arts in society.[4]

Despite this Victorian cast to Wordsworthian success, M. H. Abrams, in his 'Introduction' to the 1987 commemorative volume, *William Wordsworth and the Age of Romanticism*, can celebrate him as 'the central figure of English Romanticism [who] has exerted a revolutionary influence on all our lives'.[5] He has little trouble in collecting earlier plaudits or testimonials deferring to Wordsworth as the greatest poet of the age from Coleridge, Leigh Hunt, Blake, Keats, and Hazlitt. Wordsworth's influence is also a palpable presence in the writings of his strongest detractors, an irony he himself noted in the case of Byron. Ignorance of Wordsworth on the continent did not stop him having an indirect influence on European Romanticism vicariously through the idioms he had bequeathed to the highly popular poetry of Sir Walter Scott and Byron, especially through Canto III of the latter's *Childe Harold's Pilgrimage*.[6] Revolutionary nationalism, the political output most characteristic of Romantic enthusiasm, was fostered throughout Europe by a poetic afflatus transcending the Tory and aristocratic feelings of its authors. Wordsworth's distinctive patriotism, from the 'Lucy' poems to the final book of *The Excursion*, shared this radical impulse when transferred to countries like Italy and Greece labouring under foreign rule. Yet this openness to enthusiastic translation sounds difficult to reconcile with the uses to which Wordsworth's writings were put by later Victorian conservatism; and of the Wordsworth constructed out of those needs Arnold could write in his Preface of 1879, 'On the Continent he is almost unknown.'[7] Wordsworth's continuing romantic serviceableness, by contrast, is more easily accounted for as a strategic revision of his earlier republicanism, primarily associated with his explicitly anti-monarchical *Letter to the Bishop of Llandaff* of 1793 but also inherent in the democratic, pantheistic sympathies of that poetry of 'the still sad music of humanity' in 'Tintern Abbey'.

Critical understanding now of the Romanticism to which Wordsworth was central is beset by historical diffidence. We are wary of subscribing unreservedly to an age's image of itself, as if subscribing to an ideology. Equally, we are suspicious of the arrogance of retrospect: the prejudice of assuming that hindsight necessarily affords us a more accurate or objective view of an historical period, superior to that of its own culture. It is generally assumed that we can detect the Victorian view of Wordsworth and differentiate our own critical readings from it. However it is arguable that the complex Victorian view has persisted in obscuring Wordsworth's pivotal role in expressing a Romantic difference from and development of what went before. 'Lines written a few miles above Tintern Abbey' condenses the conflict of Enlightenment and Romantic ways of understanding within the calculatedly fictitious excerpt from an imaginary autobiography. When the poem first appeared, its extraordinary ambitions remained largely unrecognized. Sub-sequently, Victorian critics accepted that it was of a piece with Wordworth's 'philosophy', and had to be reckoned as such, the philosophy ignored or championed. The poem did not, as its first readers mostly thought, fit unexceptionably into a tradition of eighteenth-century topographical poetry, contributing to a developing fashion of psychologizing sensibility whose most influential recent practitioners were probably James Beattie in *The Minstrel* (1771–4) and Mark Akenside, whose *The Pleasures of Imagination* (1744) had recently been republished (1772). With a slight tweaking of the meaning of 'ballad' to take in the French connotation of walking (*faire une petite balade*) the poem's travelogue, literal and figurative, could also be thought in 1798 to assimilate peripatetic possibilities of the picturesque to the generic mixture ironically controlled by the other ballads in the collection (*Lyrical Ballads*) in which it first appeared. Irony was the master-trope of the brilliant group of German Romantics assembled in Jena in 1799. Also, it was the ironic treatment of character, evincing authorial superiority over rather than identification with the conventional boundaries of self, for which they commended Goethe. Coleridge famously likened Wordsworth and Goethe in their 'feeling *for*, but never *with* their characters'.[8]

The Victorian reading of Wordsworth appeared to develop this initial reception, but then retreated from its confrontation with Wordsworth's Romantic ambitions. The revealing debate between Wordsworth's Victorian readers centred round the idea of his philosophy. Francis Jeffrey and William Hazlitt had attacked Wordsworth's 'system' as perverse or politically obfuscating. For Jeffrey, Wordsworth used unsubstantiated allusions to a background in systematic thought to justify offending against generally accepted rules of poetic propriety. Hazlitt agreed, and further accused Wordsworth's 'levelling' muse or Jacobinical 'system' of allowing him to incorporate lower-class, agrarian characters – the people – in his poetry, through a show of imaginative sympathy which exonerated him from taking any further action on their behalf in real life. Matthew Arnold praised this sublimating habit which so inflated Wordsworth's range: 'Where, then, is Wordsworth's superiority? It is here: he deals with more of *life* ... he deals with *life*, as a whole, more powerfully.'[9] To translate Wordsworth's universals back into the theories from which they came, and then to relate the poem's value to the plausibility of the theories, is the mistake made by 'Wordsworthians'. In the Preface to his 1879 edition of Wordsworth, Arnold takes one of those Wordsworthians to task:

> the fervent Wordsworthian will add, as Mr Leslie Stephen does, that Wordsworth's poetry is precious because his philosophy is sound ... But we

must be on our guard against the Wordsworthians, if we want to secure for Wordsworth his due rank as a poet...His poetry is the reality, his philosophy...is the illusion.[10]

In his lucid *History of English Thought in the Eighteenth Century*, though, Stephen gave a more sensible reply to the traditional disparagement of Wordsworth's philosophical rhetoric when he claimed that, 'doctrines which men ostensibly hold do not become operative upon their conduct until they have generated an imaginative symbolism'.[11] Poetry like Wordsworth's becomes the necessary conduit of philosophical ideas which would otherwise remain obscure or would entirely lack credibility. Stephen's defence sounds stoutly empirical; but it also states a core notion of Romantic, post-Kantian philosophy. In art we grasp the otherwise inexpressible end-point of a philosophy ambitious to demonstrate our relation to a world that always exceeds our scientific differentiation of it because we belong to it in still more fundamental ways.

> An auxiliar light
> Came from my mind which on the setting sun
> Bestow'd new splendor; the melodious birds,
> The gentle breezes, fountains that ran on,
> Murmuring so sweetly in themselves, obey'd
> A like dominion; and the midnight storm
> Grew darker in the presence of my eye.
> Hence my obeisance, my devotion hence,
> And *hence* my transport.
>
> (*Prel.1805* II 387–95)

Clearly there is a doctrinal core to a passage like this, but its purpose seems rather to stress the importance of conveying some background theory by other means – in an experience by which mind is realized not in abstraction but in the intensity with which it renders back to us nature itself. 'Obeisance', 'devotion', 'transport' suggest commitments to felt experience which amply substitute for its theorization, but commitments whose full import is not understood unless the reader acknowledges their power of philosophical attorney. We can't, in other words, extract the lyricism from the philosophical rhetoric without diminishing the poetry.

Stephen's straightforward remark can be used to summon up Romantic philosophical presences usually thought to be obscure and unhelpful. Parts of Coleridge's *Biographia Literaria* appear to founder when loaded with material from the German philosopher Schelling. A twentieth-century critic as accessible as E. D. Hirsch, though, can write a persuasive book on Wordsworth and Schelling, locating Wordsworth's poetry at the heart of the European philosophical avant-garde.[12] Coleridge's philosophical disappointment with Wordsworth as expressed in a famous letter to him of 1815 sounds clumsy and importunate in its expectations:

> In short, Facts elevated into Theory – Theory into Laws – & Laws into living
> & intelligent Powers – true Idealism necessarily perfecting itself in Realism, &
> Realism refining itself into Idealism.[13]

Wordsworth had perhaps already got there more economically, wise to the fact that poetry might be able to show what philosophy could only postulate, and that the philosophical poem's supreme importance lay in fulfilling that office. Coleridge, of course, had *The Excursion* in mind, not Wordsworth's earlier work. 'Tintern Abbey' poses intepretative problems similarly liable to anachronism because the poem pre-dates whatever Coleridge might have told his friend and then collaborator of his German reading. It was in March 1801 that Coleridge announced to Thomas Poole that he had, single-handedly, broken with the British philosophical tradition, and the thought of David Hartley in particular, to take up a German-sounding one especially representative of continental romanticism.[14] In fact, though, 'Tintern Abbey' again can be argued to pre-empt Coleridge. The poem's subtle balance in which Hartleian elements, which look to the British empirical line of thought, are poised against a rhetoric of the sublime, seems already to know Coleridge's later excursions into German aesthetic philosophy and therefore to represent his transition in advance.

It is not difficult to find general and particular anticipations of the plot of 'Tintern Abbey' in Hartley's *Observations on Man* of 1749. Hartley contributes significantly to an English philosophical Enlightenment whose radical impulse parallels that of the *philosophes* in France. Although less charismatic than the tradition of Voltaire, Diderot, Holbach, and Condillac, nevertheless the line of Hartley, Priestley, Darwin, and Godwin comparably used Lockean epistemology and theories of the association of ideas to further radical causes. Wordsworth's narrative in 'Tintern Abbey' tells the story of a self constructed out of sensations which change through association from being the passive building blocks of memory into portentously energized players in transformative self-consciousness. Here is a self-sufficient materialism capable of generating spiritual categories on its own from below without any need of theological help from above. Hartley, like the Unitarian Priestley who edited him, was pious, and the Dissenting religiosity of their 'active universe' has sometimes veiled their affinities with contemporary French iconoclasts. But it is the derivation of a spiritual terminus from a base in sensations, a foundation by implication critical of other sources of the spiritual, ecclesiastical, or inspired, which allies Hartley and his followers with the Enlightenment. Equally, this comprehension of a final, qualitatively different transcendence attaches Enlightenment progressivism to romantic theories of sublimity. Hartley wrote that

> we have a power of suiting our frame of mind to our circumstances, of correcting what is amiss, and improving what is right: that our ultimate happiness appears to be of a spiritual not a corporeal nature; and therefore that death, or the shaking off of the gross body, may not stop our progress, but rather render us more expedite in the pursuit of our true end: so that if one be happy, all must: and lastly, that the same association may also be shown to contribute to produce pure ultimate spiritual happiness.[15]

Read in the light of this passage, the collectivism of 'Tintern Abbey' becomes more comprehensible, its 'still, sad music of humanity' a source of happiness not misery for the narrator because its image of the convergence of individuals, the motor-force of the entire poem, predominates over its melancholy. The self's preparation for this insight has been a progress across time through increasingly refined sensations incorporating rather than eschewing youthful, unrepresentable, animal affinities with nature, a progress itself moving towards a comparable extinction of consciousness signalling unconscious rapport:

> that serene and blessed mood,
> In which the affections gently lead us on,
> Until, the breath of this corporeal frame,
> And even the motion of our human blood
> Almost suspended, we are laid asleep
> In body, and become a living soul:
> While with an eye made quiet by the power
> Of harmony, and the deep power of joy,
> We see into the life of things.
>
> (lines 42–50)

The fact that Wordsworth then redescribes this insight as 'a sense sublime / Of something far more deeply interfused' indicates once more his Romantic view of how we retain a philosophical interest in areas philosophy points to but cannot itself articulate. The poem is an elegy for an absent cause. Just as much as does *The Ruined Cottage*, it celebrates a humanity paradoxically characterized by its inability to leave lasting memorials of its intensest feelings, experiential limits whose ultimate expressiveness is found, like Margaret's life and cottage, in its dissolution into the larger natural elements from which it arose. Precipitated out of itself, Wordsworth's self, early and late, discovers authenticity in a loss of individual consciousness, and his poetry expresses his difficult sense that he still remains a match for this new, even fatal expansion. For reductive historicism, sublimation rather than the sublime is what is really at issue here. Tintern Abbey in 1798 was swarming with beggars and the Wye valley echoed day and night to the sound of ironworks. A poetic vantage-point high enough to continue deaf and blind to this defining uproar is actually, it is argued, the view from nowhere. The poem's plot, too, is allegedly evasive. Five years back should recall a time when, the father of an illegitimate French child, exiled from his new family by France's war with his native country, he wrote a republican pamphlet too treasonable to publish and suffered a sense of alienation better summed up by the poem he wrote at the time, 'Salisbury Plain' (excerpts published in *Lyrical Ballads* as 'The Female Vagrant') than by any lines from 'Tintern Abbey':

> 'Oh! dreadful price of being! to resign
> All that is dear in being; better far
> In Want's most lonely cave till death to pine
> Unseen, unheard, unwatched by any star.'
> (lines 306–10)

The poem that replaces this with 'the hour / Of thoughtless youth' and says it 'cannot paint / What then I was' is sublimating history for its own purposes, and discrediting these purposes as a result.

Few historicists are as reductive as this, but the temptation for the rest of us to see Wordsworth's mind, in Jerome McGann's words, as having 'triumphed over its times' in a pejorative sense and Wordsworth as having 'lost the world merely to gain his own immortal soul' is strong.[16] The sublime can always be redrawn as sublimation, the view from nowhere as historical irresponsibility rather than the delegation of philosophical power to poetry. The difficulty about doing this where 'Tintern Abbey' is concerned is that such a reductio ignores the poem's Enlightenment affiliations and overlooks the connected ways in which it shows material circumstances leading to a state of indeterminacy or unconsciousness in which we have to begin again, newly born into the wider franchise of humanity, with all to play for. The poem stutters twice, impressively, just after those two moments in which it has made the most demands on the reader struggling to follow its meditative journey. After trying to 'see into the life of things' the reader is brought up short with 'If this / Be but a vain belief, yet...': a dangerous relinquishment of consciousness, a laying asleep only undertaken on the absolute guarantee of revival, now appears to lose its underwriter and be obliged to canvass alternative means of support. Spiritual solvency is subsequently recovered, and 'Tintern Abbey' departs from an alarming near-miss with the 'dreadful price of being' described in 'Tintern Abbey', but only to fall into alarming arrears yet again. The Wordsworthian 'lover' of nature has no sooner succumbed to another transport, 'A motion and a spirit', than the possibility of its mistakenness is raised: 'Nor, perchance, / If I were not thus taught, should I the more / Suffer my genial spirits to decay...' (lines 112–14). The reassurance disturbs because the preceding, persuasive afflatus had seemed to rule out of court any other care, any thought of the need for some back-up. We are suddenly reminded that the sublime is free-floating, that it supervenes precisely when reference to the world fails but a sense of affinity persists, when the individual's sense of a collective belonging continues beyond her power to distinguish her own identity. This unprecedented revolution, whose content informs the very structure of Wordsworth's poem, destabilizes its certainties and proclaims it a post-Revolutionary poem, one which patently could only be written by and about someone at the end of the Revolutionary decade. Its buoyancy, its power of self recovery or regeneration after sublime extinction, shows its progressive, Enlightened inheritance. Knowledge that its 'unremembered acts' are founded in sensation and that it is always to this empirical building-site of ideas and feelings to which it will be returned, charts the poem's direction and keeps the reader afloat.

This sublime, unmodelled openness to life releases an experience which can look very like death. After all, *The Excursion* of 1814 extolls, in the Wanderer's words 'the sublime attractions of the grave' (IV 238), and in his character it asks us to admire someone who 'could *afford* [Wordsworth's italics] to suffer / With those whom he saw suffer. Hence it came / That in our best experience he was rich...' (I 370–3). These latter lines go back to *The Pedlar* drafts of 1803–4 (MS E 328–30; RC 410) and show a lasting aesthetic adventurousness and sympathetic brinkmanship co-existing with a growing emphasis on Christian consolation. The Wanderer's rich expense of self suggests he might even be able to pay what Wordsworth's Female Vagrant calls the 'dreadful price of being'. His aptitude for sublimity makes him a match for 'the awfulness of life' (II 555), something on which he can authoritatively urge the Pastor to pronounce 'Authentic epitaphs' which 'Epitomize the life' rather than gloss it with sententiae (V 650–1). But 'Tintern Abbey', with its two main climaxes and subsequent recoveries from a kind of sensational bankruptcy resulting from vast sympathetic outlay, exhibits the same trauma, though closer, perhaps, to its original historical source.

Historicist critics have made us realize that this kind of reading of 'Tintern Abbey' must be historically reflective to be valid. Equally, this kind of reading more than covers Wordworth from historicist attacks by showing his poem's astonishingly articulate power to represent this historical moment in sensibility when Romanticism is born out of the Enlightenment's confidence in generating human experience in all its spiritual varieties from the bottom up. It is hardly contentious to argue that the French Revolution, whatever else it did, however awful, also gave unusual expression to such a sublime mixture. Its Supreme Being, its religious festivals, its extraordinary rewriting of the human calendar into the natural cycle of the year, even its paper money or questionable *assignats*, all denote a secular spirituality which replaced received spirituality with one supposedly truer to its natural origins. Its opponents excoriated what they saw as the sublimation of unacceptable political violence. And Hazlitt attacked Wordsworth's literary version of the French Revolution as 'the poetry of paradox', a breaking-down of literary hierarchies and proprieties in the interests of achieving an expression of universal humanity, a Rousseauistic realignment of poetic language with its natural circumstances or material occasions which, to Hazlitt's literary sensibility, made the cataclysmic error of assuming there really was a parallel between politics and poetry.[17]

One cannot have it both ways. Wordsworth cannot be consistently condemned both for sublimating politics and for reflecting in his poetry the sublime clearing of the ground which made possible both the continuation of the French Revolution and, also, the regrouping of its opponents whose tyrannical politics of Restoration were shortly to follow – and, it might be added, the revolutions of 1820 and later ones which followed that! But failure to appreciate the historical commentary furnished by 'Tintern Abbey' comes from the belief that any history of ideas must involve sublimation or the transmutation of historical facts into something different. Correcting this view, Wordsworth makes it his poem's subject to show that the Romantic sublime grows out of Enlightenment materialism and the spiritual indeterminacies lying at the far end of materialism's comprehensive claims to generate all experience from sensuous grounds. In this he is a formative thinker of the emergent European Romanticism. He also shows in action the Romantic sublime's role of handling those experiential extremities in a language capable of finally returning their universals to sensuous beginnings, his earlier self and the younger Dorothy, fictionalized ground-plans of the unformed love of nature from which he set out.[18]

If one reads the Preface to *Lyrical Ballads*, especially in the version of 1802, with a view to establishing Wordsworth's status as a European Romantic, two things are immediately striking: his views on the cooperation of poetry and science, and his cosmopolitanism. His cosmopolitanism is usually regarded as a Romantic excess of sympathy:

> [the poet] is the rock of defence of human nature; an upholder and preserver, carrying every where with him relationship and love. In spite of difference of soil and climate, of language and manners, of laws and customs, in spite of

things silently gone out of mind and things violently destroyed, the Poet binds together by passion and knowledge the vast empire of human society, as it is spread over the whole earth, and over all time.

(*Prose* I 141; punctuation as 1802)

Natural eagerness to relate this passage to the subjects and writing of *Lyrical Ballads* can blind us to the wider intellectual transitions it records. Again, it requires us to think Enlightenment and Romanticism at the same time. The socializing impetus, with its egalitarian respect for but levelling of geographical and cultural difference, ambitiously lays hold of a universal spirit of the laws or notion of human rights recalling the great Enlightenment ideologues from Montesquieu to Kant. On the other hand, Wordsworth argues that such equalities can only be secured by imaginative, poetic sympathies which work outside anything you might find in a code of international law or political constitution, in order to identify our growth out of a common nature. To the poet thus empowered, later distinctions even between the sane and the insane or between the healthy and the abused are not between good and bad but amount to a diversity of ways of being human. But to avoid pejorative distinctions or invidious comparisons, the poet has to slip under systematic modes of understanding once again and approach an undifferentiated, sublime graveyard of the silent and destroyed. Enlightenment leads into Romanticism, and Wordsworth once more writes a passage exemplary of this transition.

The same passage from the Preface continues with a positioning of the poet in relation to the scientist. Wordsworth's poet 'will be ready to follow the steps of the Man of Science...carrying sensation into the midst of the objects of the Science itself'. The effect seems to be the same as the one we saw Leslie Stephen think necessary for 'doctrines' to 'become operative': 'an imaginative symbolism' must be generated. This is true, but Wordsworth's ambitions appear to go further and to be more in keeping with romantic notions of science as furnishing a kind of mythology itself and not only something whose communication might be assisted by poetic expression. For,

> If the time should ever come when what is now called Science, thus familiarized to men, shall be ready to put on, as it were, a form of flesh and blood, the Poet will lend his divine spirit to aid the transfiguration, and will welcome the Being thus produced, as a dear and genuine inmate of the household of man.
>
> (*ibid.*)

Wordsworth is often thought of as not being as interested in mythology to the degree that the second generation of British Romantics were. Or, as in the great sonnet which begins 'The world is too much with us' (1802–4), he toys with the idea of affronting a base, modern, commercial realism with the startling liveliness of mythic existence:

> Great God! I'd rather be
> A Pagan suckled in a creed outworn;
> So might I, standing on this pleasant lea,
> Have glimpses that would make me less forlorn;
> Have sight of Proteus coming from the sea;
> Or hear old Triton blow his wreathed horn.

But his other uses of mythology do not necessarily share this rebarbative idealism. Book 4 of *The Excursion* has the anthropological discussion of religion and myth which so influenced Keats. And in the passage quoted from the 1802 Preface he envisages a mythologized science figured as a poetic being, correspondingly attractive of our human sympathies. This intellectual move should be understood as at one with the beliefs of contemporary philosophers like Schelling and Friedrich Schlegel that in science, above all, a new mythology was called for if scientific progress was to be achieved. The pantheism that looks back to ancient modes of belief, attacked by Heine as characteristically Romantic, has little place here where Wordsworth's poet follows 'the Chemist, the Botanist, or Mineralogist' to have their discoveries advance towards us, transfigured, part of our 'household'.[19]

Again, this seems to imply not just the popularization of science but the revelation of its human character, the *point* of the scope of investigation it has chosen. Scientists feature significantly in Wordsworth's intellectual genealogy and friendships, from Joseph Priestley, Thomas Beddoes, his assistant Humphry Davy through, of course, to Coleridge. But like Coleridge's increasingly esoteric interest in the *Naturphilosophie* of Schelling, Schubert, Oersted, Oken, and other names which do not exactly leap to the tongue of Wordsworth's readers, Wordsworth shares the fundamentally romantic idea, stemming from Kant's *Critique of Judgement* (1790), that science only makes sense when holistically conceived of as binding knower and known together within 'workings of one mind', as *The Prelude* has it in one of its scientific epiphanies (VI 568). Such figurations are far from being naive pathetic fallacies. Nor are they only pantheistic alternatives to Christian orthodoxy. Wordsworth's later more doctrinal revisions of the religious sentiments of his long poems never include substitutes for a Romantic scientific mind-set. He studied mathematics at Cambridge, and the compatibility of poetic afflatus with scientific enthusiasm is frequently apparent in the calculated atmospherics of set-pieces in *The Prelude* and *The Excursion*. Still more striking are those mineral visions of the vale of Gondo (VI 549–73) and the cave of Yordas (VIII 711–41) in *The Prelude* where it is the petrific opposite of animation which actually provides the typology and symbolism for the sublime, outer reaches of the self – a kind of paradoxically inhuman, 'unfathered' access to the ultimate boundaries of the human situation. These are the testing points for the scientific marriage desired in 'spousal verse' at the end of *Home at Grasmere* in 1800, later to find its way into the Preface to *The Excursion* as the 'Prospectus' to *The Recluse*, the theme 'but little heard of among men' of how 'The external World is fitted to the Mind'. The theme no doubt offends that transcendentalist tradition identified most closely with mid-nineteenth-century America in the figure of Ralph Waldo Emerson and recorded persuasively recently by Wordsworth's most influential twentieth-century American critics, Geoffrey Hartman and Harold Bloom. Unlike M. H. Abrams, Bloom and Hartman argue that Wordsworth falls short of fully expressing the natural homelessness of the human.[20] But Wordsworth's representative, Romantic scientism needs emphasis as well. Elsewhere, many of Wordsworth's 'spots of time' complement this ambition, but by revealing how uncanny and uneasy a meeting of mind and nature can be when scenes of apparently infinite materiality conjure up a human response characteristically sceptical of its own limits – sublime again. The 'future restoration' in which lodges the later comfort of the 'spots of time' also projects an outer boundary to which we are always aspiring – 'something ever more about to be' – an extension of ourselves whose fraughtness is often truer to the originally discomposing, uncomfortable, childhood experiences of the 'spots of time'.

Wordsworth's Romanticism can figure in those allegedly slighter moments for which he was often taken to task. The lyrics begun in 1802 look modest by comparison with the sonnets of the same year which are bold in their resumption of the past and confident in their treatment of current affairs. Poems to daisies, celandines, butterflies, and green linnets, not to mention daffodils, seemed provocative in 1807 when they were included in *Poems, in Two Volumes* as 'Moods of My Own Mind'. '*Caviare*', Walter Scott observed to Robert Southey, 'not only to the multitude, but to all who judge of poetry by the established rules'.[21] Jared Curtis, however, has alerted us to the 'experiments with tradition' which may in fact be taking place in these poems under the guise of simplicity. Wordsworth's contemporary, Anna Seward, saw this as a possibility but an unfortunate one, complaining that Wordsworth had imposed 'metaphysical importance upon trivial themes'.[22] But when in the second poem 'To a Butterfly' Wordsworth compares the alighted creature with 'not frozen seas / More motionless', the effrontery of the conceit draws attention to Wordsworth's study at that time of Elizabethan and metaphysical poetry. The imposition of meaning on the insect asks for the conceit to be read through those conventions. The immobility of the butterfly reminds one of so opposite a defining or elemental capacity for flight that it is appropriately described as a fluidity temporarily suspended. But the poem perhaps also anticipates a Tennysonian, microscopic attention to detail, a proto-Victorian relish for the potential 'treasure-house of detail' that is the butterfly, perhaps anticipated by the first 'To a Butterfly' poem of the same collection which ends with Emmeline's nervousness of brushing 'the dust from off its wings'.[23] Here, the frozen seas of the wings suggest an attention which would notice the skein of their tissue as being like a fixed grid of waves (if immobility of pose rather than iciness of colour is at issue) on which its markings sit like islands. At any rate, a metaphysical resonance is surely coupled with an observational nicety which, like the later nineteenth-century movement in painting, pre-Raphaelitism, artfully updates a once naive simplicity. Writers of the period as varied as Schlegel and Stendhal proclaimed all poetry and literature to be romantic, and while romantic syncretism (stylistically epitomized by Goethe's *Faust*) has been recognized in its larger gestures of medievalism, the cult of a pagan, classical south, or the revival of folklore, its smaller details are as important. And Wordsworth's assimilation here of a scientific niceness to fit a poetic address or apostrophe, uncannily behind and ahead of itself in English literary history, is as distinctive as his bigger Romantic sketches of natural process, memory, and nationhood. The moods of Wordsworth's own mind are only what Curtis calls an 'apparent privateness'. In the MS version of another lyric on a redbreast chasing a butterfly the poet reproaches the pursuit as if it were cannibalistic. But what might have been a moment of extreme preciosity, inviting scepticism, in fact so conspicuously recalls the language of Wordsworth's literary past as if to image a universal kinship to which, romantically, our self-consciousness ought always to aspire:

> Playmates in the sunny weather?
> Like thine own breast
> His beautiful wings in crimson are drest,
> As if he were bone of thy bone
>
> (*P2V* 76–7)

Adam's lament when he fears he will lose Eve in Book IX of *Paradise Lost*, 'Bone of my bone thou art' (IX 915) sits happily with Wordsworth's Romantic scientific habit, curious about some level on which apparent disparates actually belong to a common nature. Wordsworth's later version, published in 1807, stresses this meaning of kinship, substituting 'A brother he seems of thine own' for 'As if he were bone of thy bone.' The same point is made, more explicitly and less metaphysically no doubt, but both the dramatic contribution of the literary allusion to the meaning and the original biological curiosity are regrettably effaced as a result.

In conclusion, I have argued that to see Wordsworth's Romanticism in the round one has to overcome a prejudice extending from first reviewers to late Victorian admirers and beyond: that what is philosophical in his poetry contributes nothing to its success. To contest this assumption one should return to the Enlightenment traditions in which Wordsworth's intellect was formed and see the sublime structure of his poetry its apotheosis. The 'Ode: Intimations of Immortality from Recollections of Early Childhood', perhaps his most controversial poem, repeats the pattern of recovering in sensation a responsive, self-enhancing world which had apprently been lost through the growth of self-consciousness. The poem, as he told Isabella Fenwick, is Platonic in its presiding metaphor, not Hartleian. Yet, like 'Tintern Abbey', it inscribes on the map of one life the larger movement of intellectual history in Wordsworth's times. Read in this way, its beginning and its end are complementary by design. The spiritual sufficiency of unthinking, material experience, when 'The earth, and every common sight,/To me did seem/Apparelled in celestial light' is matched by that final lodging of our utmost expression in an object of ordinary sensation: 'To me the meanest flower that blows can give/Thoughts that do often lie too deep for tears'. Stanley Cavell thinks that the Ode tells of 'an ordinariness which a new ordinariness must replace'.[24] Cavell is our contemporary, but as a philosopher he feels compelled to trace a Romanticism in current philosophical sophistication back to a human ordinariness paradoxically achieved through scepticism of existing boundaries of the human. Or, as David Bromwich frames the conundrum, Wordsworth is, in the 1799 *Prelude*'s phrase, 'Disowned by memory' (II 445). His most native experience becomes a poetically empowering mystery he cannot 'pretend to know', including his sublimely unmastered implication in the French Revolution.[25]

The young Schelling wrote of the human spirit carrying 'within itself not only the *ground* but also the *border* of its being and its reality'.[26] The limitations we suffer are necessary if we are to have a self to be conscious of, an identity; but to know these necessary restrictions for the limitations they are is immediately to transform them into borders, demarcations we inhabit on both sides. This difficult, uncanny thought permeates European romanticism, from Schelling's *Naturphilosophie* to Chateaubriand's monumental autobiography, *Mémoires d'outre-tombe* (1849–50). And in English, it is Wordsworth who gives it its most memorable expression.

## NOTES

1 Matthew Arnold, 'Wordsworth', in *The Complete Prose Works of Matthew Arnold*, ed. R. H. Super (11 vols., Ann Arbor: University of Michigan Press, 1960–77), IX, pp. 36–54. Algernon Charles Swinburne, 'Wordsworth and Byron', *Miscellanies* (London, 1886), pp. 65–156. Stephen Gill sets the dispute in context in *Wordsworth and the Victorians* (Oxford: Clarendon Press, 1998), pp. 219–20.

2 Thomas De Quincey, *Recollections of the Lakes and the Lake Poets*, ed. David Wright (Harmondsworth: Penguin, 1970), pp. 116–17.

3 John Wyatt writes illuminatingly about Wordsworth's scientific friendships in *Wordsworth and the Geologists* (Cambridge: Cambridge University Press, 1995). See Gill's account of Wordsworth's friendship with the brilliant young mathematician, William Rowan Hamilton in *Wordsworth and the Victorians*, pp. 71–2.

4 See Richard Bourke, *Romantic Discourse and Political Modernity: Wordsworth, the Intellectual and Cultural Critique* (Brighton: Harvester Press, 1993).

5 Jonathan Wordsworth, Michael C. Jaye, Robert Woof, with the assistance of Peter Funnell, foreword by M. H. Abrams, *William Wordsworth and the Age of Romanticism* (New Brunswick and London: Rutgers University Press and The Wordsworth Trust, 1987), p. 1.

6 Robert Rehder, in *Wordsworth and the Beginnings of Modern Poetry* (London: Croom Helm, 1981), points this out as well as a general continental ignorance of Wordsworth's own work (*The Prelude* wasn't translated into French until 1949, for instance) in the context of an argument for Wordsworth's European centrality mirrored by my own chapter.

7 Arnold, 'Wordsworth', p. 37.

8 On Wordsworth's ironic use of Bürger and Sterne in *Lyrical Ballads* see Mary Jacobus, *Tradition and Experiment in Wordsworth's Lyrical Ballads [1798]* (Oxford: Clarendon Press, 1978). For the common source in *Tristram Shandy* of the German Romantic ironists and the Romantic use of irony in English, see Paul Hamilton, 'Romantic Irony and English Literary History', in Karsten Engelberg, ed., *The Romantic Heritage* (Copenhagen: University of Copenhagen Press, 1983). Coleridge's remark is from *Table Talk*, ed. Carl Woodring (2 vols.; London: Routledge, 1990), II, p. 200.

9 Arnold, 'Wordsworth', p. 48.

10 *Ibid.*

11 Sir Leslie Stephen, *History of English Thought in the Eighteenth Century* (2 vols.; London: Smith, Elder, 1876), II, p. 329.

12 E. D. Hirsch, *Wordsworth and Schelling: a Typological Study of Romanticism* (New Haven: Yale University Press, 1960).

13 *STCL* IV 575.

14 *STCL* II 706.

15 *Hartley's Theory of the Human Mind...*, ed. Joseph Priestley (London, 1775), p. 28. See H. W. Piper, *The Active Universe* (London: Athlone Press, 1962).

16 J. J. McGann, *The Romantic Ideology* (Chicago: University of Chicago Press, 1983), p. 88.

17 William Hazlitt, *Complete Works*, ed. P. P. Howe, (21 vols.; London: J. M. Dent and Sons, 1930–4), V, pp. 82–3, 162; XI, pp. 86–7; XIX, pp. 12–19. The best recent

study of Wordsworth and Rousseau is James Chandler's *Wordsworth's Second Nature: A Study of the Poetry and Politics* (Chicago: University of Chicago Press, 1984).

18 My view of the sublime here is unorthodox, although, I believe, salutary. The reader could usefully contrast it with Thomas Weiskel, *The Romantic Sublime: Studies in the Structure and Psychology of Transcendence* (Baltimore: Johns Hopkins University Press, 1976) and Frances Ferguson, *Solitude and the Sublime: Romanticism and the Aesthetics of Individuation* (New York: Routledge, 1992).

19 Heinrich Heine, *Historische-Kritische-Gesamtausgabe der Werke*, ed. Manfred Windfuhr (Hamburg: Hoffmann and Campe, 1979), Band 8/1, p. 118. A fine introduction to the culture of romantic scientists is *Romanticism and the Sciences*, ed. Andrew Cunningham and Nicholas Jardine (Cambridge: Cambridge University Press, 1990).

20 G. Hartman, *Wordsworth's Poetry 1787–1814* (New Haven and London: Yale University Press, 1964); H. Bloom, *The Visionary Company: A Reading of English Romantic Poetry* (Garden City, NY: Doubleday, 1961), pp. 120–93.

21 Scott to Robert Southey, November 1807. *The Letters of Sir Walter Scott*, ed. H. C. Grierson (12 vols.; London: Constable and Co., 1932), I, p. 390.

22 Jared Curtis, *Wordsworth's Experiments with Tradition: The Lyric Poems of 1802* (Ithaca, NY: Cornell University Press, 1971), pp. 31–2.

23 I am utilizing Peter Conrad's conceit of illustrating Victorian sensibility (*The Victorian Treasure-House* (London: Collins, 1973)) through Henry James's description of *Middlemarch* as 'a treasure house of detail, but...an indifferent whole'. The Romantics, though, were polemical in their insistence on the inherence of the whole in the detail or the infinite in the particular, hence the need for 'metaphysical' readings in both stylistic and philosophical senses.

24 Stanley Cavell, *In Quest of the Ordinary* (Chicago: University of Chicago Press, 1988), p. 71.

25 David Bromwich, *Disowned by Memory: Wordsworth's Poetry of the 1790s* (Chicago: Chicago University Press, 1998).

26 *Philosophical Letters on Dogmatism and Criticism*, translated in S. R. Morgan, 'Schelling and his *Naturphilosophie*', in *Romanticism and the Sciences*, ed. Andrew Cunningham and Nicholas Jardine (Cambridge: Cambridge University Press, 1990).

# 14

JOEL PACE

# Wordsworth and America:
# reception and reform

On the morning of 28 August 1833, a thirty-year-old American trekked up a steep road in northwest England. He was on a pilgrimage to the home of the poet who had kindled his belief in the intrinsic value of (Human) Nature. The poet's family bade him enter a 'modest household where comfort and culture were secured without any display'. Here, in a sitting room overlooking a downward-sloping garden, he awaited the master of the house. The young man was somewhat surprised when there appeared a 'plain, elderly, white-haired man...disfigured by green goggles', which he wore to soothe and protect his troubled eyes. The Englishman sat down and held forth on one of his favourite topics – America. There, society is 'being enlightened by a superficial tuition, out of all proportion [to the restraint of its] moral culture'. Getting and spending Americans lay waste their power, for 'they are too much given to the making of money; and secondly, to politics...they make political distinction the end and not the means'. In a statement that seemed paradoxical to the visitor, his host noted that 'they needed a civil war in America, to teach the necessity of knitting social ties stronger'.[1]

When the young Ralph Waldo Emerson (1803–82) made this visit to Wordsworth's home at Rydal Mount, he anticipated meeting the radically optimistic author of the *Lyrical Ballads*, but instead was bewildered by the conservative-minded man wearing green, rather than rose-tinted, goggles. After meeting Wordsworth, Emerson proclaimed that Americans had drawn an idealized portrait of the poet, who was not the free-thinker they thought him to be, but was bound by 'the hard limits of his thought' (294). Nevertheless, he noted in his account of this visit that Wordsworth 'alone, treated the human mind well and with absolute trust'. This treatment of the mind's 'divine' fabric became central to Emerson and his group of literary and spiritual reformers, soon to be known as the Transcendentalists. Wordsworth's trust in the human mind and his belief that 'we have all of us one human heart' ('The Old Cumberland Beggar') expressed sentiments of equality that became watchwords for not only Emerson and his circle, but a number of other American reformers as well.

Wordsworth once informed an American visitor that although he was known to the world as a poet, he 'had given twelve hours thought to the conditions of society, for one to poetry'.[2] Indeed, the editor of the 1888 Boston *Prelude* could proclaim quite confidently that 'Americans should claim a close relationship with Wordsworth, for he is spiritually akin to those patriots who stood by the side of Washington.'[3] America's interest in Wordsworth was quickened by Wordsworth's interest in America and the advice he gave his visitors about the need for reform. Wordsworth received over 100 American visitors who came to talk to the bard about American reforms – poetical, political, social, and religious.[4]

How did Wordsworth's name come to be associated with nineteenth-century reform movements in America? The answer lies in the several-hundred thousand pirated editions and reviews of Wordsworth printed in America. By and large, these works have been left unexamined by scholars and students of the poet, yet they contain many new and exciting points of departure and are essential to a complete understanding of Wordsworth. Stephen Gill has remarked that *Wordsworth in America* is a book waiting to be written:

> Wordsworth's poetry was being freshly set by American printers from as early as 1802; his first editor, during his lifetime was an American, Henry Reed; *The Prelude* and Christopher Wordsworth's *Memoirs of William Wordsworth* were better received in America than in Great Britain; American admirers contributed substantially to the Wordsworth memorial in Ambleside Church; the greatest private collectors of Wordsworth books and manuscripts were (and still are) Americans...Wordsworth's presence in literature and art has not been fully explored, and how much remains to be done can be indicated by the fact that at the time of writing no comprehensive bibliography exists of the publication of Wordsworth in America.[5]

This chapter briefly sketches the ways in which Wordsworth and his poetry were received in America and the roles they played in US reform movements. It begins with the first American edition of Wordsworth's verse, the 1802 Philadelphia *Lyrical Ballads*, tracing the work's reception in post-revolutionary Philadelphia. The argument then focuses on Cambridge, Massachusetts, where Wordsworth was being reinvented by the Unitarians and the faction that grew out of them, the Transcendentalists. Next, exploring several sociological lines of thought coalescing towards the turn of the century, there is cause to examine Wordsworth's role in Dorothea Lynde Dix's (1802–87) pan-American asylum reforms and the ways in which his poetry was utilized by abolitionists, women's rights advocates, and environ-mentalists, especially John Muir (1838–1914). This study concludes with thoughts on several recent critical approaches to Wordsworth, most notably Transatlantic Romanticism.

## Publication, reception, and reform in post-revolutionary Philadelphia

From the first, Wordsworth's poetics were associated with American poli-tics: in pre-revolutionary Pennsylvania, James Humphreys (1747–1810), the publisher of the 1802 Philadelphia *Lyrical Ballads*, was one of the most out-spoken critics of American independence. During the British occupation of Philadelphia, Humphreys was made 'Printer to the King'. He waged war with type and images by printing the royal arms above his name on the masthead of the *Pennsylvania Ledger*. This infuriated printers in favour of the revolution, who noted that James Humphreys owned a press 'whose weekly labors manifestly tend to . . . throw disgust on the friends of America'.[6] When Humphreys retreated with the British troops, the patriots confiscated his press and found him guilty of high treason.

When Humphreys returned to Philadelphia, he printed several revolution-ary tracts and published the *Lyrical Ballads* on paper that bore the water-mark of the American Eagle, emblem of the new country over which Thomas Jefferson (1743–1826) was presiding.[7] To Humphreys, these poems were not only a means of reintegration into America, but also a continuation of his press's engagement with radical politics. These verses exemplified the liberty and equality on which the country was founded, and it was his hope that they would also remind citizens of how much work was left to bring these principles to fruition.

Many of the underlying principles in the poems reflected the spirit of the city in which the *Declaration of Independence* had been penned and ap-proved. The Preface to the *Ballads* contained a poetical manifesto similar to that of the *Declaration*'s political one. Accordingly, it buttressed its own rev-olution: it declared a break with the poetry of his aristocratic predecessors and a democratic focus on the common woman and man, who are entitled to unalienable rights. Wordsworth expresses his 'deep impression of certain inherent and indestructible qualities of the human mind'.[8] The Preface is the declaration of independence for the citizens of the *Ballads*: Michael, the forsaken Indian woman, and many others. The ballads themselves are the voices of these characters, the representation of the under-represented. Henry Reed (1808–54) gave Wordsworth a 'copy of the first American Edi-tion of his poems – a proof of the early appreciation of them in the United States'.[9] Wordsworth replied that it 'is gratifying to one whose aim as an author has been to reach the hearts of his fellow-creatures of all ranks and in all stations to find that he has succeeded in...a distant country'.[10] The similarities between the ideals expressed in Wordsworth's poems and those on which the country was founded secured a readership for the *Ballads* in the new world; moreover, it was those same ideals that brought about a political conversion in their publisher and spurred him on to continue his press's ameliorative efforts.

The *Ballads* were written by men who, in the not too distant past, had harboured republican or 'democratic' ideals. Coleridge gave vent to these sentiments in his 1795 lectures in Bristol, and Wordsworth developed similar views in revolutionary France under the tutelage of Michel Beaupuy, captain among the republican forces. Coleridge once planned to move to America, which he assumed would be the ideal environment for realizing human perfection through democratic living. If America were meant to be the ideal place for writing *pantisocratic* literature, would it not be the place for reading it as well? John Sargent (later a Whig vice-presidential candidate) wrote to Henry Reed about the reception of the Philadelphia *Ballads*, which were 'so simple in their dress, so humble in their topics, so opposite to the pomp and strut of what had been the poetry of the times *immediately* preceding...that they touched a kindred chord in the heart'.[11]

In one set of advertisements in which Humphreys markets the *Ballads*, he notes that his publications are all 'calculated to instruct and amuse, and to instill and disseminate those Principles which cement society, and on which its general Happiness is founded'.[12] Humphreys' advertisement for the *Ballads* resounds with language of social amelioration: 'let not the name of Ballads give rise to prejudices in the minds of those who have never seen this work; for it is as much Superior to those things commonly known by that name, as happiness is preferable to misery'.[13]

Humphreys acquired a diverse American readership for the poems through a set of thoroughly 'American' characteristics. At a time when the appearance and price of a publication had political and social resonance, Humphreys' *Ballads* (which contained – in one volume – the complete contents of the 1798 and 1800 English editions) only cost a little over a dollar, or a day's wages for a labourer. In England, a labourer would have to part with a week's wages to buy the 1800 London edition. Here were poems written about (and, in part, for) the labouring class, and yet in their native country they were placed well out of the grasp of this readership. The American edition was just as politically charged as its overseas counterpart, yet it realized the Preface's ideas and ideals more so than the English editions by making use of the American publishing virtues of affordability, portability, and typographic simplicity.

JOEL PACE

Understandably, the *Ballads* made a very strong contribution to the ongoing debate over the rights of the lower classes. Wordsworth's use of their language is censured in Robert Rose's parody of Wordsworth's Preface, which is not only among the first American burlesques of the *Ballads*, but predates all published English ones as well. After Rose read the *Ballads*, he sent a parody entitled 'A Lyrical Ballad' to the editor of the *Port Folio*; the lampoon is prefaced by an explanatory letter: 'I never once had the idea that I was a poet', confessed Rose,

> till the other day, when I got a very pretty book to read, and found, that the author and I felt exactly alike. I always thought that to make verses, and them like, was right down hard; but it ain't so at all. You wouldn't, perhaps, believe it, sir, but I declare I can write as fast as any of your correspondents; besides, what I write is so vastly natural, that I'm sure you'll like it. I'm sure its better than writing about things one don't understand. However, as it an't right to say too much for one's self, you shall have a specimen of my abilities.[14]

Rose's mock preface implies that composing poetry is beyond the grasp and language of the poor. He criticizes Wordsworth's democratization of poetics through the language of 'minstrelsy', a musical form that parodied the vernacular spoken by African Americans. The speakers of such songs held nonsense discourse on political matters in an attempt to present such issues as incomprehensible to them.

The poetry of Phyllis Wheatley, like Wordsworth's, was ridiculed for its use of common language. By publishing Wheatley – who advocated Abolition and equality for slaves as well as American Indians – Humphreys subtly criticized Jefferson, who had written in his *Notes on the State of Virginia* (1787) that the 'compositions published under her name are below the dignity of criticism'. Humphreys doubtless realized that statements of equality could be inferred from several poems in the *Ballads*, including 'The Old Cumberland Beggar', which states 'we have all of us one human heart' (146). When this statement is considered in the context of Jefferson's subsequent policies towards slaves and American Indians, it echoes (and yet lays bare the hypocrisy in) the sentiments of equality he expressed in the *Declaration*. Jefferson heads the list of subscribers to a Humphreys' publication on passing laws to ameliorate the conditions of slaves; his presence on the list provides further proof of Humphreys' political reintegration.[15]

Humphreys viewed books as the very thing that 'cements' society, and this explains his Loyalist efforts to keep America from a revolution he thought would be harmful. After the war, as a convert of the new American republic, he enlisted his press in the philanthropic cause of buttressing, but also critiquing, the direction in which Jeffersonian America was moving; of the utmost importance to students and scholars of Wordsworth and Coleridge is that Humphreys chose to publish the *Lyrical Ballads* as a means of accomplishing this reform, and that it was efficacious. It is the crowning achievement of Humphreys' press that Isaiah Thomas, the most renowned patriot printer of the Revolution, forgave him for his transgressions against the budding country and referred to him as a 'good and accurate printer and a worthy citizen'.[16] Just as the *Ballads* were instrumental in converting Humphreys to the cause of America, so also did these poems play a shaping role in the conversions of William Cullen Bryant (1794–1878) and Ralph Waldo Emerson, enlisting their pens in the American literary revolution.

## Literary and religious reform

In 1810, Dr Peter Bryant purchased the Humphreys edition of the *Ballads* and brought it back from Boston to his sixteen-year-old son, William Cullen, who became one of the most popular nineteenth-century American poets. When the young Bryant was later serving out a clerkship with an established lawyer, he received a firm upbraiding from the attorney, who had caught him 'wasting his time' reading the *Lyrical Ballads*. Richard Henry Dana (1787–1879), poet and newspaper editor, replies to the attorney's expostulation, for he did not see Bryant's time as ill spent:

> I shall never forget with what feeling my friend Bryant...described to me the effect produced upon him by...Wordsworth's Ballads. He lived, when quite young...at a period, too, when Pope was still the great idol in the Temple of *Art*. He said, that upon opening Wordsworth, a thousand springs seemed to gush up at once in his heart, and the face of nature, of a sudden, to change into a strange freshness and life. He had felt the sympathetic touch from an according mind, and...instantly his powers and affections shot over the earth and through his kind.[17]

In a letter of 25 November 1837 to an American friend, R. Shelton Mackenzie, Wordsworth noted that 'several of Mr B[ryant]'s pieces have fallen in my way from time to time, some of which had merit of a very superior kind'.

Wordsworth also had this effect on Dana, as is most apparent in 'The Changes of Home', which garners characters and narrative lines from nearly every Wordsworth long poem. Bryant and Dana both applied Wordsworth's techniques of natural description to American landscape, and so created their own strain of American Romanticism. Bryant's nature description influenced Romantic prose as well, especially the Wordsworthian tales of

James Fenimore Cooper.[18] The Transcendentalist, feminist, and reformer Elizabeth Palmer Peabody (1804–94) wrote to Wordsworth to let him know that his American readers regarded him as 'the Columbus of Poetry on whom a new world has opened with its mines of solitudes – I would even say more – as the messiah of the reign of the saints – a true Christian prophet'.[19] Peabody references Wordsworth's literary reform (Columbus of Poetry) and his spiritual reform (Christian prophet) because for her circle, the Transcendentalists, literary and theological renewal went hand in hand.

Harvard Divinity School became a Wordsworthian stronghold when the Unitarians gained control of it. Andrews Norton (1786–1853), Harvard professor and social reformer, acquired as many Wordsworth editions as possible for the library. Norton and William Ellery Channing (1780–1842), the leading Unitarian reformer of religion, paid visits to Wordsworth. Channing – and this was one of the many reasons why he encouraged Emerson to make a similar pilgrimage – found Wordsworth and his poetry a 'fountain of spiritual life' (WLMS).[20]

As a student at Harvard Divinity School, Emerson was an avid reader of Wordsworth, the visionary who had opened the young student's eyes to see beyond the confines of Harvard Unitarianism; but when Emerson met his spiritual mentor, he found that the poet's vision was troubling him in more ways than one, noting that, among other things, he was 'deficient . . . in insight into religious truth'. Emerson accurately estimated that Wordsworth would not be able to sustain a movement from *Lyrical Ballads* through to culmination in *The Recluse*, the long-promised great work which certain Americans hoped would provide a panacea to society's ills.[21] Emerson's *Nature* (1836) and the Divinity School 'Address' (1838) are attempts to complete Wordsworth's unfinished task.

Eventually, Norton became aware of the heresy that Wordsworth was inspiring in students, and made every effort to stem it. His conservative Unitarian reading of Wordsworth was elucidated by his sermon on 'My Heart Leaps Up' (printed in *The Offering for 1829*). Norton's interpretation is contrasted with that of Emerson, who used a quotation from 'The world is too much with us' in his revolutionary Divinity School 'Address', which voiced the heresies conservative Unitarians most feared: that Nature and the human mind are divine. These works distilled Wordsworth's thoughts as presented in 'Tintern Abbey' (especially 94–112). Norton attempted to correct Emerson by publishing *Discourse on the Latest Form of Infidelity* (1839). Divergent interpretations of Wordsworth were at the heart of the Emerson–Norton controversy, the defining moment for Transcendentalism as well as one of the most famous debates in American theology.

Theodore Parker (1810–60), part of the graduating class of the Divinity School, referred to Emerson's 'Address' as the noblest strain he ever heard. Marginalia in Emerson's and Parker's copies of Wordsworth reveal that they both marked similar passages: poetry about Nature's revelations. Emerson's copy also reveals a marginal note that has gone undiscovered by scholars for over 170 years: in the margin below the 'Intimations Ode' Emerson remarks that the 'Ode is truly noble' and that there is 'Wonderful eloquence of sentiment . . . in the v and the xi stanzas'.[22] The fifth stanza expresses a theory of the soul's pre-existence, and the eleventh provides instructions for the spiritual perception of Nature. Differing views and interpretations of Wordsworthian Nature were debated by the Transcendental Club, which met at Emerson's home. The many works of the Transcendentalists consolidate an American literary tradition based on the revelatory experience of Nature. According to Henry David Thoreau (1817–62), these authors derived their words properly by transplanting them from Nature to the page 'with earth adhering to their roots'.[23] In an effort to keep Wordsworth abreast of this exfoliation of his principles, Peabody sent Wordsworth Emerson's *Nature* and 'Address' as well as Nathaniel Hawthorne's (1804–64) *Twice-Told Tales* (1837).

## Social reform

Peabody also sent the poet one of her own works, which documents how she and Amos Bronson Alcott (1799–1888) taught Wordsworth's 'Intimations Ode' as theological fact to young Massachusetts children in the Temple School. Alcott's readings and discussions of the poems and the students' responses to them are detailed in Peabody's *Record of a School Exemplifying the General Principles of Spiritual Culture* (1836). Wordsworth read the work and replied with the wish that her 'efforts for the benefit of the rising generation may be crowned with the success they so amply deserve'.[24] Peabody achieved success by pioneering the Kindergarten Movement in America. It was Wordsworth's 'Ode' that first drew her attention to the value of the child's perspective and she noted in her first letter to him that 'poetry is the best means to develop the nobler part of their [children's] nature . . . except *yours* I have never found any that would answer my purpose' (WLMS).

The influence of Peabody and Alcott's school is a case for transatlantic study in its own right: English educationalists founded Alcott house, a school dedicated to the education of children's minds and the reawakening of their souls. In America, several other Wordsworthian schools were established – including a Rydal Mount Seminary. Horace Mann's (1796–1859) reforms of Massachusetts schools were based, in part, on conversations with the poet. According to Mann's sister-in-law, Elizabeth Peabody, Wordsworth's poetry was able to 'connect together the heart and the intellect', and give a 'new & deeper tone...to the art of education' in America (WLMS). Peabody wove Wordsworth's verse into her epistles (on education reform) to Dorothea Lynde Dix. Dix compiled several readers for the young, including *Hymns for Children* (1825) and *Garland of Flora* (1829), which included selections from Wordsworth. Her efforts were not only literary: she converted the Dix Mansion in Boston to a school which rescued 'America's miserable children from vice and guilt and dependence on the Almshouse'.[25] Dix was inspired by a visit to the poet – as well as by his poem 'The Idiot Boy' – to embark upon her pan-American reform of asylums for the mentally ill. Dix devoted her time to visiting the mentally ill in every quarter of the United States, and found that many were kept in cages, cellars, almshouses, and jails. She, like Wordsworth, believed in the therapeutic qualities of nature; thus, the asylums she founded were surrounded by acres of woodland. She began her reform in her native state by presenting a *Memorial (to the Legislature of Massachusetts Protesting against the Confinement of Insane Persons and Idiots in Almshouses and Prisons)* (1843). In presenting something of such monumental importance, Dix needed a means of documentation that portrayed actual details and facts so as to draw out the sympathy, empathy, and understanding of her auditors. She found just such a model in the *Lyrical Ballads*. Her first victory was her memorial to the Massachusetts State Legislature, in which she presented a work, well adapted to interest humankind permanently 'and likewise important in the multiplicity and quality of its moral relations' (Preface to *Lyrical Ballads*).

What Dix found interesting in Wordsworth was his treatment of the mind, an interest that recalls Emerson's comment that the poet 'alone treated the human mind well'. Emerson's Wordsworth had unveiled the divinity of *all* human minds and souls, and in so doing he became part and parcel of the Transcendentalists' growing support of Abolitionism. Emerson mentions Wordsworth's prescient notion of American civil war, and George Ticknor (1791–1871) spoke with Wordsworth for hours on the topic. Wordsworth was also visited by Charles Sumner (1811–74), one of the most famous advocates of the cause.

The poet received an appeal for help from William P. Atkinson who, in his letter to Wordsworth, explained all his reasons for his faith in the cause and in Wordsworth's approbation of it:

> I am one of the few in this country who are actively engaged in behalf of the slave: one of those called Abolitionists...I am now, – and it is this which leads me to write you, – preparing for the press a selection of poetry, the proceeds

of the sale of which will be given to the support of lectures and papers devoted to the cause of Emancipation...I have collected many fugitive pieces, and marked many that are well known. For the latter, I have been many times to your published writings. I am now bold enough to ask of you an unpublished contributio[n.] I should not ask it for myself, but I trust your interest in a great question of philanthropy...Such a contribution from you would be of the greatest value to my undertaking.

Accept herewith the renewed acknowledgement of my obligation to you. In times of peculiar spiritual loneliness, when my mind was but half developed, my principles half formed, your words were more to me than anything save the Gospel. It is the confidence this knowledge gives me, that leads me to write you now.

(WLMS)

Wordsworth wrote the poem for the anthology although many years earlier he declined a similar request for an English collection. His support of the Abolitionists indicates that the radicalism of his earliest anti-slavery statements – 'To Thomas Clarkson, on the Final Passing of the Bill for the Abolition of the Slave Trade', 'The Banish'd Negroes', and his sonnet addressed to Toussaint L'Ouverture – was being rekindled by American correspondents and visitors. Wordsworth's praise of L'Ouverture, who had incited his fellow slaves to a bloody revolution, was translated by many Americans into support for the Abolitionist cause in the Civil War. Emerson and Thoreau were two of many Wordsworthians who spent their time writing Abolitionist manifestos; others – like Walt Whitman (1819–92), Louisa May Alcott (1832–88), and Dix – nursed wounded northern troops. Throughout the war, many northerners continued to read Wordsworth, while many southerners following the example of their leader, Jefferson Davis, creased the spines of their copies of Byron. John Greenleaf Whittier (1807–92), poet and founder of the anti-slavery Liberty Party, used Wordsworth's sonnet as a model for his own poem on L'Ouverture. In a note to *Antislavery Poems: Songs of Labor and Reform* (1848), Whittier quotes Wordsworth's sonnet in full. Wordsworth mentions the 'unconquerable mind' (14) as a power that will carry on L'Ouverture's struggle for freedom long after he has gone. Whittier, like Emerson, sees this as a call to pens and mentions the 'immortal mind' in his verse as well.

Whittier appeals to 'that strong majesty of soul / which knows no color' as one of his muses. The 'Ode: Intimations of Immortality' espouses a similar sentiment – that all souls pre-exist with God and are merely clothed with flesh; thus, all have souls exactly alike, despite differing earthly appearances with regards to colour of skin. According to this interpretation of 'The Ode', the souls of men and women would also be the same regardless of corporeal differences. Lydia Huntley Sigourney (1791–1865), famous poet and

Wordsworth correspondent, advocated women's rights in *Popular Letters to Mothers* (1838). Wordsworth entertained feminist visitors such as Caroline Kirkland (1801–64) and was aware of Sarah Green's efforts to 'adorn "Rydal Mount" Seminary with a *cluster of stars* that will not be unworthy of the *sunlike* genius of its great namesake, and to show the defamers of our sex – "how divine a thing / A woman may be made"[ – You will be crowned with] honor and praise when this transient distinction has lost its charm and value'.[26]

Most important, perhaps, was Margaret Fuller's (1810–50) combining of Wordsworth's views with Transcendentalism and feminism. Fuller was involved in many philanthropic causes, including the humane treatment of the mentally ill, female prisoners, and the blind. Like Emerson, she uses a Wordsworth quotation – in her work *The Great Lawsuit Man versus Men Woman versus Women* (1843) – that buttresses her literary liberation of women from societal roles.

Fuller's essay first appeared in the *Dial*, the Transcendentalist mouthpiece published by Peabody and edited by Fuller and Emerson. Peabody also expressed her gratitude (in a letter) to Wordsworth for his depiction of women in his poetry:

> Let me thank you in the first place for all you have sung of women (in the name of my sex) from the 'Phantom of delight' opening out into the . . . 'woman breathing Nought but breath' even unto the 'statue of soul' . . . You have done all that Milton left undone. (WLMS)

In a different letter, she explains that if Wordsworth's poetry 'moulds' American society,

> we might see *grand souls* indeed, which would do in the republic of letters . . . what they did fifty years since in politics. And it is necessary that this more interior revolution should take place, to . . . perpetuate those forms of freedom which Washington and his friends left to us . . . [S]uch a tremendous excitement begins when each takes his own destiny into his hands, & every man – I almost said every woman – does . . . (WLMS)

In this letter of March 1829, Peabody draws a parallel between notions expressed in the *Lyrical Ballads* and those of the *Constitution* and the *Declaration of Independence*. Wordsworth wrote the *Ballads* after reading Thomas Paine's revolutionary *Common Sense* and when the 'American war was still fresh in memory'. Infected by the notions of liberty held dear in revolutionary America and France, he penned poetry that would inspire Americans to attempt to bring these ideas to fruition through a 'more interior revolution'.

When Peabody substitutes 'every woman' for 'every man', she exposes an inequality that the natural end of the American Revolution would rectify. Wordsworth laid out similar thoughts in his 1800 Preface: where he advocates a change in the language of poetry to liberate it from social constructs, making it universal. Peabody looks to Wordsworth's poetry as a means of fostering these changes and thus brings to light another transformation which needs to take place – an American literary revolution, fulfilled, in part, by several Wordsworthian works: Fuller's *Great Lawsuit*, Emerson's *Nature*, Thoreau's *Walden* (1854), and Whitman's *Leaves of Grass* (1855). Moreover, these writings as well as Peabody's *Record of a School* and Dix's *Memorial* prove that Wordsworth's influence was not limited to literary reform, but extended to social reform as well – which was, after all, the original design of Wordsworth's unfinished project, *The Recluse*.

## Environmental reform

The *Prelude*, the harbinger of *The Recluse*, contains notions of the love of Nature leading to the love of humankind. Wordsworth's verses celebrate the intrinsic value of the human mind as well as Nature. Many natural scenes are embalmed by imagination, which Wordsworth viewed as everlasting. In *The Prelude*, Wordsworth transplants Nature from external reality to the landscape of the mind, which is 'of fabric more divine'. One spot of holy land that Wordsworth imaginatively safeguards (through preserving it in poetry) is the Grande Chartreuse Monastery from its occupation by soldiers during the French Revolution. In the opening line of *Descriptive Sketches*, Wordsworth writes of the monastery as 'a spot of holy ground', but when the episode is worked into 'The Tuft of Primroses', a voice speaks out against the injustice: ' "Stay your impious hand", / Such was the vain injunction of that hour, / By Nature uttered from her Alpine throne' (535–7). Nature repeats her admonition in Book VI of *The Prelude*, and also reiterates the cry ' "perish what may, / Let this one temple last, be this one spot / of earth devoted to eternity" ' (430–5).

Many preservationists, most notably John Muir, considered Wordsworth's poetry Nature's mouthpiece, speaking out against the despoiling effects of industrial revolution on the American landscape. When Muir wrote of the Sierras, he was attempting to achieve the same end as Wordsworth – their preservation, not from the gleam of arms, but of axes and saws. Wisconsin, where Muir lived after moving to America from Scotland, had fallen prey to lumber barons and was the site of near unprecedented deforestation. As founder and president of the Sierra Club, he started a movement of conservation that continues to this very day and was instrumental in developing the National Park system, which protected Yosemite Valley in California. Muir's writings are imaginative conservation tracts replete with echoes of and references to Wordsworth. Muir's textual allusions correspond to markings in the family copy of Wordsworth: 'The world is too much with us', 'Tintern Abbey', and 'Michael' are just a few of the many ecologically resonant poems Muir marked as favourites. Wordsworth's influence on the establishment of America's National Parks is parallel to his role in the foundation of the National Trust in England.[27]

Wordsworth, Muir, and Thoreau expressed the wish that the natural scenes so dear to them would be preserved. Although Thoreau did not seem to mind the railway lines which were (and are still) very close to Walden Pond, Wordsworth protested the extension of the railway through the Lake District. Sarah P. Green, founder of Rydal Mount Seminary, sent Wordsworth an epistle concerned with waterways and railways, which queried:

> Who would not lay aside the Poet's 'sibyl leaf' to have a
> 'sight of Proteus rising from the Sea;
> Or hear old Triton blow his wreathed horn'?
> Utilitarian enterprise and the mercenary speculation have converted the mighty Ocean into a highway of venal profit and wealth; and transmuted the ancient temples of Nature into fire-wood for steam-ships and railroads – there is but one step from the sublime to the ridiculous    (WLMS)

This passage quotes the poet who reacted against commerce in his lines 'Getting and spending, we lay waste our powers: / Little we see in Nature that is ours' (2–3) and warned Emerson that America was too much given to the making of money. In a missive to Wordsworth, Peabody remarks that there was a time before America

> was dammed up with paper mills and saw mills and the various other machines that deform our Yankee streamlets – and the soul cannot forget this period of its glory[.] [T]here is nature again plain-simple – *poetical* – to which your voice comes with power.                                    (WLMS)

She reinterprets the 'Intimations Ode': in this instance, the soul is Nature's.

### Rekindling Wordsworth's radicalism through Anglo-American literary relations

The success of Dix's, Emerson's, and Muir's reforms became outward manifestations of their (Wordsworthian) philosophies – a manifestation that the Wordsworth of the 1790s had hoped for, but was ultimately denied. Wordsworth's role in American reforms indicates a triumph of Wordsworthian politics, one that intermittently baffled, pleased, and displeased him. He had lived to see his views become more important to others than to himself. Nevertheless, a spark of his former beliefs was rekindled by his

American correspondents and visitors. He was unable to conclude an epistle to Reed (19 August 1837) without assuring him that the

> acknowledgements which I receive from the vast continent of America are among the most grateful that reach me. What a vast field is there open to the English mind, acting through our noble language!

The Wordsworth of the American reformers raises questions about the seemingly whole-hearted conservatism of the later Wordsworth, and perhaps gives us answers as to why he chose to leave *The Prelude*'s most radical passages intact. Perhaps Wordsworth foresaw the sympathetic reception they were to meet with in America, nearly the opposite of the immediate English reaction.

In making Wordsworth's role in these reforms the focal point of this chapter, I have of course excluded a number of other very important influences on post-revolutionary socio-cultural reform. Wordsworth was only one. But the emphasis of this essay is necessary, for Wordsworth's role in American literature and culture has been understated. His role goes beyond textual allusion and literary influence: Americans carried out activism in his name, thus realizing Wordsworth's hopeful lines in the *Preface* that 'the time is approaching when...evil will be systematically opposed by men of greater powers and with far more distinguished success'. It is a testimony to the power and success of Wordsworth's poetry that he became one of America's pre-eminent nineteenth-century prophets *and* that he continues to be read widely in America today.

Modern Eco-critics have viewed the Lake District scenes captured in Wordsworth's poetry with their own form of 'green goggles'.[28] Readings of Wordsworth that focus on historical contexts, the portrayal of race, class, and gender are among the critical lenses through which Wordsworth's poetry is currently being read. Each approach is indebted to nineteenth-century America's Wordsworth. Understanding how recent critical perspectives came to be held in common by British and American readers necessitates study not just of Wordsworth's British reception history, but of his American one as well. The study of Anglo-American literary relations is a nascent, yet burgeoning, field: one that is starting to be acknowledged by academic journals, conferences, as well as curricula, and is rife with interesting interpretative possibilities for both the scholar and student. Anglo-American Romanticism has, in the words of William Keach, 'opened up fresh kinds of transatlantic connections that make all forms of habitual national one-sidedness a serious barrier to critical advance'.[29] Wordsworth's role in the development of transatlantic (US and Canada) and transpacific (Australia and New Zealand) Romanticism remains a story largely untold, yet foretold by Peabody, who informed Wordsworth that

> you are the poet not of the English nation – but of the *English Language* – . . .
> you were sent – divinely commissioned – to all to whom this language is native –
> from the rising *beyond* the setting sun – where they are growing up under all
> varieties of circumstance. (WLMS)

In a letter to Wordsworth dated 18 March 1840, Reed also foretells Wordsworth's audience beyond the borders of the United States, hinting at a Continental (Canadian, American, and Mexican) readership; in a statement that is bound to hold true for the twenty-first century, Reed writes:

> My honoured friend, the thought is in my heart and I must give it utterance:
> this country or rather this *continent* is destined to give from it's [sic] countless
> generations in years to come readers more numerous than we can realize to
> those poems which you have composed in the hope that they might live . . .

## NOTES

1 Emerson gives accounts of his visits to Wordsworth in *English Traits* (Boston and New York: Houghton, Mifflin and Company, 1903), pp. 19–24, 294–8. Future page citations in text.
2 Quoted in F. M. Todd, *Politics and the Poet: A Study of Wordsworth* (London: Methuen, 1957), p. 11.
3 A. J. George (ed.), *The Prelude* (Boston: Heath, 1888), p. xvi.
4 Alan G. Hill, 'Wordsworth and his American Friends', *Bulletin of Research in the Humanities*, 81, no. 2 (Summer 1978), 146–60.
5 Stephen Gill, *Wordsworth and the Victorians* (Oxford University Press, 1998), p. 9.
6 *Evening Post* (16 November 1776).
7 Bruce Graver informs me that Humphreys published the *Ballads* on the heels of Robert Bloomfield's *Farmer's Boy*, which contains similar British pastoral poems with democratic overtones.
8 William Wordsworth and Samuel Taylor Coleridge, *Lyrical Ballads* (Philadelphia: James Humphreys, 1802), p. xi.
9 MS dedication from Henry Reed to Wordsworth in the poet's copy, Wordsworth Library, Grasmere. Special thanks to Robert Woof and Jeff Cowton.
10 Leslie Nathan Broughton, *Wordsworth and Reed* (Ithaca: Cornell University Press, 1933), p. 4.
11 Broughton (ed.), *Wordsworth and Reed* (1933), p. 11.
12 Patrick Kelley, *Elements of Book-Keeping* (Philadelphia: James Humphreys, 1803), p. 208.
13 Relf's *Philadelphia Gazette and Daily Advertiser* (16 January 1802).
14 Robert Rose, 'A Lyrical Ballad', *Port Folio* (1804), p. 257.
15 Bryan Edwards, *The History, Civil and Commercial of the British Colonies in the West Indies*, 4 vols. (Philadelphia: James Humphreys, 1805).

16 Isaiah Thomas, *The History of Printing in America*, 2 vols. (Worcester, MA: Isaiah Thomas, 1810).

17 Richard Henry Dana, *Poems and Prose Writings* (Boston: Russell, Odiorne, and Co., 1833), p. 148.

18 See Richard Gravil, *Romantic Dialogues, 1776–1862* (New York: St Martin's Press, 2000), pp. 69–89.

19 Dove Cottage Manuscript A/Peabody/3. Unless otherwise noted, future citation of Peabody manuscript may be assumed to be from this source. Other references to manuscripts in the Wordsworth Library will be noted in the text as (WLMS).

20 WLMS A/Channing /1.

21 William H. Gilman et al. (eds.), *The Journals and Miscellaneous Notebooks of Ralph Waldo Emerson*, 16 vols. (Cambridge, MA: Harvard University Press, 1960–82), IV, pp. 78–9.

22 MS marginalia in Emerson's copy of William Wordsworth, *Poetical Works of William Wordsworth*, 4 vols. (Boston: Cummings, Hilliard & Co., 1824), III, p. 223. Thanks to the Ralph Waldo Emerson Memorial Association; Leslie A. Morris, Curator of Manuscripts, Houghton Library, Harvard University; and Bruce Graver. Theodore Parker copy located in Boston Public Library. For a fuller discussion of Wordsworth and Emerson see Joel Pace, ' "Lifted to Genius"?: Wordsworth in Emerson's nurture and *Nature*', *Symbiosis*, 2.2 (October 1998), 125–140.

23 Henry David Thoreau, 'Walking', *Henry David Thoreau: Collected Essays and Poems*, selected by Elizabeth Hall Witherell (New York: Library of America, 2001), p. 244.

24 MS Philadelphia Historical Society.

25 Dorothy Clarke Wilson, *Stranger and Traveler* (Boston: Little, Brown and Company, 1975), p. 52.

26 John Mahoney, 'The Rydal Mount Ladies' Boarding School: A Wordsworthian Episode in America', *The Wordsworth Circle*, 23, no. 1 (Winter, 1992), 43–8.

27 See the final chapter of Stephen Gill's *Wordsworth and the Victorians*.

28 James McKusick, *Green Writing: Romanticism and Ecology* (New York: St Martin's Press, 2000); Jonathan Bate, *Romantic Ecology* (London: Routledge, 1991); Lance Newman, 'Wordsworth in America and the Nature of Democracy', *New England Quarterly*, 72: 4 (December, 1999), 517–38.

29 William Keach, 'A Transatlantic Romantic Century', *European Romantic Review*, 11, no. 1 (Winter 2000), 31.

# 15

KEITH HANLEY

# Textual issues and a guide to further reading

## Textual issues

Students of Wordsworth are confronted with an unusual array of different editions, especially of the poetry, which represent much more than commercial competition. Some of the leading issues in contemporary textual criticism have been pioneered in the conception of these editions as they have progressively sought to redefine the poet's works. So much is this so that an informed choice of texts must nowadays be the basis of any serious engagement with Wordsworth's writings.

The prevailing questions have been long standing. Wordsworth's extraordinary lifelong habits of constant revision presented his nineteenth-century editors with the problem of judging the relative status of many considerably variant readings and versions. Though his final intentions were authoritatively registered in his latest edition of *Poetical Works*, 1849–50, those readings indirectly efface previously completed works which had in many cases already produced a separate history of reception. Also, from *Poems, 1815* the poet arranged his poems according to a psychological or subject focus system which for the most part ignored a chronological reading. While Edward Dowden followed Wordsworth's final wishes in respect of versions and arrangement (the 'Aldine', 1892–3), as did Thomas Hutchinson in his edition of *Poetical Works* (the 'Oxford', 1895), William Knight attempted to reconstruct a chronological ordering in his (1882–9; the 'Eversley', revised and corrected, 1896), though the dates of composition were often uncertain, and yet to retain the final versions for the main texts.

In the twentieth century Ernest de Selincourt's collected edition (the 'Clarendon', 1941–9; revised by Darbishire 1952–9), adhered to the Dowden/Hutchinson line, (though lengthy unpublished fragments were printed in the editors' notes, and manuscript and other variants were copiously provided), and John O. Hayden has adopted the compromise favoured by Knight for his collected edition (the 'Penguin', 1977), improving on the accuracy of manuscript transcription. A much more active editorial intervention in Wordsworth's own determinations for the presentation of his texts, however, has been widely practised. A crucial departure was de Selincourt's 1926 parallel-text edition of two versions of *The Prelude*, one completed in 1805 and the other published in 1850. The extended introduction to the revised edition by Helen Darbishire (1959) on the poem's composition, revision, and ideas (comparing the pros and cons of both versions) was foundational for much subsequent discussion. Then a more radical view of the implications that had been awakened began to emerge. In *The Music of Humanity*, 1969, Jonathan Wordsworth, developing de Selincourt's practice for *The Prelude*, took the further step of printing separate versions of *The Ruined Cottage* and 'The Pedlar' from manuscript, thereby disintegrating Book 1 of *The Excursion* as it had been first published in 1814 and republished during the poet's lifetime.

The recovery/invention of these unpublished versions drew attention to the particular nature and methods of Wordsworth's composition, and it prompted a debate about the relative qualities of different versions which became a leading critical issue, especially following the *Norton Anthology of English Literature*, 3rd edn, vol. 2, edited by M. H. Abrams et al., 1974, which included the first widely available publication of Jonathan Wordsworth's 1969 text of *The Ruined Cottage* together with an even more significant first publication of what was now named 'the two-part *Prelude*' of 1798–9, arguably the poem's first stabilized version, edited by Jonathan Wordsworth and Stephen Gill.

The culmination of the new self-consciously recuperative approach to editing Wordsworth came with its principled extension to many other works in *The Cornell Wordsworth Edition*, 1975– , the most elaborate presentation to date of any writer in English, under the general editorship of Stephen Parrish. *The Prelude* was the first work to have become obviously transformed. Parrish's own 1977 Cornell volume, *The Prelude, 1798–99, By William Wordsworth*, which included a reading text with facing transcriptions of the many contributing MSS, challenged the determinacy of even the recently recovered first version, and the currency of the new editing was then widely spread by the much used and influential Norton Critical Edition of *The Prelude 1799, 1805, 1850*, 1979, textually edited by (Jonathan) Wordsworth and Gill (see Individual poems and collections below), which printed reading texts for the first time in three separate versions, including that of 1850 'as Wordsworth left it, freed from the alterations and intrusions of his executors'. Thereafter, two further Cornell *Preludes* have appeared: W. J. B. Owen's *The Fourteen-Book Prelude By William Wordsworth*, 1985, which presented the poem as it evolved in the 1830s until its first publication in 1850, and Mark

Reed's *The Thirteen-Book Prelude*, 2 vols., 1991, which presented a reading text of the poem as Wordsworth completed it in 1805–6, and a reading text of a manuscipt that was extensively revised in 1818–20.

Parrish's foreword to the Cornell series explained its ambition 'to present – for the first time – full and accurate texts of Wordsworth's long poems, together with all variant readings from first drafts down to the final lifetime (or first posthumous) printings'. The inaugural edition was Gill's *The Salisbury Plain Poems*, 1975, incorporating reading texts of different manuscript versions together with the only text that was actually authorized by Wordsworth of a work eventually published in an 1842 collection as 'Guilt and Sorrow'. Thereafter, nineteen of the projected twenty-one Cornell volumes of poetry (expanded to cover the full poetical works, with an index to follow), each offering many new such reading texts, have so far appeared (see Poetry editions below). A section on the series in *The Wordsworth Circle*, 28:2 (Spring 1997), with an historical introduction by James A. Butler, includes Parrish's latest consideration, 'Versioning Wordsworth: A Study in Textual Ethics'.

While Parrish elaborated the rationale of his series in 'The Worst of Wordsworth', *The Wordsworth Circle* 7:2 (Spring 1976), and 'The Editor as Archaeologist', *Kentucky Review* 4 (1983), it was only in Gill's first single volume selection, the Oxford Authors *William Wordsworth*, 1984, that the new principles were wholly followed so that 'for the first time a selection of Wordsworth's work [was] offered in which the poems [were] ordered according to the date of their composition [except the 1805 *Prelude*, which stands apart], and presented in texts which [gave] as nearly as possible their earliest completed state'. As a result, some manuscript versions that challenged the established textual canon, sometimes with unfamiliar titles, now became promoted for general and educational usage. Gill's Note on the Text succinctly explains why he insists that 'one *must* print a text which comes as close as possible to the state of a poem when it was first completed'.

The premises behind the procedures established in the Norton and Cornell editions had met with either enthusiasm or different degrees of scepticism from reviewers and critics. One influential and judicious response was delivered by Jack Stillinger in his article, 'Textual Primitivism and the Editing of Wordsworth', *SIR* 28:1 (Spring 1989), where he deprecated 'the effacement of the later poet' and the loss of 'some of Wordsworth's most admired writing' in Gill's selection. Nevertheless, he argued that despite 'the primitivist ideals that prompted the project in the first place', the different versions revealed in the Cornell Edition should now be admitted to the canon.

The fullest argument for the editorially equal status of different versions of the same works, published or not, was registered by Jonathan Wordsworth in the comparative contexts of the composition of other major long poems in English from *Piers Plowman* to *The Leaves of Grass* in an essay, 'Revision as making: *The Prelude* and its peers' (from *Romantic Revisions*, ed. Robert Brinkley and Keith Hanley, Cambridge and New York, 1992), while in another essay from the same collection, 'Wordsworth's poems: the question of text' (revised from *RES*, NS 34, 1983), Gill issued an authoritative reconsideration of the consequences of recent tendencies in Wordsworth editing. More recently, Jonathan Wordsworth has re-presented another *Prelude* for Penguin, 1995, comprising 'the four texts', one of which is the 150-line fragment, 'Was it for this', which was Wordsworth's first known attempt at writing the poem, and another, surprisingly, the historically received text published in 1850. The most creatively interventionist extension of the recuperative approach is Duncan Wu's edition of *The Five-Book Prelude*, 1997, which aims to reconstruct the text of what might have become the version of *The Prelude* that Wordsworth at one time projected, but that Jonathan Wordsworth had argued in 'The Five-Book *Prelude* of Early Spring 1804', *JEGP*, 76:1 (1977) was 'abandoned very suddenly ca. 10 March 1804', when it 'was either finished or within easy striking distance of completion'.

## Texts

### Poetry editions

There are three standard multi-volume complete editions: *The Poetical Works of William Wordsworth*, edited by Ernest de Selincourt and Helen Darbishire, 5 vols. (Oxford, 1941–9; revised edn 1952–9); *William Wordsworth: The Poems*, edited by John O. Hayden, 2 vols. (Harmondsworth, 1977; reprinted New Haven, CT, 1981); *The Cornell Wordsworth Edition*, General Editor Stephen Parrish. Details of individual titles in this edition, all published in Ithaca, NY, unless otherwise indicated, are as follows: *An Evening Walk, By William Wordsworth*, ed. James Averill (1984); *Descriptive Sketches, By William Wordsworth*, ed. Eric Birdsall, with the assistance of Paul M. Zall (1984); *Early Poems and Fragments, 1785–1797*, ed. Carol Landon and Jared Curtis (1997); *The Ruined Cottage and The Pedlar, By William Wordsworth*, ed. James Butler (Hassocks, Sussex and Ithaca, NY, 1979); *Lyrical Ballads, and Other Poems, 1797–1800*, ed. James Butler and Karen Green (Ithaca and London, 1992); *Poems In Two Volumes, and Other Poems, 1800–1807, By William Wordsworth*, ed. Jared Curtis (1983); *Home At Grasmere: Part First, Book First, of The Recluse, By*

*William Wordsworth*, ed. Beth Darlington (Hassocks, Sussex and Ithaca, NY, 1977); *The Tuft Of Primroses, With Other Late Poems For The Recluse, By William Wordsworth*, ed. Joseph F. Kishel (1986); *The White Doe of Rylstone, or, The Fate of The Nortons*, ed. Kristine Dugas (1988); *Benjamin The Waggoner, By William Wordsworth*, ed. Paul F. Betz (Brighton, Sussex, and Ithaca, NY, 1981); *Peter Bell, By William Wordsworth*, ed. John E. Jordan (1985); *Shorter Poems, 1807–1820*, ed. Carl H. Ketcham (1989); *Translations of Chaucer and Virgil*, ed. Bruce E. Graver (1998); *The Salisbury Plain Poems of William Wordsworth: Salisbury Plain, or A Night on Salisbury Plain (including The Female Vagrant); Guilt and Sorrow; or, Incidents upon Salisbury Plain)*, ed. Stephen Gill (Hassocks, Sussex and Ithaca, NY, 1975); *The Borderers, By William Wordsworth*, ed. Robert Osborn (Ithaca, NY, and London, 1982); *The Prelude, 1798–99, By William Wordsworth*, ed Stephen Parrish (1977); *The Fourteen-Book Prelude, By William Wordsworth*, ed. W. J. B. Owen (1985); *The Thirteen-Book Prelude*, 2 vols., ed. Mark L. Reed (1991); *Last Poems, 1821–1850, By William Wordsworth*, ed. Jared Curtis, with Associate Editors Apryl Lea Denny-Ferris and Jillian Heydt-Stevenson (1999). The two forthcoming titles in the Cornell Wordsworth are Geoffrey Jackson's *Sonnet Series and Itinerary Poems, 1820–1845*, and *The Excursion*. ed. Sally Bushell, James Butler, and Michael C. Jaye, assisted by David Garcia.

Individual poems and collections

*The Music Of Humanity: A Critical Study of Wordsworth's 'Ruined Cottage' incorporating Texts from a Manuscript of 1799–1800*, by Jonathan Wordsworth (London and New York, 1969), prints separate versions of *The Ruined Cottage* and 'The Pedlar'; *Wordsworth and Coleridge. Annotated Lyrical Ballads*, Longman Annotated Texts, ed. Michael Mason (London, 1992), prints a modernized version of the 1805 text (as finally authorized by Wordsworth); *The Ecclesiastical Sonnets of William Wordsworth: A Critical Edition*, ed. Abbie Findlay Potts (New Haven, 1922); *The Prelude, or Growth of a Poet's Mind, Edited from the Manuscripts with Introduction, Textual and Critical Notes*, ed. Ernest de Selincourt (Oxford, 1926; revised edition by Helen Darbishire, 1959); *The Prelude 1799, 1805, 1850: Authoritative Texts, Context And Reception, Recent Critical Essays*, ed. Jonathan Wordsworth, M. H. Abrams, and Stephen Gill (New York and London, 1979); *William Wordsworth: The Prelude, The Four Texts (1798, 1799, 1805, 1850)*, ed. Jonathan Wordsworth (Harmondsworth, 1995); *The Five-Book Prelude*, ed. Duncan Wu (Oxford, 1997).

Guide to further reading

## Prose editions

The standard complete edition is *The Prose Works of William Wordsworth*, edited by W. J. B. Owen and Jane Worthington Smyser, 3 vols. (Oxford, 1974), which includes items published for the first time, such as the essay on 'The Sublime and the Beautiful', but not the Fenwick notes (dictated by Wordsworth to Isabella Fenwick in 1843), which are to be found in *Wordsworth: The Fenwick Notes*, edited by Jared R. Curtis (London, 1993).

## Selections of poetry and/or prose

Owen, W. J. B. (ed.), *Wordsworth's Literary Criticism* (London and Boston, 1974), contains all the formal criticism and some important critical comments from the letters; Gill, Stephen (ed.), *William Wordsworth*, The Oxford Authors (Oxford and New York, 1984), a large selection of poetry, together with critical prefaces, notes, and letters; *William Wordsworth. Selected Prose*, ed. John O. Hayden (Harmondsworth, 1988), a scholarly, annotated selection that contains most of Wordsworth's writings in prose.

## Standard complete letters

*The Letters of William and Dorothy Wordsworth*, 6 vols., ed. Ernest de Selincourt (Oxford, 1935–9; 2nd edn, 8 vols. under the general editorship of Alan G. Hill, 1967–93):

(1)   *The Early Years, 1787–1805*, revised by Chester L. Shaver, 1967
(2)   *The Middle Years, Pt 1: 1806–1811*, revised by Mary Moorman, 1969
(3)   *The Middle Years, Pt 2: 1812–20*, revised by Mary Moorman and Alan G. Hill, 1970
(4)   *The Later Years, Pt 1: 1821–1828*, revised by Alan G. Hill, 1978
(5)   *The Later Years, Pt 2: 1829–1834*, revised by Alan G. Hill, 1979
(6)   *The Later Years, Pt 3: 1835–1839*, revised by Alan G. Hill, 1982
(7)   *The Later Years, Pt 4: 1840–1853*, revised by Alan G. Hill, 1988
(8)   *A Supplement Of New Letters*, edited by Alan G. Hill, 1993.

## Selected letters

Hill, Alan G. (ed.), *Letters Of William Wordsworth: A New Selection* (Oxford and New York, 1984; reprinted in the Oxford Letters and Memoirs series, 1990).

## Critical reception

### Full-length studies

Over 120 full-length critical studies of Wordsworth were written during the twentieth century, among which the most influential post-war work was Geoffrey Hartman's *Wordsworth's Poetry 1787–1814* (New Haven and London, 1964; 2nd edn, 1971), which is a broadly phenomenological approach to Wordsworth's developing self-consciousness, or 'consciousness of consciousness': 'a [Wordsworth] poem is...a *reaction* to...[an unusual state of] consciousness as well as its *expression*'. (The best summary is the author's own 'Retrospect' in the second edition.) Hartman's collection of fifteen mostly reprinted essays, *The Unremarkable Wordsworth* (London, 1987), represents the subsequent unfolding of his critical engagements with psychoanalysis, structuralism, and deconstruction.

Opinions obviously differ over any core short-list from this major grouping of monographs: most items concern specific works, themes, or theoretical approaches. Other studies, however, help to construct a general overview, and among these three are outstanding: Geoffrey Durrant's *Wordsworth and the Great System: A Study of Wordsworth's Poetic Universe* (Cambridge, 1970), which aims to show that Wordsworth's representation of Newton's 'great system' is 'a coherent poetic grammar' of images throughout the poetry from 1798 to 1805; Paul Sheats's *The Making of Wordsworth's Poetry, 1785–1798* (Cambridge, MA, and London, 1973), which from close readings in thought and technique infers a distinct pattern of 'three successive phases...in each of which an abrupt crisis of disappointment initiates a renewed struggle towards psychological integrity and hope'; and Jonathan Wordsworth's *William Wordsworth: The Borders of Vision* (Oxford, 1982), which brings a detailed sense of chronology and a major editor's close knowledge of manuscript materials to bear on crucial moments of creativity and other traditional visionary themes.

Full-length studies of individual works have mostly been devoted to *The Prelude* or *Lyrical Ballads*. On *The Prelude*, Stephen Gill's *William Wordsworth: The Prelude*, Landmarks of World Literature (Cambridge, 1991) offers an introductory close reading, describing the process of composition, structure, and the history of its scholarly and critical reception; Herbert Lindenberger's *On Wordsworth's Prelude* (Princeton, NJ, 1963) considers the 1805 version from various perspectives, including the language, the eighteenth-century inheritance, the blank-verse style, the relation to changing definitions of poetry, 'the social dimension', the critical reception, and the connections with European Romanticism; Frank D. McConnell's *The Confessional Imagination: A Reading of Wordsworth's Prelude* (Baltimore, MD,

1974) examines the relation to 'the tradition of Augustinian and English Protestant religious confession'; David Ellis's *Wordsworth, Freud and the Spots of Time. Interpretation in* The Prelude (Cambridge, 1985) is a psychoanalytic investigation of 'the two spots of time' (Penrith Beacon and Waiting for Horses); and Mary Jacobus's *Romanticism, Writing and Sexual Difference: Essays on The Prelude* (Oxford, 1989) is a collection of essays informed by poststructuralist, psychoanalytic, and especially feminist theories.

On *Lyrical Ballads*, Stephen Prickett's *Wordsworth and Coleridge: The Lyrical Ballads*, Studies in English Literature, No. 56 (London, 1975) offers an introduction which interprets the poems in the context of their textual history, and explores the 'creative tension' in the theoretical debates between Wordsworth and Coleridge; Stephen Maxfield Parrish's *The Art of the Lyrical Ballads* (Cambridge, MA, 1973) discusses the relations between Wordsworth and Coleridge, emphasizing Wordsworth's originality; Mary Jacobus's *Tradition and Experiment in Wordsworth's Lyrical Ballads (1798)* (Oxford, 1976) recovers the literary antecedents; John E. Jordan's *Why the Lyrical Ballads? The Background, Writing and Character of Wordsworth's 1798 Lyrical Ballads* (Berkeley, 1976) investigates aspects of the context, including the vogue of simplicity and the literary theories from which the ballads derived; John Beer's *Wordsworth and the Human Heart* (London and Basingstoke, 1978) is a study of Wordsworth's humanitarianism, particularly in relation to Coleridge's speculations and his relationship with Dorothy Wordsworth; Heather Glen's *Vision and Disenchantment: Blake's Songs and Wordsworth's Lyrical Ballads* (Cambridge, 1983) places the songs and the ballads in their immediate historical and social context to reveal the differences between two different kinds of Romantic radicalism that emerge from the vogue of 'simplicity' in eighteenth-century children's verse (Blake) and magazine verse (Wordsworth); D. H. Bialostosky's *Making Tales: The Poetics of Wordsworth's Narrative Experiments* (Chicago and London, 1984) is a detailed study of the 'experimental narratives' that aims to explain how reading them in an active and disciplined way makes them enjoyable; Susan Eilenberg's *Strange Power of Speech: Wordsworth, Coleridge and Literary Possession* (Oxford, 1992) is an exploration of the ways each poet constantly reappropriated the writings of the other in his own terms, 'generating two competing versions of literary history and intertextuality'.

Other notable full-length studies of individual works include Judson Stanley Lyon's *The Excursion: A Study* (New Haven, CT, 1950; reprinted Hamden, CT, 1970); Bernard Groom's *The Unity of Wordsworth's Poetry* (London and New York, 1966), with nine chapters chiefly concerned with *The Excursion*; James Scoggins's *Imagination and Fancy: Complementary Modes in the Poetry of Wordsworth* (Lincoln, 1966), which relates particularly to the 1815 volumes; Enid Welsford's *Salisbury Plain: A Study in the Development of Wordsworth's Mind and Art* (Oxford and New York, 1966); Kenneth R. Johnston's *Wordsworth and the Recluse* (New Haven, CT, 1984); William H. Galperin's *Revision and Authority in Wordsworth: The Interpretation of a Career* (Philadelphia, 1989), centred on *The Excursion*; Brian G. Caraher's *Wordsworth's 'Slumber' and the Problematics of Reading* (University Park, 1991); Anne L. Rylestone's *Prophetic Memory in Wordsworth's Ecclesiastical Sonnets* (Carbondale, 1991); Alison Hickey's *Impure Conceits: Rhetoric and Ideology in Wordsworth's 'Excursion'* (Stanford, 1997); and Sally Bushell's *Re-Reading The Excursion* (Aldershot, 2001).

## Recent directions: 1975–present

Over the past quarter of a century, Wordsworth's writings have increasingly become a site for the competing theoretical framings and ideological bearings which have informed the practice of literary criticism at large. Historical and political approaches have been particularly evident since E. P. Thompson's 'Disenchantment or Default? A Lay Sermon', in *Power and Consciousness*, edited by Conor Cruise O'Brien and William Dean Vanech (New York, 1969), which reviewed the phases of Wordsworth's loss of revolutionary ardour. A series of essays by David V. Erdman began with 'Wordsworth as Heartsworth; or, Was Regicide the Prophetic Ground of those "Moral Questions"?', in Donald H. Reiman, Michael C. Jaye, and Betty T. Bennett's *The Evidence of the Imagination: Studies of Interactions Between Life and Art in English Romantic Literature* (New York, 1978), which was followed by 'The Dawn of Universal Patriotism: William Wordsworth Among the British in Revolutionary France', in Kenneth R. Johnston and Gene W. Ruoff's *The Age of William Wordsworth: Critical Essays on the Romantic Tradition* (New Brunswick, NJ, 1987), and is supplemented by two related articles in *The Wordsworth Circle*, 12:1 (Winter 1981) and 19:1 (Winter 1988). James K. Chandler's *Wordsworth's Second Nature: A Study of the Poetry and Politics* (Chicago and London, 1984) examined Wordsworth's relation to Rousseau's idea of natural education and, from 1797–8, to Burke's idea of human nature nurtured by tradition, custom, and habit.

A marked turn to the revolutionary poet came with the bicentenary of the French Revolution in 1989 which prompted fresh consideration of the political positioning of the younger poet in Nicholas Roe's *Wordsworth and Coleridge: The Radical Years* (Oxford, 1988), an account of the radical background of both poets often based on new and unpublished materials, and a spate of new essay collections, including Keith Hanley and Raman

Selden's *Revolution and English Romanticism: Politics and Rhetoric* (Hemel Hempstead and New York, 1990), Kenneth R. Johnston, Gilbert Chaitin, Karen Hanson, and Herbert Marks's *Romantic Revolutions* (Bloomington, 1990), and Pauline Fletcher and John Murphy's *Wordsworth in Context* (Cranbury, NJ, 1992). John Williams also uncovered the influence of eighteenth-century British political dissidence on the poetry up to the 1805 *Prelude*, in his *Wordsworth: Romantic Theory and Revolution Politics* (Manchester: Manchester University Press, 1989). Geraldine Friedman's *The Insistence of History: Revolution in Burke, Wordsworth, Keats, and Baudelaire* (Stanford, 1996) considered the resistance of history to representation and the re-staging of the French Revolution in *The Prelude*.

The ideological analysis of Wordsworth's writings which had been broached in Marilyn Butler's general introduction to the British Romantic movement, *Romantics, Rebels, and Reactionaries: English Literature and its Background, 1760–1830* (London, 1981), took a straightforward Marxist form in Roger Sales's 'William Wordsworth and the Real Estate', from his *English Literature in History 1780–1830: Pastoral and Politics* (London, 1983), and was deepened by David Simpson's *Wordsworth and the Figurings of the Real* (London and Atlantic Highlands, NJ, 1982), which showed how the poet's mind converts sense data into ideological formations related to contemporaneous debates over political economy. The chapter on 'Wordsworth and the ideology of Romantic poems', in Jerome J. McGann's *The Romantic Ideology: A Critical Investigation* (Chicago, 1983) had a major impact on Wordsworth criticism in trying 'to define the specific ways in which certain stylistic forms intersect and join with certain factual and cognitive points of reference' in *The Ruined Cottage*, 'Tintern Abbey', and 'Intimations of Immortality'.

Gradually, the materializing tendency developed into the politically aligned but more or less theoretically distinct vogue of New Historicism, notably in Marjorie Levinson's attempt to break down assumed distinctions between the individual mind and social experience, or poetry and history, in *Wordsworth's Great Period Poems: Four Essays* (Cambridge, 1986); in David Simpson's discussion of the poet's crisis of authority, associated with a basic anxiety over the value of his own work that is detected in characteristic metaphors of property and labour, in *Wordsworth's Historical Imagination: The Poetry of Displacement* (New York and London, 1987); and in Levinson's later reading of the sonnet, 'The world is too much with us, late and soon', in 'Back to the Future: Wordsworth's New Historicism', *South Atlantic Quarterly* 88:3 (Autumn 1989), reprinted in *Rethinking Historicism: Critical Readings in Romantic History*, edited by Marjorie Levinson, Marilyn Butler, Jerome McGann, Paul Hamilton (Oxford, 1989).

The monumental culmination of this tendency was Alan Liu's *Wordsworth: The Sense of History* (Stanford, CA, 1989), which, concentrating on *An Evening Walk*, *Descriptive Sketches*, 'Salisbury Plain', *The Borderers*, *The Ruined Cottage*, and Books 9–13 of the 1805 *Prelude*, married deconstructionist and New Historicist approaches to reconstruct the history that Wordsworth's poetry denies but that finds inevitable expression in form. Another useful exposition of this approach is Clifford Siskin's 'Working *The Prelude*: Foucault and the New History' in Nigel Wood's essay collection on *The Prelude* (see Critical collections below).

These methods have not gone uncontested, however, and three different sorts of response were Helen Vendler's fierce denunciation, '*Tintern Abbey*: Two Assaults', in Fletcher and Murphy's essay collection (see above); Thomas McFarland's refutation of Levinson's methods in his *William Wordsworth: Intensity and Achievement* (Oxford, 1992); and Nicholas Roe's challenge to the political validity of New Historicism's account of the Romantic imagination in *The Politics of Nature: Wordsworth and Some Contemporaries* (London, 1992). Another critic who has recently attempted to counter the incursion of cultural theories in general into Romantic criticism is David Bromwich, whose *Disowned by Memory: Wordsworth's Poetry of the 1790s* (Chicago and London. 1998) insists alternatively on recovering the poet's 'radical humanity'.

Many ideological readings have been motivated by Anglo-American feminism. Anne Mellor's critique of Wordsworth as a patriarchal institution was sustained over a number of works, from her essay 'Teaching Wordsworth and Women', in *Approaches to Teaching Wordsworth's Poetry*, edited by Spencer Hall with Jonathan Ramsey (New York, 1986), to her chapter on 'Writing the Self / Self Writing: William Wordsworth's *Prelude* / Dorothy Wordsworth's *Journals*', in *Romanticism and Feminism* (Bloomington, 1988), where she views *The Prelude* as above all the production of 'a specifically *masculine* self', to *Romanticism and Gender* (London and New York, 1993). In her essay, 'Sex and History in *The Prelude* (1805): Books IX to XIII', in *Post-Structuralist Readings of English Poetry*, edited by Richard Machin and Christopher Norris (Cambridge, 1987), Gayatri Chakravorty Spivak argued the subtler case for Wordsworth's insidious incorporation of femininity in 'an androgynous plenitude', while John Barrell teased out the character of Wordsworth's masculinism in his essay, 'The Uses of Dorothy: "The Language of the Sense" in "Tintern Abbey" ', in his *Poetry, Language and Politics* (Manchester, 1988), with a mix of Marxism, feminism, and poststructuralist linguistics, extended in his essay, ' "Laodamia" and the Moaning of Mary', *Textual Practice*, 10:3, 1996. Another kind of French-influenced feminism, indebted to poststructuralist psychoanalysis, is employed in Mary

Jacobus's *Romanticism, Writing and Sexual Difference: Essays on The Prelude* (Oxford, 1989), which considers the relation of genre and gender in 'Vaudracour and Julia', the figure of the prostitute and the rhetorical figure of personification, and comparative representations of sexual difference in Wordsworth and Rousseau. A less censorious exploration of Wordsworth's various reationships with women into the 1820s and 1830s is Judith W. Page's *Wordsworth and the Cultivation of Women* (Berkeley, 1994).

The broader agenda of gender cricitism was opened up by Marlon Ross's *The Contours of Masculine Desire* (New York, 1989), in his chapter on 'engendering desire from the margins of masculine rivalry', concerning the power relationship between Wordsworth and Coleridge. More recently, Tim Fulford's chapter, 'Wordsworth: the "Time Dismantled Oak"?', in his *Romanticism and Masculinity: Gender, Politics and Poetics in the Writings of Burke, Coleridge, Cobbett, Wordsworth, De Quincey and Hazlitt* (Houndmills and New York, 1999), shows Wordsworth questioning the masculine sublime through his engagement with Burke, Milton, and Coleridge. A useful survey of approaches to this topic is John Powell Ward's ' "Will No One Tell Me What She Sings?": Women and Gender in the Poetry of Wordsworth', *Studies in Romanticism*, 36:4 (Winter 1997).

Language is the subject of several distinguished studies including Frances C. Ferguson's *Wordsworth: Language as Counter-Spirit* (New Haven, CT, 1977), which considers Wordsworth's speculative interest in language throughout his prose and poetry; Robert Rehder's *Wordsworth and the Beginnings of Modern Poetry* (Totowa, NJ, and London, 1981), which views Wordsworth's stylistic changes as the inauguration of 'modern' poetry; Hugh Sykes Davies's *Wordsworth and the Worth of Words*, edited by John Kerrigan and Jonathan Wordsworth (Cambridge, 1986), an original work of great range, preoccupied throughout with Wordsworth's use of words, and often related to the process of textual revision; Susan J. Wolfson's *The Questioning Presence: Wordsworth, Keats, and the Interrogative Mode in Romantic Poetry* (Ithaca, NY, 1986), which discusses the different idioms of 'the interrogative mode' in *Lyrical Ballads, The Excursion*, and *The Prelude*; Don H. Bialostosky's *Wordsworth, Dialogics and the Practice of Criticism* (Cambridge, 1992), which adopts Bakhtin to attempt a 'dialogic' synthesis of the whole tradition of Wordsworth interpretation; and Richard Bourke's *Romantic Discourse and Political Modernity: Wordsworth, the Intellectual and Cultural Critique* (Hemel Hempstead, 1993), which is 'preoccupied with the way in which poetic and political languages implicate each other . . . in the attempt to produce a legitimate sense of community in the sphere of taste and in the sphere of social value'; David P. Haney's *William Wordsworth and the Hermeneutics of Incarnation* (University Park, 1993) offers a philosophical approach in the Heideggerian tradition to relate language and thought to historical contingency and continuity; Keith Hanley's *Wordsworth: A Poet's History* (Basingstoke and New York, 2001) attempts to relate approaches from Lacan and Foucault to Wordsworth's 'discovery of the linguistic resources with which to contain the traumas of revolutionary history, public and personal'. An important collection of essays on this subject is *Romanticism and Language* (Ithaca, NY, and London, 1984), edited by Arden Reed.

Among leading methodological approaches, Paul de Man's deconstructive method became pervasive as a result of a series of essays written sporadically after his 'The Rhetoric of Temporality', in *Interpretation: Theory and Practice*, edited by Charles S. Singleton (Baltimore, 1969), which argued that the dialectic between subject and object should be 'located entirely in the temporal relationships that exist within a system of allegorical signs' as exemplified by his reading of 'A slumber did my spirit seal'. A special issue of *Diacritics*, guest edited by Andrzej Warminski and Cynthia Chase, *Wordsworth and the Production of Poetry*, 17:4 (Winter 1987), contains six representative poststructuralist essays; and a number of critics who have followed and debated like approaches (including Samuel Weber, M. H. Abrams, Tilottama Rajan, and Charles Altieri) are represented in the Critical Reflections section of *Romantic Revolutions*, an essay collection edited by Kenneth R. Johnston, Gilbert Chaitin, Karen Hanson, and Herbert Marks (Bloomington, 1990).

The theory of influence in relation to Romantic writing has been a recurrent theme in Wordsworth criticism since Harold Bloom's classic account of the effects of Milton on his successors in *The Anxiety of Influence* (New York, 1973). A chapter on Wordsworth, 'A Second Will', in Leslie Brisman's *Milton's Poetry of Choice and its Romantic Heirs* (Ithaca, NY, 1973) led to many subsequent considerations, and Robin Jarvis's *Wordsworth, Milton and the Theory of Poetic Relations* (Basingstoke and New York, 1991) is the first full-scale study of the intertextualities of Milton and Wordsworth. Lucy Newlyn's *Paradise Lost and the Romantic Reader* (Oxford, 1993) includes extensive discussions of the way Miltonic allusions to Satan and God affect Wordsworth's representation of his reaction to the French Revolution, examines Rivers in *The Borderers* as an ambivalent Satanic hero, and considers the connection between subjectivity and the myth of the Fall in *The Prelude*. Less explored is the relationship with Shakespeare, but a chapter in Jonathan Bate's *Shakespeare and the English Romantic Imagination* (Oxford, 1989) summarizes important allusions. Another consideration of Wordsworth's own Romantic construction of another forebear, who turns out to be incorporated rather than rejected, is Robert J. Griffin's *Wordsworth's Pope: A Study of Literary Historiography* (Cambridge, 1995).

The crucial poetic relationship is that between Wordsworth and Coleridge which three works in particular describe and define: three chapters in Thomas McFarland's *Romanticism and the Forms of Ruin: Wordsworth, Coleridge and Modalities of Fragmentation* (Princeton, 1981) explore the terms of their symbiosis, collaboration, and stylistic interdependence; Lucy Newlyn's *Coleridge, Wordsworth and the Language of Allusion* (Oxford, 1986) examines the two poets' partnership from 1797 to 1807 through their unconsciously aggressive uses of literary allusion; and Gene Ruoff's *Wordsworth and Coleridge: The Making of the Major Lyrics, 1802–1804* (New Brunswick, NJ, and Brighton, 1989) studies the 'intertextual genetics' of the dialogue between both poets conducted through developing composition and revision. Two notable books on Wordsworth's own urgent presence in the works of later writers are D. D. Devlin's *De Quincey, Wordsworth and the Art of Prose* (London, 1983) and Kim G. Blank's *Wordsworth's Influence on Shelley: A Study of Poetic Authority* (London, 1988). Widening the scope of Wordsworth's influence, Stephen Prickett's chapter, 'Wordsworth and the Language of Nature', in his *Romanticism and Religion: The Tradition of Coleridge and Wordsworth in the Victorian Church* (Cambridge, 1976) discusses the impact of his religious thinking. More recently, Stephen Gill's *Wordsworth and the Victorians* (Oxford, 1998) explored the poet's impact on Victorian literary and social culture, particularly in the responses of George Eliot, Arnold, and Tennyson.

Among the new tendencies, an attempt to read Wordsworth in relation to popular culture was made by Anthony Easthope in his *Wordsworth Now and Then: Romanticism and Contemporary Culture* (Buckingham and Philadelphia, 1993), and ecology, cultural geography, politicized landscape, and travel have become consistently prominent themes. Jonathan Bate's *Romantic Ecology: Wordsworth and the Environmental Tradition* (London, 1991) was a pioneering attempt to establish Wordsworth as a founding presence in 'green' politics and an originating influence on the ecological concerns of Ruskin, Hardy, Edward Thomas, and Seamus Heaney. A special issue of *The Wordsworth Circle*, 28:3, was edited by James C. McKusich, with an introduction on 'Romanticism and Ecology', and includes an essay by Heather Frey, 'Defining the Self, Defiling the Countryside: Travel Writing and Romantic Ecology'. Michael Wiley's *Romantic Geography: Wordsworth and Anglo-European Spaces* (Houndmills, 1998) finds eighteenth-century political struggles in the poet's 'utopian' landscapes, while Robin Jarvis's *Romantic Writing and Pedestrian Travel* (Houndmills, 1997) and Celeste Langan's *Romantic Vagrancy: Wordsworth and the Simulation of Freedom* (Cambridge, 1995) reveal the politics of travel, while John Wyatt explores for the first time and at length an important group of related poems in *Wordsworth's*

*Poems of Travel, 1819–42: 'Such Sweet Wayfaring'* (Houndmills, 1999). The recent bicentenary of the publication of *Lyrical Ballads* prompted two useful forms of reassessment in an essay collection on the literary milieu edited by Richard Cronin, *1798: The Year of Lyrical Ballads* (Houndmills, 1998) and a special issue of *Romanticism on the Net* 9 (February 1998), edited by Nicola Trott and Seamus Perry, http://users.ox.ac.uk/scat0385/

Readers who wish to pursue their interest in individual works or specific topics can consult the relevant bibliographies of Wordsworth criticism listed below under Chief Scholarly Reference Works. In particular, two guides will provide much relevant information from which to start: Mark Jones and Karl Kroeber's bibliography contains two indexes of authors/editors/reviewers and selected topics, and the fourth section of Keith Hanley's contains annotations of all main books and articles from 1789 to 1993, keyed to three separate indexes of Works, Subjects and persons, and Authors and editors.

## Reading list

### Contemporaneous and historical criticism

Wordsworth's historical reception can be recouped by reference to a series of works. A collection of the main Wordsworth criticism in periodicals, diaries, and letters from the specified period of the poet's life is contained in Elsie Smith's *An Estimate of William Wordsworth by his Contemporaries, 1793–1822* (Oxford, 1932). Katherine M. Peek's *Wordsworth in England: Studies in the History of his Fame* (Bryn Mawr, PA, 1943) provides an account of the development of Wordsworth's reputation throughout most of the nineteenth century, enlarged and refined by Stephen Gill's *Wordsworth and the Victorians* (Oxford, 1998). Extracts of reminiscences and various records of Wordsworth are collected in Peter Swaab's *Wordsworth, Lives of the Great Romantics by their Contemporaries*, vol. III (London, 1996).

### Principal miscellaneous critical collections

Abrams, M. H. (ed.), *Wordsworth: A Collection of Critical Essays*, Twentieth Century Views (Englewood Cliffs, NJ, 1972), is a compendium of sixteen classic essays on Wordsworth in general (I); *Lyrical Ballads* and early poems (II); *The Prelude* (III); and later poems (IV), with an introduction discriminating between the 'simple' and 'problematic' poet; McMaster, Graham (ed.), *William Wordsworth: A Critical Anthology*, Penguin Critical Anthologies (Harmondsworth, 1972), is a gathering of Wordsworth criticism from Wordsworth's day to 1971, with introductory accounts of trends for each section; Bloom, Harold (ed.), *William Wordsworth*, Modern Critical Views (New York, 1985), collects ten major essays or book extracts on Wordsworth written after 1950; Johnston, Kenneth R. and Gene W. Ruoff (eds.), *The Age of William Wordsworth: Critical Essays on The Romantic Tradition* (New Brunswick, NJ, 1987), is a collection of sixteen original essays, 'written to make the life and works of [Wordsworth]...more generally available to educated nonacademic audiences in America'; Gilpin, George H. (ed.), *Critical Essays on William Wordsworth*, Critical Essays on British Literature (Boston, 1990), offers an introductory survey on the history of the poet's reception and a collection of important essays on *Lyrical Ballads*, 'Intimations of Immortality', *The Prelude*, and miscellaneous topics, such as ecology, the Picturesque, English gardens, family guilt, sexuality, philosophy, and politics; Williams, John (ed.), *Wordsworth*, New Casebooks (Basingstoke and London: Macmillan, 1993), contains a selection of nine contemporary extracts and essays from Hartman to critics implementing Marxist, Historicist (New and Old), structuralist, feminist, and poststructuralist approaches.

### Critical collections focused on individual works

*Lyrical Ballads*: Jones, Alun R. and William Tydeman (eds.), *Wordsworth: Lyrical Ballads: A Casebook* (London, 1972), with an historical critical introduction, in three sections: (I) 'Wordsworth and Coleridge on "Lyrical Ballads"'; (II) 'A Selection of Contemporary and Victorian Opinions'; (III) 'Modern Critical Studies'; Campbell, Patrick (ed.), *Wordsworth and Coleridge: Lyrical Ballads*, Critical Perspectives (London, 1991), a very full critical survey of the history of the work's reception informed by present approaches. It contains an explanatory introduction and outline of contemporaneous magazine criticism together with trends in Victorian and later criticism.

*The Prelude*: Harvey, W. J. and Richard Gravil (eds.), *Wordsworth: The Prelude: A Casebook* (London: Macmillan, 1972), with an historical critical introduction, in three sections: (I) 'Waiting for *The Recluse*, 1793–1841', with a brief chronology of the unfinished project; (II) 'Victorian Assessments, 1852–1897'; (III) 'Modern Studies, 1926–67', the fullest section, with extracts from full-length works and journal articles. Wood, Nigel (ed.), *The Prelude*, Theory in Practice (Buckingham and Philadelphia, 1993), contains four original essays designed to demonstrate the application of 'the newest critical positions'.

*Poems 1807*. Jones, Alun (ed.), *Wordsworth; The 1807 Poems*, Casebook Series (Basingstoke and London, 1990), is comprehensive with an historical critical introduction, in three sections: (I) 'The Early Critical Reception';

(II) 'Later Critical Comment'; (III) 'Modern Studies', including extracts from full-length studies and journal articles.

## The Wordsworth circle (1970–)

Not limited to essays on Wordsworth alone, this journal provides the most consistent outlet for criticism and scholarship.

### Chief scholarly reference works

#### Bibliographies

There is as yet no full and accurate bibliography of Wordsworth's writings. Mark L. Reed is at work on this major project. Keith Hanley has attempted a listing of lifetime publications in his *Annotated Critical Bibliography*, and in his entry for the 3rd edn of the *Cambridge Bibliography of English Literature*, vol. IV. The best available descriptive catalogue is George Harris Healey's *The Cornell Wordsworth Collection. A Catalogue of Books and Manuscripts Presented to the University by Mr Victor Emmanuel Cornell*, 1919 (Ithaca, NY, and London, 1957) which contains thorough bibliographical descriptions of many Wordsworth editions up to 1955, MSS, and books of associative interest in this major collection.

A series of annotated bibliographies of Wordsworth criticism covers items from Wordsworth's day to 1993. James Venable Logan, *Wordsworthian Criticism: A Guide and Bibliography* (Columbus, 1947; reprinted 1961; and New York, 1974), covers the period *c.* 1800–1944; Elton F. Henley and David H. Stam, *Wordsworthian Criticism 1945–59* (corrected and revised edition, *Wordsworth Criticism 1945–64*, New York, 1965), includes a year-by-year chronological listing of Wordsworth criticism, annotated with selected listings of reviews; David H. Stam *Wordsworthian Criticism 1964–73. An Annotated Bibliography* (New York, 1974), is a supplement to the foregoing with additional and corrected information; N. Stephen Bauer, *William Wordsworth, A Reference Guide to British Criticism, 1793–1899* (Boston, 1978), offers annotated coverage of nineteenth-century criticism culled from a wide range of periodicals and critical studies, together with significant reviews of the latter; Mark Jones and Karl Kroeber, *Wordsworth Scholarship and Criticism, 1973–1984. An Annotated Bibliography, with Selected Criticism, 1809–1972* (New York and London, 1985), is divided into two parts: (1) standard research materials and a selection of criticism, 1809–1972, and (2) the principal section which aims to give year-by-year listings for 1973–83 and generous listings of reviews; and Keith Hanley, *An Annotated Critical*

*Bibliography of William Wordsworth* (Hemel Hempstead, 1995), comprises four sections: Editions and Manuscripts (including a full list of lifetime publications), Aids to Research, Biographies and Memoirs, and Criticism (an annotated listing of nineteenth and twentieth-century books and articles).

## Concordances

Cooper, Lane, *A Concordance to The Poems of William Wordsworth Edited for the Concordance Society* (London, 1911; rpt, New York, 1965 and 1992), keyed to Hutchinson's 1904 edition; Patricia McFahern and Thomas F. Beckwith, *A Complete Concordance to The Lyrical Ballads of Samuel Taylor Coleridge and William Wordsworth, 1798 and 1800 Editions* (New York and London, 1987), concords the first and second editions in double columns, representing the same words as found in both editions.

## Chronologies

Reed, Mark L., *Wordsworth: The Chronology of the Early Years, 1770–1799* (Cambridge, MA, 1967), gives full details of biography and circumstances of composition and revision; and *Wordsworth: The Chronology of the Middle Years, 1800–1815* (Cambridge, MA, 1975), contains a 'General Chronological List of Wordsworth's Writings with their First Published Appearances', and a more general biographical chronology for 1800–15; Pinion, F. B., *A Wordsworth Chronology* (Basingstoke, 1988), is a continuous and complete account of the principal events in Wordsworth's life, with full representation of the later years.

## Standard biographies

Moorman, Mary, *William Wordsworth, A Biography: The Early Years, 1770–1803* (Oxford, 1957; reprinted with corrections 1967, 1969), based on the editions of the poems, letters, and Dorothy Wordsworth's journals by de Selincourt and Darbishire together with some new biographical materials, contributed a heightened domestic portrait; Moorman, Mary, *William Wordsworth, A Biography: The Later Years, 1803–1850* (Oxford, 1965), is a more sustained portrait of the later poet, his family, friends, and contemporaries than any previous treatment; Onorato, Richard J., *The Character of The Poet: Wordsworth in The Prelude* (Princeton, NJ, 1971), is the classic pychoanalytic reading of Wordsworth; Gill, Stephen, *William Wordsworth. A Life* (Oxford, 1989), fully informed by advances in textual and other knowledge of the poet and his contexts, it offers a sympathetically balanced account of Wordsworth's full career; Johnston, Kenneth R., *The Hidden Wordsworth: Poet, Lover, Rebel, Spy* (New York and London, 1998) matches a freedom of speculation with much new research and highly detailed historical contextualization. Juliet Barker's *William Wordsworth: A Life* (2000) offers the fullest account since Moorman of the Wordsworth domestic circle. Duncan Wu's *William Wordsworth: An Inner Life* (Oxford: Blackwell, 2001) is the most recent scholarly biography of Wordsworth as poet.

# INDEX

# CAMBRIDGE COMPANIONS TO LITERATURE

## CAMBRIDGE COMPANIONS TO CULTURE

# DATE DUE